DEVON BULL PRINCE OF WALES:

The property of the Michigan State Agricultural College; winner of eighteen first prizes. See pages 12 and 108, of this Report.

FIFTH ANNUAL REPORT

OF THE

SECRETARY

OF THE

STATE BOARD OF AGRICULTURE

OF THE

STATE OF MICHIGAN,

FOR THE YEAR 1866.

BY AUTHORITY.

LANSING:
JOHN A. KERR & CO., PRINTERS TO THE STATE.
1866.

State Board of Agriculture.

His Excellency HENRY H. CRAPO, *Ex-Officio*,
PRESIDENT OF THE BOARD.

Hon. HEZEKIAH G. WELLS, of Kalamazoo,
VICE PRESIDENT.

Hon. DAVID CARPENTER, of Blissfield.

Hon. JUSTUS GAGE, of Dowagiac.

Hon. ABRAHAM C. PRUTZMAN, of Three River

Hon. CHARLES RICH, of Lapeer.

Hon. ORAMEL HOSFORD, of Olivet.

T. C. ABBOT, A. M., *Ex-Officio*,
PRESIDENT OF THE COLLEGE.

SANFORD HOWARD, Secretary.

JOSEPH MILLS, of Lansing,
TREASURER.

REPORT OF THE SECRETARY OF THE STATE BOARD OF AGRICULTURE.

LANSING, December 31, 1866.

To the Legislature of the State of Michigan:

In compliance with legal requisitions, the accompanying Report for the year 1866, with supplementary papers, is respectfully submitted.

SANFORD HOWARD,

Secretary of the Michigan State Board of Agriculture.

STATE AGRICULTURAL COLLEGE.

The establishment of an Institution, the leading object of which should be instruction in agriculture, and the arts and sciences therewith connected, was provided for by the constitution of the State, in the following language:

"The Legislature shall encourage the promotion of intellectual, scientific and agricultural improvement; and shall, as soon as practicable, provide for the establishment of an Agricultural school."

It was in pursuance of this constitutional provision, that the act for the establishment of the "Agricultural College of the State of Michigan," was passed.

The act of Congress donating Public Lands to the several States and Territories, for the establishment of Agricultural Colleges,—although passed twelve years after the constitution of Michigan was adopted, and seven years later than the passage of the act for the establishment of the Michigan Agricultural College,—is evidently based on the same idea as that which prompted the earlier action of this State; the declared object being "to teach such branches of learning as are related to Agriculture and the Mechanic Arts, in order to promote the liberal and practical education of the industrial classes in the several pursuits and professions of life."

No better evidence could be given of the general sentiment of the community, in reference to the long-felt want of such a system of education as that designed to be given by the proposed Institutions, than the fact that leading and reflecting minds, through years of agitation, should arrive at similar conclusions, finding expression in almost the same language.

To Michigan belongs the credit of having taken the first practical step towards the realization of what many of the people of this country had so long sought after. As the leader in the important enterprise, she has been forced to labor without guide or example, subjecting theories to the test of experience, and by this slow process elaborating a system adapted to her needs. Considering these, and numerous other difficulties, the success attained is believed to be all that could reasonably have been expected.

It seems to be expected by some persons, that the agricultural college system should at once take rank with the other collegiate systems, and exhibit at the outset all the perfection of detail and harmonious working of parts characterizing the best specimens of classical colleges. Such persons forget that the present classical college is not the creation of a single college, or of a single generation; it is the joint product of numerous college systems, experimenting through more than five hundred years; it is the result of the efforts of the first thinkers and educators in all lands, giving their best efforts to this educational problem—of mistakes rectified and errors rejected. It is the rich legacy of the past—the slowly accumulated wealth of ages of research and investigation. Compare the college of the nineteenth century, with its mountain-load of Latin, its limited mathematics, its astrology and alchemy, with the Harvard, or the Yale, or the Ann Arbor of to-day, and we see that the present classical college is not the product of a single effort, and did not spring forth like Minerva from the head of Jupiter, "adult and full-armed."

While history thus teaches us to moderate our expectations in regard to the development of new fields of instruction, ought a reasonable public, at the outset, to demand of a system essentially new, a perfection which is the result, elsewhere, of centuries of trial, experiment and change? It is natural for the human mind to demand perfection at once, and to chafe at any obstacle which holds it back from the desired end; yet the history of the past enjoins the necessity of moderation in our expectations in fields new and untried, whether in politics, literature or science.

The question now arises, has the Michigan State Agricultural College, the pioneer of the American system, made that progress in the development of a comparatively new field of instruction which the spirit of the age, and the time allotted to the solution of the problem might reasonably demand? We claim that it has in the fullest sense. It is not to be denied that mistakes have been made; but they have been corrected when discovered. Further changes will doubtless be necessary, and will be promptly made when their necessity becomes obvious. But notwithstanding the Michigan State Agricultural College has been in existence less than a score of years, instead of the centuries of the classical collegiate system, in what estimation is this College held in a nation quick to detect and expose pretentious assumption, but equally quick to recognize and honor real worth?

We have the satisfaction of knowing that it stands before the country not only as the pioneer of its class, but also as having demonstrated many important truths of which other similar institutions are availing themselves. Indeed, it is a fact, that those agricultural colleges which give the greatest promise of success, are using the Michigan Agricultural College as a model.

The growing popularity of the Institution is shown by its having received a greater number of students during the present, than in any former year—the whole number in attendance, as will be seen by the report of the Faculty, being one hundred and eight. By the report alluded to, it will also be seen, that while the number of students received was as great as could be even tolerably accommodated, the applications of a considerable number were necessarily refused, for want of rooms.

In view of this fact, the question of course presents itself, whether, if it was proper for the State to provide for the education of a small number of students, at this Institution,—a point which at the present day will not be disputed,—is it not equally proper to make provision for a larger number? It can hardly be necessary to do more than state the proposition, as it is obvious that the benefits of the Institution to the community, are proportionate to the extent to which they are diffused. It is the demand of the friends of agriculture, that the Agricultural College should take a position worthy the leading interest of our State. The College requires, as an indispensable condition of such advancement, increased dormitory accommodations. Increase in the number of students is impossible without this. If the College is denied necessary facilities, the responsibility of checking its growth and development must rest with those who refuse to grant the means. The College is now rapidly approaching a point of development which will be the realization of the hopes of its friends, but such advancement can only take place by the use of adequate means, an essential part of which is more rooms for students.

OPERATIONS ON THE FARM

for the present year have been, in some respects, less favorable than might have been expected, on account of the extreme wetness and coldness of the latter part of the season.

The wheat crop here, as in many other localities, was much injured by the winter, and by bad weather, near the time of harvest, as well as by the wheat midge,—the result being nearly a failure. Oats yielded well, but were damaged by the weather. Hay was nearly a middling crop at the first cutting; the second crop was difficult to cure, on account of the almost constant rain and cloudy weather. Indian corn, though unfavorably affected by the cold and wet weather, was much better than an average for the present year, and was but little injured by frost.

The root crop—which in the system of farm management pursued, is made important, in reference to stock keeping,—turned out well, considering the character of the soil and the season. The crop consisted of the Golden Ball, Strap-leaf, White French, and Skirving's Swede turnip, and the Long Red, and Yellow Globe Mangel Wurzel. After several years trial, preference is given to the Golden Ball turnip, for early feeding, and to the Skirving Swede turnip, and Yellow Globe Mangel Wurzel for winter and early and spring feeding.

The statement of the Farm Superintendent, will show the Farm operations more in detail. It will be seen that considerable has been done in permanent improvements. The farm-house has been removed to a more convenient site, in reference to the other farm buildings, and has been repaired. By the aid of a powerful stump machine (Parrish's), several fields have been cleared from stumps, and brought into a condition which will permit a more thorough and perfect cultivation than has ever before been practicable. Particular attention has been given to manures, and 890 wagon loads have been hauled from the barns and yards to the fields, this season.

The labor system of the students, is considered by the Farm Superintendent as on the whole, satisfactory. He says: "it is an important auxiliary in imparting instruction." By their daily labors in the field, students familiarize themselves with the principles of farm management, and naturally connect them with the subjects of their studies. They thus learn the first step towards that important desideratum in agriculture—Science with Practice.

The reports on experiments by Dr. Kedzie and Dr. Miles, herewith appended, will be found to present very interesting results. Most of the experiments will be repeated. A course designed to ascertain the relative value of roots and Indian corn for feeding sheep, is now in progress, but no definite results will be available for some months.

The live stock of the farm, of distinct breeds, may be briefly described as follows:

CATTLE.

Short-horns.—Of this breed there are on the College Farm the following animals:

Bull Fatalist, 4794, of the American Short-horn Herd-Book. He is from the noted herd of Samuel Thorne, Thornedale, Dutchess county, N. Y.; was calved Feb. 19, 1861. His ancestors on both sides for several generations, were of superior character. His sire, Second Duke of Thornedale, bred by Mr. Thorne, was exported to England, where he was sold for a sum equal to $2,000 in gold. Fatalist is of good size—weighing, in fair condition, 2,200 lbs. He is easily kept and fattens readily on ordinary food. In shape, his hind-quarters are very good; he has a good head and good limbs; his shoulders are too upright, and he lacks fulness of the fore-rib and crops.

Cow Haze, calved March 28th, 1862; bred by the late Col. F. M. Rotch, of Morris, Otsego county, N. Y. She has had two calves by Fatalist—both bulls—one in 1865, the other in 1866. The former, a promising animal, was sold when about eighteen months old, for $100, to go to Ionia county. The latter is superior in most points to the former, and is also superior to the sire in the crops and chine.

Cow Emeline, calved August, 1862; bred by J. B. Crippen, of Coldwater, and by him presented to the College. She has had two calves by Fatalist—a bull in 1865, and a heifer in 1866. The former was of only medium merit, and he was sold at a moderate price when about eighteen months old. The latter is a heifer of beautiful symmetry, a fine handler, and in all respects promising.

Devons.—Bull Prince of Wales; bred in England by Lord Portman, in 1860; was formerly owned by John Pincombe, of London, Canada West. He has taken five first prizes as the best Devon bull of any age, at the Provincial shows, and was included in the herd-prize (bull and six cows) taken by his owner, in 1862; he has also taken six first prizes at county shows, and five first prizes at township shows, in Canada West. He is an excellent specimen of the Quartley family of Devons—combining size (his weight being 1960 lbs.), with almost faultless symmetry, strong constitution, great tendency to fatten, and superior quality of flesh. Considered in all points, he is seldom excelled even in England.

Bull Ton-dog-a-nee, calved May, 1865. Sire, Cherokee; dam,

a Devon cow owned by Mr. Hart, of Lansing. He is a handsome and promising animal.

Cow Eveleen, 5th, calved March 14th, 1862; bred by the late Edward G. Faile, of West Farms, N. Y. She is small, but otherwise a good specimen of the breed. Her progeny seem inclined to grow to good size. She has had two calves by Cherokee—a bull in 1865, and a heifer in 1866. The former, an unusually fine animal, was sold when about fifteen months old, to Messrs. Ballard, of Niles, for $150. The heifer of last spring is a good one.

Galloways.—Bull Victor, bred by John Snell, of Edmonton, C. W. He took the first prize in the yearling class at the Provincial show, in 1865. He is well formed and large of his age, weighing 1640 lbs.

Heifer Blooming Heather 2d, three years old past; bred by John Snell. She is a well-shaped, hardy animal; has had one calf, which was defective in organization, and died when a day or two old. Our experience with the Galloways, thus far, supports the opinion that they will be a very useful breed for this State.

Ayrshires.—Bull Donald Dhu, calved Jan. 22, 1864; bred by Henry H. Peters, late of Southboro', Mass. He is from very superior milking stock, and is an animal of excellent points. We have as yet none of his progeny, but several cows are now in calf to him.

Cow Merryton, 4th, four years old past; bred by Mr. Peters. She belongs to a family of high reputation for dairy purposes, but unfortunately, has proved barren, and on this account has been sold to the butcher.*

---

*The animal alluded to was slaughtered by Andrew Bertch, of Lansing, on the 24th of December. Her feed had been hay and grass only, till within three weeks of the time she was killed It should be stated, also, that she was considerably reduced in flesh last winter by being kept on low diet, in the hope that it might favor her breeding. She could therefore be called no better than grass fed. Her live weight was 1,080 lbs. Dressed weight—beef, 654; hide, 68; tallow, 62 lbs—784 lbs. The weight of meat in proportion to bone and offal, was remarkably large, and its quality was very fine. The animal aided to show, what has been acknowledged wherever the breed is well known, that the Ayrshires possess good feeding properties, and make a superior quality of beef.

SHEEP.

Merinos.—There are on the farm 27 full-bloods of this breed. Several of the original stock were purchased in 1864, of Hon. Charles Rich, of Lapeer, and are of the well-known Rich stock of Shoreham, Vermont. They are a hardy family, and produce much wool of good quality. During the two years they have been on the farm, they have bred very well, although the lambs of this and other varieties of sheep, in common with many other flocks, were last spring somewhat affected with the disease called *goitre*, or "swelled neck," from which some losses were sustained.

Silesian Merinos.—The ram of this breed, which was presented to the College by the well-known importer and breeder, Wm. Chamberlain, of New York, has done well. His wool has been pronounced by one of the most experienced and judicious wool-staplers in the country, of very superior quality as broadcloth wool. As an experiment, he has been bred to grade Merino ewes to some extent, and the progeny have shown a striking improvement over the dams in quality of wool, and though the fleece is only moderately yolky, the weight is good.

The Silesian ewe, donated by Mr. Ladd, of Ohio, reared a fine lamb last year, but lost her lamb of this year from goitre.

The *Wells and Dickinson* ewes, donated by the late Hon. Jesse Edgington, of West Virginia, reared each a fine ewe lamb last year, and this year they have reared fine ram lambs by the Silesian ram.

South Downs.—Of this breed there are two rams and five ewes of different ages. Two wethers (twins) have been reared for the purpose of testing the quality of the mutton. One of them has been killed, and though only grass-fed, was very fine. The ram donated by Mr. Cornell, of New York, has been bred to the Birge ewes, and the lambs are promising. A cross has been made between a South Down ram, and grade Merino ewes, the object being mainly to obtain meat for consumption at the College Boarding Hall. The improvement of the progeny over their dams in shape and fattening tendency, is remarkable. Yearlings which had been fed only on hay and grass, were sold to the butcher, just after being shorn, at four dollars per head. The fleeces of these sheep were of good weight, in reference to the amount of actual wool, and were pronounced by the stapler before referred to, of an excellent quality for delaine goods.

Cotswolds.—Of these there are a ram and ewe. The ram took the first prize in the yearling class, at the Provincial show of Canada West, in 1865, and is a very fine animal. The ewe did not breed last season, but is expected to have a lamb next spring. The fleeces of these sheep averaged over sixteen pounds each, unwashed, and in that condition, worth fifty cents per pound—eight dollars to the fleece. It is combing wool of the best quality.

Some crosses have been obtained from the Cotswold ram and grade Merino ewes. They are lambs of last spring—are large and handsome. When they come to be shorn we shall know to what uses their wool is adapted, and what is its value.

Scotch black-faced, or Highland.—The only representatives of this breed are a yearling ram and ewe, presented to the College by Hon. Samuel Campbell, of New York Mills, Oneida County, N. Y. They are good specimens of the breed. The ewe is expected to have a lamb next spring.

SWINE.

Essex.—There are three boars and three sows, of various ages, of this breed. One boar, only, is of mature age, and he is one of the best animals of the kind to be found in the country. The younger ones are perhaps equally as good of their age. The sows are young, but very fine. This breed is held in high estimation wherever it has been proved.

Suffolk.—Of this breed there are a fine boar presented to the College by Hon. John Wentworth, of Chicago, and three sows of various ages—all good ones.

The *Chester County* variety is represented by a single specimen, a sow, presented by Mr. Court, of Battle Creek. She is a superior specimen of the stock, and a good animal.

The Farm Superintendent's statement of receipts and expenditures on the College Farm, for the year ending December 1, 1866, is as follows:

RECEIPTS.

Cash sales of produce paid to Secretary, less am't of seeds sold, $40 70,	$1,401 76	
Produce furnished boarding hall,	1,339 50	
Produce furnished farm house,	74 72	
830 lbs. of wool at 35c, (not sold).	290 50	
1,833 bushels roots, at 16c, (not sold),	293 28	
62 tons of hay, at $10, (not sold),	620 00	
740 bushels corn in ear, at 36c, (not sold),	266 40	
300 bushels oats, at 35c, (not sold),	105 00	
50 bushels wheat, at $2 (not sold),	100 00	
Corn fodder and straw (not sold),	75 00	
2 Essex pigs (not sold),	40 00	
1 short-horn bull calf (not sold),	75 00	
1 short-horn heifer calf (not sold),	75 00	
1 Devon heifer calf (not sold),	50 00	
6 grade calves, at $10 (not sold),	60 00	
2 Merino ram lambs (not sold),	50 00	
5 Merino ewe lambs (not sold),	125 00	
12 grade ewe lambs (not sold),	48 00	
12 wether lambs (not sold),	36 00	
		$5,125 16

EXPENDITURES.

Produce of last year, not used by other departments,	$1,629 00		
*Labor of men and board,	143 38		
Labor of students,	560 00		
Repairs of implements,	26 70		
Plaster,	10 00		
Seeds, $81 41, less 40 75, amount sold, ..	40 66		
Harness repairs,	10 37		
Toll,	5 20		
Blacksmith's bills,	25 48		
Expenses of stock at fairs,	49 53		
Incidentals,	32 61		
		$2,532 93	
Excess of receipts over current expenses to bal.,		2,592 23	
		$5,125 16	$5,125 16

*The balance of labor of men on farm, was paid for by team labor in other departments.

RESULTS FOR THE YEAR.

Amount of produce sold,		$2,815 98	
Amount of produce not sold,		2,309 18	
			$5,125 16
Deduct amounts as follows:			
Current expenses of farm,	$2,532 93		
Cost of permanent improvements,	905 90		
Paid for farm implements,	90 92		
" stump machine,	146 76		
" scales,	41 00		
" stock (Galloway cattle, Cotswold sheep, etc.,)	920 74		
" lumber and carpenter's work,	126 34		
" one doz. bull rings,	15 00		
		$4,779 59	
Net profit to balance,		345 57	
		$5,125 16	$5,125 16

SWAMP LANDS.

The swamp lands granted by the State to the Agricultural College, comprise 6,849.09 acres, of which a tract comprising 3,323.46 acres, called the "Big Marsh," has been withheld from sale for the purpose of improving it by drainage before putting it in market. Under the direction of the Farm Superintendent, there has been expended in ditching this tract, about $1,750. It is proposed to extend these operations next year. A tract of about thirty acres has been so far reclaimed that it would have been seeded to grass in September last, had not the unusual wetness of the ground prevented. It will be done as soon as the state of the ground will permit.

Of the lands in market, the total sales effected, amount to 1,963.46 acres, and the aggregate sum for which they have been sold, partly on credit, is $6,259 49, being an average of $3 18 per acre. The minimum price received is $1 50, and the maximum $7 50 per acre.

HORTICULTURAL DEPARTMENT.

Operations in the Horticultural Department during the present year have been quite successful. In the garden there have been 21 acres, and in the park 10 acres, under the plough. The fertility and productiveness of the soil are steadily increasing. Besides the use of composts prepared on the farm, 61 loads of stable manure have been hauled from town, the first cost of which was about 15 cents per load.

The soil of that part of the garden devoted to fruit is porous and poor, and not at all suited to the purpose. For this reason it is proposed to remove the most valuable trees and shrubs to a more favorable locality. Grapes, tomatoes, and other articles were injured by frost, and cold, wet weather. The celebrated Tilden tomato has been tried the present year in comparison with the College Seedling, the latter proving somewhat earlier. Further trial is necessary to decide on their relative merits in other respects. The New Peach-Blow potatoe, of which nearly 200 bushels have been produced this year, proves to be very valuable, its quality being excellent, and its productiveness large.

The apple orchard produced no fruit this year. Most of the trees have been set eight years; but they are growing very fast, and are less inclined to bear on that account. Beans and potatoes have been cultivated among the trees this year, not so much for the articles themselves, as for the benefit of the trees. Last spring 121 trees were set out, nearly all of which lived. The number previously set was 260—making the entire orchard consist of 381 trees.

The pear orchard has done well—the trees have made a good growth, and several of them have now formed fruit-buds.

Norway Spruce trees to the number of 350, and Arbor Vitæ to the number of 150, were set out last spring, the ultimate object being chiefly the shelter of a portion of the grounds from severe winds, which have been found quite injurious.

Considerable improvement has been made on the lawn and grounds immediately around the College Hall. Several acres on the north side, which had previously been in a very rough state, have been ploughed, graded, and seeded to grass. A small stream of water that runs through this part, has been covered, and at a point where it passes one of the main avenues, an ornamental basin has been constructed, which adds to the beauty of the grounds. A new bridge has been built over the stream, and the drives and walks of the garden, and other grounds improved.

A very creditable display of vegetables and flowers was made by the Superintendent, Prof. Prentiss, at the exhibition of the Michigan Central Agricultural Society, in Lansing, in September last. The articles were not entered for premium.

The Superintendent's statement of receipts and expenditures for the Horticultural Department for 1866, is as follows:

To cash from College treasury,	$340 49	
To cash from sales of produce of 1865,	59 70	
To labor of students,	726 33	
To unpaid bills for tools and blacksmithing,	39 50	
To keep of team 40 weeks, at $5,	200 00	
To board of hired man at $2 85,	99 75	
To balance due for labor,	26 44	
To lumber wagon,	90 00	
		$1,582 21
Deduct expenses on account of—		
Boarding Hall,	$9 65	
Buildings and wood,	92 28	
Use of team for Board of Agriculture,	6 00	
Use of team for farm,	7 00	
Use of team for sundries,	2 50	
Increased value of tools and implements,	136 26	
Outstanding bills of 1865,	22 04	
		275 73
Total ex. of the horticultural dep't proper for 1866,		$1,306 48

CREDIT ACCOUNT.

By produce to Boarding Hall,	$267 27	
By produce to farm—hay, etc.,	205 00	
By cash sales of produce,	80 00	
By produce in store,	139 75	
		692 02
Expenses above receipts,		$614 46

PERMANENT IMPROVEMENTS.

Apple orchard,	$52 89	
Park and grove,	178 87	
Drives and bridges,	49 83	
Pear orchard,	13 65	
Nursery and evergreens,	63 21	
Covered drain,	35 69	
		394 14
Expenses above receipts and cost of improvements,		$220 32

CURRENT NON-PRODUCTIVE EXPENSES.

College grounds, borders, shrubberies, etc.,	$208 66	
Experiments,	10 18	
Fair,	11 77	
		230 61
Excess of receipts from productive branches of Hort. Department, above expenses,		$10 29

DONATIONS TO THE COLLEGE, 1866.

From N. B. Rowley & Son, Detroit;
Union counter scales, from the Buffalo Scale Works Company.
From J. Covode, Cross Roads, Pa.;
Harpoon, or Finger Horse Fork.
From H. C. Foote, 15 Laight street, New York;
Right to use Foote's convertible fence.
From National Gate Company, 70 Griswold street, Detroit;
Right to use Harrah's National Gate.
From J. B. Powell, Detroit;
Right to use Palmer's Hay Stacking Machine.
From J. O. Benedict, Bedford, Ohio;
Right to use J. S. Benedict's farm gate.
From E. Ingersoll, Delta, Mich.;
Right to use Patent Portable Sheep Shed.
From M. S. Every, Clinton, Mich.;
Every's Patent Improved Sheep-feeding Rack.
From G. W. Boynton, Auburn, N. Y.;
Boynton's Improved Feed Rack, for sheep and poultry, and right to manufacture and use the same on the College farm.
From Chapman, Hawley & Co., Utica, N. Y.;
Hay Elevator, or Grappling Pitchfork.
From Hon. J. M. Edmonds, Census Reports;
Population 1 vol., Manufactures 1 vol., Agriculture 1 vol., Mortality 1 vol.
From Hon. I. Newton, Commissioner of Agriculture;

Report for 1864, 15 copies.
Monthly reports from 6 to 20 copies each.
Speech of Hon. N. P. Banks on Paris exhibition.

From Hon. A. D. Bache, of Coast Survey;
Report of Coast Survey of U. S. for 1863.

From Hon. J. M. Howard;
Package of monthly reports of Commissioner of Agriculture.
U. S. Agriculture, 1864, 2 copies.
Report of Revenue Commission on Petroleum, 2 copies.
" " Cotton, 2 copies.
Navy Register, for 1865, 2 copies.
Smithsonian Report, 2 copies.
Patent Office Reports, 1863, 2 vols., 2 copies.
8th Census Manufactures, 1860, 1 copy.
" Mortality, 1860, 2 copies.
Report on Commercial Relations, 1 copy.

From Hon. Z. Chandler;
8th Census Mortality.
Register of the Navy, 1866.

From C. B. Stebbins, Esq., Dept. Supt. Pub. Instruction;
Report on Education, 1865.

From Caleb Clark, Esq.;
Land Office Report U. S., 1865.

From Geo. H. House, Deputy Secretary of State;
Transactions of Mich. Agricultural Soc'y, for 1858.
" " " 1859.
Joint Documents, for 1865.

From E. C. Seaman, of Ann Arbor;
Pamphlets on Representation of Rebellious States, Amendment to the Constitution, etc.

From Messrs. Cooper & Wright, of Elmira, N. Y.,
Right to manufacture for use at the College, S. Keller and J. S. Good's combined Seeder and Cultivator.

From S. Hudson, of Milford, Oakland Co.;
Right to make for use at College, single and extended pointed fruit ladder.

From Smithsonian Institute, Washington, D. C.;
Vancouver and California shells, 44 species, named by the author of the British Association Reports.
Panama shells, about 32 species.
Gulf of California shells, about 50 specimens.
Duplicate shells of U. S. Exploring Expedition.

From F. L. Clements, Kensington, Oakland county;
An Indian stone axe.

From FRANKLIN NASH, of Boston, Mass.;
A whale's tooth.
From JOS. MILLS, Lansing;
Specimens of Grand Ledge coal.
From Hon. WM. H. PINCKNEY, Lansing;
A shark's jaw, from Key West.
From E. B. MILLAR, Lansing;
A shark's jaw, from East Indies.
From Prof. J. C. HOLMES;
Canker Worms;
Male and female Canker Worm Moths.
Ordway's Canker Worm tree protector.
From H. C FOOTE, Esq., of New York;
Model of Foote's Shelter Fence.
From Wm. P. SPAULDING, Esq., of Eagle Harbor;
9 specimens of iron ore from Marquette.
Specimens of copper crystals.
Calc spar containing oxide of copper.
Conglomerate rock, bearing copper.
Greenstone trap rock, from Ash beds.
2 specimens of ancient mining instruments (stone), from the Penn. mine.
From H. G. WELLS, of Kalamazoo;
Six oil paintings of fruit, the work of Miss Cornelia F. Cock, of Kalamazoo, framed.
From CALEB CLARK, Esq., of Washington, D. C.;
photograph of a painting, by Jno. H. Littlefield; subject, "The Death of Lincoln."
From Prof. J. E. TENNEY, State Librarian;
Winchell's Geological Survey of Michigan.
From MERCANTILE LIBRARY CO., Philadelphia;
43d Annual Report.
From SOCIETY OF SCIENCE, AGRICULTURE AND ART, of Milan, Italy;
A volume of papers.
From ESSEX INSTITUTE, Salem, Massachusetts;
Their Proceedings.
Historical notice of the Institute.
From Hon. JNO. W. LONGYEAR;
Transactions of California State Agricultural Soc. for 1864 and 1865;
Oration of Hon. J. A. J. Creswell, on Life and Character of Henry Winter Davis, 2 copies.
Oration of Geo. Bancroft, on Lincoln.
Patent Office Reports for 1862, vols. 1 and 2.
Revenue System of United States.
Navy Register for 1866.

President's Message, 8.
Report on Coinage, Weights and Measures.
Report of Gen. Grant.
Report of Committee on Reconstruction.
Report of Committee on Mineral Lands.
Letter of Secretary of Interior.
U. S. Coast Survey for 1862 and 1863, (2 copies of each), and other papers.

From Professor OSCAR CLUTE;
Olmstead's Philosophy.
Bartlett's Synthetic Mechanics.
Theo. Parker's Experience as a Minister.
Worthen's Cylopædia of Drawing.

From Capt. E. B. WARD, of Detroit;
Specimens of iron manufactured from the Lake Superior ore, bent cold to show toughness of fibre.
Specimens of steel manufactured by pneumatic method, from Lake Superior ore.
Specimens of iron.
Specimens of slag, firestones.
2 specimens of native silver and copper, 1 of quartz crystals and azurite.

From H. B. WILLIAMS, of New England mine;
Specimens of hematite ore and of specular ore.

From G. D. JOHNSON, of Lake Superior mine;
Suite of specimens of iron ores from that mine.

From Capt. MERRY, of Jackson mine;
Specimens of hematite and specular ore.

From J. A. HUBBARD, of Houghton;
Crystals of copper.
Crystals of amethystine quartz.
Massive quartz.

From AYERS STOCKLEY, of Rockland;
Specimens of copper bearing rock.
" crystals of calc spar.
" crystals of stibbite.
" oxide of copper.
" stamp copper.

From J. MUELLER;
Specimens of native silver and copper.

From Dr. G. L. BRUMSCHWEILER;
Collection of copper bearing rocks.
Crystals of native copper.
" spar.
" native silver.

Crystals of chlorite, etc.

From THOMAS WALKER;

Specimens of mineral coal.

Slate overlying coal.

Petrifactions, etc.

From J. B. and J. W. WALDO;

Specimens of coal, slate, etc.

From Hon. C. L. FLINT, Sec'y Mass. Board of Agriculture;

Agriculture of Massachusetts for 1864.

" " 1865-6.

From Hon. JOHN H. KLIPPART, Sec'y Ohio Board of Agriculture;

Ohio Agricultural Report for 1862.

" " 1863.

" " 1864.

" " 1865.

From Hon. S. L. GOODALE;

Agriculture of Maine for 1865.

From the respective publishers, the following papers and magazi[illegible] been presented to the College:

Hovey's Magazine of Horticulture.

Prairie Farmer.

Western Rural, bound vol., 1866.

Wisconsin Farmer.

American Farmer.

Rail Road Record.

The Monthly Magazine.

Lansing Republican.

Bay City Journal.

Flint Citizen.

Michigan Argus.

Ann Arbor Journal.

Sturgis Journal.

North-Western Christian Advocate.

And from other than the publishers:

Detroit Advertiser and Tribune, tri-weekly.

" Free Press, "

" Post, "

New York Evening Post, semi-weekly.

" Tribune, "

The Congregationalist.

The Christian Register.

The Western Rural.

The Rural New Yorker.

From the STUDENTS;

The Round Table.

Every Saturday.

From Hon. ISAAC NEWTON, Commissioner of Agriculture;

Package of white Swedish oats.

2 packages of Brewers' Delight barley.

Package of Hertfordshire Hero barley.

" Page's Prolific barley.

" Chevalier barley.

3 packages early Boughton wheat.

2 " white Mediterranean wheat.

From Hon. J. M. HOWARD;

1 package Chevalier barley.

1 package barley.

From Mrs. JNO. W. LONGYEAR, plants for borders, viz.;

Forsythia Vendissima.

Spiraea Lindleyana.

Rubus Odoratus.

Kerria Japonica.

Fellenburg Rose.

From Messrs. WEBB & WOOD, of Jackson;

Fine collection of Fuschias, Begonias, Geraniums and other bedding plants.

SANFORD HOWARD,

Secretary of the Michigan State Board of Agriculture.

SECRETARY'S ACCOUNT.

Receipts for the year ending December 1, 1866.

1866.		
Dec. 1.	From State Treasury, at sundry times,	$15,000 00
"	Swamp Land sales,	1,094 27
"	Stock, sales and use,	1,264 96
"	Farm, sales of produce,	655 15
"	Garden, "	82 38
"	College bills paid by students and others,	5,187 01
"	House rent,	290 00
"	Sale of books,	318 93
"	Sales of sundries,	18 85
		$23,911 55

The following disposal has been made of the above receipts:

1866.		
Dec 1.	Certificates on State Treasurer put into hands of Jos. Mills, Treasurer of College,	$15,000 00
"	Cash paid over to Treasurer at sundry times,	6,833 55
"	To balance,	2,078 00
		$23,911 55

NOTES.—The amount reported above as receipts from sale of farm produce and sale and use of stock, exceeds the sum reported by the Superintendent of farm, by $477 65, the amount of warrant No. 627; the sum appeared in the Superintendent's account as an order given by farm to Boarding Hall, on A. Bertch, to whom the stock was sold, for meat; and a warrant was subsequently drawn. Additional sales, before Dec. 1st, give an additional $210 order to be credited the farm, and charged the boarding hall.

Of the above receipts from students, $395 is for matriculation, and belongs to the library fund.

Payment of outstanding warrants diminishes the balance given above to $934 97. See "Indebtedness of College," on another page, for outstanding accounts for which no warrants have yet been drawn.

SANFORD HOWARD,
Secretary.

TREASURER'S REPORT.

Joseph Mills, Treasurer, in account with State Board of Agriculture.

DR.

1865.			
Dec.	1.	To balance from old account,	$ 436 57
1866.			
Jan.	2.	To cash of State Treasurer,	4,000 00
Feb.	22.	" S. Howard, Secretary,	304 00
March	8.	" " "	800 00
"	12.	" State Treasurer,	4,000 00
"	29.	" S. Howard, Secretary,	279 34
April	4.	" " "	1,121 76
"	14.	" " "	303 19
May	31.	" " "	254 93
		" State Treasurer,	4,000 00
June	30.	" S. Howard, Secretary,	1,135 93
July	19.	" " "	1,000 00
Aug.	25.	" " "	890 24
"	30.	" " "	34 24
Sept.	7.	" State Treasurer,	3,000 00
"	13.	" S. Howard, Secretary,	547 65
"	21.	" " "	162 27
Dec.	1.	To balance to new account,	384 49
Total,			$22,652 61

CR.

By paid warrant No. 450	$ 149 99
" " 451	81 01
" " 452	19 10
" " 453	41 98
" " 454	382 87
" " 455	119 31
" " 456	65 82
" " 457	200 33
" " 458	224 82
" " 459	11 75
" " 460	75 15

By paid warrant	No. 461	$100 00
"	" 462	173 02
"	" 463	90 84
"	" 464	123 53
"	" 465	215 33
"	" 473	148 33
"	" 474	133 47
"	" 475	147 79
"	" 476	66 67
"	" 477	75 00
"	" 478	60 00
"	" 479	48 00
"	" 480	75 00
"	" 481	44 77
"	" 482	50 00
"	" 483	162 50
"	" 484	156 25
"	" 485	32 00
"	" 486	125 00
"	" 487	50 00
"	" 488	56 66
"	" 489	223 02
"	" 490	222 17
"	" 491	208 34
"	" 492	150 00
"	" 493	102 21
"	" 494	75 00
"	" 495	23 00
"	" 496	30 00
"	" 497	70 00
"	" 498	125 00
"	" 499	106 00
"	" 500	300 00
"	" 501	150 00
"	" 502	650 00
"	" 503	28 20
"	" 504	400 00
"	" 505	136 90
"	" 506	38 36
"	" 507	92 50
"	" 508	90 00
"	" 509	67 23
"	" 510	12 50
"	" 511	27 50

By paid warrant No.	512	$116 53
" "	513	48 94
" "	514	23 60
" "	515	200 00
" "	516	468 75
" "	517	268 33
" "	518	162 50
" "	519	125 00
" "	520	250 00
" "	521	250 00
" "	522	125 00
" "	523	100 00
" "	524	300 00
" "	525	86 42
" "	526	39 16
" "	527	100 00
" "	528	200 00
" "	529	36 00
" "	530	11 75
" "	531	24 23
" "	532	400 00
" "	533	63 50
" "	534	500 00
" "	535	18 17
" "	536	200 00
" "	537	55 00
" "	538	100 00
" "	539	12 25
" "	540	10 45
" "	541	40 50
" "	542	9 79
" "	543	100 00
" "	544	100 00
" "	545	117 40
" "	546	14 88
" "	547	16 50
" "	548	312 50
" "	549	208 33
" "	550	108 33
" "	551	166 67
" "	552	166 67
" "	553	66 67
" "	554	83 34
" "	555	137 50

By paid warrant No.	556	$83 34
" "	557	105 00
" "	558	39 42
" "	559	650 00
" "	560	15 88
" "	561	66 18
" "	562	21 44
" "	563	150 00
" "	564	12 90
" "	565	21 99
" "	566	100 00
" "	567	100 00
" "	568	150 00
" "	569	25 00
" "	570	21 26
" "	571	50 00
" "	572	41 67
" "	573	12 65
" "	574	20 95
" "	575	234 37
" "	576	100 00
" "	577	279 92
" "	578	150 00
" "	579	17 38
" "	580	400 00
" "	581	2 75
" "	582	40 20
" "	83	39 09
" "	584	64 00
" "	585	100 00
" "	586	7 00
" "	587	50 00
" "	588	150 00
" "	589	250 00
" "	590	57 00
" "	591	41 67
" "	592	275 00
" "	593	150 00
" "	594	175 00
" "	595	100 00
" "	596	42 74
" "	597	250 00
" "	598	50 00
" "	599	195 75

By paid warrant No.	600	$124 92
" "	601	13 19
" "	602	6 03
" "	603	3 10
" "	604	234 37
" "	605	50 00
" "	606	51 90
" "	607	41 67
" "	608	23 80
" "	609	11 00
" "	610	10 00
" "	611	30 00
" "	612	50 00
" "	613	50 00
" "	614	50 00
" "	615	162 50
" "	616	312 50
" "	617	200 00
" "	618	150 00
" "	619	112 50
" "	620	100 00
" "	621	105 00
" "	622	50 00
" "	623	24 00
" "	624	375 00
" "	625	33 75
" "	626	125 00
" "	627	477 65
" "	628	4 00
" "	629	16 43
" "	630	39 20
" "	631	100 00
" "	632	100 00
" "	633	50 00
" "	634	200 00
" "	635	41 67
" "	636	275 00
" "	637	100 00
" "	638	300 00
" "	639	175 00
" "	640	50 00
" "	641	30 00
" "	642	100 00
" "	643	100 00

By paid warrant No. 644	$50 00
" " 645	150 00
" " 646	105 00
Total	$22,652 61

Cr.

Dec. 1.	By balance from old account,	$384 49

JOSEPH MILLS, *Treasurer.*

Lansing, Dec. 1, 1866.

WARRANT STATEMENT of the Secretary of the State Agricultural College, for the year 1866.

1865.	Number.	To whom Drawn.	Object.	Amount.
Dec. 14	478	Sanford Howard,..	Cuts for Report for 1865,............	$60 00
" 14	479	T. C. Abbot,......	Advertising opening of term,........	48 00
1866.				
Jan. 2	480	Geo. T. Fairchild,.	Salary to Jan. 1, 1866,...............	75 00
" 4	481	E. B. Millar,......	Provisions for Boarding Hall,........	44 77
" 4	482	S. S. Rockwell,....	Boarding Hall,.....................	50 00
" 4	483	R. C. Kedzie,......	Salary to Jan. 1, 1866,...............	162 50
" 4	484	T. C. Abbot,......	Salary,...........................	156 25
" 4	485	Ivison,Phinney&Co.	Books,............................	32 00
" 13	486	Sanford Howard,..	Salary to Jan. 1, 1866,.............	125 00
" 20	487	Geo T. Fairchild,..	Salary,...........................	50 00
" 20	488	C. C. Stowe,.......	Salary, final settlement,............	56 66
" 23	489	M. Miles,..........	Farm department and ditching,......	223 04
Feb. 8	490		Farm department and ditching,......	222 17
" 8	491		Salary,...........................	208 34
" 8	492		For expenditure as Supt. of Farm,....	150 00
" 9	493	Oscar Clute,......	Salary to Jan. 1, 1866,...............	102 21
" 17	494	Geo. T. Fairchild,.	Salary to Jan. 1, 1866,...............	75 00
" 17	495		For books for Library,..............	23 00
" 19	496	S. S. Rockwell,....	Salary,...........................	30 00
" 19	497		Salary in full,......................	70 00
" 19	498		Boarding Hall,......................	195 00
" 19	499		Boarding Hall, final account,.........	106 00
March 12	500	E. A. Sheldon,....	Steward, Boarding Hall,.............	300 00
" 15	501	R. C. Kedzie,......	Salary............................	150 00
" 19	502	E. A. Sheldon,....	Boarding Hall,......................	650 00
" 19	503	Lansing & Clark,..	Blacksmith's work,................	28 20
" 20	504	M. Miles,.........	Purchase of span of horses,..........	400 00
" 20	505	T. C. Abbot,......	Advertising,.......................	136 90
" 20	506	E. W. Mills,.......	Foreman of farm, salary in full,.....	38 36
" 20	507	T. C. Abbot,.......	Expenses of Board meetings:	
			Mr. Gage,..................$49 15	
			Mr. Carpenter,............. 25 85	

WARRANT STATEMENT—Continued.

1866.		Number.	To whom Drawn.	Object.	Amount.
March	20		T. C. Abbot,......	Ex. of B'd meetings—Mr. Rich,.$17 50	$92 50
"	24	508	Robt. Bercham,...	Wagon for garden department,.......	90 00
"	26	509	Lansing & Clark,..	Blacksmith's work,.................	67 23
"	26	510	T. C. Abbot,......	Salary to Jan. 1, 1866,...............	12 50
"	26	511	Abner Brown,....	Repairs in Boarding Hall,............	27 50
"	27	512	A. N. Prentiss,....	Salary to Jan. 1, 1866,...............	116 53
"	28	513	T. C. Abbot,......	Books and express for College,.$34 52	
				Exchange and office book,...... 3 40	
				Postage,........ .... 11 02	48 94
March	28	514	Francis Raymond,	Stationery,..........................	23 60
April	2	515	E A. Sheldon,....	Furniture for Boarding Hall,...$18 50	
				Repairs,...................... 11 00	
				Expenses,......................170 50	200 00
April	2	516	T. C. Abbot,......	Salary to April 1,....................	468 75
"	2	517	M. Miles..........	Salary to April 1,....................	268 33
"	2	518	R. C. Kedzie,......	Salary to April 1,....................	162 50
"	2	519	Sanford Howard,..	Salary to April 1,..................	125 00
"	2	520	A. N. Prentiss,....	Salary to April 1,....................	250 00
"	2	521	Oscar Clute,.. ...	Salary to April 1,....................	250 00
"	2	522	Geo. T. Fairchild,..	Salary to April 1,....................	125 00
"	6	523	E. A. Sheldon,....	Boarding Hall, ...	100 00
"	9	524		Boarding Hall, ...	300 00
"	9	525	R. C. Kedzie,.....	Chemicals,....................$79 52	
				Repairs, ... 6 90	86 42
April	14	526	M. Miles,.........	Farm department and ditching;......	39 16
"	14	527		Farm department,..................	100 00
"	18	528	E. A. Sheldon,....	Boarding Hall,...................... ..	200 00
"	23	529	T. C. Abbot,.... .	Advertising,........................	36 00
"	23	530	Wm. Moots,.....	Repairs in Laboratory,..............	11 75
"	23	531	T. C. Abbot,......	Refunded to students,......... $7 80	
				Repairs,...................... 7 20	
				Secretary's office expenses,.... 9 23	24 23
April	26	532	M. Miles,.........	Farm department,..................	400 00
"	28	533	E. A. Sheldon,....	Boarding Hall,....	63 50

WARRANT STATEMENT—Continued.

1866.		Number.	To Whom Drawn.	Object.		Amount.
April	28	534	E. A. Sheldon,....	Boarding Hall,........................		$500 00
May	10	535		Boarding Hall,........................		18 17
"	10	536		Boarding Hall,........................		200 00
"	14	537	M. Miles,.........	Moving farm house,..................		55 00
"	14	538		Farm department and ditching,......		100 08
"	15	539	M'Ewen&Burnham,	Repairs on garden wagon,...........		12 25
"	15	540	Lansing & Son,....	Blacksmith work,....................		10 45
"	15	541	Elwanger & Barry.	Evergreens,...........................		40 50
"	15	542	A. Brown,........	Making desk,.................	$8 00	
				Making bee boxes,............	1 79	9 79
May	16	543	R. C. Kedzie,.....	Salary,................................		100 00
"	16	544	Geo. T. Fairchild,.	Salary,................................		100 00
"	24	545	T. C. Abbot,......	Expenses of board,..................		
				A. C. Prutzman,...	25 20	
				H. G. Wells,..................	24 75	
				O. Hosford,...................	12 00	
				Chas. Rich,...................	16 50	
				Justus Gage,.................	22 00	
				D. Carpenter,.................	16 95	117 40
May	29	546	R. S. Robson,.....	Ticking and sheeting,................		14 88
"	29	547	S. R. Greene,.....	Boxes for Secretary's Reports,.......		16 50
"	29	548	T. C. Abbot,......	Salary to June 1,.....................		312 50
"	29	549	M. Miles,.........	Salary to June 1,...		208 33
"	29	550	R. C. Kedzie,......	Salary to June 1,.....................		108 33
"	29	551	A. N. Prentiss,....	Salary to June 1,.....................		166 67
"	29	552	O. Clute,..........	Salary to June 1,.....................		166 67
"	29	553	Geo. T. Fairchild,.	Salary to June 1,.....................		66 67
"	29	554	Sanford Howard,..	Salary to June 1,.....................		83 34
"	29	555	E. A. Sheldon,....	Salary to June 1, ...		137 50
"	29	556	A. F. Allen,.......	Salary to June 1,.....................		83 34
"	29	557	W. W. Daniels,....	Salary to June 1,.....................		105 00
June	5	558	E. A. Sheldon,.....	Boarding Hall,........................		39 42
"	5	559		Boarding Hall,........................		650 00
"	13	560	A. N. Prentiss,....	Furniture for College,...............		15 83

WARRANT STATEMENT—Continued.

1866.		Number.	To whom Drawn.	Object.		Amount.
June	13	561		Horticultural department,...........		$66 18
"	18	562	E. A. Sheldon,.....	Boarding Hall,......................		21 44
"	18	563		Boarding Hall,.........		150 00
"	20	564	Frederick Stearns,	Chloride of lime, ...		12 90
"	21	565	R. C. Kedzie,......	Chemicals,..................		21 99
"	21	566	M. Miles,.........	Farm department,..................		100 00
"	22	567	Geo. T. Fairchild,..	Salary, ...		100 00
"	22	568	R. C. Kedzie,......	Chemicals,..........		150 00
"	22	569		Chemicals,............................		25 00
"	25	570	J. L. Harris,......	Flower pots,......		21 26
"	27	571	Sanford Howard,..	For Essex swine,....................		50 00
"	27	572		Salary,..............................		41 67
"	28	573	R. C. Kedzie,......	Chemicals,.........		12 65
"	28	574	T. C. Abbot,......	Refunded to students,.........	$3 30	
				Repairs,......................	7 90	
				Advertising,.................	4 90	
				Secretary's office expenses,....	5 75	20 95
June	28	575	T. C. Abbot,......	Salary,..............................		234 37
"	28	576	E. A. Sheldon,....	Boarding Hall,......................		100 00
July	2	577	M. Miles,...... ...	Farm department,..................		279 92
"	2	578		Farm department,...................		150 00
"	16	579	E. A. Sheldon,.....	Boarding Hall,......................		17 38
"	16	580		Boarding Hall, ($6 50 furniture),.....		400 00
"	16	581	Wm. Moots,..	Repairs in laboratory,...............		2 75
"	16	582	F. M. Cowles,.....	Carpet for farm house,..............		40 20
"	20	583	M. Miles,.........	Farm department,.		39 09
"	20	584		Farm department,..................		64 00
"	20	585		Salary,..............................		100 00
"	20	586	A. N. Prentiss,....	Expenses on College Hall,............		7 00
"	20	587		Horticultural department,...........		50 00
"	23	588	E. A. Sheldon,.....	Boarding Hall,......................		150 00
"	31	589		Boarding Hall,..		250 00
August	2	590	N. Parish,........	Stump puller,........................		57 00
"	3	591	Sanford Howard,..	Salary,..............................		41 67

WARRANT STATEMENT—Continued.

1866.		NUMBER.	TO WHOM DRAWN.	OBJECT.	AMOUNT.
August	6	592	Geo. T. Fairchild,.	Library and books,..................	$275 00
"	13	593	M. Miles,.........	Farm department,.....................	150 00
"	14	594	E. A. Sheldon,.....	Boarding Hall,.......................	175 00
"	14	595		Boarding Hall,.......................	100 00
"	15	596	R. C. Kedzie,......	Chemicals and making shelves in lab.,	42 74
"	15	597	A. N. Prentiss.....	Salary,..............................	250 00
"	15	598	Oscar Clute,.......	Salary,..............................	50 00
"	21	599	M. Miles,..........	Farm department,....	195 75
"	21	600		Farm department,.....................	124 92
"	22	601	Sanford Howard,..	Money refunded to students,.........	13 19
"	22	602	T. C. Abbot,......	Postage and exchange,...............	6 03
"	22	603	R. C. Kedzie,......	Repairs and exchange,...............	3 10
"	22	604	T. C. Abbot,......	Salary,..............................	234 37
"	23	605	M. Miles,.........	Farm department,....................	50 00
"	30	606	Nathan Parish,....	Stump puller,........................	51 90
"	22	607	Sanford Howard,..	Salary,..............................	41 67
"	30	608	A. C. Pautzman,..	Expenses attending Board meeting,...	23 80
"	30	609	H. G. Wells,......	Expenses attending Board meeting,...	11 00
"	30	610	O. Hosford,.......	Expenses attending Board meeting,...	10 00
Sept.	1	611	R. C. Kedzie,.....	Refunding house rent,...............	30 00
"	1	612	T. C. Abbot,......	Refunding house rent,...............	50 00
"	1	613	E. A. Sheldon,.....	Boarding Hall,.......................	50 00
"	1	614	M. Miles,.	Salary,..............................	50 00
"	4	615		Salary to Sept. 1,..................	162 50
"	4	616	R. C. Kedzie,......	Salary to Sept. 1,..................	312 50
"	4	617	O. Clute,..........	Salary to Sept. 1,..................	200 00
"	4	618	Geo. T. Fairchild,.	Salary to Sept. 1,..................	150 00
"	4	619	E. A. Sheldon,....	Salary to Sept. 1,..................	112 50
"	4	620	A. F. Allen,.......	Salary to Sept. 1,..................	100 00
"	4	621	W. W. Daniels,....	Salary to Sept. 1,..................	105 00
"	4	622	M. Miles,.........	Farm department,....................	50 00
"	7	623	Home Ins. Co., N.Y.,	Insurance on barns,.................	24 00
"	10	624	E. A. Sheldon,....	Repair of sewer,............. $37 27	
				Boarding Hall,............... 337 73	375 00

WARRANT STATEMENT—Continued.

1866.		Number.	To whom Drawn.	Object.		Amount.
Sept.	10	625	A. N. Prentiss,....	Garden department,.................		$33 75
"	12	626	E. A. Sheldon,....	Boarding Hall,.....................		125 00
"	12	627		Boarding Hall,......................		477 65
"	12	628	S. R. Greene,......	Work in laboratory,.................		4 00
"	12	629	A. N. Prentiss,....	Horticultural department,...........		16
"	12	630		Horticultural department,...........		39 20
"	17	631	E. A. Sheldon.....	Boarding Hall,......................		100 00
"	21	632	T. C. Abbot,... ..	Salary,.............................		100 00
"	25	633	A. N. Prentiss,....	Horticultural department,...........		50 00
"	28	634	E. A. Sheldon,.....	Boarding Hall,.................		200 00
Oct.	2	635	S. Howard,.......	Salary to Oct. 1,....................		41
"	4	636	E. A. Sheldon,.....	Boarding Hall,......................		275 00
"	11	637		Boarding Hall,......................		100 00
"	20	638		Boarding Hall,......................		300 00
"	20	639		Boarding Hall,......................		175 00
Nov.	3	640	A. N. Prentiss,....	Horticultural department,...........		50 00
"	12	641	R. C. Kedzie,......	Coommencement expenses,..........		30 00
"	13	642		Salary,.............................		100 00
	13	643	A. N. Prentiss,....	Salary,.............................		100 00
"	13	644	Oscar Clute,.......	Salary,.............................		50 00
"	13	645	Geo. T. Fairchild,..	Salary,.............................		150 00
"	13	646	W. W. Daniels,....	Salary,.............................		105 00
"	30	647	M. Miles,..........	Farm department,...................		539 07
"	30	648		Farm department,...................		9 88
"	30	649	E. A. Sheldon,.....	Salary,.............................		150 00
"	30	650		Boarding Hall, final account,.........		5 52
"	30	651	P. N. Gallup,.....	Work in garden,.....................		5 00
"	30	652	T. C. Abbot,......	Refunded student,............	$1 56	
				Laboratory,..................	52	
				Advertisement,...............	30	
				Postage, office expenses,......	17 75	20 13
"	30	653	R. C. Kedzie,......	Commencement expenses,............		9 50
"	30	654	P. N. Gallup,......	Labor in garden,....................		21 44
Total,...						$20,767 06

SUMMARY OF WARRANT ACCOUNT OF 1866.

Salaries,	$7,709 20
NOTE.—This embraces unpaid salary account of 1865. A part of the salaries for 1866 is still unpaid.	
Books,	364 52
NOTE.—Books are purchased for library and to sell again to students. The amount above given exceeds receipts for books by $45 59.	
Boarding Hall, running expenses	7,093 85
NOTE.—Of this sum the College pays, by paying wages to the students for their labor, $2,234 17; cash receipts from students, less matriculation fees, $4,792 01. The amount yet to be received from students is fully sufficient to cover the balance of current expenses above cash receipts and wages ($67 69), as well as all indebtedness of the College on account of the Boarding	
Secretary's office, expenses traveling, reports, &c.,	76 50
NOTE.—The Secretary had a balance of $206 01, Jan. 1, 1866, which accounts for the smallness of the warrant account for this year.	
Advertising, insurance and commencement expenses,	288 70
Chemical laboratory, repairs, shelves and chemicals,	354 02
Repairs about buildings other than Boarding Hall,	49 50
Chloride of lime and copperas,	12 90
Furniture for College Hall, chairs, &c.,	15 88
Expenses of State Board of Agriculture,	255 45
NOTE.—A portion of these expenses is still unpaid.	
Postage, envelopes, stamps, post office box,	37 86
Stationery and blank books,	30 42
Personal expenses of President, and exchange and express,	7 75
Refunded to students,	25 85
Refunded house rent,	80 00
Stump puller,	108 90
Essex swine,	50 00
Furnishing farm house,	55 08
NOTE.—The cottage that stood empty, near the apple orchard, has been removed, fitted up, and is now occupied by the foreman of the farm.	
Unclassified blacksmith bills,	105 88
NOTE.—$10 45 for 1866, the rest for 1865.	
Wagon for Horticultural Department,	102 25
Desk and bee boxes for Horticultural Department,	9 79
Flower pots " " "	21 26
Evergreens " " "	40 50

Horticultural Department,		$339 00
NOTE.—Of this there was paid—		
For labor, $219 69		
" College Hall, 7 00		
" blacksmithing, 9 45		
" seeds, 38 05		
" cultivator and other implements, 33 94		
" manure, 9 91		
" paint, wagon and harness repairs, stationery, &c. 20 96	$339 00	
Expended by Superintendent of farm, as follows:		
Swamp land—		
Ditching on big marsh,	$394 75	
Grass seed,	8 35	
Expenses of surveying, superintending and sales,	16 85	
		419 95
Stock—		
Span of horses,	$400 00	
Galloway cattle and Cotswold sheep,	413 11	
Essex pigs,	6 53	
Devon bull, expenses and freight,	51 10	
Exchange,	16	
		870 90
Moving and repairs of farm house	$109 13	
Furniture for "	57 83	
		166 96
NOTE.—The person who contracted to move the house got severely injured; a good part of the removal was effected by the farm hands and teams.		
Implements for farm—		
Horse rake,	$31 14	
Set of measures for sheep barn, freight on horse fork, sheep rack, shovels..,	11 30	
		42 44
Repairs on wagon and mower,		22 70
Implements on wood account and permanent improvement account—		
Paid by farm Superintendent on stump puller,	$34 01	
Axes and helves,	20 05	
		54 06
Repairs on horse power		22 75
Seeds—		
Clover,	$16 50	
Vetches,	7 66	
Roots,	23 25	
Wheat,	32 50	
		81 41
Pumps,		22 00

Feed—		
Oil cake and freight,	$50 66	
Mill feed, corn and hay, and freight and expense...	338 86	
		$389 52
Expense at fairs with stock,		49 53
Expenses for College—		
For library, purchase of books,	$28 80	
" museum, jars, &c.,	12 87	
" Boarding Hall,	6 90	
" tent, copperas, register,	29 20	
		77 77
Office expenses—		
Revenue stamps, stationery, pass-book, ink, chimneys, twine, &c.,		11 60
Blacksmithing,		1 80
Lumber—		
For sheep barn,	$14 62	
Shingles, farm house,	2 25	
Plank,	97 89	
		114 76
Halters, harness repairs, whip, bull halter, brooms, medicine for sheep, marking materials for sheep, and other incidentals on account of care of stock,		15 59
Lime, plaster, nails, salt, toll, putty, machine oil, soap, &c.,		43 29
Current expenses of farm house,		85 69
Carpenters' work for sheep yards and other objects,		53 70
Labor—		
For current expenses of farm,	$492 52	
" wood account,	153 03	
" permanent improvements,	148 16	
" Boarding Hall,	68 20	
" College,	33 76	
		895 68
Making total cash expenditure by Sup't of farm		$ 3,442 00
Total amount of warrant account		$20,767 06

INDEBTEDNESS, DECEMBER 1, 1866.

Salaries of officers,	$1,527 08
Expenses of the members of the Board of Agriculture, in attending meetings of the Board, about	225 00
Blacksmith bills,	49 17
Museum expenses and small account for paint,	57 56
Harness repairs,	7 52
Furniture for College and farm house, &c.,	27 50
Printing catalogues, warrant book, labor account, binding for library, and the like,	179 95
Hardware bills, implements and the like,	384 73
On account of Secretary's office,	150 00
Boarding Hall bills,	186 05
Farm house bills,	258 47
Expenses relating to purchase of stock,	400 00
	$3,453 13
Subtract funds in hands of Secretary of the College, December 1, 1866,	934 97
Indebtedness,	$2,518 16

ESTIMATES FOR 1867-8.

Salaries, including and Steward, Foreman Assistant Chemist,	$10,575 00
Debt at date, Dec. 1, 1866,	2,518 16
Expenses of meetings of Board of Agriculture,	500 00
Salary of Secretary Howard,	500 00
Fxpenses of the Secretary of the Board and College,	500 00
Labor of students,	2,500 00
Expenses of hired hands, three on the farm and one in the garden, with their board, and all current expenses of farm house,	2,200 00
Expenses of Horticultural Department, grounds, lawns, orchards, manures, tools, seeds, &c., but *not* including a green house and propagating house, which, however, the College very much needs,	500 00
Postage,	50 00
Printing, binding, &c.,	175 00
College Hall expenses, lights, office expenses, repairs, museum, freight, teaming for College, &c.,	500 00
Furniture, hardware, insurance, &c.,	400 00
Farm implements, tools, &c.,	500 00
Permanent improvements on farm above receipts, fencing, piggery, &c.,	1,000 00
Other incidentals, rebuilding ice house and wood shed, that have been destroyed,	1,000 00
	$23,418 16
Same for 1868, less indebtedness,	20,900 00
	$44,318 16

The College should repay an indebtedness to its library fund of $500.

REPORT

OF THE

FACULTY OF THE STATE AGRICULTURAL COLLEGE.

[EXTRACTS.]

The past year has been, in many respects, a pleasant and successful one in the history of the College. The number of students has been greater than during any previous year, there being 108 on the roll. Not all these have been in attendance at once, for the dormitories, when crowded to their utmost capacity, will accommodate but 82 students. When a student has from any cause been obliged to leave the Institution, others have stood ready to take his place, thus keeping the number full. More than thirty applicants have been denied admission.

The number of dormitories in the Boarding Hall which can be occupied by students, is 19. During the past two years two rooms in the College Hall have been occupied by students, though at some inconvenience to the College. Of these twenty-one rooms for the use of students, nineteen have been occupied by four students each; the remaining two by three students each. The necessity that four students should occupy a room, has been an evil to the College since its first opening. It is an evil which only increased accommodations can remove.

The greatest need of the College at present, is more dormitories and enlarged arrangements for boarding. It is believed that if the College had accommodations for one hundred and fifty students, it could have that number in attendance the coming year, and that the number of applications will soon be much greater than that. The rooms of the present Boarding Hall could be so altered as to give a commodious kitchen, laundry, and dining hall for one hundred and fifty students; also rooms for the use of the steward and the necessary help, spare bed-rooms, and dormitories for a few students. The class rooms, with the exception of the laboratory, would need no alteration, in order to accommodate one hundred and fifty students.

INCREASED FACILITIES IN THE LABORATORY.

The need of a new Laboratory must be apparent to any one who considers the necessity of *abundant light and free ventilation* in a laboratory devoted especially to chemical analysis. Facility in chemical analysis often depends entirely upon good light, as the evidence of the presence or absence of a given substance is found often in delicate shades of color, or in the existence of precipitates, which can be seen only in a good light. The present Labratory, 27x50, is lighted by two windows, and the tables are so arranged as to intercept a large part of the light. Some improvement has been secured by throwing the Balance Room into the Laboratory and thus securing a third window, but even now the supply of light is entirely inadequate in the best weather, and on cloudy and stormy days the students must frequently suspend their analyses. There are no means of securing good side light in the present Laboratory, without injuring the architectural appearance of the Hall, and no opportunity whatever of securing sky light or vertical light, which is very important.

The facilities for ventilation are equally unsatisfactory. With a large class of students working in the poisonous and corrosive vapors and gases of a Laboratory for three hours each day, with the contamination of the atmosphere arising from so many lamps constantly burning, good ventilation becomes a vital necessity. This cannot be secured in the present building. And not only is the Labratory unhealthy from this cause, but the rooms over the Laboratory are rendered unwholesome and offensive from the same cause.

Not only is the room unfitted for a Laboratory, but it is

insufficient for the College with the present number of students, and will be entirely inadequate when increased dormitory accommodations will allow all to come to the Agricultural College who desire to do so. The tables in the Laboratory afford room for sixteen students, and this present year there are nineteen in Analysis. The surplus had to be placed in unusual and inconvenient positions to pursue their researches. What arrangements can be made for the prospective Sophomore class of next year with its twenty-eight students, in addition to the students in the Select Course, who may wish to pursue Chemical Analysis, the Faculty will not attempt to say; but it is evident that the Laboratory is insufficient, and that that insufficiency must become more embarrassing with the growth of the College. It is therefore earnestly recommended to the Hon. Board of Agriculture, that they will take steps to secure at an early date, the erection of a building for a Chemical Laboratory, adequate to the present and future wants of the Agricultural College.

COURSE OF INSTRUCTION.

So long as there is no larger corps of Professors than at present, there can perhaps be no marked change for the better, in the course of instruction. The departments of Geology and Entomology should be organized at an early day. They are departments of great importance in a course of agricultural instruction, and would be of much value to the College, and to the State. Instruction has been given in them during the present year.

FACILITIES FOR INSTRUCTION.

The attention of the Board has heretofore been called to the fact that a green-house is essential to a thorough course in Botany and Horticulture, and to the prosecution of many important experiments. To the representations already made, the Faculty has at present noting further to add.

Geology cannot be properly pursued until the Geological cabinet contains typical specimens of the different kinds of rocks, and a suite of fossils sufficient for purposes of illustration. The present meagre collection is quite inadequate, and means should be taken for its improvement.

For the use of the classes in Animal Physiology, Zoölogy, and Stock-Breeding, there should be a collection of skeletons, manikins, and casts of man and the domestic animals; also a collection of dried and alcoholic preparations.

Besides the green-house mentioned above, a woodshed, ice-house and piggery are much needed. The present woodshed and ice-house have always been unsightly, and are now so dilapidated as to be of no further use. The ice-house should be constructed in time to be stocked with ice the coming winter. A set of globes is very much needed for use in nearly all the classes.

The advantage to the College of a few hundred dollars judiciously expended in the purchase of books, can hardly be over-estimated, for the library is very deficient in all departments. Works on gardening and farming are best represented, but these are by no means numerous.

REPORT

OF EXPERIMENTS IN AGRICULTURAL CHEMISTRY FOR 1866.

The Professor of Agricultural Chemistry, to whom was assigned, by the Honorable Board of Agriculture, certain experiments with composts of muck and night-soil, and upon the relations of the volatile constituents of manures to vegetable growth, submits the following report:

The compost of muck and night-soil was formed April 12th, using three parts of muck, and one of night-soil. The compost was thoroughly turned and mixed, May 4th, again May 18th, and finally, May 31st.

The ground upon which the compost was used in prosecuting the experiment, was a piece of light, sandy soil, in the vegetable garden. It had not been manured in two years past, and was greatly exhausted by previous cropping. The ground was plowed and harrowed, May 31st, preparatory to planting the corn. It was carefully measured off into rows, three and one-half feet apart each way.

The seed corn used was a white dent. It was soaked in simple water for twenty-four hours previous to planting. It was planted June 1st. Seven rows of the corn received two shovel fulls of the compost in each hill; the ground and compost being mixed before planting. It was afterwards found that the mixing was imperfectly done, and in consequence of the large amount of the compost underlying the corn, the growth was unhealthy for several weeks after it came up. The result would probably have been more satisfactory, if half the amount of compost in each hill had been used, and the mixing more thoroughly performed.

The 9th row received no manure at or preceding the time of

planting, but a small handful of plaster was scattered over each hill, June 12th. The 10th row was treated in the same manner, except that it received on the 12th of June, a teaspoonful of salt instead of plaster. The 11th and 12th rows received no dressing of any kind, serving as a basis of comparison for the rest.

To test the effect of the volatile constituents of manures, nine jugs ($1\frac{1}{2}$ gallons each) were filled two-thirds full of manure, six with horse-dung, two with hen-dung, and one with urine, and sufficient water added to the dry manure to wet it thoroughly. In the mouth of each jug a lead tube $\frac{3}{4}$ inch diameter and 20 inches long, was fastened air-tight, and the open extremity inserted in the middle of a hill of corn, passing down three inches below the surface, so that the volatile products of the fermentation of the manure might be conveyed to the soil sustaining the hill of corn, and its effects upon the growth of the corn might thus be ascertained.

These jugs were placed by their respective hills June 6th, as soon as the corn came up, and were left undisturbed during the whole period of the growth.

The corn was cultivated June 14th, and hoed June 16th; cultivated the second time June 22d, and hoed June 25th. It was cut Sept. 26th and 27th, and husked October 16th, and both corn and stalks carefully weighed, with the following results:

The two rows without any dressing, gave 50 lbs. 8 oz. corn, and 137 lbs. 8 oz. stalks, or 27.29 bushels per acre of corn, and 5,201.61 lbs. stalks.

The row top-dressed with salt, gave 21 lbs. 4 oz. of corn, and 85 lbs. of stalks, or at the rate of 22.96 bushels per acre of corn, and 6,430 lbs. of stalks.

The row receiving a top-dressing of plaster, gave 18 lbs. 12 oz. of corn, and 69 lbs. 8 oz. of stalks; at the rate of 20.26 bushels of corn, and 5,257 lbs. of stalks per acre.

The nine hills with the jugs, gave 9 lbs. 7 oz. of corn, and

22 lbs. 12 oz. of stalks, or at the rate of 53.27 bushels per acre, and 4,021.3 lbs. stalks.

The seven rows receiving the compost of muck and night-soil, yielded 486 lbs. 8 oz. of corn, and 710 lbs. of stalks, or at the rate of 75.33 bushels of corn per acre, and 7,668 lbs. of stalks.

In these experiments the soil seems to have been so destitute of organic matter, as to have derived no benefit from the top dressing of salt and plaster. The compost of muck and night-soil, caused a marked improvement in the growth of the corn, an improvement strikingly evident to the eye even at a distance, while the corn was growing. The increase of corn was over forty-six bushels per acre, and of stalks, 2,466 lbs. The increase of grain per acre from the volatile products of the manure, as shown by the experiments with the jugs, was twenty-six bushels, or a gain of more than 87 per cent.

To test the relative absorption of the volatile products of decomposition in manures, when placed on the surface of the ground or buried beneath it, I instituted the following experiment: I spread upon the surface of the ground, to the depth of one inch, a layer of fresh horse-manure, and another similar layer of hen-manure; I also buried the same quantity of hen-manure in the soil, covering it to the depth of four inches. On the surface of all these plots thus prepared, I placed a plate containing dilute sulphuric acid, to absorb and retain any ammonia which might be produced by the fermentation of the manure, and which might escape into the air, and thus come in contact with the acid. To confine such volatile matters, and also to protect the acid from the effects of the weather, I placed over each one a barrel inverted.

This experiment was instituted June 12th. While I was enjoying my vacation by a trip up Lake Superior, the covering of the barrel over the manure buried four inches deep in the soil, blew off, and that part of the experiment failed.

The contents of the plates under the other barrels were analyzed August 8th, and the quantity of ammonia ascertained in each. The acid in the plate over the horse-manure lying on the surface of the ground, contained 1.96 grains of ammonia, or at the rate of 6.44 lbs. per acre. The acid in the plate over the hen-manure contained 3.453 grains of ammonia, or at the rate of 13.8 lbs. per acre. The unfortunate accident to the third barrel prevented any comparison of relative loss by placing on surface or by burying beneath surface.

The importance of settling by definite experiment, the questions arising from the relations of volatile matters of manures to vegetable growth, and of absorption by soil when placed on its surface or buried beneath it, would justify repeating and extending these experiments.

R. C. KEDZIE.

Agricultural College, Nov. 12, 1866.

REPORT

OF EXPERIMENTS IN PRACTICAL AGRICULTURE.

To the President of the State Agricultural College:

The following report on experiments in practical agriculture, for the year 1866, is respectfully presented:

EXPERIMENTS IN THE APPLICATION OF TOP-DRESSINGS TO GRASS LANDS.

This is a continuation of the experiments commenced in 1864, and continued in 1865. (See report of Sec'y for 1864, page 117, and for 1865, page 235.)

No additional fertilizers have been applied since the commencement of the experiments, in 1864.

The first crop this season was cut in the forenoon of July 11th, and put up in small cocks in the afternoon. The cocks were opened July 12th, and hauled to the barn in good order, in the afternoon. Care was taken to secure uniformity in the curing of each piece.

The clover, which comprised the largest portion of the crop last year, has nearly all disappeared, the crop of the present year being in the main timothy.

The results this season are given in Table 1, showing for each piece the rate of yield per acre, the gain per acre, the gain per cent., and the kind and amount, per acre, of fertilizers applied in 1864:

TABLE 1.

Subdivisio	Yield per acre in lbs	Gain per acre in lbs.	Gain per cent. in lbs.	KIND AND AMOUNT, PER ACRE, OF TOP-DRESSINGS APPLIED IN 1864.
No. 1.	1,388.83	....	....	None.
No. 2.	1,720.00	331.12	23.80	Two bushels of Plaster.
No. 3.	1,602.22	213 34	15.36	Five bushels of Wood Ashes.
No. 4.	1,780.00	391.12	28.16	Twenty loads of Muck.
No. 5.	2,157.77	768.89	55.36	Twenty loads of Muck and 3 bush. of salt.
No. 6.	2,431.11	1.042 23	75.04	Three bushels of Salt.
No. 7.	2,600 00	1,211.12	87 20	Twenty loads of Horse-manure.
No. 8.	2,333.33	944.45	68 00	Twenty loads of Cow-manure.

The first crop was quite uniform on each of the subdivisions. The second crop was not cut, as it did not make a uniform growth, and on most of the subdivisions the timothy was replaced to a great extent by weeds, that interfered with the further progress of the experiment.

The result of the experiment for the three years, (1864, 1865, and 1866,) is shown in Table 2, for each subdivision, the total yield per acre, the total gain per acre, the total gain per cent., and the kind and amount per acre, of fertilizers, applied in 1864, at the commencement of the experiment:

TABLE 2.

Subdivisions.	Total yield per acre in pounds.	Total gain per acre in pounds.	Total gain per cent. in pounds.	KIND AND AMOUNT, PER ACRE, OF FERTILIZERS APPLIED IN 1864.
No. 1.	8,74	......	......	None.
No. 2.	13,226	4,484	51.29	Two bushels of Plaster.
No. 3.	12,907	4,165	47.64	Five bushels of Wood Ashes.
No. 4.	13,816	5,074	58.04	Twenty loads of Muck.
No. 5.	14,819	6,077	69.51	Twenty loads of Muck and three bushels of Salt.
No. 6.	13,969	5,227	59 79	Three bushels of Salt.
No. 7.	14,986	6,244	71.42	Twenty loads of Horse-manure.
No. 8.	14,564	5,822	66.60	Twenty loads of Cow-manure.

EXPERIMENT IN THE APPLICATION OF MANURES TO CORN.

For the purpose of ascertaining the best method of applying manures, a piece of land of apparently uniform quality was selected, in the north-west corner of Field No. 5, and divided into plots of one-tenth of an acre each, designated by numbers from one to eight.

The soil, a clay loam, was summer-fallowed in 1864, and sowed to winter wheat, which was harvested the 14th of July, 1865.

Manures were applied as follows:

Plot No. 1. Five loads of horse-manure plowed under.

" " 2. Five loads of cow-manure plowed under.

" " 3. No manure.

" " 4. Five loads of horse-manure on the surface after plowing, and harrowed in.

Plot No. 5. Five loads of cow-manure on the surface after plowing, and harrowed in.

Plot No. 6. No manure.

" " 7. Five loads of horse-manure on the surface after harrowing, and before planting.

Plot No. 8. Five loads of cow-manure on the surface after harrowing, and before planting.

The plots were plowed on the 15th of May, to the depth of six inches, and planted on the 16th. The corn was of the variety known as white dent, planted in drills four feet apart, running north and south. A space of eight feet was left between the plots, so as to prevent the manure on each plot from affecting the adjoining plots on each side.

The preparation of the soil before planting, and the after cultivation were the same on each plot, and care was taken to have the work performed each day, distributed uniformly over each plot of the experiment.

The corn was cut up and put in stooks on the 22d of September. After the stalks were thoroughly dried, the corn was husked and the stalks and corn were each carefully weighed, with the following results:

TABLE 3.

Plot.	KIND OF MANURE AND MODE OF APPLYING.	Weight of corn in ear, pounds.	Weight of Stalks, pounds.
No. 1.	Horse-manure plowed under,......	328½	346
No. 2.	Cow-manure plowed under, ...	310½	330
No. 3.	No manure,...............	291	290
No. 4.	Horse-manure on the surface, dragged in,.................	252	304
No. 5.	Cow-manure on the surface, dragged in, ...	257	260
No. 6.	No manure,..	231	28
No. 7.	Horse-manure on the surface after dragging, ...	230	356
No. 8.	Cow-manure on the surface after dragging, ...	350	348

Two pieces, No's 3 and 6, were left without manure, as a standard of comparison.

The remarkable difference in the yield of these plots could not have been predicted from an examination of the land before planting

So far as we were able to judge from a careful inspection of each piece, there was no difference in quality or texture of soil.

Experience has, however, shown that in field experiments such variations in the yield of unmanured plots, are not uncommon, even when a chemical analysis has shown that the elements of the soil are the same in the different plots under experiment.

From this fact it will be seen that it is difficult to obtain a reliable standard of comparison by which the results of field experiments may be tested.

The larger the pieces experimented on, the greater the danger of fallacy from these obscure differences in the properties of soils.

Accuracy can only be secured by a frequent repetition of the experiments, and the unmanured plots should at least equal in number the plots on which the manures are applied.

One of the best methods of determining the relative fertility of experimented plots, would perhaps be, to weigh accurately the preceding crop on each piece that is to be used for experimental purposes.

The standard thus obtained would certainly be of great value, and in connection with a system of small, unmanured plots, frequently repeated, it would add very much to the reliability of results.

I would recommend that the piece of land south of the Boarding Hall, which has been used for experiments in top-dressing grass land, be sowed to oats in the spring, (without manure,) and divided into permanent plots, of one-tenth of an acre; the crop grown upon each to be carefully weighed, and put on record as a standard of comparison for other experiments that are to follow.

EXPERIMENTS IN FEEDING PIGS.

Three Essex sow pigs of the same litter were fed cow's milk for four weeks; the amount consumed being carefully weighed each day, and the pigs weighed each week.

At the commencement of the experiment, July 21st, the pigs were eleven days old; their feed up to this time having been the same as during the experiment.

The results are given in Table 4, showing the weight of the pigs at the beginning of each week, the milk consumed each week, and the gain each week:

TABLE 4.

NUMBER OF THE PIGS.	1ST WEEK.			2D WEEK.			3D WEEK.			4TH WEEK.		
	Weight of pigs July 21st.	Milk consumed in lbs. & dec.	Gain in lbs. & tenths.	Weight of pigs July 28.	Milk consumed, lbs.	Gain in lbs & tenths.	Weight of pigs Aug. 4th.	Milk consumed, lbs.	Gain in lbs & tenths.	Weight of pigs Aug. 11th.	Milk consumed, lbs.	Gain in lbs & tenths.
No. 1, ...				6.25		3.00	9.25		3.00	12.25		4.00
" 2, ...	14.50	79.19	11.00	9.75	106.94	5.50	15.25	129.94	3.50	18.75	141.81	4.25
" 3, ...				9.50		5.00	14.50		4.50	19.00		5.75
Total, ...	14.50	79.19	11.00	25.50	106.94	13.50	39.00	129.94	11.00	50.00	141.81	14.00

The following table shows the average amount of milk consumed each week, for each pound of live weight, and the gain per cent. of live weight, for each week:

TABLE 5.

1st. Week.		2d Week.		3d Week.		4th Week.		Av. for 4 Weeks.	
Average am't of milk consumed for each 1 lb of live w't of animal.	Gain per cent.	Average am't of milk consumed for each 1 lb. of live w't of animal.	Gain per cent.	Average am't of milk consumed for each 1 lb. of live w't of animal.	Gain per cent.	Average am't of milk consumed for each 1 lb. of live w't of animal.	Gain per cent.	Average am't of milk consumed per week for each 1 lb. of live weight of animal.	Average gain per cent.
LBS.		LBS.		LBS.		LBS.		LBS.	
3.96	75.86	3.32	52.92	2.92	28.20	2.49	28.00	2.98	46.25

From this it is seen that the average amount of feed consumed for each lb. of live weight, and also the gain per cent. are constantly diminishing as the animals increase in size.

This agrees with results obtained by Mr. Lawes, in feeding pigs, who found a "rapid decrease in the rate of consumption of food to a given weight of animal as it fattens."

In the following table, the average amount of milk required to produce 1 lb. of increase of live weight, is given for each week of the experiment:

TABLE 6.

	1st week.	2d week.	3d week.	week.	Average for 4 weeks.
Average amount of milk consumed to produce 1 lb. of increase of live weight,...............	7.20	7.92	11.81	10.13	9.25

By referring to Table 4, it will be seen that the gain per week was less in proportion during the third week of the experiment.

This is accounted for by a slight derangement of the digestive organs, that was observed during this week, as shown in a tendency to constipation.

This explains the larger amount of milk consumed the third week of the trial, to produce 1 lb. of increase, than was required to produce the same amount of increase the fourth week.

By making a proper allowance for this variation in Table 6, the results would seem to indicate that the amount of feed required to produce a given increase of live weight, is greater as the animals increase in size.

It is to be regretted that the experiment was not continued for a greater length of time. After the 18th of August, it was thought best to furnish the pigs with some vegetable food, in addition to the exclusive milk diet to which they had been restricted.

For want of suitable facilities for weighing the mixed food, the experiment was closed at this date.

Pig No. 1 was sold soon after the close of the experiment.

Pigs No. 2 and 3, have been weighed several times since the close of the experiment, with the following results:

	Aug. 25th.	Sept. 8th.	Dec. 25th.
Pig No. 2 weighed.........	29 lbs.	42¾ lbs.	139 lbs.
" " 3 "	29¾ lbs.	45¾ lbs.	154 lbs.

At the date of the last weighing, it will be seen that the pigs were 5½ months old.

Respectfully submitted.

M. MILES.

College Farm, Dec. 28th, 1866.

CHARACTERISTICS OF THE SEASON OF 1866.

The season of 1866 will be long remembered for some of its peculiar characteristics; especially will it be remembered by the farmers of Michigan, as well as those of other portions of the country, for its untoward influence on some of their most important interests. A dry and rather cold winter was followed by a cold spring, the two latter months of which were marked by drought, and the prevalence of high, blasting winds. Vegetation was kept backward. Toward the latter part of May and the coming in of June, a favorable change occurred in regard to moisture, which caused grass to rapidly improve. But June was cold for a summer month. July brought the first hot weather, and it might be added, the only hot weather of the season. Several days, from the first to the twentieth of the month, were unusually hot, the thermometer rising above 90° in the shade. With August the weather relapsed into its cold habit, and at the close of the month people were heard to remark that it had been the coldest August they ever knew. We barely escaped frost, the mercury running down to within two degrees of the freezing point, while the mean temperature for the month was 62° 60 min.,—more than three degrees below that of the corresponding month of 1865, which was rather cool. The month, like the three succeeding ones, was remarkable for cloudiness, and to this was attributed the absence of frost. The low temperature, however, checked the growth of most plants; it particularly retarded the filling of Indian corn, and was an important cause of the damage of that crop by frost, in the following month.

It was hoped that with September would come warmer weather, as was the case in 1865, but the hope was not realized.

The autumn set in with even more clouded skies and a more ungenial temperature. Indian corn lingered along, making little progress toward maturity, till on the night of the 14th there came a frost which did much injury to the crop, and on the night of the 21st, a harder frost occurred, which nearly ruined many fields. The injury was not confined to this State, but extended to Northern Illinois, Wisconsin, and other parts of the country in the same parallel.

The month was not only remarkable for cloudiness, but for the prevalence of rain storms, which in some parts of the country, particularly in Western Ohio and Eastern Indiana, caused disastrous floods, which sweeping through some of the most fertile valleys, destroyed an immense amount of Indian corn. The quantity of rain noted as having fallen at Urbana, Ohio, from the 17th to the 20th of September, was 7.43 inches, and the quantity for the month was 15.88 inches, or more than one-third the annual average for that locality.

Michigan was visited by no such floods, though the quantity of rain that fell was large, and the unusual cloudiness and dampness was very unfavorable to securing late crops of oats and spring wheat; and much grain which was stacked was lost or greatly damaged, by heating and sprouting. The sowing of winter wheat was delayed fully two weeks, in many cases, by the wet weather, much of it not being got in till the first week in October. The mean temperature for the month (September) was 55° 80 min., a striking contrast with that of the corresponding month of 1865, which was 67° 66 min.

October, with the exception of its first week, gave us as little sunshine as the previous month, and with November, the "melancholy days" have been so numerous as scarcely to admit a gleam of sunshine. In fact the mud has been so deep and soft, that farmers have had difficulty in passing with teams over their fields, to gather in their late crops. The roads have been so "hard to travel," that comparatively little produce has been taken to market, during the latter part of autumn.

The following summary of the quantity of rain, in inches, falling from May to September, inclusive, for the years 1864, '65, '66, is taken from the Meteorological Journal kept at the State Agricultural College, by Prof. R. C. Kedzie:

Months.	1864.	1865.	1866.
May,	2.087	1.872	3.478
June,	3.050	3.552	5.366
July,	1.025	3.906	4.194
August,	.395	3.381	3.442
September,	3.528	4.792	5.806
Total,	11.543	17.403	22.285

The entire rainfall for the years 1864 and 1865, was 28.840 inches for the former, and 29.821 for the latter. The average annual fall for this locality is thirty inches; so that in the five months above noted we had more than two-thirds of our annual amount of rain. The percentage of cloudiness for the autumnal months, as will be seen by Prof. Kedzie's tables, comprised in this volume, was unusually great, four to five successive days of total cloudiness several times occurring, and in one instance—23d to 29th October, inclusive—no less than seven such days in succession.

A very large portion of our country and the British Provinces of North America have been visited by frequent and heavy rains during the autumn, and, what is quite remarkable, the British Islands and a considerable portion of Continental Europe, have been similarly affected, causing much injury to crops and doing other damage.

YIELD OF CROPS.

The wheat crop came out of the winter in very bad condition over the southern portion of the State, and more or less so in other portions, except where protected by a considerable depth of snow. So complete was the destruction, that late into May many wheat-fields presented more the appearance of fallow-ground, than that on which a crop had been sown. Clover was nearly as badly killed as wheat. Some fields were plowed up and planted to corn, or sown to spring grain. The rains of the latter part of May and first of June, had the effect of resuscitating more of the plants than might have been expected, and those which finally grew up produced a fair quantity of grain, which, where not injured by rain, was of good quality. But the yield for the State was considerably below an average—precisely how much below, there is, at present, no means of ascertaining.

In regard to the yield of this crop for the whole country, the Commissioner of Agriculture, in his report for October, makes the following remarks:

"The estimate for the present year, now nearly complete, will not vary much from 143,000,000 bushels, showing a small percentage of decrease, [the crop of 1865 being put down at 148,522,829 bushels,] which is fully compensated by the comparatively superior quality of the grain. This is ten millions of bushels more than the crop of 1859, and is within five millions of a product in proportion to the increased population.

"The diminution in the south is more apparent. The estimates point to less than seventeen millions of bushels in the eleven States hitherto unreported—a fraction less than five-tenths of the crop of 1859.

"It is worthy of remark, in connection with the diminution of the three past seasons, that the wheat crop of England has been likewise deficient since 1864.

"The California wheat harvest, of which little mention has been publicly made in connection with the present crop, is excessive. In 1860, the product of this young State was nearly six millions of bushels. Now, it is seriously claimed by leading California agriculturists that the surplus for export will be nearly double that quantity.

"It is evident that the entire wheat crop will exceed by several millions that of 1859, when the yield was reported at 173,104,924 bushels. Then there were five and a half bushels to each individual; in 1866 the estimates point to five bushels to each inhabitant. There is no ground then for apprehensions of scarcity, and little excuse, in the amount of crop, for starvation prices."

Oats gave a large yield over a great part of the country, but the quality of the grain and straw was, in many cases, deteriorated by bad weather, in curing. The Commissioner of Agriculture considers the general yield extraordinary, and the quality excellent. The indications point to an increase from 171,497,072 bushels in 1859, to 271,912,595 in 1866.

The cultivation of *Barley* appears to be rather on the increase in the State. The yield the present year was generally good.

Indian Corn was greatly injured by frost, through the central and northern portions of the State A greater breadth than usual was planted, which in the southern and south-western counties, will probably aid somewhat in making up the deficiency in other sections. The Commissioner of Agriculture observes, that although this crop has suffered from frost, and from heavy rains, the aggregate product is the largest ever chronicled in the country. In this State the loss of the corn-fodder, by injury from frost, is a serious one, as it ordinarily takes the place of hay in wintering stock, to a considerable extent.

Potatoes have done well considering the unfavorable conditions which affected them. They made a luxuriant growth, and though the extremely wet weather prevented their being taken from the ground at the usual time, comparatively little complaint has been heard of rot. The sandy soils produced a large crop, which proves to be of excellent quality.

It should be remarked that the potatoe crop is already one of the most important in the State. Besides its great value for home consumption, the annual returns of its exportation are by no means small. It was stated that more than one million of dollars worth of potatoes were shipped from Detroit alone, last spring. The prices realized by the farmers were from sixty to eighty cents per bushel. As large quantities were sent from the western portion of the State, to Chicago, and many also to Toledo, it is reasonable to suppose that the entire quantity exported, was more than two millions of dollars' worth.

A large extent of the soil of the State is well adapted to the production of potatoes, and the quality is generally so superior that Michigan potatoes are specially called for, where they have become known. There is reason to expect that a demand for them, both from the East and West, will continue.

Apples, taking the State at large, gave a rather small yield. Some neighborhoods, however, were favored with a good crop. As usual, the demand for them has been good, and prices satisfactory. Shipments have been made to the eastern markets, and to Chicago.

Peaches generally failed, except along the shore of Lake Michigan, or within the influence of the lake. There the crop was good, and the profits of it large.

Grapes did not generally succeed so well as in 1865. In some favored localities, however, several of the earlier varieties ripened well.

INJURIOUS INSECTS.

THE CANKER-WORM,

Which was mentioned in my report for 1865, as having appeared in Calhoun county, in this State, continued its ravages in that locality the present year. During the first week in June I visited several orchards in the neighborhood of Marshall, in which the insect was found. Although it is gradually spreading, it was not so numerous this year, in some of the orchards where it has been longest established, as it was in 1865. The cause of their diminution in their old haunts is obscure. It is possible that in some instances the ground was overstocked last year—that is, the foliage may not have been sufficient to carry to maturity all the worms which fed upon the trees—and that many of the starved larvæ died before they reached the perfect state; or it may be that the frosts and unusually cold weather which occurred last spring, soon after the insects hatched, destroyed many of them.

I could not learn that means, either of destruction or prevention, had been much used. Edwin Wilson, of Marengo, whose orchard has suffered most, dug the earth away from the trees in the fall of 1865, and put around each tree a peck of strong wood ashes, which lay there until the trees leaved out last spring, when they were spread about. It was supposed that the ashes had killed the insect to some extent; but it does not appear that the decrease in the number of worms this year, as compared with the last, is any greater in this orchard than in others where no ashes or anything else had been applied.

Gideon Townsend, of Marshall, whose fine orchard was completely defoliated in 1865, put round his trees, in the spring of that year, a good mulch of straw, as a manure. He allowed swine to run in the orchard in the fall, and they rooted in the straw almost constantly. His poultry, too,—barn-yard fowls and turkeys,—were busy day after day, scratching in the straw and earth about the trees, from which they appeared to obtain food which they liked. It is probable that the pigs and poultry destroyed many canker-worms in the pupa state. The worm, as it drops from the branches to secure for itself a lodgment in the ground, where it may undergo its transformation, generally moves towards the tree, so that the chrysalids are generally found within a comparatively small distance from the trunk.

The effects of the ravages of the insect on the trees, in the orchard above mentioned, are already very obvious. In Mr. Wilson's orchard, the trees on which the canker-worms first appeared, in 1862, are totally dead. Several other trees in this orchard are nearly dead; and the vitality of all is evidently weakened.

In regard to means of prevention, nothing in particular can be offered in addition to what was spoken of in my report for 1865. We have had the experience of another year with the different kinds of "tree-protectors," that have been invented. In the Eastern States, particularly in Massachusetts, where the articles have been more fully tried than in other sections, the conclusion has been reached, that they are not an entire protection against the ascent of the female insect. Such, at any rate, is the statement of the editors of the Massachusetts Ploughman, and New England Farmer. According to the Ploughman, the strip of sheep-skin, with the wool on, fastened as a belt round the tree, has been as effective as anything. As this is a cheap article, within the reach of every farmer, its use may be safely advised. The strip of skin should not be less than two inches wide, and the wool should be three-fourths of an inch, to an inch in length. To guard against the ascent of the insect in the fall, or in mild weather in the winter, the belt should be put round the trees in the early part of November. It may be fastened to the trunk by a few tacks, and where it does not set perfectly close to the bark, cotton, or tow, or clay mortar should be forced in, care being taken that no space is left through which the insect could pass. It has been suggested that saturating the wool with kerosene oil would render it a more effectual barrier to the insect's progress. This might readily be tried with a few trees, and the effect of the oil observed.*

It is earnestly hoped that measures will be speedily adopted for checking the spread of this destructive insect. It appears from statements which I have received from Mr. T. T. Lyon, of Plymouth, that the insect has appeared in the neighborhood where he resides, and it may be that it has been established in other parts of the State. Still, there is reason to believe that at the present time there are only a few small colonies of it within our borders. This being the fact, we might be induced to adopt the suggestion of the New England Farmer, and try the "stamping out" process,—as has been done with pleuro-

---

*Since the above was written, I have received the following from Prof. J. C. Holmes, who spent the summer of the present year, as well as that of 1865, in a section of Massachusetts where the canker-worm has formerly done great injury, and where various inventions have been tried to check its ravages:

"With regard to tree protectors, I think that nothing that can be got up to prevent the canker-worm from injuring the trees, will be of any utility unless people give it more attention. The protector (Ordway's) I sent to the Agricultural College, I know has proved effectual where it has been applied, and care taken that cobwebs are not so formed as to make a bridge for the moths to walk upon. You know spiders form their webs upon trees in all directions. If they stretch their webs from the trunk of the tree below the protector, up over the edge of the protector to the tree above, the moths will pass along upon the webs about as readily as if there were no protector there. A gentleman in Massachusetts said to me: 'If this thing is properly put on and proper attention given to it, my experience is that it is perfect; but if put on in a careless, slovenly manner, and no subsequent attention given to it, it may as well not be put on, as it will be useless.' This is the testimony of people in canker-worm districts, respecting many of the arrangements in use to protect their trees from injury by this pest. Mr. Fred. Putnam, a naturalist, told me that with him it was a perfect protection. He had placed it upon trees where for some years he had had a large crop of canker-worms but no fruit. Now he has no canker-worms but good crops of fruit. I do not know but one protector is as good as another, or as efficacious as another, provided the same care and attention be given to each. One object is to get the one that will prove effectual at the least expenditure of time, money and labor.

"Tarring is somewhat laborious and requires a great deal of attention, but may be made perfectly effectual; yet that mode is, in some respects, objectionable. The arrangement of a box at the surface of the earth, filled with tar, and a trough of oil fastened to the sides is a good arrangement, but there are objections to it. Last fall I saw trees in a canker-worm district that were well protected in this way, full of splendid fruit."

pneumonia and rinderpest in cattle,—if we were not constantly liable to new importations of the insect.

Certain things, however, may be safely advised. The first and most important is, that all the trees whose vitality is much weakened by the defoliation which they have suffered, should, when the next generation of insects is fairly hatched, be cut down and cast into the fire. Their value, so far as regards fruit-bearing, is at an end, and their lives will soon be so, even if they are let alone. The action recommended would destroy the greater portion of the insects in the infected districts, because it would sweep off the greater portion of the old trees. The younger ones could be more easily managed. To all of these the sheep-skin belts should be applied.

It may be well to give a word of caution in regard to the use of pretended specifics against this and other insect enemies; such as putting sulphur into the trunk of the tree, with the view of poisoning worms that eat the foliage. This is an old humbug, which has gone the rounds of the newspapers as often as it has been forgotten, for the last fifty years. The secret nostrums which are advertised as *death* on caterpillars, &c., are probably no better than sulphur used as above specified. Some of the Eastern papers advertise a substance called muriate of lime; which the vender claims is both a manure for the tree and a destroyer of the canker-worm and other insects; but the most careful experiments show that the latter effect does not follow the prescribed use of the substance.

THE WHITE GRUB,

So called, was very abundant in various portions of the State. The insect alluded to is the larvæ of a species of beetle belonging to the genus *Melolonthæ*. In its perfect state it is called the May-bug or May-beetle, and closely resembles the European cockchafer.

In the latter part of July, and in August, the grubs were very numerous in old meadows and pastures. Attention was turned to them in the first place by spots of sward becoming dead, as if killed by drought. Knowing that we could not have had dry weather enough to kill grass, the writer made an examination of some of the dead turf, finding that the grass-roots had been so thoroughly eaten off an inch or two below the surface that the turf could easily be rolled up like a carpet. The worms confined their eating chiefly to grass of different species, carefully rejecting every root of clover. It is known, however, that they sometimes do much damage to nurseries by eating the roots of the young trees, and they sometimes do great injury to strawberry plants.

This insect has at various times been very destructive in different parts of this country. Its period of existence in the worm or larvæ state is not, perhaps, accurately known. That it lives in this state three years, entomologists generally admit, while some say it continues in it four or five years. It is principally during the last season of its existence in the larvæ state that its destructive habits are particularly noticed. It then approaches near to the surface of the ground, and cuts off the roots of grass, as above described.

In dry seasons the damage it does to grass is very great, as it completely kills the sward. They were so numerous in many places last summer, that on turning up the dead turf, from ten to a dozen full-sized grubs were found to the square foot.

The damage done by this insect this year was less than it would have been if the latter part of summer and autumn had been dry, instead of very wet, as they were. Seeds of grass, clover, &c., which lay on or near the surface of the ground, germinated, and the young plants grew with such rapidity that in a few weeks the ground, previously almost without a shade of greenness, became in many places covered with a new sward.

This insect is sometimes injurious to Indian corn and wheat, and sometimes injures potatoes, gnawing cavities in the tubers, on which account it has been called the "potato-grub," or "potato-worm." Within the past ten or twelve years it has been very destructive, as I am informed, to various crops in the neighborhood of Schoolcraft, on Prairie Ronde, in this State. In 1864,

I witnessed the devastation it had spread over the corn-fields of that fertile region—the loss of the corn crop having been so great to some farmers that they were obliged to sell their hogs in a lean state, because they had not the means to fatten them. It generally prevails most on "the black soils," or those containing much vegetable matter, and hence the prairie is well adapted to it. I was told that since the grubs had first attracted attention in the section referred to, they had re-appeared in great numbers, doing much damage about every third year. This would seem to indicate that they grow from the egg to the full sized grub, in three years. As before remarked, it is only during the last season of their existence in the larvæ state, that their inroads on vegetation are specially striking. Most of the grubs that were to be seen here during the past summer and autumn, were nearly full grown, being about as large in diameter as the stem of a common clay pipe, and somewhat more than an inch in length, of a dull white color, with a pale-red head. They will probably appear in great numbers as "May-beetles," about the last of May or first of June, 1867. They ceased their ravages quite suddenly, early in the month of September. Where great numbers of them might have been seen on the first of this month, scarcely one could be found a week later. They had undoubtedly descended into the ground, where they will be transformed to beetles. Harris says: "At the close of their third summer (or as some say, the fourth or fifth) they cease eating, and penetrate about two feet deep into the earth; there, by motions from side to side, each grub forms an oval cavity, which is lined by some glutinous substance thrown from its mouth. In this cavity it is changed to a pupa by casting off its skin. In this state the legs, antennæ and wing-cases of the future beetle are visible through the transparent skin which envelopes them, but appear of a yellowish white color; and thus it remains until the month of February, when the thin fibre which encloses the body is rent, and three months aferwards the perfected beetle digs its way to the surface, from which it finally emerges during the night."*

The beetle is of a chestnut-brown color, about nine-tenths of an inch in length, its greatest breath nearly equal to one-half its length. It flies chiefly in the evening, frequently entering houses where windows or doors are open, and whirling about candles or lamps. The insect lives but a few days after its appearance in the beetle state, during which time it sometimes injures trees by feeding on the leaves, the foliage of the cherry being most frequently attacked. It is seldom, however, that complaint has been made of damage being done by the insect in this stage, although the European cockchafer is represented to be very destructive as a beetle.

Means of destroying the insect or avoiding its ravages.—In all its stages it is preyed upon by various animals, but the earth with which it is covered during its larvæ state, affords a pretty effectual protection against most of its enemies. In the beetle state it secretes itself in the day time, though it is found to some extent and eaten by various birds, especially crows. Toads catch the beetles as they come out from their hiding places at twilight. Skunks devour great numbers of them in spring, and great numbers of the grubs through the season—their numbers being, perhaps, more diminished by this animal than by all other causes. Hogs and poultry will eat the beetles and grubs voraciously. Barn-yard fowls scratch for them, and, where they are plenty, find many. But hogs, when their rooting powers are unabridged by rings or "hog tamers," can destroy the insect to the best advantage. When the grubs are near the surface of the ground, hogs could readily obtain them in abundance, and would probably fatten on them. In former years I have known great numbers of the grubs to be picked by hand from plowed fields, persons following the plow for that purpose. No doubt an immense slaughter of the grubs might be made by turning hogs into fields where the grass has been killed.

*Treatise on insects injurions to vegetation, pp. 22 and 23.

Where the ground has been thoroughly overrun with the grubs, it is frequently advisable to plow it, and either sow it to winter wheat or rye, or re-seed it to grass. For pasture it would be merely necessary to sow grass seed the last of August or first of September, and harrow it in with a light harrow—even a bush-harrow would answer the purpose. Or, if rains should fall about the time of sowing, the seed would germinate very well by being merely sown on the surface. For meadows, it would be advisable to plough the ground in most cases, in order to obtain a uniform sward and an even surface. The soil will break up very mellow, affording a good seed-bed for grain.

Some people suppose that by plowing the ground late in the fall, the insect is killed by frost. It is hardly probable that this result takes place to much extent. According to Harris, the larvæ descend into the ground at the approach of winter, to a greater depth than is reached by the plow.

PRINCIPLES OF BREEDING.

[It is within a comparatively late period only, that any attempt has been made to lay down rules for breeding domestic animals. Bakewell,—a hundred years ago,—seems to have been the first to reduce the subject to a practical system. The striking improvements which he effected, attracted the attention of the whole civilized world. But beyond the opportunity of studying the examples which he presented, the public derived little actual knowledge from his labors; he merely showed things as *done*, without showing *how* they were done. The results which he attained were, however, well calculated to excite investigation, and it was natural that thinking minds should be led to inquire into the principles involved.

One of the most valuable papers that has been brought out on this subject, was from the pen of Sir John S. Sebright, in 1809, and was addressed to Sir Joseph Banks, under the title of "The Art of Improving the Breeds of Domestic Animals."

Believing that the perusal of this essay may be both interesting and instructive, to many readers, it is herewith re-published, accompanied by such notes and observations as seem pertinent to the subject.—S. H.]

I have not the presumption to think that I can throw any light upon the art of improving the breeds of domestic animals, which is now so well understood in this country; but in obedience to your commands I print these observations, to which I am sensible you have attached more value than they deserve.

The attention which gentlemen of landed property have, of late years, paid to this subject, has been extremely beneficial to the country; not so much by the improvements which they themselves have made, as by the encouragement which the professional breeders have received from their patronage and support, without which they could not have carried the breeds of cattle and sheep to the perfection which many of them have now attained. They have, likewise, been the means of making the best breeds known in every part of the kingdom, and of transporting them to districts where it is not probable they would have been introduced but through their agency.

The Duke of Bedford, Mr. Coke, [afterwards Earl of Leicester,] and some few others, have not only been the liberal patrons of the professional breeders, but have themselves made great improvements in the breeds to which their attention has been directed. The same success has not, in general, attended gentlemen in this pursuit; the best breeds, after having been obtained by them at a great expense, too frequently degenerate in their hands from mismanagement. They conceive that if they have procured good males and good females, they have done all that is necessary to establish and to continue a good breed, but this is by no means the case.

Were I to define what is called the art of breeding, I should say that it consisted in the selection of males and females suited to breed together, in reference to each other's merits and defects.

It is not always by putting the best male to the best female, that the best produce will be obtained; for should they both have a tendency to the same defect, although in ever so slight a degree, it will in general preponderate so much in the produce as to render it of little value.

A breed of animals may be said to be improved when any desired quality has been increased by art, beyond what that quality was in the same breèd in a state of nature. The swiftness of the race-horse, the propensity to fatten in cattle, and the fine wool in sheep, are improvements which have been made in particular varieties of the species to which these animals belong. What has been produced by art, must be continued by the same means, for the most improved breeds will soon return to a state of nature, or perhaps defects will arise which did not exist when the breed was in its natural state, unless the greatest attention is paid to the selection of the individuals who are to breed together.

We must observe the smallest tendency to imperfection in our stock, the moment it appears, so as to be able to counteract it before it becomes a defect; as a rope-dancer, to preserve his equilibrium, must correct the balance, before it is gone too far, and then not by such a motion as will incline it too much to the opposite side.

The breeder's success will depend entirely upon the degree in which he may happen to possess this particular talent. Regard should not only be paid to the qualities apparent in animals, selected for breeding, but to those which have prevailed in the race from which they are descended, as they will always show themselves sooner or later, in the progeny; it is for this reason that we should not breed from an animal, however excellent, unless we can ascertain it to be what is called *well bred;* that is, descended from a race of ancestors who have, through several generations, possessed in a high degree, the properties which it is our object to obtain.

The offspring of some animals are very unlike themselves; it is therefore, a good precaution to try the young males with a few females, the quality of whose produce has been already ascertained. By this means we shall know the sort of stock they get, and the description of females to which they are the best adapted.

[This is sound advice. The best evidence we have, *in advance,* as to the character of the stock an animal may get, is the character of his ancestors; and herein consists the value of pedigree. But it sometimes happens that two animals of precisely the same blood, will get quite dissimilar stock. The only *positive* evidence then, as to the value of an animal as a stock-getter, is the character of his progeny. When this is proved to possess the properties desired, the pedigree of the parent is of no consequence, further than as a means of showing the properties of the family.—S. H.]

If a breed cannot be improved, or even continued in the degree of perfection at which it has already arrived, but by breeding from individuals, so selected as to correct each other's defects, and by a judicious combination of their different properties, (a position I believe, that will not be denied,) it follows that animals must degenerate, by being long bred from the same family, without the intermixture of any other blood, or from being what is technically called bred *in-and-in.*

Mr. Bakewell, who certainly threw more light upon the art of breeding than any of his predecessors, was the first, I believe, who asserted that a cross was unnecessary, and that animals would not degenerate, by being bred in-and-in, which was at that time the received opinion. He said, you could but breed from the best. Of this there can be no doubt; but it is to be proved how long the same family, *bred in-and-in,* will continue to be the best.

No one can deny the ability of Mr. Bakewell, in the art of which he may fairly be said to have been the inventor, but the mystery with which he is well known to have carried on every part of his business, and the various means which he employed to mislead the public, induce me not to give that weight to his assertions, which I should do to his real opinion, could it have been ascertained.

Mr. Meynel's fox-hounds are likewise quoted as an instance of the success of this practice; but upon speaking to that gentleman upon the subject, I found that he did not attach the meaning that I do, to the term in-and-in. He said that he frequently bred from the father and the daughter, and the mother and the son. This is not what I consider breeding in-and-in; for the daughter is only half of the same blood as the father, and will probably partake, in a great degree, of the properties of the mother.

Mr. Meynel sometimes bred from brother and sister; this is certainly what may be called a *little close*, but should they both be very good, and particularly, should the same defects not predominate in both, but the perfections of the one promise to correct in the produce, the imperfections of the other, I do not think it objectionable; much further than this—the system of breeding from the same family cannot, in my opinion, be pursued with safety.

Mr. Bakewell had, certainly, the merit of destroying the absurd prejudice which formerly prevailed against breeding from animals between whom there was any degree of relationship. Had this opinion been universally acted upon, no one could have been said to be possessed of a particular breed, good or bad; for the produce of one year would have been dissimilar to that of another, and we should have availed ourselves but little of an animal of superior merit, that we might have had the good fortune to possess.

The authorities of Mr. Bakewell, and of Mr. Meynel being generally quoted, when this subject is discussed, I have stated why I reject that of the former altogether, and that the latter, in point of fact, never fairly tried the experiment.

I do not find that any of the many advocates for breeding in-and-in, with whom I have conversed, have tried it to any extent; they say that it is to perfect animals only, that the practice applies; but the existence of a perfect animal is an hypothesis I cannot admit.

I do not believe that there ever did exist an animal without some defect, in constitution, in form, or in some other essential quality; a tendency, at least, to the same imperfection, generally prevails in different degrees, in the same family. By breeding in-and-in, this defect, however small it may be at first, will increase in every succeeding generation; and will at last, predominate to such a degree as to render the breed of little value. Indeed, I have no doubt but by this practice being continued, animals would, in course of time, degenerate to such a degree as to be incapable of breeding at all.

The effect of breeding in-and-in may be accelerated or retarded, by selection, particularly in those animals who produce many young ones at a time. There may be families so nearly perfect, as to go through several generations, without sustaining much injury from having been bred in-and-in; but a good judge would, upon examination, point out by what they must ultimately fail, as a mechanic would discover the weakest part of a machine, before it gave way Breeding in-and-in will, of course, have the same effect in strengthening the good, as the bad properties, and may be beneficial, if not carried too far, particularly in fixing any variety which may be thought valuable.

[In the latter paragraph, two very important points are comprised, viz: the necessity of selection in breeding stock, and the declaration that breeding in-and-in strengthens the good as well as the bad properties, &c. The advantage of having many animals from which to select breeding stock, is very great. In chickens of the same brood, or in pigs of the same litter, there will frequently be much variation. If there are many, we may select the good and reject the bad ones; if there are but few, and they happen to be bad, breeding from them is almost sure to result in degeneracy. The advantage of range for selection, is simply that we have the greater chance to obtain animals of the best quality.

If it be admitted that the good properties of animals may be strengthened by in-and-in breeding, it is certainly a strong argument in favor of the practice. There is no doubt of the fact.

Where both parents possess any particular property in an unusual degree, it is likely to become intensified in the progeny. The object, therefore, should be to endeavor to obtain animals which possess the properties we want in the highest degree, and which are at the same time free from defects—S. H.]

I have tried many experiments, by breeding in-and-in upon dogs, fowls and pigeons: the dogs became, from strong spaniels, weak and diminutive lap-dogs; the fowls became long in the legs, small in the body, and bad breeders.

There are a great many sorts of fancy pigeons; each variety has some particular property which constitutes its supposed value, and which the amateurs increase as much as possible, both by breeding in-and-in, and by selection, until the particular property is made to predominate to such a degree, in some of the most refined sorts, that they cannot exist without the greatest care, and are incapable of rearing their young, without the assistance of other pigeons, kept for that purpose.

The Leicestershire breeders of sheep have inherited the principles, as well as the stock of their leader, Mr. Bakewell. He very properly considered a propensity to get fat, as the first quality in an animal destined to be the food of man. His successors have carried this principle too far; their stock are become small in size, and tender, produce but little wool, and are bad breeders.

[This remark, in regard to Leicester sheep, is doubtless more strikingly applicable at the present day, than at the date of this essay. Some breeders, have however, avoided the defects alluded to in the preceding paragraph—have procured in their stock good size, constitution and weight of wool. It does not appear that a change of blood has been necessary to effect this. The celebrated Leicester flock of Mr. Valentine Barford, of Foscote, Northamptonshire, England, may be referred to as an instance of successful breeding from very close affinities. A particular account of the breeding of this flock has been kept since the year 1783—rams of Bakewell blood only having been used from that period; and since 1810, Mr. B. has, as he states, bred from his own flock, "sire and dam, without an interchange of male or female from any other flock." I had an opportunity of examining several specimens of this flock a few years since. They certainly exhibited no evidence of degeneracy, but were of good size and almost faultless symmetry. In a note appended to a printed pedigree of his flock, Mr. Barford says: "This flock being bred from the nearest affinities, commonly called breeding *in-and-in*, has not experienced any of those ill effects frequently ascribed to the practice. The males and females have been paired on principles upon which it is believed improvement depends; have been kept entirely in a state of nature; fed upon *vegetable food only*, [probably meaning grass, hay and roots,] and are open to inspection at all times of the year." S. H.]

By selecting animals of one property only, the same effect will, in some degree be produced as by breeding in-and-in; we shall obtain animals with the desired property in great perfection, but so deficient in other respects as to be, upon the whole, an unprofitable stock. We should, therefore, endeavor to obtain all the properties that are essential to the animals we breed. The Leicestershire sheep prove that too much may be sacrificed, even to that most desirable quality in grazing stock—a disposition to get fat at an early age, and with a small quantity of food.

Many causes combine to prevent animals, in a state of nature, from degenerating; they are perpetually intermixing, and therefore do not feel the bad effects of breeding in-and-in; the perfections of some correct the imperfections of others, and they go on without any material alteration, except what arises from food and climate. The greatest number of females will, of course, fall to the share of the most vigorous males; and the strongest individuals of both sexes, by driving away the weakest, will enjoy the best food and the most favorable situations for themselves and for their offspring.

A severe winter, or a scarcity of food, by destroying the weak and unhealthy, has all the good effects of the most skillful selection. In cold and barren countries, no animals can live to the age of maturity, but those who have strong constitutions; the weak and the unhealthy do not live to propagate their infirmities, as is too often the case with our domestic animals. To this I attribute the peculiar hardiness of the horses, cattle and sheep bred in mountainous countries, more than to their having been inured to the severity of the climate, for our domestic animals do not become more hardy by being exposed when young, to cold and hunger. Animals so treated will not, when arrived at the age of maturity, endure so much hardship as those which have been better kept in their infant state.

If one male and one female only, of a valuable breed, could be obtained, the offspring should be separated, and placed in situations as dissimilar as possible, for animals kept together are all subjected to the effects of the same climate, of the same food, and of the same mode of treatment, and consequently to the same diseases, particularly to such as are infectious, which must accelerate the bad effects of breeding in-and-in.

By establishing the breed in different places, and by selecting, with a view to obtain different properties in these several colonies, we may perhaps be enabled to continue the breed for some time, without the intermixture of other blood.

If the original male and female were of different families, by breeding from the mother and the son, and again from the male produce and the mother, and from the father and the daughter in the same way, two families sufficiently distinct, might be obtained; for the son is only half of the father's blood, and the produce from the mother and the son, will be six parts of the mother and two of the father.

[This expression, in connection with what was said in a preceding paragraph respecting the breeding of Mr. Meynel's fox-hounds, indicates that the author of this essay considered breeding in-and-in to consist only in breeding from animals of precisely the same blood. Many persons regard breeding from the father and daughter, or mother and son as in-and-in; but Sir John says distinctly, that he does not consider it so. S. H.]

Although I believe the occasional intermixture of different families to be necessary, I do not, by any means, approve of mixing two distinct breeds, with the view of uniting the valuable properties of both. This experiment has been frequently tried by others as well as by myself, but has, I believe, never succeeded. The first cross frequently produces a tolerable animal, but it is a breed that cannot be continued.

If it were possible, by a cross between the new Leicestershire and Merino breeds of sheep, to produce an animal uniting the excellencies of both, that is, the carcass of the one with the fleece of the other, even such an animal so produced would be of little value to the breeder; a race of the same description could not be perpetuated, and no dependence could be placed upon the produce of such animals; they would be mongrels—some like the new Leicester, some like the Merino, and most of them with the faults of both.

[Taking this language in connection with what follows, it is plain that the author does not object to crossing distinct breeds and breeding the issue back to one of the parent stocks, for he says he has no doubt that better stock may be obtained from a Merino ram and South Down ewes than from the same ram and Merino ewes—the aim being to obtain wool similar to the Merino. It is the attempt to perpetuate the stock of the first cross—the *half-and-half* stock—that is regarded as impracticable. There can be no more difficulty in retaining a certain degree of Leicester blood in a stock, than the same degree of South Down blood.—S. H.]

Merino rams are frequently put to South Down and Ryeland ewes, not with a view of obtaining the good properties of both kinds, but from the difficulty of procuring Spanish ewes, and with the intention of obtaining the Merino blood in sufficient purity, for every practical purpose, by repeatedly crossing the female produce with Merino males.

I have no doubt but that better stock may be obtained, in a few years, in this manner, from a large flock of well chosen ewes, than by breeding, at first, from a small number of the pure Merino blood, (and many of them cannot be obtained,) for the great advantage to be derived from the means of selection afforded by a more numerous flock, will more than compensate for the little stain of impure blood, which would be insensible in a flock, crossed in this manner, for four or five generations.

The introduction of Merino sheep to this country opens a fine field for improvement. It has been ascertained that neither the sheep nor the wool sustain any injury from the change of climate or pasture, and the absurd prejudice that Merino wool could be grown only in Spain, is fortunately eradicated.

In comparing the Merino sheep with the South Downs, which are allowed to be the best of our short-wooled breeds, the former have very much the advantage, both as to quantity and quality of wool; but, I believe, the latter would produce by far the greatest quantity of meat, from a given quantity of food, which is the criterion by which we determine the relative value of all animals as grazier's stock.

[It should be remembered that this essay was written at the time when attempts were being made to introduce the Merino sheep into England. They were not numerous, and hence the difficulty alluded to of obtaining the ewes. It is scarcely necessary to remark that the Merinos failed to become established in England; not because the sheep or wool sustained "any injury from the climate or pasture," but because of their deficiency in the return of meat for the food consumed.—S. H.]

Taking the gross produce, both of wool and of carcass, at the present prices, the Merino breed may perhaps be the most profitable; but should it be generally introduced, fine wool would become cheaper, and mutton dearer; it is therefore not easy to form a conclusive opinion upon this subject.

Great improvements may undoubtedly be made in the Merino breed, as to their disposition to get fat. Their advocates say, with truth, that the South Down sheep were but a few years ago, as imperfect in shape as the Merinos now are; but they should recollect, that a disposition to fatten at an early age was always the characteristic of the South Down breed, even in its most unimproved state, and that it was from its possessing this very essential quality that so much attention has been paid to it.

It is well known that a particular formation generally indicates a disposition to get fat, in all sorts of animals; but this rule is not universal, for we sometimes see animals of the most approved forms, which are *slow feeders*, and whose flesh is of a bad quality, which the graziers easily ascertain by the *touch*. The disposition to get fat is more generally found in some breeds than in others. The Scotch Highland cattle are remarkable for being almost all *quick feeders*, although many of them are defective in shape. The Welsh cattle have but little disposition to get fat; not from being particularly ill-shaped, but because they are almost invariably what the graziers call *bad handlers*.

We must not, therefore, suppose that the bad shape of the Merino sheep is the sole cause of its being so ill calculated for the purpose of the grazier.

An observation which Dr. Jenner made to me about ten years ago, (the truth of which has since been confirmed by my own experience—that no animal whose chest was narrow could easily be made fat,) applies particularly to the Merino sheep, who are in general contracted in that part, and it is well worth the attention of those who wish to improve this breed.

Perhaps the great secretion of yolk, so essential to the production of fine wool, and which is excessive in the Merino sheep, may be incompatible with the fattening quality.

I have always found the fineness of the fleece in exact proportion to the quantity of yolk it contained. Those who are unaccustomed to examine wool, may consider this as a certain criterion of its quality; for although the hair of some dry fleeces may be fine, it will always want the elasticity which is so much valued by the manufacturer.

[The finest wool which the author of this essay had seen, was probably the Merino, as produced by the Spanish sheep introduced into England. Finer wool has since been produced by the Saxon and other sub-varieties of the Spanish Merino, and with much less yolk than is common with the latter. The so-called American Merino has *more* yolk than the original Spanish, but not finer wool. Experience has proved that the greatest quantity of yolk does not accompany the finest fleeces.—S. H.]

It is to be regretted that so little attention has been paid to the improvement of British wool, and particularly to that of the short-wooled breeds. A fine fleece is not only more profitable to the owner, but from the closeness of its texture, and the quantity of yolk it always contains, is a much better protection to the sheep in bad weather, than the open and hairy covering, which too generally disgraces our flocks.

This extraordinary negligence in the sheep-breeders may, in some degree, be accounted for, by the manner in which the wool trade is carried on. The *growers* are seldom well acquainted with the value of this article, or indeed with its quality, and the *buyers* find their account in fixing a general price every year, for the wool of each breed, without making any distinction between the very different quality of the pile of different flocks.

It is likewise the custom, in many parts of England, for the growers to deliver their wool to the buyers, upon their engaging to give them the highest price of the year; such bargains (and they are very general) are of course strong inducements to the purchasers not to give the full value for any wool that may be offered to them, of a superior quality.

The fineness of the fleece, like every other property in animals of all kinds, may be improved by selection in breeding. The opinion that good wool could only be produced in particular districts, is a prejudice which, fortunately, no longer exists. Climate, food and soil, have certainly some effect upon the quality of wool, but not so much as is generally supposed. The fleece is affected by the degree of nourishment which the animal receives, and by the quality of pasture on which it is fed. If sheep are highly kept, their wool will become less fine, but in other respects, its quality will not be deteriorated. The wool of a starved sheep may be apparently fine, but it will be brittle and of little value to the manufacturer.

A regular supply of food to the sheep is essential to the growth of good wool; for that part of the hair which grows when the animal is in a high state of flesh, will be thick, and that which is grown when it is reduced by hunger, will be weak and thin; and consequently, the thickness of hair will always be irregular, if the animal passes from one extreme to the other.

The alteration which may be made in any breed of animals by selection, can hardly be conceived by those who have not paid some attention to this subject. They attribute every improvement to a cross, when it is merely the effect of judicious selection.

I have often been told that from the beautiful shape of Mr. Elman's South Down sheep, they must have been crossed with the New Leicester; and that from the fineness of their wool, they must have been crossed with the Merino breed; but I do not conceive that even the skill of this very distinguished breeder could have retained the good shape of the former, without any appearance of the character of its wool or the fine fleece of the latter, without the deformity of its carcass, had he crossed his flock with either of these breeds.

It may as well be contended that the white pheasant, which is now become very common, was produced from a cross with a Dorking fowl, whereas, it was one of those accidental varieties which sometimes occur, and which has been perpetuated by selection. The same may be said of the endless variety in the color, shape and size of rabbits, ducks and pigeons, in a domesticated state; a variety, produced by the art of man, and which did not exist in these creatures in their natural state.

A greater proof, I conceive, of what may be effected by selection and perseverance, cannot be adduced.

There is, perhaps, no means by which the breeds of animals can be so rapidly and so effectually improved, as by its being the particular business of some breeders to provide male animals for the purpose of letting for hire. Our horses could never have arrived at the degree of perfection which they have now attained, but from the facility which has been afforded to every one, by the public stallions, of breeding from the best horses of every description, at a moderate expense.

The breeds of sheep to which this practice has been applied, have attained great perfection, while those which have never been attended to by persons in this particular business, show no signs of improvement.

No trouble or expense will be spared by those who expect to derive profit, not from the quantity, but from the quality of the animals which they breed. The competition which must always exist between breeders of this description, will be a never failing stimulus to exertion.

The common farmer, who seldom sees any stock but his own and that of his neighbors, generally concludes that his own have arrived at the summit of perfection; but the breeder who lets for hire, must frequently submit his male animals to the inspection of the public, and to the criticism of his rivals, who will certainly not encourage any prejudices he may entertain of their superiority.

In this trade, as in every other, there ought to be a regular gradation; those, for example, who hire a male for eighty guineas, will be amply repaid by letting seven or eight for twenty guineas each, as will those who hire for twenty guineas, by letting several for five or six.

Thus, each, besides the improvement of his stock, will receive a fair remuneration, and every breeder have the means of selecting the male he thinks best calculated for the females he may happen to possess.

The same effect will not be produced by the sale of male animals; for we are induced to keep a male we have purchased at a high price, although we may not be entirely satisfied with his produce, but by hiring, we endeavor to select a male every year, with the properties in which our females are deficient, and which we think calculated to correct the faults which, from time to time, arise in our stock.

These observations are the result of many years' experience, in breeding animals of various descriptions. But the life of man is not long enough to form very decisive conclusions upon a subject which is so little understood, and which is darkened by innumerable prejudices. Many experiments must be tried, to establish a single fact; for nature is sometimes so capricious in her productions, that the most accurate observer will be frequently deceived, if he draws any inference from a single experiment.

I have freely stated my opinions, without considering them as conclusive, and shall be much gratified if they induce others to direct their attention to a subject which appears to me of great importance to the agricultural interests of this country.

The importance of this subject will justify the addition of a few remarks in reference to one or two points. There is abundant evidence that the most successful breeders have bred both from close affinities, and from crosses, according as either promised to aid in the accomplishment of their objects. The history of the Warlaby, or Booth tribe of Short-horn cattle, as given by Capt. Carr, in the Farmers' Magazine for April, 1864, may be cited in illustration. In speaking of the herd of Mr. Thomas Booth, which was mainly the foundation of the herds of the late Messrs. John and Richard Booth, Capt. C. says:

"Having judiciously selected the best animals procurable of both sexes, Mr. Booth was careful to pair such, and such only of the produce of these unions as presented, in a satisfactory degree, the desired characteristics, with animals possessing them in equal or greater measure, and unsparingly to reject, especially from his male stock, all such as were not up to the required standard. Having by these means succeeded in developing and establishing in his herd a definite and uniform character, *he sought to insure its perpetuation by breeding from rather close affinities*, as in his opinion the only security for the unfailing transmission, and transmission in an increased ratio, of these acquired distinctions to the offspring. In tracing the pedigree of these herds it will be seen that from the earliest period the same system of breeding from close relations which was followed by the Collings, was followed by the Booths. An examination of the pedigree of Lady Maynard (*alias* the cow Favorite) will show to what a length the system was carried by the early breeders, and how closely the first families of the Colling strain were allied to the Booth tribes. Further proof of this may be found in the pedigrees of the earliest bulls used by Mr. Thomas Booth, viz: Twin-Brother-to-Ben, Suworrow, Albion, Pilot, and Marshal Beresford. Thus, Twin-Brother-to-Ben was own uncle of Red Rose by Favorite, the dam of Pilot; and Red Rose is own sister to Styford, the sire of Suworrow. Suworrow was by a son of Favorite, and his dam was by Favorite. Albion, purchased at Mr. Charles Colling's sale, in 1810, and an excellent sire—was by a bull which was both a son and a grandson of Favorite; his dam was by a son of Favorite, and his granddam by a son of Favorite. Pilot, bred by Mr. Robert Colling, was by Major or Wellington. Major was by a son and grandson of Favorite, and his dam by Favorite. Marshal Beresford was by a son and grandson of Favorite."

The following extracts from Capt. Carr's history show that some of the finest catttle of the Messrs. Booth, were derived from crosses:

" Albion is said to have done more good in Mr. Booth's herd than any other of the earlier bulls, notwithstanding that he had through Washington (674), the *alloy*, [or Galloway blood,) which was the term of reproach cast upon Lady by Grandson of Bolingbroke and her descendants, in the early days of Short-horn breeding. The offspring of Albion were in general very round, compact, and near the ground."

[Mr. Richard Booth expressed verbally to me, a few years since, his opinion of the great value of Albion, in improving his father's herd.—S. H.]

"Isabella and her descendants brought the massive, yet exquisitively moulded fore quarters into the herd, and also that straight underline of the belly for which the Warlaby animals are remarkable. That such a cow should have had but three crosses of blood is striking evidence of the impressive efficacy of these early bulls, and confirms Mr. Booth's opinion that four crosses of really first-rate bulls of sterling blood, upon a good market cow of the ordinary Short-horn breed, should suffice for the production of Short-horns fit to compete with the possessors of twenty quarterings. And indeed in later times, Mr. Booth's cow Princess Elizabeth, the dam of Queen of the Isles, and her sister Princess Mary, abundantly verified the truth of this tenet. Nor can many herds boast of a better Short-horn than was Mr. Booth's cow British Girl, though only third in descent from a red Galloway cow. She was level, round and compact, and had very graceful fore-quarters. In British Girl's daughter, British Rose, by Prince George, and her granddaughter, Wild Rose, by Lord of the Valley, though reared as hardily and frugally as West Highlanders, the visitor to Warlaby will find all the excellencies that mark the high-caste Short-horn. They more than verify a remark of Mr. Robert Colling's, after the sale of his own and his brother's herd: 'Give me,' said he to Mr. Wiley, of Brandsby, 'my sight and my touch, and in half-a-dozen years I will produce as good a herd as I or my brother have sold off. I would do this by the use of well bred bulls on good market cows.'"

It is common to refer to the intermarriage of cousins in the human family, as showing the degenerating tendency of the union of parents related to each other. That degeneracy results from some such unions is undeniable. Where both parents, whether related or not, possess the same defects, the offspring may be expected to exhibit the defects in an increased degree. But that there is no natural law which necessarily produces degeneracy from the union of relations, is evident from the fact that in many cases no such result follows from such causes. It is a well established fact that among the Arabs the marriage of cousins has always been practiced. Burton, in his "Journey to Medina and Mecca," says: "The national type of the Bedouins has been preserved by systematic intermarriage. The wild men do not refuse their daughters to a stranger; but the son-in-law would be obliged to settle among them, and this life, which has charms for awhile, ends in becoming wearisome. Here no evil results are anticipated from the union of first cousins, and the experience of ages and of a nation, may be trusted. Every Bedouin has a right to marry his father's brother's daughter before she is given to a stranger; hence 'cousin,' in polite phrase, signifies a wife. Our physiologists adduce the Sangre Azul of Spain, and the case of the lower animals, to prove that degeneracy inevitably follows breeding in. Yet the celebrated Flying Childers, and all his race, were remarkably bred in. There is still, in my humble opinion, much mystery about the subject, to be cleared up only by the studies of physiologists. Either they have theorized from insufficient facts, or civilization and artificial living exercise some peculiar influence, or Arabia is a solitary exception to a general rule. The fact which I have mentioned is patent to every Eastern traveler."

THE DEVON BREED OF CATTLE.

ITS HISTORY AND CHARACTERISTICS.

It is a singular fact that although almost every quarter of the globe possesses one or more indigenous species of the ox tribe, it is impossible to name the natural locality of the domestic race, or say where its domestication was first effected. It is agreed by naturalists that the numerous breeds or varieties of the latter, although presenting wide differences in size, shape and other points, are properly included in one species—*Bos taurus*. Of its original subjugation by man we know nothing. It is at least doubtful if within the historic period any strictly wild cattle have existed, that could justly be considered the parent stock of any tamed breed. In making this statement, the fact is not overlooked that there are in Britain cattle which have long been called wild, particularly the herd kept at Chillingham Park, Northumberland, England, and that at the old Cadzow or Chatelerhault Park, Lanarkshire, Scotland. But the question has not been settled whether these cattle belong to a stock originally wild, or to a domesticated one, which, having in early times been allowed to roam at will in an uncultivated country, lost their tameness to a considerable extent, and whose offspring, produced in this state of liberty, approximated from generation to generation more and more to the wild type. Some have argued, not without semblance of reason, that the ancestors of the Chillingham cattle were introduced by the Romans, and contend that though two thousand years may have elapsed since they were transferred from Italy, their descendants in England bear many marks of similarity with the cattle of the Campagna of Rome—a breed of undoubted antiquity.

But if we cannot trace our domestic cattle to an undoubted wild stock, there is no question that some breeds are very old, having been in the possession of the inhabitants of the countries where they are found at the earliest period of which we have any account of them. Such breeds may therefore be called aboriginal, in contradistinction to those whose origin is known.

Three distinct tribes or stocks of cattle appear to have existed in the British Islands from time immemorial, viz: 1, the Long-horns, which originally occupied the low flat lands of England and similar parts of Ireland, and were remarkable for the enormous length of their horns, their bulky frames and thick hides; 2, the Middle-horns, represented by the cattle of Devonshire, Herefordshire, Wales and the Scottish Highlands; 3, the Polled cattle, represented by the Galloway and other hornless breeds, and of which the semi-wild stock of Chatelerhault Park may be the oldest type. Martin says of these three classes, "they are of untraceable antiquity in our Islands." The Short-horns are believed to have been introduced from the Continent.

The similarity in the shape and general characteristics between the West Highland and Devon, and the wild cattle of Chillingham, has long been noticed. Vasey, in his "Delineations of the Ox Tribe," says: "The Chillingham cattle are *white*, and the Highland cattle or Kyloes are generally *black;* but with this exception the same description might almost serve for both breeds. * * * Indeed, so great is the similarity, that the Kyloe appears only to be a black variety of the Chillingham ox, and the Chillingham only a white variety of the Kyloe."

The author of the "Complete Grazier," a work written sixty years ago, in his list of breeds, places the wild stock of Chillingham at the head, and the Devons next, remarking in regard to the latter that they are "descended from the wild race." Youatt observes: "Every one who has had the opportunity of comparing the Devon cattle with the wild breed of Chillingham Castle, has been struck with the great resemblance in many points, notwithstanding the difference of color." But it is well known that color is not one of the most permanent characteristics of animals. It is not altogether invariable, even in wild races, as we see by the tendency to white, or *albinage*, in various species of quadrupeds and birds. One of the first changes resulting from the subjection of wild races to domestication, is in many cases, variation of color. The domestic turkey is the offspring of the wild, which in its natural state, is nearly as uniform in color as any other bird. Its period of domestication of course extends no further back than the settlement of America by Europeans; yet it long since broke into nearly as many shades and variations of color as the common barnyard fowl. Wild ducks which have been tamed, have frequently exhibited striking changes of color, after being bred in a domestic state for a few generations. It is true that domestication does not produce such results in all species. The wild or Canadian goose, for instance, retains without variation, its original markings, from generation to generation, in a state of tameness.

The wild cattle of Chillingham and Chatelerhault are generally white—are sometimes said to be *uniformly* white. But the keepers of these cattle state that they occasionally produce calves which are not white; they are spotted and sometimes wholly black. Such are soon put out of the way. So, too, with the Highland cattle; though black is the prevailing color, there are not unfrequently animals of lighter shades, and sometimes those of clear white. If it were wished to effect a general change in the color of these cattle, it might probably be accomplished by selecting for propagation those which deviate most from the common shade.

The Devons, in common with all the middle-horned British breeds, seem to have undergone comparatively little change for a great length of time. When the Romans, under Julius Cæsar conquered England, fifty years before the Christian era, they found the native Britons in possession of large numbers of cattle, on whose milk and flesh they lived to a great degree, neglecting the cultivation of the soil. Cattle formed "their riches," as the rein-deer are said to form the riches of the Laplander. In an unsettled state of society, with constant danger of outside enemies, "that property only was valuable," as has been aptly observed, "which might be hurried away at an invader's approach." The country, for centuries, was frequently overrun by hostile armies, before which the populatian of the western districts retired, taking with them to the fortresses of North Devon and Cornwall, or to the mountain fastnesses of Wales, many of their cattle. "In this manner, probably," says Youatt, was preserved the ancient breed of British cattle. * * * As for Scotland, it, in a manner set its invaders at defiance; or its inhabitants retreated for a while, and soon turned again on their pursuers. They were proud of their country and proud of their cattle, their choicest possession; and there, too, the cattle were preserved, unmixed and undegenerated. Thence it resulted that in Devon, in Sussex, in Wales and in Scotland, the cattle have been the same from time immemorial; while in all the eastern coast the breed of cattle degenerated, or at least lost its original character; it consisted of a variety of animals, brought from every neighboring and some remote districts, mingled in every possible way.

"The slightest observation will convince us that the cattle in Devonshire, Sussex, Wales and Scotland are essentially the same. They are middle-horned; tolerable but not extraordinary milkers, and remarkable for the quality rather than the quantity of their milk; active at work, and with an unequaled aptitude to fatten. They have all the characteristics of the same breed, changed by soil and climate and time, yet little changed by the intermeddling of man. We may almost trace the color, namely, the red of the Devon, the Sussex and the Hereford, and where the black alone are now found the memory of the red prevails."

It is conceded on all hands that the Devon is one of the oldest and purest of British breeds of cattle. The Devon oxen have long been esteemed for beauty of form, for usefulness in labor, and for the readiness with which they produce beef of fine quality. Their value for the yoke is due in a great degree to their superior intelligence. "Knowledge is power," no less in oxen than in men. Youatt, comparing the Lancashire and the Devon ox, says: "The former has just wit enough to find his way to and from his pasture; the latter rivals the horse in activity and docility, and often fairly beats him out of the field in stoutness and honesty in work. He is as easily broken in, and he equals him in attachment and gratitude to his feeder." The Devon ox quickly understands what is required of him, and at once proceeds to do it with ease and dispatch.

The adaptedness of Devon oxen to the yoke was formerly one of the principal points for which the breed was recommended in England; and in America it still constitutes an important merit. But in England the labor of the horse has been almost entirely substituted for that of the ox. The ox has at the same time become relatively more valuable for beef than formerly. Hence it results that the changes which have taken place in the Devon breed of cattle of late years, are such as tend to render the production of beef its leading characteristic. The propensity to fatten is increased, and a greater weight of meat in proportion to the bone is obtained, than was yielded by the old stock. By regarding chiefly the points which relate to fattening, it is not unlikely that in many cases the stock has lost something of its former activity and muscular power, as well as something of the faculty of secreting milk. The breed, it is true, was never noted for quantity of milk; but the milk in respect to richness was not excelled by that of any other cows except those of the Channel Islands, and perhaps the Kerry; so that for the production of butter the breed occupied by no means an inferior position. Until beef came to be regarded as more profitable than milk and its products, in the districts where Devon cattle were kept, herds of cows of this breed were devoted to dairy purposes; and a quarter of a century ago, Mr. Bloomfield, a tenant of the Earl of Leicester, in Norfolk, had a herd of twenty cows which produced for a year, an average of two hundred pounds of butter per head. Youatt quotes from a correspondent who kept Devon cows, the statement that ten of them averaged, in summer, sixty pounds of butter per week. He refers to another correspondent as saying of the Devon cow that, "the quality of the milk is good, and the quantity remunerative to the dairyman." Youatt adds: "Such, however, is not the common opinion; they are kept principally for their other good qualities."

But it may be as well to state here, that the dairies for which a portion of Devonshire has been somewhat famous, are not supported by cows of the breed which it is the object of this article chiefly to describe. There have always been in the county two varieties of cattle, known as the North and South Devons—the former of smaller frame and truer form than the latter, more uniform in general character, and regarded as the older type. The North Devon has always been considered as the best for labor and for the shambles, while the South Devon, or as they are frequently called, the South Hams cattle, have had the preference for dairy purposes. Youatt says: "A South Devon cow has been known, soon after calving, to yield more than two pounds of butter per day; and many of the old Southern native breed are equal to any Short-horns in the quantity of their milk, and far superior to them in its quality." The breed has sometimes been crossed with the Guernsey, Alderney and Jersey, by which the richness of the milk has been improved, and the value of the stock for butter-making increased. But these cattle are not held in very high estimation, and sell at only low prices compared with those which the North Devons bring. It appears that attempts have been made to improve the dairy properties of the North Devons by crossing. Youatt says he was informed by Mr. Roberts, of South Molton, that this breed had been crossed with the Guernsey, and that the consequence was the stock became more valuable for the dairy, but was so much injured for the plow and for the grazier that the breeders were zealous to preserve the old stock in its native purity.

The first importation to this country of cattle known to be of the genuine North Devon breed, was a bull and several heifers sent by Mr. Coke, of Holkham, Norfolk, to Wm. Patterson, Esq., of Baltimore, in 1817. An impression has prevailed quite generally, that most of the cattle introduced into New England by the early settlers, were Devons. Hence it has been the practice of some persons to speak of the common cattle of that section, as "New England Devons." From the Colonial records, it appears that the cattle which were imported from Europe were from various sections of Britain, and some from the Continent. Several years since, the writer had the opportunity of examining the first records of the Plymouth (Mass.) Colony, in reference to the importation of cattle. It appears that the first cattle in the Colony were brought by Edward Winslow, in the ship *Charity*, in March, 1624. They consisted of one bull and three hiefers. Others arrived shortly aftewards in the *Jacob*. They were distributed among the settlers according to a plan agreed upon, and in recording the disposition made of the animals, they are described. Thus, "four black heyfers, that came in the *Jacob*," are spoken of, and "black cows that came at first in the *Ann*," "the great white-back cow brought over in the *Ann*," "the white-bellied heyfer," "the red cow," &c. Most of these colors do not indicate affinity with the Devon breed; they indicate rather relationship to the cattle of Cornwall, and some of the Welsh breeds. But the largest importation of cattle by the first settlers of New England was made into the Plantations of Massachusetts Bay, in 1629, and consisted of 115 head. It is said "they were mostly ordered by Francis Higginson, formerly of Leicestershire, whence several of the animals were brought." In the early days of the New Hampshire colony, an importation of cattle was made from Denmark. It thus appears that the cattle first introduced into New England were from different sections, and were quite diverse in blood and characters. With the exception of some animals imported into Connecticut, there is no evidence that any were brought from Devonshire. The stock which gave rise to the cattle formerly well known in Connecticut as the "Farmington Reds," is said by persons who have examined into its history, to have been shipped from Plymouth, England.

This is a port in the south of Devonshire, and the Farmington Reds, so far as the writer has any knowledge of them, bore more resemblance to the South Devon than to the North Devon.

Since the importation of 1817, before spoken of, the North Devons have been constantly increasing in America. The Patterson herd, of Maryland, constituted the nucleus from which the breed was for several years mainly disseminated; but numerous other importations from various English herds—including some of the highest reputation—have been made of late years, and the breed may be considered as established in this country. There is reason to believe that where the Devons are judiciously bred and properly cared for, they will continue to be a profitable stock. It is important, however, that their characteristics should be understood, as otherwise more may be expected of them than will be realized.

It has already been remarked that it is for beef chiefly that the Devons are now kept in England. It is in reference to this that the breed has been *improved*. Probably it is less valuable for labor and for milk than it was before the propensity to fatten acquired its present ascendency. But in this country one of the principal recommendations of the breed is the value of the oxen for labor. Hence it is in those sections where oxen are worked to a considerable extent, that the Devons have been mostly kept, though their hardiness and activity render them better fitted for exposure and for thin pastures than the Short-horns. No ox of his size equals the Devon in ability to labor; he is very active and strong for his weight. Youatt says: "Four good Devon steers will do as much work in the field or on the road as any three horses, and in as quick and often quicker time."

It is not merely for the *amount* of work which the Devon ox performs that he is prized; the style in which he does it, his handsome form, fine color, graceful carriage, and the little attention he requires from his driver, all serve to enhance his value even as a beast of burthen. In fact, but one objection is made to him, and that is, he lacks the weight which is required for the heaviest work. The objection, as applicable to full-bloods, must be to some extent admitted; they are not generally as large as would be desirable for all kinds of work, though some of the breed have size enough for any duty required of a working ox; and by attention to this point in the selection of breeding stock, there would be no difficulty in obtaining animals possessing the requisite weight and strength.

In this country, however, the Devons have not become so numerous that many full bloods are subjected to the yoke. The bulls are used for crossing, and the *grade* bulls, of various degrees of Devon blood, are castrated when young and reared for oxen. Cows which will produce half-blood oxen of sufficient size, are readily obtained, and by due attention to the selection of half-blood cows, oxen of three-fourths blood, not lacking in size may be bred.

Youatt said of the North Devon cattle, in 1835: "This aboriginal British breed is a very valuable one, and seems to have arrived at the highest point of perfection of which it is capable. It is heavier than it was thirty years ago, yet fully as active. Its aptitude to fatten is increased rather than diminished; and its property as a milker could not be improved without probable or certain detriment to its grazing qualities."

There is no doubt that the average weight of the Devons when slaughtered, has been increased since Youatt made the above remark; but it is not so certain that they are "yet fully as active" as formerly. Since that remark was made, the use of oxen for labor, in England, has been almost entirely given up, and the breeders of Devon cattle have mostly thrown out of the scale of points, whatever had no relation to fattening. It may not be that the frame of these cattle has of late years been much enlarged; but the tendency to lay on flesh has been increased—the flesh being thicker, and of greater amount, in proportion to the bone. The ordinary weight of oxen of this breed, in England, four to five years old, is 800 to 900 pounds, beef only; but *show* animals have attained the weight of 1400 pounds, and upwards. In respect to quality of flesh, the Devons stand very high, being excelled only by the mountain breeds of Scotland and Wales, and the Kerries of Ireland.

As has already been intimated, an important object in keeping Devon cattle in this country, is the working of the oxen. Hence the points of activity and muscular strength must be duly regarded. More attention should be paid to size, in the selection of breeding stock, than has usually been given to this point. Still, symmetry should by no means be sacrificed to size. Bulls may be obtained which will weigh, in fair condition, at mature age, from seventeen to nineteen hundred pounds, and in some instances more, while they are not lacking in any of the special merits of the Devon breed. The bull Prince of Wales,—owned by the Michigan State Agricultural College, a brief description of which is given on the 12th page of this volume, and a portrait of which forms the frontispiece,—may be referred to as a specimen of the kind of bulls alluded to. Such an animal, broken to the yoke, would probably show that he has weight and strength enough for any duty required of an ox. Of course there is no reason why oxen of the breed should not attain as great or greater size than the bulls.

Considerable has been said in regard to securing higher dairy qualities in the Devons. They might unquestionably be obtained; but it would be at the sacrifice, more or less, of their fattening tendency and value for the yoke, as has been found to be the result whenever the same thing has been attempted in England. In this State the value of the Devons for making beef and for labor, will probably be regarded as about equal at the present time, milk standing in a subordinate position. It is not unlikely that the price of beef will in future render it expedient to place the fattening tendency relatively higher in the scale than it now generally stands. Where dairying is pursued as a special business, the Devons will not be adopted; some breed that is cultivated with particular reference to that object should be chosen.

FRUITS ALONG THE EASTERN SHORE OF LAKE MICHIGAN.

Every year seems to add proof to the idea that the eastern shore of Lake Michigan is one of the finest fruit sections in the country. In my report for 1865, pages 13 to 16, some remarks were given in reference to the production of fruits in a portion of Ottawa county. I am indebted to Rev. L. M. S. Smith, editor of the Grand Haven *Union*, for facts of interest respecting the fruit crop of that neighborhood for 1866. A society called the Lake Shore Horticultural Association has been formed, which held its first annual exhibition at Mill Point, on the 27th of September last. Mr. Smith writes that only a partial report has been made by the Association on the growth and sale of fruit, and that relating only to the town of Spring Lake. From this document Mr. Smith collates some facts, as follows:

"During the past season there have been gathered and sold, as the produce of Spring Lake, ten thousand baskets or boxes of peaches, averaging from one-third to one-half bushel each—probably 4,500 bushels. Geo. G. Lovell, Esq., one of the proprietors of the largest orchard in that town, informs me that his peaches brought him an average of two dollars and a half per box. If this holds true of the other orchards, the value of the peach crop for the year was $25,000.

"Apples, pears, plums, grapes, and all the varieties of small fruits flourish here. But few large orchards of either have yet come into bearing. On a comparatively small scale, all these kinds of fruit have been tested for many years. I had peach trees in bearing in Mill Point, in 1851. These trees are yet producing fruit, and for fifteen years have never failed to produce it every year. I never saw finer apples, nor so large and beautiful ones, of the several kinds I have tested, grown in any other place. I say this, fully realizing the import of the words. The Baldwin grows much larger here than in Western New York, and I have kept them, without special care, until the first of July. I have also kept in the same way, the Black Jilliflower, so noted for becoming dry and mealy in the winter, until the last days of May, and they remained juicy and fresh to the last."

From statistics gathered by the Lake Shore Horticultural Association, and published in the Grand Haven *Union*, it appears that there were growing at Mill Point in the year 1866, of trees, vines, etc., the following:

Apple trees, 7,604; of which 2,819 are in bearing; 2,000 from two to three years old, and 2,785 set out in the spring of 1866.

Pear trees, 1,286; of which 400 are in bearing; 400 from two to three years old, and 486 set out in the spring of 1866.

Plum, apricot, nectarine and quince trees, 755 of each.

Grape vines, 18,693; of which 1,700 are in bearing; 2,000 from two to three years old, and 14,993 set out in the spring of 1866.

Currants, 8,500 bushes; raspberries, 1,000; blackberries, 500; strawberries, 4 acres.

There were said to be in course of preparation for fruit, to be ready by the spring of 1867, 337 acres—enough to admit 53,640 trees, and 16,500 vines, allowing nine-tenths of the land for trees, and one-tenth for vines.

From a communication to the Grand Haven *Union*, it appears that there were growing in the township of Grand Haven, in the year 1866, the following:

Apple trees, 2,450; peach trees, 4,585; pear trees, 962; plum trees, 345; cherry trees, 300; quince trees, 259; grape vines, 2,878; currant bushes, 4,649; New Rochelle (Lawton) blackberry bushes, 500; nursery trees, 5,000. The grapes consist of Isabella, Catawba, Clinton, Delaware, Hartford Prolific, Concord, Iona, Massachusetts White, Adirondac, Israella, Allen's Hybrid, Elsingburgh and Diana. The apples, pears, and peaches, comprise the leading varieties cultivated in the Northern States.

A communication from Henry S. Clubb, Secretary of the Lake Shore Horticultural Association, published in the November number (1866) of the Monthly Report of the Agricultural Department, Washington, D. C., contains an interesting description of a portion of the lake shore country. It is herewith subjoined:

The general character of the eastern shore of Lake Michigan, for from six to ten miles east of the lake, is sandy, and close to the lake the white sand is whirled into the most fantastic shapes by the lake storms, in some cases forming hills almost as white as snow, and running from two to four hundred feet above the level of the lake. These hills are partially covered with forest trees, consisting of pine, hemlock, beech, maple and oak, with a small growth of cedar, and in the valleys black oak is occasionally to be found.

Most of these hills are full of roots (apparently growing from the solid ground beneath) of a wild grape-vine, which sometimes produces a small black grape, of no particular value where cultivated varieties can be obtained. The highest hills have a strong growth of these vines at their summits, and consequently the roots must in some cases be from 200 to 400 feet in length, keeping pace in their growth with the white sand on the hill.

Back from the sand-hills are numerous small lakes, or bayous, varying from one to six miles in extent, around which are sloping banks of sand, with here and there a substratum of white marl. In some of the small valleys there is an occasional swamp of black soil. This, however, is a scarce article in this sandy region, and such spots are held at high prices, being adapted for market-gardening or meadow-land. Around the small lakes, on the sloping banks, and on the table-land of only moderate elevation, the peach and the grape appear to have found their natural position, and lands which a few years ago would not sell at five dollars an acre, now command from ten to fifty dollars per acre, and in close proximity to shipping ports, much higher rates.

Corn is seldom grown here in large quantities, and neither wheat nor grass can be obtained, except on the rare spots above mentioned, in sufficient quantities to make their cultivation profitable. Rye and buckwheat are more successful.

The growth of peaches along this shore was, we believe, commenced at St. Joseph, Berrien county, about fifteen years ago, and the success of the experiment there has been the means of extending the peach culture along the lake shore as far as Manistee, and experience has shown that in some seasons, when St. Joseph fails to obtain a crop, the more northern localities succeed beyond all expectation. The season just past has shown this in a remarkable degree, and the theory explaining it is that while St. Joseph is so located that the prevailing wind, the southwest, only passes over a small portion of the lake, and that portion frozen, the wind from the same direction at Grand Haven, and north of here, sweeps over the surface of the unfrozen lake for a distance of one hundred miles, and is thus modified in its temperature. Our meteorological friends here, record in the severest winters, several degrees in favor of Grand Haven over the temperature of St. Joseph.

The Lake Shore Horticultural Association held an exhibition or fair last month, and to show what kinds of fruit are the most successful in this locality a brief report of the awards of the committee on fruits is given below:

Apples.—The premium for the largest variety of apples was taken by Judge Hathaway, of Nunica, a village east of the sandy lake shore region, so that this locality will not claim any pre-eminence in the production of this fruit, although some fine apples were exhibited by our lake shore growers.

Grapes.—The premium for the best pound of grapes was awarded to John W. Cook, Esq., of Grand Haven, to whom belongs the credit of being the pioneer in fruit growing in this vicinity, which may be regarded as the centre of lake shore fruit culture. Mr. Cook has not only proved the adaptability of this locality for peaches, but also for grapes. To the Delaware was awarded the first premium, the only grape which at that period, October 3, could claim to be agreeably ripe. September was this year unusually wet, and had the fair been held the latter end of the month, instead of the beginning, grapes would have exhibited to much greater advantage, although it would have been too late for peaches. A bunch of the Hartford Prolific, exhibited by J. V. Hopkins, Esq., of Mill Point, would have taken the second premium but for the lack of the requisite quantity; as it was, the premium was awarded to Hunter Savidge, Esq., for a fine box of Concord. The Isabella, exhibited by the same amateur, was nearly equal to the Concord. The Catawba should be placed last on the list of grapes adapted to this locality.

The exhibition may be said to have placed the old established grapes for this section in the following order, the earliest being placed first: The Delaware, Hartford Prolific, Concord, Isabella, Clinton, Catawba. The most recent varieties, Iona, Israella, Diana, etc., not being on exhibition, cannot be said to have been fully tested in this locality. We have, however, seen at Mr. Cook's residence, in Grand Haven, a very fine specimen of the Diana, which shows that it is a good grape here, although its relative earliness will not, we think, place it higher in the list than the Concord or Isabella.

The premium for the best exhibition of grapes was awarded to Hunter Savidge, who, we believe, exhibited all the varieties in the above list. This gentleman, in connection with his partner, Dwight Cutler, Esq., of Grand Haven, has a vineyard of about three-fourths of an acre on the south shore of Spring Lake, with a decided inclination towards the north, and a blind fence on the west. For perfect neatness and good order we have never seen the equal of this model vineyard. Its trellises run north and south, and are about seven and a half feet in height. Not a blade of grass or a weed of any kind is visible among the vines, and the whole is raked as even as a newly made seed-bed. The production of this little vineyard four years after planting was about $800 worth of grapes—one year ago. The yield this year has been fully equal in quantity, we believe, although the price is probably less, in consequence of the prevalence of the cholera in Chicago, the best market for this region of country.

There are numerous other vineyards in different stages of growth, and in another year the competition among lake shore grape growers will become quite sharp and interesting. Considerable tracts of land are being cleared for vineyards, and the eastern shore of Lake Michigan bids fair to rival, in a few years, the famous southern shore of Lake Erie. Grape growers from Ohio have visited this locality and expressed the opinion that it is preferable to their own section, in consequence of the superior protection on the north side, which is furnished by a dense growth of evergreen timber. The fact that Lake Michigan never wholly freezes over, and that the prevailing winds are southwest, west, and northwest, gives this locality a decided advantage for grape culture.

Peaches.—The premiums for the best exhibition of peaches were taken by Mr. Lovell and Mr. Eames, the former of Mill Point, and the latter of Ferrysburg, a village on the opposite side of Spring Lake. The early and late Crawfords and the Stump-the-World could not be excelled by anything we have ever seen from North Carolina, Delaware, or New Jersey, in the New York markets.

The shores of this little inland lake are becoming the favorite resort of fruit growers. Peaches and grapes appear to grow here with equal success and profit. The peach orchard of Mr. Lovell is a model of its kind. It contains about thirty acres, running parallel with and alongside of the Detroit and Milwaukee railroad. When this beautiful crop was on the trees this year, we understand Mr. Lovell was offered $25,000 for the orchard, and that sum was refused. This orchard is on land which ten years ago was covered with a scrubby growth of oak and did not appear worth clearing; yet, we understand, but little manure has been applied. The trees are kept trimmed and free from worms, and the ground loosened by cultivation.

Mr. Reed, of Mill Point, exhibited a fine seedling which resembled the Crawford's Early, but which appeared sweeter to the taste and fully equal in size. It was named Reed's Imperial by the committee. Several seedlings of fine quality were also exhibited by Mr. Eames, who had the largest variety of peaches on exhibition.

One of the finest, and we believe, the oldest orchards in this vicinity is that of Mr. Hezekiah Smith, situated on an arm of Spring Lake, known as Smith's bayou. There are over twenty acres of apples and peaches. Mr. Smith has taken the premium several times at the county fair for the best peaches; this year the exhibition occurred between the perfection of his Early and Late Crawfords, being too late for the former and too early for the latter. We visited the orchard, and must say we have seldom witnessed trees in better condition.

The method of packing grapes and peaches generally adopted here is to pack the former in boxes of half-inch planed pine boards, containing about ten pounds to the box, while the peaches are placed in crates made of rough lath and holding about half a bushel.

The wages paid during the gathering and packing season were, for women, one dollar per day.

The prices realized this year for grapes were from 12½ cents to 25 cents per pound, and for peaches from 50 cents to $3 per crate—the former price for common seedlings, and the latter for the best Crawfords.

A communication to the *Prairie Farmer*, from a correspondent at Muskegon, Mich., after giving a description, somewhat similar to that given by Mr. Clubb, above quoted, of the lands immediately on the lake shore, proceeds to make some remarks on the advantages of the section for fruit growing, from which the following extract is taken:

Nearly all the fruit orchards already set, are on the smooth lands, but the opinion is fast gaining ground that the rough lands, from being nearer the great lake, and offering every variety of aspect on high ground and consequent immunity from late spring frosts, will prove the surest and most valuable land, especially for peaches and grapes.

Scattered through this tract are found beautiful valleys, or ampitheatres, of from five to twenty acres in extent, with southern and eastern slopes admirably adapted for the grape, and northern and eastern ones for peaches.

Here are all the conditions which your correspondent J. W. C. says the Delaware grape imperatively requires—a light, dry, rich, warm soil; or, if anything is lacking to make it rich enough, it can be cheaply supplied in the form of the animal fertilizers now manufactured in Chicago.

The climate of this whole region, extending from St. Joseph to Grand Traverse Bay, is so modified by the air from the great lake, that only at the extreme north and south limits of it is the blossom bud of the peach injured by the cold winter. In this vicinity which is opposite the broadest expanse of the lake, the thermometer has never been known to fall lower than ten degrees below zero, while several degrees lower are necessary to injure the peach bud. The oldest peach trees around here have never failed to bear.

But the *profits* of fruit-growing depend not merely on the facilities for *producing* it, but on easy and cheap access to a good market. Chicago is, and always will be, the principal market for the fruit from the Eastern Shore, and daily steam communication the only reliable means of transit. From this port there are already two lines of steamers permanently established, which furnish daily access to Chicago, starting late in the afternoon, and reaching Chicago early in the morning, providing the very best conveyance for fruit over a highway which cannot be monoplized by a greedy company. Fruit from here and Grand Haven will arrive in market in perfect order at a trifling expense for freight. These two ports possess excellent harbors, and shipping facilities superior to any other points on this shore—a matter which will not be overlooked by the intelligent fruit grower in search of a location. Many have already made beginnings in fruit culture in this vicinity—still there is plenty of good land, at comparatively low prices, waiting to be transformed into fruitful and lucrative orchards and vineyards.

QUESTIONS CONNECTED WITH THE ROTATION OF CROPS.

A LECTURE DELIVERED BEFORE THE HIGHLAND AND AGRICULTURAL SOCIETY OF SCOTLAND, BY DR. ANDERSON, CHEMIST TO THE SOCIETY.

There is probably nothing which has been more frequently insisted on, of late years, than the advantages which agriculture has already, and is yet destined to derive from the active co-operation of science and practice, nor will any one—now that the true relation of the two are recognized—and it is understood that they are not antagonistic, but advance in the same direction, though by different paths—be inclined to doubt the importrnce of the progress agriculture has made since it came to be regarded as a scientific art. Differences of opinion may, no doubt exist, as to the extent of the influence which science has exerted on its progress; but no one can hesitate to attribute to it a certain effect, while those who are most familiar with the subject, and most capable of following science through the details of practice, will most fully recognize the changes it has effected. The results which have occurred are exactly those which may be anticipated, when an art that has been slowly advanced by the gradual accumulation of experience in a purely empirical manner, calls in to its aid, a branch or branches, of knowledge which have already examined the same subject from a different point of view, for it thus obtains new tools, which if properly used, enable it to accomplish what would have been impossible without their assistance.

The instant an art begins to be cultivated in a scientific spirit, it is no longer content with the mere observation of facts, but seeks for their explanation, and is thus enabled to make them the starting-point of further progress. Up to the end of the last, or beginning of the present century, science and practical agriculture had never come in contact, and the former had shot far ahead of the latter, so that when Davy, and other chemists, directed their attention to agricultural questions, they were able to throw light on much that was previously obscure, and to make many important practical suggestions, the utility of which is best proved by their thorough incorporation with the daily practice of agriculture. These, and the subsequent statements of Liebig, have led to the impression that science must be in a condition to unravel all the difficulties encountered in the field. But this is only possible in the event of science maintaining its position in advance of practice, and though this has hitherto, and probably always will be the case, in a general sense, yet it is obvious that there may be circumstances under which the opposite may occur, for practice may be led into particular channels of observation, which science has no special inducement to follow, and a whole mass of facts may be accumulated, which it is unable at once to explain, and which it can only clear up by a series of elaborate inquiries made for that special purpose. In addressing the members of the Highland Society, I have more than once adverted to this point, and explained that as the practice of agriculture is not perfect, neither are the sciences on which it depends, and that there are many matters still obscure, and for the full explanation of which we may have to wait until much additional information is obtained. The truth is, that while science, in the main, is in advance of practice, and has discovered many facts for which we have been as yet unable to find practical use, and which we are, therefore, in our ignorance, pleased to call unpractical, there are other facts established by empirical observations in the earliest periods of agriculture, for which no satisfactory explanation has yet been discovered.

Among these subjects I reckon the rotation of crops, to some points in relation to which, I propose to direct your attention on the present occasion. I do not intend to discuss it in full, for that would carry me far beyond the limits of an address, but rather to point out some of the difficulties encountered; to show how the explanations hitherto offered—some of which are extremely ingenious—have failed, as I cannot help thinking they have done, and to suggest the importance of minute observations of all facts likely to throw light upon it. It is unnecessary to refer to the early period at which the necessity for a rotation of crops was observed, further than to remark that the Romans had some idea of it, and that it had reached a condition not very different—in principle, at least—from its present state, long before any attempt was made to study agriculture as a science. The earlier explanations given, were of a very loose and unsatisfactory character. Even Davy himself, usually so clear and lucid, scarcely throws any light upon it, and we owe to Decandolle, the first consistent view of the subject. He supposed that plants growing on the soil, are entirely devoid of the power of selecting their food, but sucked up by the roots everything they met with, and these substances, circulating through them, those which are useful are retained, and those which it cannot assimilate, are again excreted by the roots, that is, by the same organs by which they were originally absorbed. After the plant had grown for some time in the soil, these excrementary substances accumulated in that part of it occupied by the roots, in such quantity as to impede its growth. His idea appears to have been that those substances were not in themselves injurious to the plant, but rather that being accumulated in the soil the plant obtained among the substances, it absorbed a disproportionately large quantity of the materials it was incapable of assimilating, and too small an amount of those which constituted its food, and therefore languished and died. But the substances which one plant rejected, he supposed to be perfectly capable of assimilation by another, so that the growth of the first not only formed no impediment to the second, but might actually promote it, by gathering together the very elements it required. It is to be observed that he considered the substances which acted in this way, to be normal constituents of the soil, which were not poisonous to the plant, but exerted a negative influence, by taking the place of those it was capable of digesting and turning to account.

This view was subsequently modified by Macaire Princep, who made a series of experiments by growing plants in water, and examining the substances excreted by the roots. He found that peas and beans communicated a brown color to the water in which they grew; that the little sponge (*Euphorbia peplus*) excreted a green resin of very acrid taste, and several other plants produced particular substances distinguished by taste or smell. When the plant which had produced these excretions was withdrawn, and replaced by another of the same kind, it refused to grow, although no such effect was produced on a different species. A corn plant, for example, would not only grow, but flourish in the water which refused to support a pea or bean. It is to be noticed that the views entertained by these two observers were not identical, for the excretions obtained by Macaire Princep, were not constituents of the soil, but substances elaborated within the plant and got rid of through the roots. They had, however, this much in common, that both assumed the existence in the soil of substances excreted by the plants which prevented the growth of the same, but did not affect that of another species. These poisonous matters, however, were supposed to be capable of decomposition, and thus a soil which had become poisonous to a particular plant, after a time lost its noxious effect, and became capable of producing it again.

This view is undoubtedly extremely ingenious, and explains many facts; but it is so totally opposed to many others equally familiar and well established, that it is surprising that it should ever have met with the support it actually received. If it were correct, it ought to be entirely impossible to obtain two or more successive crops of the same kind, while in reality, nothing is easier. It may not generally be economically advantageous to do so, but by proper manuring it is perfectly possible to obtain two successive wheat or barley crops on the same soil; and this is even sometimes done, although I need scarcely say it is not considered good farming. In this there is certainly nothing incompatible with Decandolle's view because it may be said that the manure used restores more or less completely the balance between assimilable and unassimilable substances in the soil, and the plant is no longer compelled to take the latter in disproportionate quantity. But how are we to explain those cases in which crop after crop of wheat has been taken from the same soil, as was done with the virgin soils of America, and is still practiced in Hungary and some other countries? If Macaire Princep's view is correct, two successive crops of the same kind ought to be an impossibility, for the poison which prevents the growth of the second is there, and cannot do otherwise than act. His explanation is, therefore, incompatible with facts observed in the field, and it has not stood the test of experimental investigation.

Another observer, Braconnot, repeated Princep's experiments, and found that if the roots of the plants grown in water were entire nothing was excreted, but that if they were injured, substances similar to those observed by Princep were soon found in the waters. If it be the proper juices of the plants which were thus excreted, it is quite obvious that no poisonous effects can be produced by them, for in the process of green manuring an entire crop is plowed into the soil without injury to another of the same kind succeeding it. The views of Decandolle and Macaire Princep therefore fell to the ground, and were replaced by the much more probable idea that successive crops refuse to grow, not on account of the accumulation of any substances in the soil, but because they remove from it some elements necessary to their growth. This explanation is, in the first place, much more natural than the other, and it accordingly appears to have occurred to many observers, and was used to explain the appearance of fairy rings by supposing the toadstools took from the soil some substances which they required, and no longer finding them, advanced from centre to circumference in search of the necessary food. The nature of the substances thus removed was not then understood, and we owe to Liebig the development of this view which became possible when the facts of chemistry had increased. He insisted more strongly than any one before his time on the importance of the mineral constituents of plants. The older chemists believed that these substances were quite fortuitous, and that the plant sucked up from the soil like a sponge, everything it came in contact with, and Decandolle's view was so far founded on this idea. But the numerous ash analyses which had been made in the interval between his time and that of Liebig, enabled the latter to show that this was not correct.

Now when plants are burned it is found that the composition of ash they leave behind, is not consistent with the idea that they work up anything their roots encounter in the soil, but that each plant takes up those substances which it more particularly requires, and yields an ash which is about identical in composition, whatever be the soil in which it grew. After a sufficient number of analyses of the ash had been accumulated, Liebig began to classify plants, according to the preponderating constituents of their mineral portion. It is found that in the straw of a cereal, for instance, a proportion yields an ash, of which about two-thirds of the ash consists of silica, and that the grasses generally are very similar in composition. But when other plants are burnt, such as the tobacco plant, pea-straw or clover, the ash they yield is extremely poor in silica, but rich in lime. And again, if we burn a portion of the turnip plant, the ash contains abundance of potash, while the lime and silica are there in only small quantities. These facts seemed to afford an indication of necessity for a rotation of crops. It is well known that a number of the constituents which plants require, are found in the soil, in an available condition, in extremely small quantities; that silica, for example, which is an abundant element of every soil, is not all in a condition in which the plant can absorb and assimilate it, but that only a minute fraction of that found in it, is in a condition fitted for being taken up by the plant. If a cereal, however, is grown, it takes up at once the silica which it requires. It exhausts a great part of the supply of that element existing in the soil, and in an available form; hence a similar crop growing there cannot flourish, because it does not receive that substance in sufficient quantity. If, however, a plant which requires no silica, be grown after one which requires a great deal of it, then gradual changes take place in the soil, converting a quantity of the unavailable silica, into an available condition, and when a certain time has elapsed, there has been a sufficient accumulation of that particular substance, to serve for the supply for another crop.

So, again, if a lime-plant be grown again with success, it may so completely exhaust the available lime, that another crop immediately following it, cannot grow; but if after one or two seasons, another supply of that element has been brought into an available condition, advantage may be taken of it by changing the crop. It is obvious that this is a very ingenious explanation of the necessity of a rotation of crops; and if it be carried still further, not merely restricting it to the ash of the plant, but including also their organic constituents, it is found that there are circumstances bearing on it, in relation to them also. If, for example, we grow the turnip, which is a broad-leafed plant, and after it take a cereal of narrow-leafed plant, which exposes a very small surface of green matter to the atmosphere, the conditions of the growth are very different in the two cases. It is well known that certain constituents of plants are absorbed from the air, and it is generally supposed that the broad-leafed plants take from it a larger quantity of carbonic acid (and it is alleged also, of nitrogen, though that is more doubtful) than the narrow-leafed plants; that the turnip, which may be taken as an example of the former, is mainly dependent on the air, and a cereal, which exemplifies the latter class, is mainly dependent on the soil. A cereal, it is therefore supposed, cannot be grown for a succession of years without manure, because it exhausts very rapidly the supply of the particular organic food, although it exists in the soil. But if this view, which is unquestionably an extremely ingenious one, be carefully examined, we find many difficulties in the way. In the first place, the distinctions which Liebig in the first instance drew between the substances containing silica and so forth, is by no means so marked as was originally supposed. A cereal, no doubt takes silica from the soil in large quantities; but if we look at other plants, such as the bean, the turnip, &c., it is seen that there is far from being that amount of difference that might be expected. Liebig, for instance, calls the bean a lime-plant, but it can only be so described, if we look simply at the straw by which the bean is supported. The error lay in not comparing the entire plants with one another, but only one of their organs. In bean-straw, no doubt the quantity of lime is very large; but if we look at the seed of the bean itself, we find it is very poor in lime. And hence it is clearly necessary not to look at the stems only, but at the entire plant, and not even at the entire plant only, but at the total produce per acre.

In fact, it is not enough to say that one plant is rich in lime and another poor in it; the question is, what quantity of lime is taken from an acre of land? And when by different plants an average crop of the ordinary farm plants is examined, it turns out that the relative quantities of different mineral matters removed from the soil, does not differ so much as we might anticipate. No doubt cereals differ from every other plant, insomuch as they take a large quantity of silica; but on the other hand, if we come to examine the effect of the repeated growth of crops, it appears that the cereals are less affected by repetition on the same soil, than any other kind of crop whatever, although if this view we are discussing be correct, they ought to be most immediately affected by it. There are many other facts that strike at the root of this view. If it be true that the successful growth of any particular plant, depends on its finding in the soil a very large quantity of the particular substances it requires, it must necessarily follow that if we begin the rotation with the turnip, and produce annually a large crop, we necessarily remove from the soil, a very large quantity of mineral matters, and we ought to impoverish the soil to an appreciable extent, and render it less capable of supporting the subsequent crops of the rotation; while on the other hand, if the turnip crop be small, it would follow that the quantity of these mineral matters removed from the soil being also small, the soil itself should be in a condition the next year, to produce a larger crop, whatever that crop may be, than it would have been, if it had produced an extremely large crop of turnips. In practice, however, the very reverse is the case. I apprehend that no point is better established than this: that if a farmer commences his rotation with a poor crop, all those that follow are also small; although under these very circumstances, if this explanation be correct, they should be the largest.

Looking still fqrther into the matter, we encounter a great number of facts, some of them of an extremely remarkable kind, which require consideration. The points to which I am about to advert, are many of them of an obscure kind, and I shall have some difficuity in putting them, in a clear and satisfactory way before you. They are mainly deducible from some experiments and observations made by Messrs. Lawes and Gilbert. These observers, as is well known, have experimented with the same crop on the same soil, for a number of years, both with and without manure, and they find it possible to grow wheat for sixteen years in succession, with comparatively little diminution in the amount of the crop. It may be said that this continued growth of wheat is due to the fact that their soil is extremely rich in the substances that wheat requires. But see what occurs when another plant is taken. Beans may be cultivated for twelve successive years, and a crop may be produced, but not without a very conspicuous diminution. If the quantity of nitrogen in the bean be taken as the test of the crop, it appears that during twelve successive years it will draw from the soil, an average of nearly 48 lbs. weight of nitrogen; but the first six crops of beans averaged 70 lbs., and the last six 26 lbs. of nitrogen, so that there is a very considerable diminution in the quantity. But see how important is the difference in the total quantity. The wheat crop during these successive years removed on the average, only about 24 lbs. of nitrogen, while the beans abstracted 47 lbs., or nearly twice as much.

In the case of clover again, they have found that by no means can they produce more than three or four successive crops. They may manure the crop as they please; apply to it any kind or any quantity of plant food, but nothing they can do will enable them to increase the number of crops of that plant which can be grown in succession. No principle or system of preparing or manuring the land that they could adopt, had any effect, and the diminution in the amount of produce is extremely remarkable, for they found that the second crop of clover, with the wheat intervening, was only about one-ninth of that produced in the first year. Here it is very clear that the amount of plant food did not affect the produce, and that a supply of the necessary elements is not all that is required.

Going still further, more remarkable results attract our attention. When ten crops of beans were grown, one after another, without manure of any kind, they found that the average of nitrogen removed from the soil, was 34.7 lbs. per year. If they employed mineral manure, the average quantity removed was 51.1 lbs. Now, with ten crops of wheat taken in succession, without manure, the average quantity of nitrogen drawn from the soil was 23.4 lbs. But if they took five crops, with five intervening years of fallow, they found that at the end of the ten years, that the five crops of wheat had withdrawn almost the same quantity of nitrogen, as the ten crops in ten successive years, so that, alternating a year of fallow with every year of wheat, had the effect of doubling the amount of the crop. The total amount of nitrogen removed by the ten crops in these ten successive years, was 234 lbs., and the total amount removed in the five years of fallow, with five of crop, was 219.3 lbs., or a difference of about 14 lbs. Each crop in the ten successive years drew 23.4 lbs., and with five years of fallow and five years of crop, the average amount drawn was 43.9 lbs., and dividing these by two, we get the average over the ten years, which was 21.9 lbs.

The experimenters next proceed to grow wheat, with alternate crops of beans—five crops of beans and five of wheat, in place of the fallow, as in the preceding experiment. Now, these five crops of wheat, alternated with those of beans, yielded 235 lbs. of nitrogen by the end of the ten years, just about the same as when the ten crops were successively grown; but during the intermediate years, the beans were engaged in abstracting nitrogen from the soil and air, and they had actually withdrawn 48.9 lbs. of nitrogen every year, so that the taking away of that element from the soil, by the five crops of wheat, did not prevent the beans taking exactly the quantity which they required. You will thus perceive that the ten crops of wheat contained a certain quantity of nitrogen; that five crops of wheat with five of fallow, contained about the same quantity, and that five crops of wheat and five of beans, took much more than double the quantity, for the wheat took as much as if there had been no beans, and the beans took the quantity they required. Now here is a fact of which we had no previous definite idea at all. I do not apprehend that practice offers us any definite facts of this kind, and in making these experiments Messrs. Lawes and Gilbert have opened up an entirely new field of observation.

In the experiments to which I have referred, the soil was left in its original condition, no manure being employed; but they found that if they added manure, especially mineral manure, the result was that the five crops of wheat when alternated with five crops of beans, gave 207 lbs. of nitrogen, and the five crops of beans which alternated with them, yielded 227.2 lbs., the proportion in this case being not larger, but actually smaller than where no mineral manures were employed. Now how are we to explain this? If we look at it, we see very distinctly that the question with regard to the mineral matters contained in the manure, throw no light whatever upon it. Here is a plant, the wheat, which takes a certain quantity of material from the soil, and it does not seem to matter how that wheat is grown. It is immaterial whether ten successive crops be taken, or five; with beans intervening, exactly the same result is obtained; and if there be thrust in between five of wheat, five of another plant, we get all its produce, as it were, over and above the wheat. It would appear, then, that there are some advantages in growing crops alternated in this way, for beans when grown ten times successively, do not yield so large a quantity, as when put between successive crops of wheat.

Take these facts how we may, it must be admitted that they seem to indicate that the rotation of crops is a far more complicated question than has been supposed, and that if proper explanation is to be found for it, a class of facts to which but little attention has been hitherto paid, must be taken into consideration. It appears indubitable that it is not a question to be explained by merely looking to the chemical nature of the food to be supplied to plants; that it is not a purely chemical, but to a great extent a physiological question; and that it is not enough to look at the plants as machines, taking in a certain quantity of food, but that they must be viewed as beings, endowed with certain functions which are not the same in every particular plant. And if we come to look at it in this point of view, a very great deal must be considered as depending on the manner in which the plant grows.

I think one reason why alternation of crops is beneficial is, that certain crops spread their roots in the superficial, while others penetrate into the deeper layers of the soil, so that a shallow-rooted crop exhausts from the upper part of the soil, certain substances which it requires, and another crop which must derive its food from the same layer, following it, does not find these substances in sufficient quantity, and it becomes necessary, to thus take advantage of the supplies contained in the lower soil, by growing a deep-rooted immediately after a shallow-rooted plant, until such time as a new supply of available food has accumulated at the upper part; and this is what actually occurs in practice, a shallow generally following a deep-rooted plant. But even this is far from explaining all the facts observed, and it seems necessary to go a little further and look upon some plants as having a much greater assimilative power than others—that such a crop as the turnip, for example, can readily take food from the soil, when in a condition in which it may be totally inaccessible to another plant; and I am inclined to think that a great deal of the failure of the clover plant is due to this, and that the clover may be described as a plant of nice digestion, which requires to have its food in certain conditions, in which it exists in the soil in but small quantities, and this would help to explain why we seldom see clover abundant in the second year. The land may be well planted with it the first year, but bye and bye it disappears, and next season perhaps the field shows not the slightest trace of it, although it supplies abundant food for grasses, and would support cereals very readily if they were grown upon it. There are a great many other points which appear to me worthy of consideration, but you will observe that the great difficulty we have in regard to this subject, is that we must talk of it, to a great extent, in a speculative way. There are few definite facts to go upon, and I feel very strongly that until they are supplied, it is impossible to explain or even discuss, many points relating to it. It may also be anticipated that much time must elapse before the necessary facts are amassed, for they are not of a kind likely to be obtained in the ordinary practice of agriculture. They must be obtained by actual, deliberate experiments made for the purpose—not confined to one, but extending over many years—and requiring great care and a very great expenditure. They should be something like these experiments of Mr. Lawes, made with great skill, carried on during successive seasons, at a cost of time and labor, on which few private individuals, and none of our present public institutions, could possibly venture. Therein lies the great difficulty we have to encounter.

PRECOCITY OF DEVELOPMENT IN ANIMALS.

[It is well known that one of the chief aims with many breeders of stock in England and in this country, is early maturity. This is especially the case in reference to cattle and sheep destined for the shambles. In some breeds the system of forcing the growth by highly nutritious food, has been carried to such an extent, that there can be no doubt of its injurious results on the constitution and health of the animals. It will be admitted that there are advantages in early maturity; but it is worthy of consideration, whether these advantages are not often obtained at the sacrifice of other properties of paramount importance. Animals, like plants which grow rapidly, are less firm in tissue and decay sooner, than those of slow growth. "Soon ripe, soon rotten," though an adage of our "rude forefathers," is expressive and truthful. The Leicester sheep, which are fattened for the butcher at twelve to fourteen months old, and are often "full mouthed" at two to two and a half years, are *old* at four or five; while some of the mountain breeds that do not mature till their fifth year, are often vigorous at the age of eighteen or twenty. Another point which seems not to have received the attention it deserves, is whether the flesh of animals that are killed at an early age is as nutritious as that of those which require more time to attain a proper state of ripeness; for the true question is not the number of pounds, but the amount of nutriment produced at the least expense. As embracing some remarks on this subject, which many persons may read with advantage, whether fully agreeing with them or not, the following essay by Professor Brown, V. S., published in the Journal of the Bath and West of England Agricultural Society, is herewith appended.]

In dealing with any subject of importance it is desirable to avoid confusion at the outset, by affixing a precise meaning to the terms employed. This is especially the case with reference to "Precocity of Development," since it is quite possible that what one man may consider to be rapid, another may regard as comparatively speaking, tardy. What we really mean by the term "Precocity of Development," is the premature occurrence of the ordinary signs of maturity, in size, appearance, and general qualities. But how are we to decide whether an animal's arrival at maturity is premature or not? By ascertaining the time required for perfect development in a wild state, before definite attention was paid to the means of accelerating growth.

The originals of our several breeds cannot be found, nor has their history been very minutely traced for us: but enough has been recorded by careful observers to prove that a change has taken place in the capabilities and characteristics of most breeds of animals, coming under the denomination of Stock. So generally admitted is this view, that its denial would be taken as an imputation upon the breeders of the present time. Universal assent will, therefore, probably be accorded to the proposition that varieties of animals, distinguished as cultivated or improved breeds, arrive at maturity earlier than their originals did, when existing under less artificial conditions. Starting from this point it is required to determine *what effects follow this production of premature maturity, whether beneficial or otherwise.*

As bearing upon this question, we may adduce the maxim, that whatever is rapidly produced is by consequence wanting in stability. In support of this idea, instances without number might be drawn from mechanics and from natural history. It seems, indeed, to be a settled point, that every work in nature or in art, to be properly elaborated, requires a certain amount of time to be devoted to its construction; whilst an attempt to accelerate its completion, always results in some radical omission or defect; so that under all circumstances it would be accepted as a legitimate apology for faulty performance, that sufficient time had not been allowed for the proper arrangement of the necessary parts. In the vegetable kingdom it is proverbial that plants of slow growth are the most durable, whilst plants that are produced in a single night, may wither in the next day's sun. In animals, not only are the tissues subject to the operations of this rule, but even the intellect, which precociously matured is rarely lasting, seeming by its very vigor to exhaust itself. Thus we are told that the prodigy of six years is often the imbecile of twenty. The explanation of these phenomena is scarcely possible; no more so, indeed, than is that of the primary properties of matter, whether hardness, transparency, affinity or polarity.

It must be accepted as a general rule that certain combinations, possessing durability, can only be effected under proper conditions, time being one of the essentials. Thus, in the absence of the proper amount of time; or of any other essential circumstance, the results although apparently perfect, lack the power to resist the various destructive influences to which they are exposed, and hence the combination soon ceases to exist. So far, the argument is in support of the general idea; but on the other side of the subject there is someting to be urged. In the first place, it is alleged with truth that there is no direct proportion between the time occupied in the development of the fœtus and the average duration of the animal's life after birth. Thus man, whose fœtal life continues for nine months, has a longer average existence than the horse, whose fœtal life extends to eleven months; and further, in reference to other animals, including birds and fishes, discrepancies are constant. Next, it may be remarked, that the time required for affecting permanent combinations is not definitively fixed, and therefore it becomes difficult, if not impossible, to determine what is premature development and what is not. The first objection is unanswerable, and so far affects the general proposition, as it proves it to be open to exception. The second objection is readily disposed of by remarking that experience will determine the requisite time under all circumstances. Thus the period required for the proper developement of the fœtal structures is fixed in each case, and has not, so far as we know, been influenced by change of circumstances, nor in any degree been subject to variation.

If we could accelerate the process of fœtal growth, it would then be easy to decide the general question, how far such change would affect the subsequent duration of the animal's life; but in the absence of such power, we are compelled to leave the problem unsolved, and proceed to the particular proposition which more immediately concerns us, viz: *the influence of external circumstances in relation to the growth and development of the animal tissues after birth.*

Here again, the question of time returns in reference to the attainment to maturity, and again the answer must be given in accordance with experience. Arrival at the adult period is determined by certain indications, sufficiently definite to be universally recognized, and to remove all difficulty about the time of its occurrence, the animal is fully grown, the permanent dentition is complete, and all the physical qualities are perfect. At this period the assimilative functions seem to lose some of their activity; and the deposition of new materials under perfectly healthy conditions, is about equal to the waste of the tissues, preserving something like uniformity of size for a time; as age advances nutrition becomes still less active, and often less material is deposited than suffices to supply the waste, and a decrease in bulk is the result. This, however, being influenced by various circumstances, is not an invariable consequence.

Natural development presupposes a healthy condition of system, sufficient food, and the full exercise of every organ; such conditions, in fact, as ordinarily exist in nature. In association with these favorable circumstances, there will be others of an opposite tendency, whose operations, however paradoxical it may appear, is conducive to the desired result. In the discussion of these opposing influences, we shall find much that is of practical value.

DEVELOPMENT OF THE ANIMAL UNDER NATURAL CONDITIONS.

In the wild state, where domestication has no influence, and man's interference is not felt, the conditions of existence are very materially different from those which are artificially established. Weak and diseased animals are placed in the most unfavorable position. Where healthy animals owe their preservation to their capabilities of flight, the maimed have slight chance to escape destruction; and, in general terms, where full vigor of all the animal faculties is indispensable to the preservation of existence, there is present a natural and constantly-operating agency for the destruction of defective animals, who, under other conditions, might exist and perpetuate their defects.

On this grand principle depend all the essential differences between natural and artificial conditions of life. In nature there is a guarantee in some considerable degree for healthy development; while under domestication much is left to be determined by judgment or caprice. Naturally, therefore, we may conclude that a healthy state of the organism will, as a rule, characterize the majority of animals under natural circumstances.

As the conditions of existence influence the animal's qualifications and tendencies, we may still further conclude with safety that there will be a proper exercise of all those capacities, which become more developed as they are more actively employed. In this way the strongest and most perfect animals enjoy the largest share of the advantages of their position, while the weakly ones are most affected by destructive agencies, such as inclemency of season, scarcity of food, and predatory attacks from larger animals.

It is not contended that an entire exemption from injury or disease is a condition of the natural state of existence. Animals suffer from accidents of various kinds, and are sometimes found affected with disease; but it is most important to observe that any radical defects are not likely to be perpetuated, because the circumstances under which the animal is placed lead to his destruction so soon as he ceases to possess the qualifications necessary for resisting the adverse influences by which he is surrounded. It is scarcely necessary to illustrate this statement, although numberless instances at once present themselves. An animal whose freedom of movement is interfered with becomes an easy prey to his pursuer, while the predatory beasts under like circumstances are incapable of providing food for themselves.

Radical defects, it is apparent, can only be extended to a certain point, and that not a very remote one; for the reason that their general extension would diminish, and ultimately exterminate the race, by depriving it of the qualities on which its existence depends.

Every animal in a state of nature has to seek its own food, and in so doing preserves the due proportion between the waste and reparation of his tissues. The food on which he subsists, again, contains in natural combination the elements which he requires, and which his organs are capable of appropriating. Certain portions are devoted to the support of his flesh, while other parts furnish the necessary supply of fat; any excessive accumulation of one or the other being prevented by the healthy activity of the excretory organs. By exertion, by respiration, by exhalation from the skin, by secretions from the liver and kidneys, the old and worn-out materials are removed, and by digestion of the elements taken by the animal as food, new materials are prepared, and in the course of the circulation of the blood deposited to compensate for the waste. So long as all these conditions continue in perfection, so long as the old materials are removed and the functions are all active, and the animal obtains a due supply of proper food, it is difficult to realize the possibility of the occurrence of disease, except from the action of some violent mechanical or chemical cause.

During the growth of the tissues many circumstances influence the development of particular parts. In animals whose mode of existence necessitates speed, for pursuit or flight, the respiratory organs, with the organs of progression, will indicate the possession of the capability; the habit of rapid movement naturally leading to a preponderance of those parts which are most necessary for the perfection of the quality; under the same circumstances the circulation will be very active, and hence the organs in this system will be proportionately developed. Activity of respiration, circulation, motion and secretion, are opposed to excessive accumulation of tissue, particularly of fatty tissue, as well as to great bulk of body. It is merely begging the whole question to say that these things are denied the animal because they would encumber his movements; they are absent because the habits of his life occasion the development of organs whose healthy exercise is opposed to such accumulations; quick movement, active respiration and excretion being destructive actions, are of necessity incompatible with excessive deposition.

Domestication essentially modifies the condition of existence, the change being in exact proportion to the difference of the animal's previous habits, as compared with his present mode of life. How decided the variation really is will be apparent upon a very cursory review of the new circumstances under which he is placed.

DEVELOPMENT OF THE ANIMAL UNDER ARTIFICIAL CONDITIONS IN A STATE OF DOMESTICATION.

Instinct, which guides the wild animal in the choice and pursuit of his food, and volition, which regulates his movements, are alike rendered powerless by the new conditions of his existence. It is no longer for him to determine when he will seek provender, or what kind of aliment he will select. A superior will is substituted for his own, and he has now no choice but to eat and drink, more or less, according to his possessor's judgment.

Seldom, in thinking upon the differences between the wild state and domestication, do we quite realize the change in its completeness; how entirely in nearly every particular the circumstances are altered. The animal's character may remain the same, but his power of action, his individuality, is lost; if he has been accustomed to depend for his food upon his bodily strength and activity, he is now to remain quiescent until supplied with what is deemed necessary for his sustenance; if formerly he was in a state of ceaseless motion, he must now rest until permitted to move. Scarcely one of his qualities can now be spontaneously displayed.

Of the positive influence of the artificial system of treatment no more satisfactory evidence can be adduced than is afforded by the changes observed in the development of the teeth of the domesticated breeds as compared with the production of those organs in animals placed under more natural conditions.

M. Gerard, in his work upon teeth, places the completion of permanent dentition in the ox at four-and-a-half to five years; that of the sheep from four to four-and-a-half years; of pigs, two and two-and-a-half years. That his statements are founded upon observation no one will doubt who considers his professional position. As early as 1846 the occurrence of a remarkable case on the Continent excited considerable attention. In "The Veterinarian" for 1847, M. Renault comments upon this case in a letter dated August, 1846. After remarking on the importance of admitting the influence of early feeding and careful selection of breed upon the dentition, he adduces the instance of a certain bull (Antinous) who, at an adjudication, extorted universal admiration on account of his fine quality, but was refused the prize on the ground that the conditions specified that the candidate should be but *two years* of age, whereas the animal, from the condition of his teeth, was four years old and upwards, and the opinion was corroborated by several veterinarians, who all certified the bull to possess all his permanent teeth. Ultimately satisfactory evidence was given that the animal was really no more than two years old. M. Renault commenced a series of inquiries upon the point in question, stating his conclusions as follows:

"Uniformly where the ox species has experienced the ordinary kind of management and feeding, wherever food, however good, has been given as ordinary nutriment, and not for forcing or fattening; in all such parts of the country, dentition follows the ordinary course, as indicated by writers upon the subject.

"But these rules, the result of long and accurate observation, and correct and well founded at the time when and in the countries where they were made, are no longer applicable and true in regard to certain individuals and certain breeds.

"Indeed, thanks to a better system of management and feeding of cattle, and to judicious and advantageous crossings, it is certain that for some years past many of our bovine races have experienced in their form, and especially in their precocity of development, unmistakable amelioration.

"Whatever may be the cause of this remarkable aptitude in certain breeds to acquire their growth early, it is readily conceivable that such precocious development can not be confined to any particular organs. If every one has not equally participated in it, at least they are all more or less affected by it. Above all, the digestive system—the part called in to play an important part in the preparation of such apitude, since all must essentially result from the nature and action of alimentation—must be one of the first to undergo important modifications.

"Physiologically, therefore, it may be argued, we must admit that the use of teeth and dentition ought to be earlier in subjects weaned at so early an age, and so soon fed with substantial food."

Twenty years have passed since these observations were made, and animals have continued to progress in their aptitude to fatten, and their precocity of development, as witness some of our best horses and oxen at two years old, sheep at one year, and pigs at six months.

DOMESTICATION NOT ONLY MODIFIES THE CONDITIONS OF DEVELOPMENT, BUT IT EFFECTS IMPORTANT ALTERATIONS IN CIRCUMSTANCES UNDER WHICH DISEASE IS PRODUCED AND EXTENDED FROM ONE GENERATION TO ANOTHER.

Disease in the wild animal finds its limitation in the general probability of the subject falling a victim to the numerous adverse influences, which he is incapable of combating. In domestication these adverse influences lose much of their power, or are sensibly modified by the institution of measures intended to combat their effects. Defects, which in a natural state would render the animal incapable of living, and which, if perpetuated, would ultimately lead to the extinction of the race, are, under the new conditions, fostered and extended, and take the name of "hereditary" or "transmitted" diseases, running through whole generations, or occasionally ceasing for a time only to burst out again with renewed violence.

It would be doubtless a reproach to our humanity if the weaker animals did not receive more care and consideration than the stronger; but who fails to comprehend that this course of procedure, the opposite of what is true in nature, must ultimately be injurious to the race, however conscientious we may be in adopting it? Singularly enough the details of the natural system which are often harsh, even relentlessly cruel, in our estimation, tend to the universal progress; while our efforts, dictated by humane consideration and undeniably productive of immediate individual or limited good, have often the tendency to produce universal deterioration.

Wild animals will not be expected to improve under the treatment they meet with in domestication at the commencement; not until they have become perfectly habituated to the new mode of existence are they likely to accommodate themselves to the change. The time required to effect this will vary, but several generations must pass before the wild original progressively passes into the domesticated animal, who now possesses so few of his native qualities as to be incapable of existing under conditions which were formerly essential to the continuance of his race.

During the transition from the wild state, and when the new variety, "the domestic animal," is established, numerous circumstances may be brought to bear with important influence upon the development. Reverting to what has been stated under "development in the natural state," we find the modifying circumstancs to be, selection, the strong having the advantage; destructive influence tending to remove the weak and diseased; food possessing the elements of nutrition and respiration in due proportion; and legitimate exercise of all the organs of the body. All these are in greater or less degree under our control when animals become subject to our influence.

Selection we can arbitrarily arrange according to our ideas of fitness or our object in the production of new characters; the various destructive influences we can ameliorate, if not remove; the elements of food we can apportion with almost chemical exactness, whether we desire an excess of fat or flesh-producing materials; and most of the organs of the body are directly or indirectly under some degree of control.

Experience and observation having demonstrated the possession of a power to influence the animal's qualities and physical conformation, it becomes immediately a matter of inquiry, how far it is possible to proceed. Experiments dictated by fancy or founded upon calculation are made, with variable results; new facts are discovered, and a gradual progress is made towards the foundation of a system. According to the object desired will the aggregate result be apparent; one aims at producing bulk and physical strength, another speed and lightness; a third sees a special gain in color, or some particular line in conformation.

It would far exceed our limits were we to attempt an extensive examination of the subject; nor would any advantage accrue, as the animals with which we are more immediately concerned afford sufficient evidence for the support of our argument; we have only to point to the existing breeds to prove what changes may be effected by attention to the circumstances which influence development.

Advancing rapidly to the practical section of the subject, it may be advantageous to indicate the position we have been endeavoring to establish.

At the commencement we explained the meaning attached to the term "Early Maturity," and referred to general observation and experience to prove that in cultivated breeds maturity is attained more rapidly than under natural conditions. In considering, in the next place, the universal idea that what is rapidly produced is wanting in durability, we found it necessary to accept the fact as established by general observation, and explained, on the principle, that permanent combinations can only be effected under proper conditions, time being one of the essentials. The differences between the circumstances of the natural and domestic states were next discussed, as affecting the development of the tissues, the general conclusion being deduced that important modification of form and quality may be effected by regulating the condition of the animal's existence, according to the object we have in view.

It being conceded that there is a possibility of controlling the animal's development, and producing such alterations of physical form and qualification within certain limits as may be determined upon, it is very important that the power should be exercised with circumspection. How far this is the case will appear as we proceed.

Whatever minor objects may be kept in view in cultivating certain kinds of animals, there is ample evidence to prove that the paramount one is to lose as little time as possible in fitting the animal for his intended purpose. Without any qualification that statement must be made; in obedience to the spirit of the age, everything must move rapidly to its destination, and animals, as well as machines, must be brought to the greatest perfection in the shortest space of time; failing which, in either case, no superiority in other respects can save from condemnation.

Imagine a breed of sheep, furnishing mutton of a quality hitherto unknown, rich in nutriment and of rare flavor, but insipid and unwholesome, until the animal had reached the age of four or five years; not the possession of all the qualities in excess that make the best varities valuable, could render such a breed popular, save with the wealthy epicure. Extend the same reasoning to horses; establish a breed possessing every requisite, opposed by the single objection that the animal must be six years old before he could be used, and the extinction of the race would be certain. Further illustration can not be necessary to prove what hardly any one can doubt, that the tendency of the whole system of the present day is to force animals by every available means to a premature adultism; and to call into active exercise the powers which are yet imperfect, for the reason that one important condition, TIME, is wanting. Upon different animals this forcing system will produce results varying, in some degree, according to the characteristics of each; there are, however, certain inevitable consequences which affect all in a nearly equal degree. These may be termed the general results, while the others having reference to each breed may be distinguished as the particular results.

GENERAL RESULTS OF THE FORCING SYSTEM.

Early maturity, if legitimately attained, is doubtless a desideratum; but in the anxiety to exceed the ordinary rate of development, too little regard is paid to the possible production of disease. Animals are highly fed, kept in a warm temperature, denied a proper amount of exercise, and yet no ill results are anticipated; and, in the event of active disturbance supervening, there is immediately a wondering inquiry as to the cause, as if every circumstance in the animal's treatment did not deserve the title.

Taking the whole system of management, we find all the conditions tending to the same results: the food, the stationary position, and the warm temperature, all unite to diminish expenditure and facilitate excessive deposition. Of these three, the food supplied exerts the most decided influence, by furnishing an abundant material for the support of the body. Fatty tissue becomes abundant enough in a comparatively short time; but the muscular structure does not experience any improvement, on the contrary it deteriorates. This fact universally admitted is worthy of profound consideration. The food contains more elements than necessary for the development of muscle (flesh) as well as of fat; the various oil-cakes and all kinds of grain on which animals are fed, contain a large per centage of flesh-forming elements, as well as a quantity of the elements which form fat; so that if the two were equally assimilated and deposited, the animals would show as much flesh in proportion as fat. Instead of this being the case, fat elements are invariably assimilated in far larger proportion than the elements of flesh. Not only so, but more remarkably still, the fatty tissues encroach upon the flesh and other parts, leading to a fatty condition of all the muscles, the fibres of the heart, the structure of the liver, and nearly every part of the body where the deposition can possibly occur.

Reasoning upon this preference for the one tissue over the other, we are required to remember that flesh or muscle is a highly organized structure, possessing vital properties; that all the movements of the animal body, the action of the heart, the motions of the digestive organs depend upon the exercise of the characteristic power of muscular contraction.

For the proper development of this important and extensively-diffused structure, not only is nutriment necessary, but also bodily exercise, which improves the circulation, increases the secretions, and by aiding the removal of worn-out tissues, assists the development of the new. The conditions, however, which are essential for the growth of muscle are absolutely opposed to the deposit of fat, which is not a highly organized tissue, which has no vital functions, but is a chemical substance simply deposited in a membrane of most simple construction.

Fat plays a very important part in the system; but its offices are solely chemical or mechanical. It forms in many parts soft cushions, it regulates the temperature of the body by offering the escape of heat, and its most important duty is to furnish elements for the support of respiration; elements which may combine with the oxygen of arterial blood, and by the results of the combination contribute largely to the heat of the body.

The destruction of fatty elements will be in direct proportion to the activity of respiration, circulation and excretion; consequently exercise is opposed to the accumulation of fat, and rest favors it. An animal at rest does not inhale any large amount of atmospheric air; his circulation is slower than it would be during exertion; excretion is diminished, therefore there is but little destruction of fatty elements. If under these circumstances an abundance of those elements is given in the food, a large amount is stored up in the system, in various parts, even to the exclusion of muscle or flesh, which cannot be developed although its elements are largely consumed; because there is an absence of those healthy conditions of respiration, circulation and excretions, which are indispensable for the elaboration of so vital a structure.

An objection may possibly be made to the use of the word disease as applied to mere excess of healthy tissue. It may be urged with apparent justice, that a certain proportion of fat is necessary in the most perfect state of health, and that therefore there can be no very serious evil in an excess of what is harmless or even desirable. We have no desire to escape this position by advancing the language of schools upon the subject of disease; but accepting the popular idea of the matter, let us suggest in reply that a small quantity only of fat is necessary, that its excess increases the size of the body without any advantage being gained; that when it usurps the place of other tissues it interferes with the functions of those parts; that a heart in such case cannot properly distribute the blood; a liver so affected cannot secrete healthy bile; and that if these functions are imperfectly performed, the system must suffer according to the extent of the derangement.

In reply to the general objection that the material whose excess is characterized as disease is itself a healthy tissue, it may be observed that no structure is more healthy or of more importance to the animal than bone, and yet nothing can be conceived more dire than its deposit in the brain or the heart, or more serious than its encroachment upon other parts; a structure, however necessary in due proportion and in proper place, is even on this principle injurious in excess, or when out of its proper situation.

Nitrogen or flesh-forming elements being present in considerable quantity in most kinds of food used for fatting animals, it is necessary to account for their consumption in the animal economy. The flesh being rather lessened than increased, it follows that the nutritive elements are not properly appropriated: the question then arises—What becomes of them? Many substances that would be injurious, or at best useless in the system, escape digestion by reason of their insolubility and are expelled as excrementitious; not so, however can we get rid of all the nutritive elements of food which are digestible, and although when given in excess a large proportion may pass unassimilated, a larger proportion is digested and taken into the circulation.

Without assuming any power of tracing the nitrogenized elements through the digestive process, we may form a very natural conjecture as to their destination from one fact, viz.: that in fat animals there is always a large increase of the fibrin of the blood. Whatever may be the actual relations of this material to the nutritive function, it will not be necessary now to decide; but its chemical relation to the nitrogenized elements of food lends a sanction to the idea that it is derived from them.

An animal in perfect health, undergoing regular and proper exercise, and receiving a due quantity of food to supply the wants of the system, has no more than one or two parts of fibrin in 1,000 parts of blood; but lessen the activity of the muscular system, or impair the nutritive function, and the proportion is immediatly increased. Give an excess of food, and at the same time diminish the wants of the system by so arranging the animal's position that there shall be the least expenditure; and the fibrin will rise to six or seven parts in 1,000. An inflammatory attack leads to the same result by its interference with the nutrition, and, curiously, in extreme debility the same excess is noticed, the animal in such case literally feeding on its own tissues; thus in each instance the immediate result of non-deposition of flesh or muscle is excess of fibrin in the blood.

The state of comparative inactivity in which the animal is kept is favorable to the production of debility. Important functions, as circulation, respiration and excretion, are sluggishly performed; the various organs, receiving therefore an insufficient supply, lose their tone, and in course of time decrease. The diminution of a structure from disease is a fact familiar to most people; even an injury, which necessitates the inaction of an arm or leg for a few weeks, will be attended with a very perceptible decrease of bulk. Alterations so apparent in the short space of a week or two enable us to form some idea of the effects of rest continued for months, and prevent our being much surprised at the statement, that parts when entirely thrown out of use in process of time, disappear.

Thus the animal is not only receiving an injurious excess of food, but he is also placed in a position least likely to favor a healthy condition of the system. The muscular structures suffer most; but the respiratory, circulatory and secreting organs also experience considerable injury; the inaction is only comparative, as all these parts continue to perform certain offices; but healthy activity is impossible under the circumstances of the animal's position.

The general result of the forcing system may be summed up in a few words:

By excessive feeding fat accumulates upon the surface and in the interior of the body, encroaching upon more important tissues. The blood at the same time becomes charged with the fibrinous element.

Inactivity tends to the diminution of muscle, and impairs the functions of respiration, circulation and excretion, upon which depend the purification of the blood, the removal of effete products, and the proper action of the various vital functions.

Tissues are rapidly deposited, and are by consequence deficient in stability.

The animal prematurely attains his full growth, and as far as appearance is concerned, his perfect development.

PARTICULAR RESULTS OF THE FORCING SYSTEM.

It might be imagined that the desire to accelerate the growth of the animal and increase the bulk of the body by the deposit of fat would be limited to the breeds that are employed for human food. Not so, however, in fact: the same anxiety to economize time affects treatment of the horse, as well as that to which the ox, sheep and pig are subjected. The horse-breeder finds it as little to his advantage to keep his colts in a natural state until they gradually attain the adult period before he sends them to market, as the breeder of other stock does. Society demands young, sleek and well-fed animals to draw its carriages and curvet in its parks; it also affects young animals and despises the older and more muscular subjects, whose anatomy is too apparent to gratify its taste. Society's demand is met by the producer to the very letter: the fairs are thronged with horses in every stage of adolescence and obesity.

Upon a superficial view of the subject, it may seem very meritorious to be able to bring two and three years old horses into the market, presenting all the matured characters of the adult; but looking upon it in the light of experience, what are the real advantages? The horse is ready for use two years before he might be expected; granted this to be true, the advantage is merely a pecuniary one on the side of the dealer; can it be said that the animal's tissues are in a better condition for work at this early period? Are the two years added in reality to his working life, or is any thing to be urged in favor of the system beyond the fact that time is saved at the commencement, and thus the markets are supplied to a certain extent with tolerably good animals, who, if kept back for two years, would leave a considerable hiatus to the inconvenience of the purchaser? Giving full weight to this very meagre defense, we can only conclude that something must be radically wrong with our system of breeding and rearing horses to necessitate the premature employment of them to meet the demand, which cannot be supplied in a more legitimate manner.

It is not sought to underrate the disadvantages to the breeder, that a longer keeping of the animal would occasion; such as the risk of illness, injury, or death, added to the inevitable expenses of maintenance. This difficulty, however, is only accidental: it would seriously affect an individual, but, were it the custom not to work horses before the age of five or six years, the extra expense incurred would naturally be met by a corresponding increase of price.

Of the disadvantages of the forcing system in relation to horses we have constant and ample proof. Let any candid inquirer ask himself to what the efforts to *improve the breed* amount. On the turf, in the field, on the road, and in the stable, the object seems to be to discover how much strain upon his organism a young animal can bear. Will any one seriously hold the belief that early and severe training on the one side, excessive stimulating food on the other, and lastly, work often beyond an animal's powers, are under any circumstance calculated to improve the qualities of the individual or the race? The solution of the question is given by our daily observation of the liability of these young animals to disease, and their rapid prostration under its influence; of the universal prevalence of lameness from derangements of feet and joints; of the rapidity with which the system succumbs to the effects of work; and of the mortality attendant upon maladies which in older animals are combated without difficulty. Latterly it is remarkable how quickly debility supervenes upon an attack of a comparatively simple affection. We should cease to find it curious that such is the case did we remember that the majority of young and fat horses, probably all of them, are suffering from fatty disease of the heart, liver and other organs.

In the event of the animal escaping the first difficulties of his entry into active life, these diseased parts, under the effects of exercise and moderate feeding, are ultimately restored to a tolerably healthy state in most instances; but should he be unfortunate enough to be attacked by any inflammatory or congestive disease at the commencement, or be subjected suddenly to active exertion, the chance of his recovery from the prostration which results are indefinitely diminished by the state of the most vital organs in his body.

Without advancing a step further in the inquiry, or entering upon details which to the amateur would be tedious, enough has been adduced to prove that one particular result of the "forcing system" is to diminish the stamina of the most valuable of domestic animals, to abridge the period of his active usefulness by prematurely exhausting his powers in his youth, and to induce such a state of organic disease, that the resistant power of the system is lessened and the mortality largely increased. To compensate for the actual loss sustained, we can only discover that animals, by acquiring a precocity of development, become saleable at an early age, and so a deficiency in the supply is avoided, while the risk involved in keeping them for the period requisite for them to attain maturity is removed from the breeder to the purchaser.

PARTICULAR EFFECTS OF THE FORCING SYSTEM UPON CATTLE AND OTHER STOCK.

One very important and fundamental difference between horses and cattle lies in the fact of the latter being cultivated for human food in some form, while the former are only valuable according to the extent and duration of their physical powers. This distinction at once establishes two perfectly separate principles of action in reference to the cultivation of the horse for his mechanical qualities, and the breeding of cattle and other stock for the support of the people. Incidentally, cattle of all kinds are valuable in other respects; but it will be conceded that the essential object of their cultivation is the one we have advanced.

Under these circumstances an apparent defense of the forcing system is at once established. As the object is to supply meat for the people, the more rapidly it can be produced the better. Admitting the general truth of this proposition, it is nevertheless unfortunately requisite to insist upon certain qualifications, the main being that the amount of nutriment is of higher importance than the quantity of material that may be classified as food; hence, unless it can be shown that the meat thus rapidly produced is equal in alimentary quality to the flesh of the mature animal, the advantage to the consumer is only imaginary. Primarily, then, the point to be decided is, does the meat of the young animal, rapidly forced to full growth as it may be, possess the nutrient quality of that of the naturally matured animal some years older? If the previous reasoning is not altogether false, the question is at once answered in the negative. On the general principle first laid down, that whatever is rapidly produced is of necessity imperfect in some of its parts or properties, the notion is inconsistent; and on the further ground of the preponderance of the fatty tissue over the nutritious, it cannot be maintained. By the common sense of the practical observer, as by the inductive reasoning of the scientific man, the same reply would be given. Analysis and direct experiment upon the feeding properties of the two kinds of meat would alone establish the position beyond cavil; but there would be a savor of the ridiculous in the idea of a man gravely conducting a series of experiments to determine which animal would furnish the largest amount of available nutriment—a sheep of one year that had been forced by artificial treatment to his full growth, or one that had been left to acquire maturity upon a good pasture during the space of four or five years.

Animal food is a necessary of life, according at least to the prevailing belief; and it may be urged with some force that the supply must be made to meet the demand. The answer to this is easy. Were animals bred and treated with more regard to a healthy condition of the various organs, their liability to disease would be materially diminished and their power to resist it augmented, and the extraordinary losses which are sustained every year in our country would no longer be a reflection upon our argriculture. The readiness with which animals yield to the influence of epizootic maladies has long been a subject of remark, and we do not underrate the virulence of the disease nor the importance of any measure which shall tend to prevent its importation, when we insist that a great part of the mortality is due to the predisposition of the animal's system, permanently established by our methods of breeding and management.

It is very curious to the physiologist to note how perfectly we have come to tolerate the existence of an evil; and even to claim it as an advantage: to hear the common talk and read the every-day remarks, it would seem as if "fat" were really the essential element of our food. "Lean meat" sounds unpleasant enough in the ears of the epicure, suggestive as it is of deficiency of food or disease. A fine fat beast, on the other hand, establishes a feeling of confidence in the healthy condition of the animal. Food is estimated according to its power of fattening with rapidity, and breeds become famous in inverse ratio to the time they take to develop fatty tissue.

To attempt to combat the general idea upon this subject would be futile, the more so as it is essentially founded in truth. Leanness is typical of diseases and wretchedness, as its opposite is of health and prosperity. It is not expected of the people that they should discriminate analytically; but the practical man, who does not desire to misrepresent the principles advocated, will understand the difference between the meagre subject whose condition is radically bad, and the well-developed animal whose muscular system is in the most perfect state of development and health, and whose fatty tissues are subordinate but in due proportion to the other structures of his body. Preponderance of fat of necessity diminishes the amount of human food, not merely because the material is non-nutritive and incapable of repairing the tissues, but for the still more obvious reason that the major part of it is not consumed at all, as the process of cooking causes a large proportion to melt and run off comparatively as waste.

Again, the advantage is entirely on the side of the producer, who finding a certain and easy method of increasing almost at will the bulk of the animals required for consumption, very naturally avails himself of the materials which promise such desirable results; enabling him to prepare his stock for market with convenient rapidity, and at the same time to meet the public demand for fat meat, which the public will not eat, but feels constrained to ask for as the only guarantee that the animal was healthy and well-fed.

Hence the forcing system leads to the development of two palpable evils in regard to the animals which furnish meat for our consumption; it produces flesh or muscle deficient in nutrititive quality, and furnishes in addition a large proportion of material, which is almost valueless as food, and is really not consumed excepting in very small quantities. Besides these disadvantages attending the present system of feeding and management, there are others even more serious, viz., the interference with the animal's health. This point has been considered in the general result; the particular consequences, however, are very apparent as affecting cattle, sheep and pigs, as the condition induced which in the horse is remediable by exercise and proper dieting, in the other animals is fostered designedly until the beasts are placed in the hands of the butcher. Further, the influence of the want of exercise is felt in a particular degree by the organs of the respiratory system, occasioning loss of tone in these parts and rendering them peculiarly susceptible to diseases of the congestive order.

From the individual the consequences are extended to the breed. The property of acquiring early maturity is transmitted as other qualities are, and in the endeavor to perpetuate peculiar capabilities and characteristics of form necessary to preserve the race, the temptation to breed from animals of the same family is very strong; in fact these artificial qualities can be cultivated to the highest point by no other means. Gradually under such a course the natural characteristics of the animal body are lost, and in their stead are developed others which are incompatible with absolute health, to wit, muscle wanting in firmness, excess of fatty tissue, defective secretion, loss of tone of the respiratory and circulatory organs, fatty disease of liver and heart, predisposition to disease, and want of power to resist its effects. On the other side, he may place the rapid increase of the bulk of the animals, aiding to keep the supply of meat at a certain average; and compensating to some extent for the enormous yearly losses resulting from disease, acting upon animals eminently predisposed to its attacks.

Accustomed as we are to speak of the great improvements that have taken place in the various cultivated breeds, it is not to be supposed that we can at once accept the idea that all the work has been in vain, and that in our endeavor to advance we have only succeeded in retrograding; indeed, it is not likely that such an admission will be made by any men who are personally concerned. Opinions differ widely upon all subjects, and whether an object be legitimate or not it will find defenders. If by improvement of the breeds of cattle, sheep and pigs, we mean the rapid growth of the animal, the early development of fat and the attainment to premature maturity at the expense of the perfection of the organism, then the system has succeeded. But to say that our efforts have tended to improve the health of our animals, to diminish the liability to disease, to produce a larger supply of nutritious food for the people, is to make an assertion which is opposed to all the evidence bearing upon the subject.

Practically, what is to be deduced from all that has been advanced—assuming it to be true? It is not with any idea of altering the present system that we have discussed the question: the motives for continuing the same course are too urgent in our commercial age to be easily set aside. On what plea will the breeder retain his sheep until they are four years old, when he can dispose of them at nearly the same price to the butcher soon after one year? That the four-year-old mutton is better for the people might weigh with him as a philanthropist, but would offer meagre consolation for the pecuniary disadvantage he would sustain. Under exceptional circumstances, the value of fleece may constitute a reason for keeping certain animals for an extra season or two; but speaking as we are in reference to the cultivation of animals for meat, there are literally no practical reasons likely to induce the breeder and feeder to keep them beyond the time absolutely necessary to force them to the condition in which they will be considered fit for the butcher.

At last, therefore, we can only deplore the state of affairs without even indulging the hope of a change for the better. In spite of everything that can be urged, cattle *will be* overfed and disease *will be* induced. Horses *will be* brought early to the markets in a state of plethora, and the result *will* continue to be premature decay.

But there is some satisfaction in knowing even the worst; at least it is preferable to acting under an universal delusion. We are ready to admit that remarkable results have followed the efforts to improve the breeds of stock, results not satisfactory in the main, but not the less decided. We accept the proofs of what can be achieved by systematic attention to a definite object; but we do not the less contend that the system has been carried too far. The principle has been all along that of the railroad; the struggle to drive onward rapidly at all risks, even without considering them. The cry has been for the animal that will be the first ready for the carriage, the saddle, the dairy or the butcher, and so far the demand has been answered; at what cost we have endeavored to show. Whatever respect may be accorded to our suggestions, we may at least ask that the "forcing system" shall no longer exist under a false designation, that men shall not in future speak of the artifical induction of disease, of premature development, and of systematic degeneration, under the imposing terms—CULTIVATION AND IMPROVEMENT.

THE CATTLE PLAGUE, OR RINDERPEST.

[The prevalence of this disease in Great Britain during the last two years has caused no little anxiety in our country. Fortunately, our Government, by prohibiting the importation of cattle, has thus far secured for us immunity against the destructive malady. An article in my report of last year showed to what immense losses various European countries have been subjected by this fearful scourge. By this last visitation, England and Scotland are said to have sustained a loss of 200,000 head of cattle; and although the disease was supposed, at the time of this estimate, to have been eradicated, we have news of its reappearance in one or two districts. It is to be hoped that the disease will not be introduced into this country, but it is proper for our people to understand something of its character. The subjoined article is from the pen of A. J. Murray, now of Detroit, lately Professor of Veterinary Surgery in the Royal Agricultural College, Cirencester, England, and the writer of the first work on the Cattle-Plague published in Britain. It will be read with interest.]

The history of this disease is interesting to every American farmer, who feels an interest in anything which occurs beyond his own neighborhood. Though it is to be hoped that this fatal malady may never be brought to America, yet it must be remembered that Britain had, until the late outbreak, enjoyed an immunity from its ravages for nearly a century and a quarter. The British people and government had, consequently, no experience of the disease, and much valuable time was lost in vain and futile efforts to cure it. The first work written on the Cattle Plague, after its appearance in Britain, proceeded from my pen, and in it the very fatal character of the disease and its extreme contagiousness, were emphatically pointed out. Had the preventive measures recommended by me, been adopted and rigidly enforced by the British government, the progress of the Cattle Plague would have been checked, and the national loss would consequently have been comparatively slight. Individual efforts were, however, of but little avail, as the majority of the agricultural and political journals ridiculed those who recommended slaughtering the diseased animals to check the disease; and they insisted that the disease was amenable to treatment. No journal did so much towards misleading the public, as the London *Times*. The tone of authority with which their articles were written, was only equaled by the ignorance of the writers.

Great difference of opinion exists as to the nature of the Cattle Plague. From the opportunities which I have had of making *post mortem* examinations, I have been led to discard the idea of the disease being typhoid; I think that it has rather the character of typhus fever. Dr. Smart, of Edinburgh, who had opportunities of making many *post mortem* examinations, thinks that the disease is analagous to the scarlatina of man; while Dr. Murchison, of London, who was employed by the British government to investigate the nature of the disease, regarded it as the analogue of small-pox in man. For this latter opinion, there is not a vestige of foundation, as I never saw an eruption of any kind, in upwards of 120 cases, which I have been called to inspect; nor do I see any grounds for concluding that this disease is analagous to small-pox, from the *post mortem* appearances which I have observed.

Though the disease most frequently affects the ox species, it is capable of being transmitted to sheep; yet, fortunately, they do not readily contract the disease. The malady exists continually in the steppes of Russia, hence it has been called the steppe murrain or steppe disease; but notwithstanding the attention which scientific men have given to the subject, the exact conditions which produce the disease have not as yet been ascertained. The following extracts from my pamphlet explain the contagious nature and history of the disease. It is very clear that this disease is not of "spontaneous origin." If it is, all the efforts which are at present being made to check it are worse than useless.

The terms infection and contagion are applied to the transmission of a disease from one animal to another by direct or indirect contact. They are also applied to the action of miasmata proceeding from a sick animal. On passing into the body of a sound animal, the morbid element increases until it disorders the functions and produces disease; and it accordingly receives the name of virus, or contagious principle. In a disease like the Cattle Plague, the virus is contained in the air expired by the animal, in the exhalations from the body, in the urine, fæces, and all the other excretions. Death does not destroy the virus: though the animal dies, the virus lives. Porous animal and vegetable matters, such as straw, hay, wool, hides feathers, animals, human beings, may become depositories of the contagious principle. Crowding animals together, and bad ventilation, favor the extension of virulent emanations, and render them more intense. According to the observations of Abildgaard, the atmosphere of contagious typhoid does not extend beyond twelve or eighteen feet; and this agrees with the observations of Jessen, who has seen a healthy herd separated from infected beasts by a river twenty-five feet in breadth, without any of them contracting the disease.

The trade in hides may transmit the disease from one country to another; and it is stated by Layard that the malady was introduced into England, in 1744, by an English tanner purchasing infected hides in Holland, and bringing them over to England. In 1774 the disease was carried into France by the importation of infected hides.

The area of the disease is also extended by the movements of armies. Thus in 1794 the disease was introduced into Italy by the cattle forming the convoys of the Russian army, and in the course of three years it destroyed three millions of Italian cattle.

When the disease exists in a country, it may be transmitted in such a variety of ways that it is often difficult, and sometimes impossible, to trace its mode of origin. If it appears suddenly in a district, and if its mode of origin is not satisfactorily traced, it is immediately said to have originated spontaneously. Such a conclusion is unwarrantable, as we are simply in the position of being *unable to ascertain* how it has been propagated. I visited many of the London cow-houses during the present outbreak of the disease, and I found that in those instances in which the cow-sheds were free from the disease, there had been no recent purchases of stock, and in all the places where the disease had shown itself (with one exception) there had been recent purchases of stock from the Islington cattle-market. I saw a cow suffering from the malady in this cow-shed, and was informed that there had been no purchases of stock for two months. In this case, however, the disease might have been transmitted by any of the men who attended on the cows visiting an infected cow-shed, and thus acting as carriers of contagion. It must not be imagined that the disease can only be communicated by the sound animal being brought into close proximity with the diseased one, and that if this is not done the disease cannot arise from contagion. Dogs, sheep and other animals may also act as carriers of contagion, when they have touched or approached infected cattle.

If infected animals are turned into a field, the saliva and excretions which are deposited on the grass will communicate the disease to any sound animals which may afterwards be placed in the same field. The remains of food which has been eaten by diseased beasts, or the litter on which they have stood, may also be a means of communicating the disease.

HISTORY OF THE DISEASE.

Accounts are given of the havoc produced by the extension of the Cattle Plague from the Russian steppes at very early periods of European history. During European wars, armies marching from infected countries have carried the disease wherever they went. Accounts of its ravages are given as early as the days of the Emperors Theodosius and Charlemagne; but we will pass over the earlier accounts, and refer briefly to its ravages of more recent times.

This malady was introduced in England in 1744 for the first time. Its mode of origin was doubtful: by some it was said to have been introduced by the importation of two calves from Holland, where the disease was then raging; and, according to the other account, it was brought to this country by an English tanner purchasing a parcel of diseased hides in Zealand. It committed great havoc, destroying hundreds of thousands of cattle, but seems to have disappeared about 1757.

Buniva states that during the wars of the French Republic with Austria and Russia, during 1793, 1794 and 1795, of which Italy was the theatre, the Rinderpest appeared among the cattle of that country, and in those three years destroyed between three and four million animals.

In 1796 the typhoid fever appeared among the oxen forming the convoys of the French army stationed on the banks of the Rhine. The disease, which was not at first regarded as contagious, propagated itself with great rapidity among the cattle in the department of Bas-Rhin. It soon invaded Alsace, Lorraine, Belgium, Picardy, the Vosges and Franche-Compté. From this last point it penetrated into Switzerland, returned to France by Bourgogne, and almost reached the gates of Paris. During this period the mortality in the twenty-eight French departments exceeded 140,000.

According to the estimate of Dr. Faust, the Cattle Plague destroyed in France and Belgium alone, between the years 1713 and 1796, not less than 10,000,000 of horned cattle.

Delafond states that when the allied armies entered France in 1814 and 1815, the Hungarian and German cattle which they brought with them introduced the Cattle Plague into the country. The malady was soon communicated to the French cattle; and almost all of the departments, except that of the Loire, which was occupied by the French army, suffered from the ravages of typhoid fever.

The Cattle Plague appears to have been limited to Russia until 1827, when, in consequence of the invasion of the Turkish dominions by the Russian army, the area of the disease was extended into that country. It afterwards extended into Prussia, Saxony, Hungary and Austria, and committed great havoc in those countries before it could be extirpated.

In 1841 it was introduced into Egypt by the importation of 200 cattle from Caramania, in Asia Minor, and in the course of three years it destroyed 350,000 head of cattle. The scourge at length disappeared, after having destroyed nearly all the cattle of the country.

During the Crimean war some infected cattle were purchased for the use of the British and French armies; and the disease, having thus been introduced, extended rapidly, and destroyed great numbers of cattle.

In 1857 fears were entertained in this country (Britain) lest the Rinderpest should be introduced by the importation of foreign cattle. As it was deemed necessary to ascertain whether the disease actually existed in those countries from which cattle were exported to Britain, Professor Simonds was sent to the countries stated to be infected, for the purpose of investigating the matter. It was then found that Belgium, Holland, Denmark, Mecklenburg, Hamburg and Lubeck were free from the disease, but that the malady had very recently existed in some portions of Silesia, near the Polish frontier. It was found, however, that the disease had not disappeared from Austria: the disease existed in the Cracow division of Galicia, at the villages of Zabrzez and Kamienca, near the Polish frontier. The outbreak of the disease in those villages was due to the introduction of ten steppe cattle, which had been purchased at a cattle-fair in the Lemberg division of Galicia, and they formed part of a large drove which had been brought from Russian territory. The disease at that time was limited to a small part of the Austrian frontier adjoining Poland, so that there appeared to Professor Simonds to be but little probability of its extending into this country.

In Britain the destructive progress of the disease has ruined many an industrious and thriving farmer, while others have escaped with heavy losses. The disease had almost been crushed out in Britain, when, unfortunately, a recent outbreak of it in Yorkshire, Lancashire and Cheshire has given additional evidence with what an insidious and obstinate enemy the farmer has to contend. As the Rinderpest is still producing havoc among British cattle, I am not at present in a position to state the loss which it has occasioned.

I also annex an account of the symptoms and *post mortem* appearances, taken from my pamphlet:

SYMPTOMS OF THE DISEASE.

An animal will not usually show symptoms of the disease immediately after having been exposed to contagious influence. The period which intervenes between exposure to contagion and the development of the symptoms is termed the period of incubation, and varies from four days to a fortnight, though it has not been proved that the disease may not remain dormant in the system for a longer time. The disease is first indicated by dulness and want of appetite; the animal then ceases to ruminate. The pulse, which is weak, increases to 70 or 80 per minute in severe cases; the animal drinks water readily at all stages of the disease. The respiration becomes slightly increased. In cows the secretion of milk diminishes rapidly after the appearance of the disease. There is a mucous discharge from the nose, and a watery discharge from the eyes, frequently fœtor of the breath, and frequently ulceration of the palate and the inside of the lips. There is occasionally a slight cough. Diarrhœa sets in, and the fæces have a dirty yellow color, and are not unfrequently tinged with blood; the skin along the back is sometimes emphysematous; the patient becomes rapidly emaciated, and dies in from twelve hours to eight or ten days. Those animals which live beyond the fourth day of the attack not unfrequently survive; but in the majority of fatal cases the animal does not survive the third, and in many cases dies on the second day of its illness. The animal's gradual restoration to health is indicated by cessation of diarrhœa, by its showing an inclination to eat, by its gradually beginning to ruminate, and by the secretion of milk commencing.

POST-MORTEM APPEARANCES.

The morbid changes produced by the disease chiefly affect the digestive system. The mouth, pharynx and larynx present yellow patches, which are produced by the disintegration of the mucous membrane and the effusion of lymph. The gullet, rumen and reticulum are usually healthy. In some cases the contents of the third stomach are hard and dry, and closely packed between the folds of that organ; but in numerous cases the manyfolds present a normal appearance. The mucous membrane of the abomasum, or fourth stomach, presents a red, congested appearance, and in many parts its follicles are filled with lymph. The terminal portion of the mucous surface of the small intestines, as also the cæcum and colon, have yellow patches distributed over them, produced by the effusion of lymph. Payer's glands are frequently, though not invariably, ulcerated. The only change to be observed in the liver is effusion of lymph on the sides of the gall-ducts. The internal sur. face of the gall-bladder is also studded with yellow patches o a nature similar to those of the intestines.

The blood contained in the heart and blood-vessels does not coagulate after death, owing to its deficiency in fibrine; and the brain and spinal cord present no traces of structural disease, but the quantity of fluid in the vertebral canal and in the ventricles of the brain is larger than usual. The lining membrane of the bronchial tubes is frequently congested, and the mucous membrane of the vagina inflamed.

With regard to the treatment of this disease, my experience coincides with that of all conscientious observers who have had extensive experience of the Cattle Plague. I was the first to propose the use of dilute sulphuric acid, in connection with vegetable tonics; but though it was used extensively by myself and others, it did not prove a successful treatment. I also adopted the system of giving laxatives in the early stage of the disease, following them up by the use of stimulants; but I did not find that this system of treatment was attended with success. From the experiments made by Professor Polli, of Milan, on the neutralizing effects of sulphate of soda on blood poisons, great hopes were entertained of the efficacy of this agent. I did not find, however, that sulphate of soda and chlorate of potash, which was also strongly recommended, produced any other effects than the agents before mentioned. I also vaccinated a number of cattle, *at the special request* of the owners, (as I had no faith in vaccination as a preventive); but the utter uselessness of vaccination in either diminishing the virulence of the disease, or preventing animals being seized with it, was very soon shown to the public. Its uselessness was not recognized by the public, however, before large sums of money had been spent in vaccinating thousands of cattle throughout the country.

The most important practical matter for the American farmer to think over is—Whether or not there is a probability of the Cattle Plague being imported into the United States? This is a question of immense national importance, and cannot receive too attentive and anxious a consideration. Immunity from the Cattle Plague can only be secured by stopping the importation of cattle and sheep from all countries in which the Cattle Plague prevails, and the prohibition should continue six months after the Cattle Plague shall have been declared, on good authority, to have ceased to exist in such countries.

A. J. MURRAY, M. R. C. V. S.

Detroit, Mich., 59 Monroe Avenue.

NEW CROPS.

SORGHUM AND ITS PRODUCTS.

This crop seems to have been quite as unfavorably affected by the peculiarity of the season of 1866 as any other. I am indebted to John Richard, Esq., of Tecumseh, for the following facts:

"The Sorghum crop this year has been generally poor, the yield of syrup having been much smaller than last season. The same causes that operated to produce a poor corn crop throughout the country, have had a still greater effect upon the Sorghum crop, for the plant, being of slow growth during the first half of the season, requires favorable weather during the months of August and September to perfect it. This we did not have this year; consequently the crop was poor, comparatively speaking, although the crop has by no means been a failure. A large amount of syrup has been manufactured in the State, much of it of a good quality, but generally darker in color than in former years.

"The amount of syrup manufactured in the State this season may safely be estimated at *800,000 gallons, the same as last year, the excess of acres planted this year over last making up for the deficiency in yield.

"The demand for Sorghum syrup is steadily on the increase, and it will no doubt use up all this year's crop, together with the balance of the last year's crop on hand. The farmers are by no means discouraged by the results of this year. Unforeseen causes may injure any crop, and the Sorghum crop is no more liable to injury than any other. The early varieties of

*In last year's report the quantity of syrup was, by mistake, stated at 400,000 gallons. It should have been 800,000.

cane have done the best this year, a result altogether unusual, but not surprising, when we take into consideration the unfavorableness of the latter part of the season. The early varieties had more nearly reached maturity when the cold weather began, and consequently were not injured to the extent that the late varieties were.

"The result of this year does not argue against the late varieties of cane, but it may establish the expediency of planting both the early and late varieties, and in this way being prepared for either long or short seasons. Usually, the late varieties of cane are the most profitable, yielding double the quantity of syrup and of a much better quality than the early varieties.

"The cane-growing interest is still extending further north. We have flattering accounts of its successful cultivation and the manufacture of syrup from Genesee, Ingham, Barry and Allegan counties, notwithstanding the prevailing opinion that the climate of these counties would not admit of the growth of Sorghum.

"Much injury is done to the Sorghum interest by the many worthless evaporators that are palmed upon the community. People buy them simply upon the recommendation of the owner of the patent right, without any evidence that they have ever produced a good article of syrup. The continuous process of evaporation can be shown to afford the greatest advantages.

"Those engaged in the cultivation of Sorghum should be very careful to procure good seed. The sale of poor seed has been the cause of numberless failures. A little care will obviate this difficulty, as good seed can always be procured by applying at the proper sources.

"On the whole, the Sorghum interest is fast increasing, and Sorghum syrup must hereafter be reckoned as one of the staple products of Michigan. Those who have given it a thorough trial, would not be willing to part with it as an article of profit and as an article of domestic economy. I cannot do better than to append an extract from a letter received from Wm.

Clough, of Cincinnati, editor of the *Sorgho Journal*, to the Cane-Growers' Association of Michigan:

"'The cane enterprise has received an extraordinary impulse from the results of last year, (1865), and we cannot doubt that we shall witness a large increase in the number of cultivators and in the quantity of cane planted. The enterprise has now become one of immense magnitude, and is producing something like a revolution in dietetical economy. Many families now consume more sweets in one year than they formerly used in a decade, and in most cases this increase has been attended with corresponding diminution in the quantity of butter and animal food consumed. This change in the domestic regimen has in no case been attended with injurious results; on the other hand, many who use Sorghum syrup freely, contend that the general health of their families has been promoted by its use. It would, perhaps, be difficult to determine the extent to which sweets can be appropriately used as food, but it is quite safe to say that the limit is not easily reached, and that cane-growers are in no danger of making more of the article than the country will buy and use at fair prices for years to come. I think it devolves upon us now, having demonstrated that syrup can be made, and made profitably, from our canes, to give our attention more particularly to the quality of the article. It is a notorious fact that a large portion of the syrup made in the country is miserable stuff. We need to encourage and promote, as far as possible, a higher general standard of excellence in this product.'

"Sugar can be made from any of the Sorghum or Imphee canes, but the syrup of the Otaheitan variety seems to granulate more readily than any other. This branch of the business has not yet attained the perfection which the syrup-making has, although much progress has been made during the past season. J. T. Weeks, of Jackson county, has never failed to make sugar when he has attempted it. B. M. Merrill, of Galesburg, had Otaheitan cane, the syrup from which granulated before it left the evaporator. Time will no doubt develop results in this direction which will greatly exceed the expectations of the warmest friends of the Sorghum interest."

HOPS.

The cultivation of hops has been followed in some parts of this country for many years, with varied success. In districts where the soil and climate are favorable and the culture and management of the crop have been good, the profits have been generally satisfactory.

Within the past few years the price of hops has risen greatly, which has stimulated their production, and caused their cultivation to be introduced into new sections. In various parts of Michigan hop-fields have lately been formed, and under present prices the crop is likely to become one of great importance. Much, however, will depend on the judgment exercised in the selection of the soil, and on the skill and care applied in the cultivation and curing of the crop. The season of 1866 was in some respects unfavorable to the hop, especially in its being too wet and cold, and the crop having in many instances been more or less injured by frost.

The following observations from an intelligent and successful hop-grower, will be read with advantage by many persons interested in the subject:

MANCHESTER, Mich., Dec., 1866.

TO SANFORD HOWARD, *Secretary of the Michigan State Board of Agriculture*:

In complying with your request to furnish for your Report some remarks in regard to my experience in hop-culture in Michigan, I would say that I came into the State for the first time in the spring of 1864. On arriving here I began to look about to see what the soil was adapted to produce, and what would afford the best returns for labor. Having been reared in a hop-growing district, although not a practical hop-grower, I decided to commence the cultivation of that crop. I visited several localities where hop-yards had been started, for the purpose of procuring roots, but without success. Not relishing the idea of being foiled in my object, I sent to some friends in New York for roots, and succeeded in obtaining, in a damaged condition, enough to set seven acres. Owing to the dry season, and to the injury the roots had received, I only saved about two thousand hills, which were poled in due time. Two thousand hills is about the right number for two-and-a-half acres, although mine were scattered over seven acres.

The first crop yielded 3,785 pounds of cured hops, which would be a trifle over 1,500 pounds to the acre, if the hills stood properly. I sold them at the store-house, soon after harvest, for 47 cents per pound, amounting in the aggregate to $1,778 95. In 1866, I had what would stand on seven acres, allowing no miss-hills, although they were scattered over ten acres. The latter part of the gathering season was very unfavorable, and there was considerable loss in the heavy rains and winds. The yield, however, was 9,000 pounds. Of this amount, 2,000 pounds were second-class, and 7,000 pounds were first-class. I sold the second-class at the store-house for 50 cents per pound. Those of the first-class I sent to New York, and have not yet received full returns from them; but am quite sure they will sell for 65 cents, at which rate they will amount in the aggregate to $5,550.

So far as I have been able to form an opinion, I think the average yield of hops in this State would not fall below 1,000 pounds to the acre, and the average price would not be below 35 cents per pound. My own experience induces the belief that the climate of Michigan is well adapted to the growing of hops, and with good soils and good culture, 1,500 pounds per acre might be produced. Suppose the price of good hops should fall down to 20 cents per pound, (which I think is not likely to be the case), the receipts would be $500. If we assume that it would cost half that sum to grow and cure them, ready for market,—which in my opinion is more than it would cost,—it would still leave quite an income for the use of the ground.

A few hints in regard to the localities and soils best adapted to the growing of hops: 1. I would select soils that are naturally dry, or made so by under-draining, and of a sandy or gravelly character, though a slight mixture of clay would be no detriment. 2. Make the soil rich by applying such quantities of barn-yard manure as would cause it to produce a good crop of Indian corn. It should be free from stumps and large stones. 3. Choose, if possible, sites where there are surrounding objects of greater elevation than the hop grounds, such as belts of timber, or higher land, though the latter should be half a mile away, so that the wind which comes from over the plains of the West may have something to break its force before striking the hops. Exposure to severe gales when the hops are nearly ready for harvest is very disastrous.

I have experimented, somewhat, in growing hops on different kinds of soils. I have grown them on what might be termed black muck. This soil produces a great growth of vines, but the hops are of light weight in the bale, and in wet seasons are liable to blight and mildew. I have also grown them on very sandy soils. They produce a quick growth, and the hops mature early, are large and bright, and of excellent quality; weigh well in the bale, but at best will not produce more than 1,200 pounds to the acre. I have had the best yields from gravelly soils with a mixture of sand. This kind produces a great growth of vines, which arm out well, and set thickly with hops of good size and quality, and weigh heavily in the bale. A good yield would be 1,500 pounds to the acre, though with good cultivation 1,700 to 1,800 pounds are frequently obtained. I have had the different kinds of soils under cultivation in the same season, and the results were as stated.

GEO. P. OATLEY

The following facts are collated from an essay on hop-cultivation, lately delivered before the Maidstone Farmers' Club, England, by Mr. Troutbeck. Relating, as they do, to a district which has for many years been noted for the production of large quantities of hops of the finest quality, it is probable that their perusal may be to some extent beneficial to the hop-growers of Michigan:

In looking at the analysis of the hop, we may safely conclude it is one of our most exhausting cultivated plants, both in respect to the organic and mineral constituents which it extracts from the soil; and when chemistry informs us of the largeness of phosphoric acid and potash which, as well as nitrogen, is received from the soil, we naturally conclude that the most fertile soils should be chosen for its cultivation.

On our heavy soils, clay has been shown to be the active substance in retaining manure; and our light soils that are sandy and gravelly, not possessing sufficient clay, these are expected to be less retentive of manure. Soils of the former description are said to hold manure; on those of the latter description it must be applied more frequently and in smaller quantities than on stiff soils. I believe the most important feature, and actually required in our heavy soils, where natural drainage is defective, is efficient drainage. We have many interesting confirmations of the advantages from facts that may be gathered from the best managed farms in the Weald of Kent. In the undrained land we find the manure is carried off the surface into the water-courses; and when the land is drained the manure is preserved. It is dissolved by rain in the upper strata, and becomes more perfectly distributed and brought into contact with the active soils below; and on these farms hops are cultivated with success. On our rich deep loams, in the Weald of Kent, where I have observed hops are cultivated with success, much benefit has been derived from thorough drainage, and by abundant stirring of the soil, the absorbing powers of which are greatly augmented by continued exposure to atmospheric influences.

Coming to the cultivation of the hop, whatever is worth doing at all is worth doing well; and in preparing land for growing hops, my own experience has taught me that after selecting the land, the most important consideration is drainage. When land has not good natural drainage, it should he thoroughly drained. On the majority of our lands, I am not in favor of a less depth than four feet. On our heavy lands, where they are stiff, adhesive, with power to retain moisture, the class which, as I have before observed, have a great affinity for ammonia and the retention of manure, we find them inclined to be cold, and sometimes expensive and difficult to prepare and cultivate; but when properly cultivated, form some of our most fertile hop-gardens in producing quantity. The faults are more confined to the mechanical structure than the want of the necessary ingredients. On these soils I would certainly thoroughly trench, and attend as far as practicable to loosening and stirring the subsoil, and if I found drainage required I would run the mole plough diametrieally in an opposite line to the line of the drains.

In this, as in all other cases in preparing land for hops, I would avoid burying the surface soil, and as to how far it may be desirable to mix some of the surface soil with some of the subsoil, depends upon circumstances. On our heavy clays, we frequently find a deficiency in lime and phosphoric acid. In many cases I have seen most satisfactory results from applying a compost made of lime and vegetable mould—the cleansing of ditches and ponds and fresh-burned lime, and I believe the addition of bone-dust or half-inch bones would greatly increase the fertilility and improve the quality of the hop. There is little doubt that the use of bulky manures is decidedly to be recommended, as well as to correct the mechanical structure of the soil, which is important.

We have the hop plant thriving for many years in some particular spots. Hops have been grown for years in succession, until at last they become worn out. We have most striking examples of this on several farms, when, after the plant had been grubbed and the land brought into the usual rotation of crops in tillage, it has been restored and the productive powers for the support of the plant have become repaired. I believe the falling off of the hop plant is mainly, but not entirely, due to the gradual extraction from the soil of a certain quantity of that inorganic matter on which the plant thrives. The object of manuring is to restore the inorganic matter; and the object of chemical analysis is first to ascertain what substances are deficient in the soil, and next to supply them. It is also important for the hop-grower, as well as the agriculturist in general, to be acquainted with the nature of the soil he cultivates as to the presence of any pernicious substance, that its effects may be counteracted, as well as to the supplying of any substances necessary for the growth of plants wanting in it. In the present state of chemical science, I believe no certain system can be devised for improving lands independent of experiment; but there are few cases in which the labor of proper analytical researches will not be amply repaid by the certainty with which they denote the most practical and best methods of amelioration.

The hop plant, (indeed any plant,) is a complex matter made up of a great variety of substances. For example, when we burn the hop-vine and find the quantity of ash left behind, we are struck with the smallness of the quantity, for in every thousand parts we have not more than five parts remaining. It is despoiled of its organic matter. We are aware that the atmosphere is the great reservoir for the organic substance existing in old plants, and which they can always draw on to a comparatively unlimited extent. These substances exist in the air; while the substances which are found in a small quantity in the plant, exist only in the soil, and can only be drawn from that source.

When we turn our attention from the plant to the soil, we find that the substances most essential to the hop exist in the smallest proportions in the soil, viz., phosphoric acid, lime and potash. If we direct our attention to any particular substance, as potash or phosphoric acid, and examine the composition of a fertile soil, we are impressed with the fact that what the plant requires in a large proportion, the soil only contains to a trifling extent, and the importance is at once forced upon us to supply those things which are deficient.

In applying manure, our object is to obtain from the soil a larger quantity of produce than it would yield in a state of nature; and we are to obtain this larger produce partly by tillage and partly by the use of suitable manures. Manure operates in supplying matters which the plant requires, as well as opening out the stores which exist in the soil, and places them in condition available to it—the great reservoir of matters which only slowly becomes available in our fertile soils—the object being to encourage these changes, so that the plant can assimilate and take possession of them, and this is one of the most important functions of which farm-yard manure is capable.

Farm-yard manure made from hop-vines, is not only a source of food to the plant, but is one of those which opens up the storehouse of unavailable food. While it is undergoing decomposition, it is yielding certain substances capable of acting upon the soil, and of transferring from the unavailable to the available category—of putting in that condition in which the plant can absorb them—the matters of which it is in need. I believe well-made and well-managed farm-yard manure from fattening animals, when the hop-vine is employed in part as litter, to be one of the best and most perfect manures, inasmuch as it contains every substance which the plant requires; it is directly or indirectly the vegetable matter, restoring to the soil those very substances which have been removed from it; and hence it is that we may attribute in part, but not entirely, the success of many of our hop growers.

But farm-yard manure has its defects, and one of them lies in the fact that the matters it contains are not at once available to the crop. Take for example, hop-vine; it contains all the constituents which the hop plant requires; but place it upon the soil as a manure, and we find the substances contained are locked up in a condition in which they are incapable of absorbtion, and before they can be made available they must form a complex into a simple state by virtue of decomposition. What we want is not only to supply food to the crop, but to supply it in such a form as can be returned to us as rapidly as possible in the form of a crop; and in order to obtain such a result we must resort to the use of manure in proper condition, which, in the case of farm-yard manure, is obtained by decomposition. The substances of the plant are rapidly brought into an available position, and which change is produced most actively when the dung is heaped up and allowed to get hot, as in a dung-heap; and nothing accelerates the uniform decomposition more than putrid urine in liquid manure. Hence the advantage of a liquid manure tank in the neighborhood of the manu e-pit. It not unfrequently happens that decomposition is very much retarded by leaving manure in our yards, or spread over a large surface; indeed, we have examples where it stops altogether, and then the farm-yard manure is as useless and inert as anything can well be. There is doubtless a severe loss in the management of farm-yard manure, in the drainage of manure in yards as well as that from manure heaps. It is to be looked upon with regret that streamlets of strongly colored water should run away from the dung-heap.

Experience has shown us that while all the constituents of a plant are equally necessary, it has also shown us that certain substances are more likely to become deficient in some soils than others, and that the one above all others likely to become exhausted is ammonia; hence the necessity of continuing to cultivate our hop soils with extraneous substances; and practice has established the importance of employing certain compounds, rich in nitrogen and phosphoric acid. All our manures recently employed are to a greater or less extent supplies of ammonia and phosphoric acid, which form the composition of the two important fundamental classes of artificial manures, viz.: phosphatic and nitrogenized. As far as my present experience goes, phosphatic manures tend to promote the quality of the hop, but not the quantity.

Among these manures I will enumerate fresh bones, bone-dust, bones treated with sulphuric acid, phosphatic matter of

Saldanha Bay, and Patagonian guano. Animal matter of all descriptions, rape-cake, farm-yard manure, nitrogenized matter, such as wool, blood, flesh, Peruvian guano, soot, woolen rags, shoddy, putrid animal substances, horn shavings, glue refuse, &c., are all very conducive to the growth of the hop plant. In poor sandy or thin porous soils, the preceding matters should not be used alone, but in conjunction with bone dust; or better still, with dissolved bones accompanied with a dressing of farm-yard manure.

On our light lands, we know manure lasts for a shorter time than it does in heavier soils; and the reasons for this are, that in an open soil the air has access and decomposition goes on with greater rapidity on such soils. On the other hand, decomposition is slow on heavy soils, but from the nature of the soil the products of decomposition are retained. Ready-formed ammonia, or ammoniacal salts, such as sulphate of ammonia, is a substance highly soluble in water, and I believe should not be used for hops; it is even dangerous to apply too much Peruvian guano, on account of the excess of ready-formed ammonia, of which it contains from 10 to 12 per cent. Experience has shown us that if we pour a solution of sulphate of ammonia upon a heavy soil, such as I have alluded to, it takes possession of the ammonia, retains it, stores it up in the condition in which it is available and useful to the plant. But if we pour the solution on clear sand, we find the water which passes through contains all the ammonia; and one of the important features in applying manure to the hop plant, or any other crop, is the power of the soil to retain the food the former adds, as well as supplying it. We have many examples where ammoniacal manures, or any other substances very soluble and powerful, cause in wet weather a very vigorous growth, which receives a sudden check in dry weather, and the crop ripens unequally; the color of the sample is injured, and mould and fungi follow.

All very soluble matters, however good as manure, must be applied in a very diluted state, or else they do harm and are apt to produce disease. In cases where the hop-grower is compelled to use any substance very soluble and powerful, I believe the best mode is to divide it into small quantities and apply it at various times during the season. In the case of soils that are inclined to be light, or lands rich in phosphate, I would use sparingly of substances rich in ammonia. I would resort to a mixture, which, although not containing much ammonia, is capable of leaving it. I would use the following proportions: One-and-a-half cwt. of dried blood, eight cwt. of shoddy and a half cwt. of Peruvian guano; or five cwt. of rape-cake and three cwt. of dried blood. On the other hand, on soils inclined to be heavy, lands which are deficient in phosphate, I would use nitrogenized substances sparingly, and resort to phosphate, which I believe should be made soluble, at least in part. Probably one of the following mixtures would answer well, in the proportion of three cwt. of superphosphate of lime and two cwt. of dried blood; or four cwt. of dissolved bones (real bone-dust), treated with one-third of sulphuric acid; or, farm-yard manure and vines and bone-dust; or three cwt. of superphosphate and three cwt. of rape-dust.

Experience has taught me that if we try to cultivate hops on a light soil, we do not act wisely in using substances rich in ammonia, such as Peruvian guano. We find better results from bones, or Bolivian guano, which contain a large quantity of phosphates and a small quantity of ammonia. On the other hand, we have examples of hops being cultivated on heavy soils by means of Peruvian guano; whereas on light soils this manure is always thrown away. I do not say that the use of Peruvian guano is always the best practice on heavy soils, but that the results from its application to the hop on heavy soils are better than on light soils. The application of farm-yard manure is a question upon which a variety of opinions exist among practical men. For hops, I am strongly in favor of applying the manure in a rotten state. When it has been allowed to rot carefully, I recommend getting it into the soil, and on our heavy soils during autumn, as by so doing I believe there is the least loss.

Hop-houses and Hop-boxes.—The following article, written by H. H. Potter, of Sauk county, Wisconsin, for the Prairie Farmer, with the accompanying cuts, for the use of which I am indebted to the proprietors of that paper, furnishes valuable ideas in regard to curing hops:

Hop houses in the West are almost invariably built of wood, in the ordinary balloon style of framing. For yards of three to six acres, 20x40 ft. is a convenient size for a hop house. The building, which, of this size, is divided in the centre, the lower floor into a kiln and press (and store) room, each 20x20 feet, the floor above into a dry room and store room of equal dimensions, should rest upon a wall so as to give draft-holes, one foot in height by two in width, on each of the four sides of the kiln under the sills.

The Kiln should be bricked up, or, which answers equally as well, lathed and plastered. The kiln floor is a ground floor on which the stove stands, the main stove-pipe rising up in the centre of the room and running back to within three feet of the wall opposite the chimney, where it divides, the two branches passing around the room in a square (as shown in the following diagram) at a distance say of three feet from the walls until they enter the chimney; the pipe to be ten-inch pipe all around. The pipe should be at least five feet below the kiln-cloth. The cloth should be from thirteen to fifteen feet from the ground floor. For a kiln of this size a four foot stove is required.

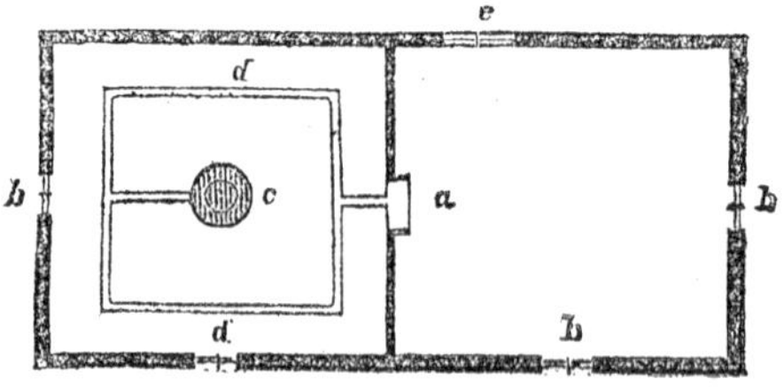

The Press and Store Room, 8 feet between joints, requires a tight floor. A door leads from this room into the kiln, for carrying in fuel, &c.

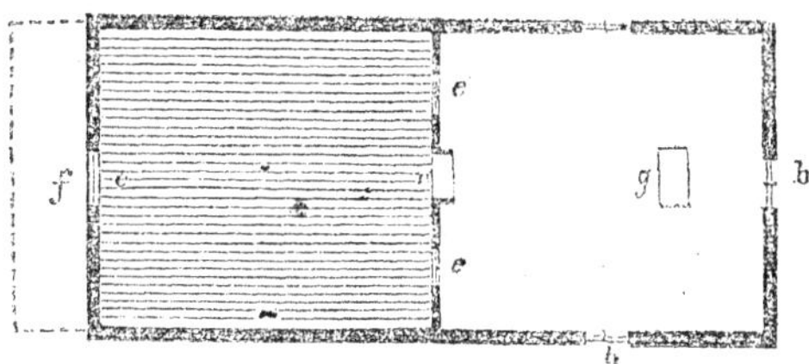

SECOND FLOOR.

The Upper Store Room is reached by a flight of stairs from the press room. A slide or trap door in the floor of this room, say a foot by two feet, allows the hops to pass down into the press room or press.

The Drying Floor needs to be three feet higher than that of the store room, and is formed of slats one by one and a quarter inches, placed edgewise one and a quarter inches apart; over it is spread a cloth of half-pound burlaps; heavier than this is objectionable. On each side of the chimney, which should be entirely within the store room, making no break on the kiln-cloth, are doors two feet wide by four feet high, through which to shovel out the dried hops. On the opposite side of the room a door opens on a platform, the floor of which is of six inch wide boards, placed two inches apart, to admit air under the sacks of green hops which, in the drying season, will constantly be standing on the platform. These sacks may be hoisted with block and tackle, or carried up a flight of stairs; a window above the door will admit sufficient light. It is well to plaster this room up to the eaves.

The cowl or ventilator stands on the ridge of the roof over the centre of the kiln. The size of the ventilator should be sufficient to allow the steam to pass off freely.

With a kiln of this size last season, I dried two kilns daily, of from 50 to 60 boxes each—the picking of from 40 to 50 hands; in yards of eight to ten acres it is usual to employ a greater number of hands than this, but for a ten acre yard a larger store-room than I have described would be necessary. I have described a hop-house erected by me last summer, 20x 40 feet, 10 inch sills, 16 feet studding, under one roof, quarter pitch, at a cost of $400. As mentioned in my last letter, I employ this building for many other purposes than that for which it was erected.

In another common style of hop house the kiln is higher between joists, with a four-square roof running to a point, surmounted by the ventilator, the press and store-room, forming a wing with common roof.

The press in ordinary use throughout this section, and the best I know of, is the Harris Press, the cost of which is $55.

The size of hop boxes in this State is fixed by law at seven bushels, but the term hop box applies indiscriminately to a box of which four statute boxes form compartments, as shown in the following diagram.

Each compartment is three feet long, eighteen inches wide, by two feet deep, in the clear, holding, by accurate measurement, seven bushels and one peck; the three corner posts, one and one-half inches square, in each compartment, take out the peck as near as may be. The four outside corner posts run down eight inches below the bottom of the box, forming legs.

The handles, one inch thick, two inches wide and eight feet in length, are nailed to the side of the box. The box itself is made of half-inch stuff. There has been more inquiry as to the dimensions of hop-boxes than upon almost any point connected with hop picking. This proves to be the most convenient box in use.

Explanation of Diagrams.—Fig. 1—a, chimney; b, window; c, stove; d, pipe; e, door.

Fig. 2—f, platform; e, doors; g, slide; b, window; a, chimney.

RAYMOND'S HAY AND STRAW ELEVATOR.

Among the various horse-pitchforks that were brought out at the trial of implements instituted by the New York State Agricultural Society at Auburn, last summer, was the one known by the above name, and exhibited by Chapman, Hawley & Co., of Utica, N. Y. It was awarded the second premium at the trial alluded to. On this occasion, at the first test, 2,720 lbs. of hay was pitched off in 13 pitches, in 5 minutes and 30 seconds. At the second test, 2,485 lbs. of hay was pitched off in 11 pitches, in 5 minutes and 10 seconds.

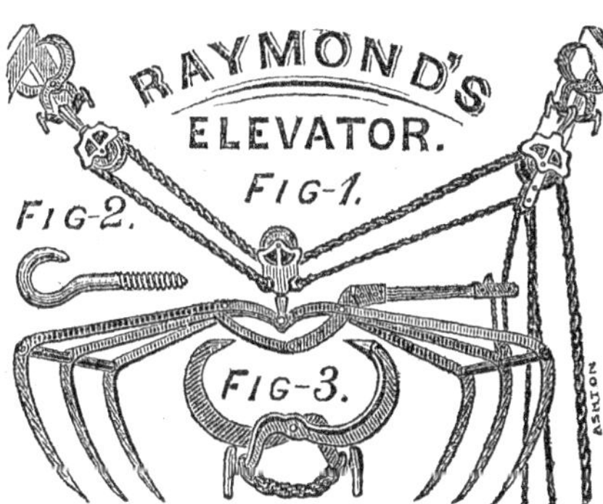

Figure 1, gives a very good idea of the construction and manner of rigging this implement for use. It consists of two three-pronged forks connected by a hinge. The prominent advantages claimed for it are, 1st, That it grasps the substance to be moved, and that therefore there can be little or no scattering, and that unbound grain, straw, and fine hay can be taken up with it. 2d, That after elevating, it will convey its load any required distance across a large mow, or the length of a long stack, and discharge it in good shape for removing with a hand fork. 3d, That no boards or slides are needed, as by means of a guy-rope it may be elevated almost perpendicularly nearly to the height of the pulleys, and then allowed to move over the mow or stack; consequently the stack can be kept level and its sides remain undisturbed,

Messrs. C., H. & Co., gave the weight and price of their fork and the apparatus belonging to it to the judges at the Auburn trial, as follows:

Weight 34 lbs.; price $20, with three hooks and pulleys; grapples $3. The manner of rigging this fork and the management of the blocks and tackle, undoubtedly confer upon it important advantages. The report of the judges says: "We award unqualified praise to the clamps used with this implement, which we understand to be secured by letters patent. By the aid of these, the blocks can be attached to the rafters from the floor, without a ladder, and can be removed with the greatest facility from place to place at any time."

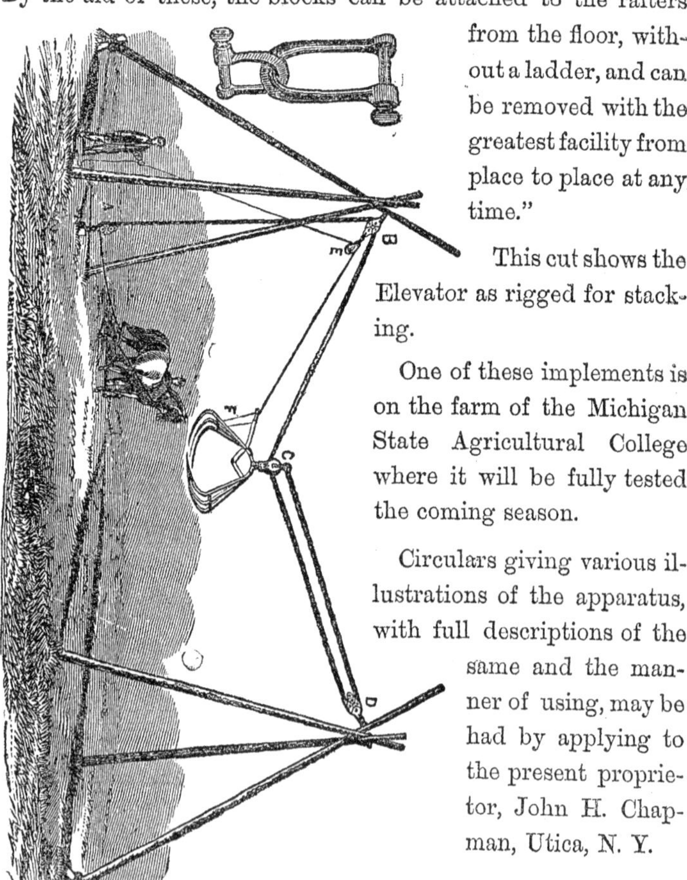

This cut shows the Elevator as rigged for stacking.

One of these implements is on the farm of the Michigan State Agricultural College where it will be fully tested the coming season.

Circulars giving various illustrations of the apparatus, with full descriptions of the same and the manner of using, may be had by applying to the present proprietor, John H. Chapman, Utica, N. Y.

THE FACTORY SYSTEM OF CHEESE-MAKING.

It is a gratifying fact that the making of cheese on what is called the factory system, has been commenced in Michigan. There is no reason why the business may not be as profitable here as in States to the eastward of us, and there are some reasons why it may become more so. All the cheese made in this State for sometime to come, can be sold here, and it can be sold in a greener condition than the New York dairymen can sell theirs; so that something is saved in the labor of curing, and something in weight, while the price is equal to that obtained for the older cheese of the Ohio and New York dairies. Land is also much cheaper here than in New York.

Rufus Baker, of Fairfield, Lenawee county, Mich., has kindly submitted for publication in this report, some account of a cheese factory of which he is the proprietor. His remarks are as follows:

The township of Fairfield is located six miles south of the city of Adrian, which is on the Michigan Southern Railroad, and is about 80 miles from Detroit. The township is devoted mostly to grazing and the cultivation of Indian corn. There have been about one hundred and thirty-five tons of cheese made here this season, there being some private dairies beyond the reach of the factories.

About two years ago, I turned my attention to the subject of building a cheese-factory; and in the Autumn of 1865, I visited in company with a neighboring townsman, several Ohio factories. I also visited some New York factories last January, and from those I formed the plan of my factory. I commenced my buildings in January, 1866, and completed them about the first of May. Commenced making cheese on the 23d of April, and closed November 17th. We used the milk from 230 cows, on an average.

The cost of my fixtures for manufacturing cheese, has been near $3,500, all told, their capacity being for about 300 cows—would enlarge if I should have more than that number. I think it hardly an object to give you a description of the buildings, as it would be better for a person who wished to start a factory to make examinations for themselves.

I have found the manufacture of cheese to be very remunerative when made a primary business, and I might say very unprofitable when made secondary.

There has been delivered at my factory this season, 970,931 ℔s. of milk, from April 23, to November 17th, inclusive, or 4,221 ℔s. milk for each cow—making 112,420 ℔s. of green cheese, and allowing the cheese to shrink 10 per cent. (which is a fair estimate), would give 101,198 ℔s. of cured cheese—483 ℔s. per cow. I am compelled to *estimate* the shrinkage, as our cheese is not yet all cured; but former experience with a private dairy, is, that 10 per cent. shrinkage is enough to allow.

The probabilty is that our cheese will bring an average of 16 cents per ℔. I have sold all but about nine tons, some sales running as high as 18 cents through the latter part of September and fore part of October. I receive for manufacturing, a cent and a half per pound, the patrons furnishing each his proportion of salt, rennets, bandages or sacking, grease, &c., with boxes for the cheese, all which amount to a trifle over two cents per pound. Each patron also bears his proportion of the expense of selling, of which a committee of three have charge.

I cannot recommend the starting of factories with the number of cows that I have, for it does not pay for the labor and investment. A factory should work up the milk from at least 400 cows to make cheese-making profitable. The factory system seems to have worked a revolution in the cheese-making business, although cheese has borne better prices since the introduction of that system than before. Should a specie basis in our currency be reached, we will not look for over ten cents per pound for cheese; and should the number of new factories now talked of be built, the probability is that our State will be supplied with all the cheese that will be wanted here.

At the present time cows are very high, and are difficult to be obtained. I know a lot of six that were sold on the first of November at $60 per head, within the circuit of my factory.

I do not know that I can answer your inquiries in regard to the various cheese-factories in the State; but will give the following, in the order, as I understand, in which they commenced operations:

Fairfield Factory, 230 cows, Rufus Baker, proprietor; post-office address, Fairfield, Mich.

West Fairfield Factory, 300 cows, Samuel Horton, proprietor; post-office address, Adrian, Mich.

Ypsilanti Factory, locality not known, S. H. Salisbury, proprietor; post-office address, Ypsilanti, Mich.

I understand there is a factory in Livingston county, but I know nothing about it, and cannot learn that they have any cheese in market.

If there are any others in this State, I have not heard of them.

RUFUS BAKER.

Fairfield, Mich., Dec. 14, 1866.

The principles of cheese-making are beginning to be regarded with so much interest by the people of Michigan, that they will undoubtedly be glad to avail themselves of many important facts brought out in the address of X. A. Willard, Esq., before the American Dairymen's Association, at their annual meeting at Utica, N. Y., 1866. The following extracts are presented:

No branch of farming to-day offers prospect of better or more permanent remuneration than the dairy. It has become a vast and wide-spread interest.

Born and living among dairymen, and for the last 15 years engaged upon my farm in cheese-making, I have watched with intense interest its progress, and have given the subject some thought. I feel deeply the nscessities of the age—the necessity of more and better markets for our products—the necessity of higher skill, and more science in their manufacture.

In the old days, cheese was not considered fit for market until fall or winter; it was packed in rough casks and peddled in the home markets at four, five, or six cents per pound. All the operations of the dairy were rude and undeveloped. The milking was performed in the open yard. The curds were worked in tubs and pressed in log presses. Everything was done by guess, and we had no order, no system, and no science in conducting operations.

The dealers who first broke ground in the trade are still living, and by no means old men. Looking back to those times, what truly wonderful and splendid results have been accomplished. *Now* we begin to see order and system where there was nothing put chaos. Instead of a few cheeses in casks, peddled here and there, we have cars, canal-boats and ships, freighted with the product of herds which are numbered by thousands. And yet to-day we are but at the commencement of dairy farming, and only at the threshold of a great interest that is to have a controlling influence on the wealth and prosperity of the nation.

SPECIALTIES IN FARMING.

There is a class of agriculturists who argue against specialties in farming, who advise the dairymen to go into a mixed husbandry, urging that greater profits would be realized, our lands improved, and that there would be less money thrown away in the transportation of material for food and raiment to different parts of the country.

I envy no section of country its prosperity. If the grain men can grow rich by raising grain or by a mixed husbandry, and the sheep men can make money by growing wool, or the grape region by producing grapes, I am glad that it *is* so, and trust as each section becomes wealthy it can afford to pay us a good round price for our dairies, while we in turn will buy their products, and as for the money lost in transportation, let that go; it may help to enrich a very useful class, who are not producers, but who, we hope, will have the good taste to buy and eat freely of our products.

A mixed husbandry may be advisable, and even necessary upon some farms; but if our soils are adapted to grazing, and we are doing well by the dairy, why be diverted from the main business? Men seem to forget that nearly every crop, except grass, has a thousand enemies to contend with—insects innumerable, frosts, rains, drouths and blights, while grass, being a natural product of the soil, scarcely ever fails in the dairy region, under decent treatment, to yield fair returns.

WASTE.

A good deal has been said about waste in cheese-making. Let us examine this point and see wherein the loss lies. In this matter it would be desirable to have the exact figures, since vague speculations and guess-work it is evident will not be fully satisfactory to practical men, who have for years been engaged in the manipulation of milk.

Unfortunately we have not a series of chemical analyses for determining this matter. It is true the English chemists have analyzed milk from time to time, but it varies so much in quality at different seasons of the year, and upon different farms, that it would be impossible to arrive at correct conclusions by taking English statements.

Thus Haidlen gives milk as having 87.3 parts water, 3 of butter, and 4.82 parts casein. Milk analyzed Oct. 21st, 1860, by Prof. Voelcker, of the Royal Agricultural Society of England, makes 100 parts contain 83.90 of water, 7.62 of butter, 3.31 of casein, 4.46 milk sugar, and .71 of mineral matter, (ash.) That analyzed by him on August 7th had 87.40 of water, 3.43 butter, 3.12 casein, 5.12 milk sugar, and .93 mineral matter.

Suppose we take the October milk, the amount of butter and casein in 100 pounds of milk would be 10.93, or nearly 11 pounds. Good cheese, besides the butter and casein in its composition, should contain when cured from 35 to 40 per cent. of water, about 1 per cent. of milk sugar, lactic acid and extractive matter, and 4 per cent. of mineral matter, (ash.) The amount of well-cured cheese then which should be made from a hundred pounds of milk of the character analyzed in October, if the butter and casein were all extracted should be about 15½ pounds. That is, 11 pounds butter and casein, 4 pounds water, and ½ pound mineral matter, milk sugar, &c. The August milk, on the above basis, should furnish 6.55 of butter and casein, 3 pounds water, and ½ pound milk sugar and mineral matter, making only about 10 pounds.

So how are we to arrive definitely at losses, without going to the factory or private dairy and analyzing the whey from time to time? That there are great losses in factories and dairies all are well aware. I have seen hogsheads of whey-butter that had been collected at factories, and cream upon vats forming a crust almost thick enough to bear a man.

This waste of thousands and thousands of dollars goes on annually, and patrons rest satisfied under the impression that it is a matter of necessity. There are factories where no attention is given to a careful manipulation of the curds. The rake and agitator are in the hands of persons who use them among the tender curds as they would toss grass in a hayfield. Again, portions of the curd are left to pack and melt from excessive heat, and when taken up in the hand, present a ropy, stringy appearance, all of which must result in a great loss to patrons.

My friends, you may not thank me for standing here and telling unpleasant truths, but it would be base in me to gloss over facts, giving you and the public the impression that no losses were being sustained in the dairy region. Some may have the idea, that the larger the quantity of poor cheese thrust on the market, the better it will be for those making a superior article. This is not so. The poorer cheese, on account of the less price which it brings, depreciates the price of the good, since the market always takes advantage of every opportunity to spring a trap upon producers and reduce prices. It is not the consumers who do this, but the speculators, who are always on the watch to make a good thing in their transactions. I shall presently have more to say on this head, in the discussion of butter manufacture in connection with the cheese dairy.

FLAVOR.

There has been improvement during the year in the matter of flavor, among a large number of factories and private dairies. Dairymen and dealers have labored assiduously, and sought more, the past year, after knowledge in improved processes of manufacture than ever before. It is an important feature in the year's operations, and shows what we are able to do in the future by persistent effort in this direction. Had not this effort been made, and the general character of our cheese improved, prices would have fallen at least three or four cents lower. Some people have thought it wonderful that the home trade has been so active, taking such large quantities of cheese. It is because American cheese has been better, has been made more attractive and palatable than formerly.

Our people are accustomed to good living, and are willing to pay a good price for a really good article; but it is useless to try and force upon them a mass of poor, spongy and putrid rubbish, such as was manufactured a few years ago. Such may perhaps be sold in limited quantities to a certain class at very low rates, but that is not the class we want to reach. It is those who have plenty of money, and are nice about their food.

These persons do not hesitate at a difference of three, four, or five cents per pound on an article like cheese, if it suits. It is on this point of flavor and quality, that our efforts in the future must be directed. There is always room for improvement even among our best factories, and further efforts must be made in this direction. From experiments made during the last season, it appears that flavor is improved not only by the process of manufacturing, but by curing in sunlight and a moderately moist atmosphere, ventilation and temperature, of course, being properly attended to.

In manufacturing there are several points that are important to insure high flavor. The first is pure, clean, sweet milk when it goes into the hands of the manufacturer. If we are to arrive at the highest excellence in flavor, manures and dirt, or the droppings of an unclean udder, with filthy hands, must be kept from the milk. The pails and all the utensils used should be kept scrupulously clean. The nature of milk-ferments is very imperfectly understood by most dairymen.

It is wonderful what a small quantity of ferment will taint a large quantity of milk. Ferments are most active at a temperature between 70 and 100 degrees. Essential to fermentation are sugar, on an equivalent convertible into it, water, heat, leaven, or yeast, and air. Cold diminishes it, and water at a temperature of 212 degrees or at boiling heat destroys it.

One of the curious things about ferments is, that they are capable of reproducing themselves in large quantities; that is, they produce in other matters with which they are brought in contact, changes similar to those which they themselves undergo. It will be seen, then, that when the careless dairymen has not properly cleaned his pails or cans with boiling water, or when he has been milking with dirty hands, or is not careful to exclude milk that happens to be feverish, diseased, and partly decomposed, he is adding the leaven or yeast which, when deposited in the vats and brought to a heat favorable for its rapid development, is of great damage, and causes the manufacturer trouble in securing flavor. Sometimes these ferments are of such a bad character and proceed so rapidly, that the curds become filled with gas and float upon the surface of the whey before they are of proper texture for the press. This makes bad work, and often results in the loss of cheese.

I have had but little experience in floating curds, and shall not try to point out the best manner in which they should be treated. But it would seem that some means should be immediately taken to check the progress of fermentation. This can be done in a measure by diminishing heat, or, by the addition of salt. I have tried two methods, and in both have been successful in obtaining a firm cheese, but of course, of unequal flavor from that of good milk. First, by drawing the whey, cooling with sour whey and salting; and again, simply by cooling and salting. In both instances the curds were pressed two days, and cheese cured in a temperature between 50 and 60 degrees. I do not pretend to give a rule for others to follow, but am only giving my own experience. The subject is alluded to here with the view of fastening this bad condition of milk upon the guilty parties—unclean, negligent dairymen, or those in their employ. If some of our manufacturers of dairy apparatus would furnish us with a light wooden pail, nicely lined with tin, and having on the inside a concave bottom, much trouble would be obviated in securing better milk, because such pails could more easily be kept sweet and clean, and would not allow of small particles of milk adhering so readily to the surface of the pails, and especially at the sharp angles made by the bottom and sides.

Such pails would pay for themselves during the first season's use, in the less labor of cleansing, and if they could be generally introduced would save manufacturers a vast deal of trouble, together with thousands of pounds of bad-flavored cheese. The common wooden pail cannot be kept sweet and clean except with extraordinary care; and from an examination of these utensils from time to time, I am satisfied, that much of the bad milk at factories arises from ferments induced by particles of old milk adhering to some parts of the pail, and thus communicating its properties to the fresh milk.

A mere rinsing in cold water, or even with warm water, will not clean pails properly. Nothing but boiling water and scrubbing with salt and with some implement by which the corners may be reached, will destroy these particles of matter by which ferments are induced.

Some people are extremely slovenly and dirty about their

milking, and when the number of such are taken into account, it is a wonder, often, how manufacturers have been so well able to maintain a decent flavor. Cheese is often badly tainted from this source, and it is one of the crying sins that calls loudly for redress. In regard to animal heat or a condition of the milk in that state, some claim that it is of no account in cheese-making; but from carefully conducted experiments, it is believed that milk made up, warm from the cow, is more or less prejudicial to fine flavor, since such milk contains more ammonia and animal odor than that which has been subjected to a process of cooling. In the processes for condensing and desicating milk, the cooling of the milk in order to get rid of the ammoniacal gas, has been found to be of imperative necessity in securing a fine flavored product, and although the necessity may not, perhaps, be so great in cheese-making, still an excess of ammonia has a tendency to give cheese an unpleasant, pungent taste, and render it liable to be more easily thrown out of flavor while curing. Experiments during the past season, although not carried so far as may have been desired, give satisfactory evidence that, if the morning's milk could be properly cooled as it comes from the cow, a finer flavored cheese would be obtained.

The heating process, whether of the milk or the curds, should be very slow and uniform. Steam vats are objectionable unless constructed so as to get an uniform temperature through every portion of the milk. This is a matter which has not been sufficiently urged.

High heat in any portion of the milk gives it a scorched flavor, besides injuring its quality in other respects. It is of the utmost importance that heat, when employed in any operation, should be slow, gradual, uniform, and never higher than 98 degrees or 100 degrees. Of course milk in proper condition is here presumed. When otherwise, variations in the process must be adopted, and among the several evils the least chosen.

RENNET.

Much of the bad flavored cheese comes from tainted rennet. There is too little attention paid in obtaining clean, sweet, healthy rennet. The difficulty of obtaining good rennets is great, and will continue to be greater, it is feared, from year to year. Some action ought to be taken by this convention, in disseminating correct knowledge through the country in regard to the selection and curing of rennets. The rennets obtained from large cities like Boston and New York, are for the most part of a very bad character. Many of the calves when they arrive in the city are in a starved condition, and the stomach of the animal highly inflamed. When thus saved it is already on the point of decomposition, and becomes poisoned with putridity. To inoculate human food with such an element, is death among consumers, thus injuring the sale of good cheese through fear. Cases of poisoning from the eating of factory cheese have occurred during the past summer. The cheese, when analyzed by the chemist, was found to contain a virulent poison. And it is not improbable that it was the result of using putrid rennet. Should cases of this kind occur *frequently* in the home market, it would soon sensibly affect sales.

People outside the dairy region should in some way be made acquainted with the manner of selecting and curing the stomach of the calf. The stomach, if healthy when taken from the animal, is nearly white. The contents should be turned out, and all specks or dirt wiped off with a cloth, and the skin thoroughly salted inside and out. It may then be stretched on a hoop or crotched stick, and should be hung in a dry room with only moderate heat. When taken out in summer, it should not be dried in a hot sun. There are many curious things about the rennet that are shrouded in mystery, and are not understood by the chemist. As far back as 1859, in an article published in the "Dairy Farmer," I gave it as my opinion, that the theory of Prof. Johnston and other chemists on the action of rennet was incorrect. Since that time Dr. Voelcker, of the Royal Agricultural Society of England, expresses similar views

He says: "Scientific and practical writers on milk have stated that the casein is held in solution by a small quantity of alkali; that when in warm weather milk curdles, lactic acid, which is always found in sour milk, is formed from a portion of the sugar of milk; and this lactic acid by neutralizing the alkali which holds the casein in solution, causes its separation from the milk. Rennet is supposed to act as a ferment, which rapidly converts some of the sugar of milk into lactic acid. Whether, therefore, milk coagulates spontaneously after some length of time, or more rapidly on the addition of rennet, in either case the separation of the curd is supposed to be due to the removal of the free aikali by lactic acid.

"This theory, however, is not quite consistent with facts. The casein in milk cannot be said to be held in solution by free alkali, for although it is true that milk often has a slightly alkaline reaction, it is likewise a fact that sometimes perfectly fresh milk is slightly acid. We might as well say, therefore, that the casein is held in solution by a little free acid, as by free alkali. Newly-drawn milk, again, is often perfectly neutral, but whether milk be neutral, or alkaline, or acid, the casein exists in it, in a state of solution, which cannot, therefore depend on an alkaline reaction.

"We all know that milk, when it turns sour, curdles very readily. It is not the fact that a good deal of acid curdles milk, which I dispute, but the assumption that the casein in milk is held in solution by free alkali.

"The action of rennet upon milk, then, is not such as has been hitherto represented by all chemists who have treated of this subject. Like many other animal matters which act as a ferment rennet it is true rapidly induces the milk to turn sour, but free lactic acid I find makes its appearance in milk after the curd has separated, and not simultaneously with the precipitation of the curd.

"Perfectly fresh and neutral milk, on the addition of rennet, coagulates, but the whey is perfectly neutral. I have even purposely made milk alkaline, and yet succeeded in separating the curd by rennet; and what is more, obtained a whey which had an alkaline reaction.

"What may be the precise mode in which rennet acts upon milk, I do not pretend to explain. I believe it to be an action which as yet is only known by its effects. We at present are unacquainted with the precise chemical character and the composition of the active principle in rennet, and have not even a name for it."

I may remark here that the stomach of the calf, when subjected to freezing and thawing, seems to be increased in its strength and efficiency—a curious fact not heretofore made known.

Mr. Dwyer, of Springfield, Illinois, gives an account of a practice adopted in Switzerland, and which the Swiss cheese-makers deem important in the coagulation of milk for cheese-making. After the rennet is added to the milk, gold pieces are dropped into the vat, which it is stated acts as an electric, or in some way as an agent, to modify the condition of coagulation and the curds, so as to improve the flavor of the cheese. I have alluded to it here, because the idea is new to us. It may be a mere whim, or it may have some foundation for usefulness, and at least can be no injury as a suggestion for future experiments. I trust there is no one here but will be willing to make experiments, however much his faith may be that he has arrived at the acme of the art of cheese-making.

The man who, in this age, wraps himself up in the notion that there is nothing more to be learned, is a poor, vain mortal, whose days of improvement are over, and who would gain nothing even from the teachings of an angel.

An untainted atmosphere, sunlight, ventilation, temperature and moisture, are each and all important in securing flavor and desirable qualities in cheese. Some of these points need not be dwelt upon here.

The idea of making nice cheese among the intolerable stenches arising from decomposing slops, the foul odors of excrements from the pig-sties, and emanations from diseased hogs, may be entertained by some, but it is one of those rare pieces of skill which we have yet to see accomplished. How far taste may be perverted to select an article manufactured under these conditions, and *call* it good, we are unable to say; but there never has been, and never will be, a manufacturer who can lead the market, whose establishment is surrounded by filth, and where no attention is paid to cleanliness in conducting operations.

We are entering upon a grand field of improvement, but it is useless for patrons to expect that everything is to be accomplished by manufacturers. The factories must be overhauled, hog-pens torn down or removed, so as not to stand in near proximity to the buildings, the whey and slops properly conducted away, and everything about the premises kept sweet and clean. This point was alluded to in my address before the New York Cheese-Makers' Convention, last year; and if patrons could *only* see the great necessity of taking immediate action in this matter, so that better cheese and better prices be had, they would not only be helping themselves, but doing a great service to the whole dairy public.

COARSE CURDS—MOISTURE, ETC.

I am not prepared to say that any better *flavored* cheese can be made by the "coarse curd process" than by the fine curd; but by the coarse curd a greater quantity is obtained, and of a richer quality, that is, having more butter. A proper managemant of the acids is, of course, presumed in either process.

Many have an idea that the more butter we retain in the curds the better must be the cheese. This is hardly correct. A certain proportion of butter, mingled with the casein, is doubtless needed to suit the general taste; but there are other things requisite to make cheese palatable, besides butter and clean flavor. One of these is moisture. A cheese may be fine in flavor, and very rich in butter, but if dry and crumbly, it is far less palatable than one that has only half the quantity of butter and the requisite moisture nicely distributed throughout. This character of cheese is always sought after, and, when flavor is maintained, always pronounced prime, whether in the home or foreign market.

Our most delicious fruits are in a great part made up of water. An addition of sugar would not improve them, but on the contrary greatly deteriorate from their flavor and palatableness.

One of the great arts in cheese manufacture, and one in which our skill in the future must be directed, is in this matter of moisture. How to distribute it through the curds in the right proportion, and how to manage so that it may be retained until it reaches the consumer.

Dr. Voelcker's analysis of the finest English Cheddar Cheese when six months old, showed that it *then* contained nearly 34 per cent. of water; and he remarks that it did not contain near so much butter as its appearance, rich taste and fine mature condition seemed to imply; and thanks to Mr. Harding's skill and experience, had a much fatter and more mellow appearance and richer taste than a specimen which actually contained 2½ per cent. more butter.

The best American cheese analyzed by him, he says, was as nice cheese as could be desired; in flavor it much resembled good Cheddar. This cheese contained 2½ per cent. more butter than the English sample made by Mr. Harding, and only a fraction above 27 per cent. of water, or seven pounds less water, to the hundred weight of cheese, than the English Cheddar.

Here then we are actually losing seven pounds in the weight on every hundred pounds, besides throwing away two pounds of butter, and yet obtain an inferior article to that of Mr. Harding.

This matter of moisture has not been studied by Amenican cheese-makers; and one of the chief tests of the skill of manufacturers in the future is to be the production of a rich-tasting, fine-flavored mellow cheese, from milk not particularly rich in butter.

The peculiar mellow appearance of good cheese, says Dr. Voelcker, though due to some extent to the butter which it contains, depends in a higher degree on a gradual transformation which the casein or the curd undergoes in ripening.

"The curd is hard and insoluble in water, but by degrees it becomes softer and more soluble, or speaking more correctly, gives rise to products of decomposition, which are soluble in water. Now, if this ripening process is *badly conducted*, or the original character of the curd is such that adapts itself but slowly to this transformation, the cheese when sold will be, comparatively speaking, tough, and appear less rich in butter than it really is; whilst in well made and perfectly kept cheese this series of changes will be rapidly and thoroughly effected. Proper ripening thus imparts to cheese a rich appearance, and unites with the butter in giving it that most desirable property of melting in the mouth. On examining some cheese deficient in this melting property, and accordingly pronounced by practical judges defective in butter, I nevertheless found in them a very high per centage of that substance, clear proof that the mellow and rich taste of cheese *is not entirely, nor indeed chiefly, due to the fatty matters which it contains.*"

When whole milk cheeses are made, it is believed that this point can be better reached by the "coarse curds system," and the proper management of the acids, than by the fine curds. The point to be reached is, to retain the largest amount of moisture that the cheese is capable of holding so nicely mingled with its other constituents as not to collect in drops, and at the same time preserve the cheese compact and solid, so as to fill the tryer without any indication of porosity. The complaint against factory cheese, of its dryness, has been common, and the losses, in quantity from this source, want of moisture, have been very large.

Water is a very cheap material, and if, as it has been proved by analysis, the English cheese, with its 7 pounds more of water per 100, is better than ours, is it not important that this 7 pounds of water be retained, and go into the farmer's profits?

A dollar and fifty cents lost on every 100 cheese is a very important item.

The construction of the dry-house is very important. In our hot, dry weather, evaporation is very rapid. We understand the fact perfectly that England has a moist atmosphere, and yet no one seems to try to improve our cheese-curing rooms. We follow blindly after the old plan, and if the cheese gets out of flavor and the quantity falls short of what was expected, we go to blaming the manufacturer. Doubtless some of them deserve censure; but, my friends, it is not right to pile up all the blame at his door, for so far as my observation goes, both patrons and proprietors of factories ought in justice to take a good share.

Our dry-houses should be constructed not only so as to preserve an even temperature, but secure an atmosphere that has a certain amount of moisture in it, so that evaporation from the cheese should not be too rapid in hot, dry weather. We need our dry-rooms constructed in such a way that whenever it is desirable to hold cheese a month, six weeks, or longer, we can do so without meeting losses from shrinkage and having the cheese get out of flavor.

Trees about the dry-houses do service in equalizing temperature, and securing the desired object. Water in some shape, in hot weather, either by sprinkling upon the floor, or in tubs, I have found in part a prevention of too rapid evaporation from the cheese, as well as for keeping it in flavor. There is no time now, even if I had the ability, to describe minutely buildings best adapted for curing cheese, and can only give you facts and subjects for thought, which are to be considered and worked up and improved at your leisure.

BUTTER FACTORIES.

It has been shown that the finest flavored and most palatable cheese is not necessarily that which is richest in butter; and, perhaps, in this connection, it will not be out of place to speak of butter-making in connection with the manufacture of cheese.

In my tours among the New York factories, it could not but be plainly seen that immense losses are annually sustained in the waste of oily particles carried off in the whey during the process of cheese manufacture. And it may be observed that the loss generally has been in the butter particles. The casein is heavy and sinks to the bottom of the vats, carrying down the oily particles entangled in its meshes.

When the curds are cut very fine, some portions of course escape, but it is the butter, (which in good milk is equal and often in larger proportion than the casein), that we have been trying to save. However wonderful the skill of the manufacturer, he has not yet been able to retain all the oily particles of the milk, but a considerable proportion slips through his fingers and passes off in the whey. The butter or oil, as you are aware, is in globules, each one of which is encased with a pelicle or thin coating of casein. The richer the milk the more difficult it is to retain the butter.

When there is comparatively but a small per cent. of butter in the milk, a careful manufacturer has no difficulty in holding nearly every particle of the oily matter; and hence to work up milk to the best advantage with our present imperfect knowledge of cheese-making, a portion of the cream must be removed.

Butter is always worth double, treble, and often quadruple, the price of cheese. Now take these facts together:

1st. Our cheese is richer in butter than need be.

2d. We cannot retain it all in the curds, even if we would.

3d. The price of butter is greatly in excess of cheese.

What do these propositions prove?

They prove that we have been annually throwing away millions of dollars, without benefiting anybody or anything, except perhaps the pigs. It is a waste which all of us have been aware of for a long time, but in our blindness were unable to see clearly how to remedy. It can be remedied by the establishment of *Butter Factories*, in connection with cheese manufacture.

This modification of our system promises to be the leading feature in future operations of the dairy. It is another progressive step, and will do much to ensure a permanency to the factory system, since a great many farmers have no conveniences for conducting the business thus complicated, nor would the additional work required be likely to find favor with the family household.

One of the leading arguments of the factory system has been the advanced price obtained for factory cheese over that made in families. But the private dairies this year, by improving their make and style, have been able to obtain sales very nearly, if not quite, up to the factories. In some sections patrons have become dissatisfied, and talk of returning to the old system, and it is evident that unless a moneyed inducement can be held out, many will do so, and some of the factories must go down. But by the system of butter and cheese making together the factories spring at once ahead of private dairies, and will be able to pay patrons, after deducting all expenses of manufacture, carting milk, etc., more money than they could possibly realize by making up the milk at home after the old system. This gives a lift to the factory system beyond the expectations of the most sanguine

The plan admits of various modifications in the manufacture of cheese. Thus some can turn their attention to purely skim-milk cheese, and others only partially so. The question of course will occur to what extent the cream may be removed from the milk, and yet a nice mellow, palatable cheese be manufactured. This opens up a vast field for skill and science in cheese-making. But from the analysis of Dr. Voelcker, heretofore given, and facts gathered in my visit to Orange county, N. Y., it is believed that a portion of the milk may be kept twelve, and perhaps twenty-four hours, then skimmed and added to the morning's mess, and from this mixture as nice an article of cheese made as under our present system of letting the cream pass off to the whey tubs.

I went down to Orange county in November, and made an

examination of the butter and skim-milk cheese-factories recently established in that section. On my return, a lengthy report, embracing a minute description of their processes, was given in the Utica *Morning Herald*, and has been so widely copied by the agricultural press that it is presumed you are all familiar with its leading features. We have something to learn from the Orange county dairymen, and their processes in the management of milk open up a wide field for us to experiment upon, and on which to make improvements. They understand the management of milk, in some respects, better than the cheese dairymen. The Orange county farmer has no difficulty in keeping milk sweet for 36 hours, and that, too, during the hottest weather. The milk is carted in old-fashioned milk-cans to the factories, and drawn off into pails 8 inches in diameter, and from 20 to 22 inches deep. These, on being filled within 5 inches of the top, are immediately set in the springs. Perhaps to a full understanding of this matter I cannot do better than to give here a description of the parent butter factory in Orange county, which is under the management of Mr. Alanson Slaughter, a member of the New York Cheese-Makers' Association. The factory is located in the town of Wallkill, and although some improvements have been made in other factories recently erected, the general features and principles in conducting operations are alike.

The main building consists of a two-storied structure, arranged on a plan similar to our cheese factories. Below are the vats, presses, etc., for making cheese, and above is the dry-room. On one end of this building is erected the spring house, containing two rooms—one 12 feet by 16 feet, and the other 14 feet by 24 feet. In the more modern factories there is but one spring room. It has windows and doors for ventilation. The packing and churning room is a separate building, 12 feet by 24 feet, and stands opposite the spring room, with a narrow alley between. Adjoining to and connected with this is a horse-power for churning, and a store-room. The establishment receives the milk from 400 cows, and, after the cream is taken from the milk, the milk is made up into skim cheese. Vats are constructed about the springs for holding the water. They are three in number, 12 feet long by six feet wide, set down even with the floor, and with racks in the bottom for holding the cans. The water flows up through these racks and above them to the depth of 17 inches. The pails are 22 inches long and 8 inches in diameter, and, as fast as the milk is received, they are filled within 5 or 6 inches of the top, and immediately placed in the water. Care is taken that the surface of the milk in the pails is not above that of the water in the spring. The pails are set close together, and one spring will hold 2,040 quarts of milk. The spring should have a sufficient flow of water to divest the milk of the animal heat in less than an hour. Mr. Slaughter regards 56° as the highest temperature that the water of the spring should be for conducting operations with success. He has not yet determined the precise temperature of water best adapted for obtaining the most cream, but is satisfied from his experiments that the natural temperature of the water should not be below 48° nor above 56°. He says, as much cream—and that of better quality for butter-making—can be obtained by setting the milk on the above plan, than shallow in pans. The object is to expose as little of the surface of the milk as possible to the air, and that surface should always be in a moist atmosphere, in order that the top of the cream may not get dry, which has a tendency to fleck the butter and injure its flavor.

The milk of one day is left in the spring till the next morning, when it is taken out, the cream dipped off, and put immediately in the churns. In removing the cream, a little tunnel-shaped cup, with a long, upright handle, is used. It is gently pushed into the pails, and the cream dipped off. It is very expeditiously effected, and the milk line easily determined by the blue appearance of the milk. The cream, in fall and spring, is churned sweet. In summer the cream is dipped into the same pails, returned to the spring, and kept there till it sours. As fast as the cream is removed, the milk in the pails is emptied into the vats for making skim cheese.

THE CHURN-ROOM AND CHURNING.

The churning is done by horse-power. The churns are the common barrel and half-dash churn, four in number, and are placed on each side of the power, so as to be all worked together. About 50 quarts of cream are put into each churn, and each then receives a pail of cold spring water, and the mass is brought to a temperature of 63 or 64 degrees. In warm weather ice is sometimes broken up and put in the churn, to reduce the temperature to 56 degrees; but it is deemed better to churn without ice, if the temperature does not get above 64 degrees in the process of churning, as butter made with ice is more sensitive to heat. It is, however, a less evil to use ice than to have the butter come from the churn white and soft. It requires from forty-five minutes to an hour to churn, when the butter should come solid, and of a rich yellow color. It is then taken from the churns, and thoroughly washed in spring water. In this process the ladle is used, and three times pouring on water is generally all that is required. It is then salted, at the rate of one pound and two ounces of salt to twenty-two pounds of butter. In making winter butter, a little more salt is added at the last working. The butter, after having been salted and worked, is allowed to stand till evening, and is then worked and packed in sixty pound pails, and shipped twice a week to New York. In hot weather, after the butter is salted and worked over, it is taken to the spring and immersed in the water, where it remains until evening, when it is taken out and worked over and packed. For winter butter, a small tea-spoonful of pulverized saltpetre and a large table-spoonful of white sugar are added to the twenty-two pounds of butter at the last working. No coloring matter is used in the butter at this establishment.

The butter is worked on an inclined slab, with beveled sides running down to the lower end, and within four inches of each other. A long wooden lever, so formed as to fit into a socket at this point, is used for working the butter. It is a very simple affair, and does the work effectually. In churning, the dashers are so arranged as to come within a quarter of an inch of the bottom of the churn, and rise above the cream in their upward stroke. When butter is packed in firkins none but those made of white oak are used. These firkins are very handsomely made, and are tight, so as not to allow the least leakage. Before using they are soaked in cold water; after that in hot water, and then again in cold water.

After being filled with butter, they are headed up, and strong brine poured in at the top, so as to fill all the intervening spaces. The pails for holding the milk in the springs are thoroughly cleaned each day with soap, rinsed in spring water, and put on a rack to dry. In furnishing a factory, two pails are allowed for each cow, as it is necessary to have a double set.

THE SKIM CHEESE.

In making the cheese the milk is set at 82 degrees; highest heat 96 to 98 degrees, and three pounds of salt to 100 of curd. The curd is pressed in 16-inch hoops, and cheese made about four inches high. We bored a number, and tested their quality. They were of good flavor, and by no means unpalatable, though, of course, inferior to pure milk cheese. These cheeses are shipped to warm climates, and may go to China in exchange for tea. Their value has been constantly increasing, as the markets have been opened for this character of cheese, and it has sold this year, a part of the time, for as much as our best factory, and sometimes in advance.

It is believed, if the quantity could be increased, other markets would be opened, so that the cheese would always sell for as much as the pure milk cheese, and perhaps in advance of it, since it seems to be better adapted to warm climates, and better suited to the tastes of people living under a burning sun, where less fat is required than in our cold climate.

RECORD OF RESULTS FROM A GIVEN QUANTITY OF MILK.

Mr. Slaughter has only from time to time made a record of a single day's work—his books being arranged for monthly statements. Among the single day's results are the following:

On May 18th, from 3,512 quarts of milk, *wine measure*, there was produced 213 pounds of butter and 560 pounds of cheese; May 26th, from 3,300 quarts of milk, 210 pounds of butter and 550 of cheese; September 12th, from 3,128 quarts, 200 pounds of butter and 546 of cheese; October 14th, from 2,027 quarts of milk, 120 pounds of butter and 407 pounds of cheese.

Take the result for instance of May 26th. The 3,300 quarts of milk by our system, allowing two pounds to the quart and nine pounds of milk to the pound of cheese, would make 730 pounds of cheese; but by this Orange county process we get 210 pounds of butter and 550 of cheese, or 760 pounds, being a product of 30 pounds more than with us. But the 210 pounds of butter alone, at the price it brought in the fall would give the Orange county farmer more than we got for the same quantity of milk made up into cheese, leaving him the 550 pounds of cheese as clear gain.

ADVANTAGES OF THE SYSTEM.

I do not know the prices obtained for Orange county butter and cheese in the spring and early part of summer, and do not pretend to give the exact figures, but it will be readily seen that the advantages of the system in conducting the dairy are very great.

From experiments made at the Orange County Milk Association, Mr. Allison, the superintendent, states that during the summer it takes on an average 14 quarts of milk, wine measure, to make a pound of butter and two pounds of cheese. Estimating a quart of milk, wine measure, to weigh 2 pounds, it will be seen that 28 pounds of milk yields 3 of butter and skim cheese, or one pound from 9⅓ pounds of milk.

At this establishment, in addition to the spring-room, there is a cellar 12 feet by 14 feet, with walls nicely laid up with stone, and extending into the bank at the rear end of the building. Here the butter is stored in summer as soon as packed, where it remains until ready to be shipped.

ORGANIZING BUTTER-FACTORIES.

The factories are managed on a little different plan from those in the central counties of New York. The farmers of a neighborhood join together, and erect the buildings, each one paying in proportion to size of farm, or number of cows from which milk is to be delivered. After the structure is completed and furnished, a superintendent is chosen, and help hired for running the factory, and the expenses are shared by stockholders in proportion to the amount of milk delivered. Repairs, additions, &c., from year to year, are added to the expense account.

Last year, at the Wallkill Creamery Association, the expense account for labor amounted to a fraction above two mills per quart, and the gross proceeds from sales gave to the farmers five cents and two and a half mills per quart, wine measure. The cost of erecting a factory, and furnishing it throughout, for four hundred cows, is estimated at $10 per cow.

LABOR EMPLOYED.

At the Rockville Milk Association, besides the superintendent, three hands are employed at the factory—two men and one woman. The butter-maker and his wife get $50 per month, and find themselves in board, &c.; the remaining hand gets $20 per month and board. At all these factories Ralph's Oneida vat is in use for cheese-making, and gives universal satisfaction.

THE CAPTAINS MARKETING BUTTER.

The manner of marketing butter differs from that practiced in other sections. Consignments are not generally made directly to the New York dealers; but shipments are intrusted to "captains," as they are called, or persons who make it a business to collect freight and take it in charge to New York, making the sales and returning the proceeds to the manufacturer.

These captains go with their freight twice a week, are men of standing and responsibility who are well posted in the trade, and know how and where to obtain the best prices. They receive a commission for their labors, and find it for their interest to make good bargains, otherwise they would lose the confidence of those intrusting freight to their charge, and would therefore be displaced. These captains often receive proposals for large lots of butter, which are submitted to the factories, when they are rejected or accepted, as seems best to the parties interested.

Large profits are realized by the farmer, since the milk is more thoroughly worked up, and with less loss, while at the same time the butter product will bring from three to four times more than it would if made into cheese. Good butter is needed, and will readily sell for a high price in all our cities. We are opening up another market for cheese, by furnishing the kind that will keep well on long voyages and in hot climates, and of a precise character demanded by the people of those climates.

THE SYSTEM APPLIED TO CHEESE-FACTORIES.

To many of our cheese-factories the addition of a spring-room, churn-room, and the necessary implements for butter-making, need cost but little, and the additional labor, with an ordinary factory, would be covered by one person, and in some instances could be carried on with the usual force employed. That the butter will bring a high price in market can not be doubted, since skill in manufacturing will be sought after, and a prime article "never goes begging."

The public necessities demand several butter-factories in every cheese-producing county, to manufacture for home consumption. And as the quantity of skim-cheese increases, new markets will be opened, and these, while they have a tendency to continue renumerative rates, must also operate advantageously on other styles of cheese, by reducing the quantity of these kinds and rendering them comparatively scarce.

I do not advise every factory rushing at once into the manufacture of skim-cheese. This would be to overdo the business, and cause a failure by throwing upon the market too much of this kind of cheese. But it would be safe for those factories that have nice water and locations suitable for erecting spring-rooms to add them to the factory, and commence a series of experiments to determine what proportion of the butter may be removed from the milk, and yet retain a quantity sufficient to produce a rich, mellow and high priced cheese. As to the value of skim-cheese, all of you know what the quotations were in the fall. When the Orange county skim-cheese was selling at 18½ cents, the best factories of Herkimer and Oneida brought but 17½ to 18c.

The whole matter at this time is crude and undeveloped, and must be worked out in the future.

In no art can we expect to reach the highest standard of excellence at one grand stride, but by degrees, progressing little by little; and if we can only advance with the same rapidity that has marked our course for the last few years, the most sanguine of those seeking improvement will have no cause to complain. Skim-milk cheeses can be manufactured so as not to be unpalatable even here, but they are particularly adapted to the taste of those living under a burning sun, who do not require, and whose stomachs will not bear rich oily food. Such cheese, too, is better adapted for keeping, and pound for pound is of more nutritive value than whole milk cheese. The celebrated Parmesan cheese is prepared from skim milk, and it is believed if a sufficient quantity of skim cheese could be manufactured so as to make it more an object for transportation, a most profitable trade could be opened in countries lying in the torrid zone—China, Japan, the countries in southern Europe and Asia, the West India Islands and some of the States of South America.

NUTRITIVE PROPERTIES OF CHEESE.

The reason why skim-milk cheese is more nutritous than that made from whole milk, is because, divested of most of its butter, it contains a greater proportion of casein or nitrogenized food. Recent writers affirm that nitrogenized foods are alone capable of conversion into blood, and of forming organized tissues, that in fact *they* only are the foods properly so called. The non-nitrogenized foods, of which butter or fat is one, are pronounced incapable of transformation into blood, and are, therefore, unfitted for forming organized or living tissues. They are, nevertheless, essential to health, and Liebig asserts that, their function is to support the process of respiration, (by yielding carbon and hydrogen, the oxydation of which is attended with the development of heat,) and some of them, he states, contribute to the formation of fat. These non-nitrogenized foods he calls elements of respiration. They consist of fat, starch, gum, cane sugar, grape sugar, sugar of milk, pectine, bassorine, wine, beer and spirits. The nitrogenized foods or plastic elements of nutrition are vegetable fibrin, albumen, casein, animal flesh, and blood. It has been found by experiments on animals, that gum, sugar, starch or butter, cannot alone preserve the health or life of animals. Magendie found that dogs fed exclusively on sugar and water died in from 31 to 34 days; and similar results were obtained with butter and gum. Tiedeman and Gemlin have comfirmed Magendie's statements. In the report of the Gelatine Commission, of the French Academy of Sciences, it is stated that a dog, fed on fresh butter only, continued to eat it irregularly 68 days. He died, subsequently, of inanition, although in a remarkable state of *embonpoint*. During the whole of the experiment he exhaled a strong ordor of butyric acid, his hair felt greasy, and his skin was unctuous and covered with a fatty layer. At the autopsy all the tissues and organs were found infiltrated with fat. The liver was in a state, called in pathological anatomy, fatty. By anlaysis, a very large quantity of stearine, (margarine,) but little or no oleine was found in it. Into this organ, therefore, there had been a kind of infiltration of fat.

Non-nitrogenized foods support the process of respiration by yielding carbon and in some cases hydrogen, to be burnt in the lungs, and thereby to keep up the animal temperature. This is the reason why fatty foods are relished, and are even necessary in cold climates, and also why they are repulsive to persons living in the torrid zone, where heat is supplied to excess by climate.

It will be seen, therefore, that casein is the chief nitrogenized constituent of milk. It is highly nutritious, and it is from this source that the development of the tissues is effected in young animals which feed upon it. "The young animal," says Liebig, "receives, in the form of casein, (which is distinguished from fibrin and albumen, by its great solubility and by not coagulating when heated,) the chief constituents of the mother's blood. To convert casein into blood no foreign substance is required, and in the conversion of the mother's blood into casein, no elements of the constituents of the blood have been separated.

"When chemically examined, casein is found to contain a much larger proportion of the earth of bones than blood, and that in a very soluble form, capable of reaching every part of the body. Thus, even in the earliest period of its life, the development of the organs, in which vitality resides, is, in the carniverous animals, dependent upon the supply of a substance identified in organic composition with the chief constituents of its blood."

These facts have been alluded to, because there is a misapprehension generally in the minds of many, in regard to the nutritive properties of cheese. It is considered, to a great extent, as merely a luxury, when the facts show that there is no article of food in common use that is so nutritious. Professor Johnston states that a pound of cheese is more nutritious than two pounds of beef; and as it contains no bones, and scarcely any waste, it *is*, and always has been, a very cheap article of human food; in fact furnished a great deal too cheaply. When our people begin rightly to understand that a pound of nice cheese is not only one of the greatest luxuries of the table, but at the same time *twice* as nutritious as the same weight in steak, perhaps they will be willing to pay us prices in proportion to its real value.

What we need at this time is, that our people be made acquainted with the finer grades of cheese, and also that, as an article of food, it is highly nutritious, and, therefore, more economical than other kinds of food, such as butter, etc., which are regarded as necessary. That cheese is one of the cheapest articles of diet is well understood, *practically*, by the working men of England. They can make a good hearty meal upon bread and cheese alone, and find that on such a diet, for at least one meal of the day, they are enabled to endure hard and exhaustive labor quite as well as on the more expensive diet of animal flesh.

Efforts should be made to induce the general government to purchase cheese for the army and navy of the United States, and when its healthfulness, its nutrition, its universal relish, its ease of transportation, and economy, are taken into account, it is a wonder why it has not long since been more universally used in filling up rations for the army. But in order to reach these ends, dairymen and cheese manufacturers and home dealers should be united and stand firmly together. Let us act in concert, and make an effort not only for the improvement of American cheese, but for extending our markets, and for better prices.

STYLES OF CHEESE.

In this connection of markets a word may be offered in reference to the styles of cheese for the coming year. Many of our factories and family dairies continue to make a large-sized cheese. They have the old hoops on hand, and cannot see the reason why large cheeses should not be as saleable and command as high a price in the market as formerly. There are some advantages in making large cheeses—they take less bandage, require less labor in handling while curing, and the expense of boxing is less than when made smaller. To these may be added less waste in shrinkage. All these points are well understood by cheese-makers, and they therefore make an effort to retain the old styles. Unfortunately for them, the markets step in and reject the old styles, giving preference to the smaller size. They do not absolutely command dairymen to stop making large cheeses, but they say plainly, and have done so all summer, if you continue to persist in this course, you must take a less price as a consequence. The time has been when large cheeses would outsell the smaller; but it was not because of the size, but for the simple reason that the quality was generally better. When quality was alike, the smaller cheeses have always been worth the most money. The reasons are obvious. The smaller cheeses are more easily handled; there is less loss from breakage or accident; there is less waste in cutting, and they are more saleable to persons purchasing for family use.

We may remark here that in England the shops for retailing cheese are often kept by women, who are unable readily to handle a heavy cheese. In the home trade large cheeses have always been objectionable, on account of heavy handling, loss from breakage, skippers, and the waste from drying, during the time employed for cutting up and selling small quantities at retail.

Now there is some reason on the part of consumers in regard to all this, and dairymen must conform to the requisitions of the markets. The past season the smaller dairies, by improving in their manufacture, have been able to outsell the larger dairies, even though the cheese was of equally fine quality, because the size was not desirable.

The factories should be provided with hoops, to make various styles, so as to suit the markets. For exportation to England two styles are in favor—the Cheddar, pressed in 15½ inch hoops, making a cheese about 12 inches high; and the flat cheese, about 5 or 6 inches thick, pressed in 15, 16, or 17 inch hoops. These latter are also desirable for the home trade. But the home trade demands yet another style of cheese, pressed in 8, 10, and 11 inch hoops, and weighing from 10 to 20 pounds. When the smaller sized cheeses are made, they may be put up without bandage, and packed in square or oblong boxes, several together, thus greatly reducing the expense in getting them to market. A greater discrimination it is believed will be made the coming year than ever before in styles of cheese, and both factories and private dairies should fix upon a style best suited to the market which it may be desirable for them to supply. But one thing is certain, the day of large cheeses is over, and if factories persist in making such, they must expect to be outsold by small family dairies, and the tendency of this will be to break up the factory system, since farmers will not pay from one and a half to two cents per pound for having their cheese made in factories, and see the private dairies outselling them at one to two cents per pound.

The home trade promises to be large the coming year. Our people are beginning to find that nice, palatable cheese can be manufactured, and while they are willing to pay a good round price, they will insist that it be put up in a shape that insures the least loss to consumers.

REARING CALVES.

I feel that I ought not to close without alluding to another matter of great importance to dairymen—a matter that has too long been neglected. It is the necessity of breeding and rearing stock for the dairy.

I have already drawn largely on your patience and good nature, and shall not inflict further by discussing the breeds best adapted for dairy stock. This is a matter which may be left for individual preference and experience. But the question has occurred, whether some plan might not be fixed upon whereby the whey at factories could be used to advantage for rearing calves. We have reached a point where something must be done to replace the stock that has been swept away during the war. Milch cows are now extraordinarily high, and must continue so for some years to come, or until a surplus can be made up by raising stock for this purpose. Dairymen should have commenced raising calves from their best milkers at the commencement of the war, and our herds now would have been kept up to the maximum standard as to numbers and quality, instead of being mixed up with a heterogeneous compound of miserable scrubs—mere refuse stock—gathered from all over the country, and pushed into the dairy region, and sold at monstrous prices. But it is too late now to go back to "by-gones," and the question is, how best to get out of our present difficulties.

Why cannot calves be fed upon whey at factories, each farmer, if necessary, erecting stalls and inclosures for a certain number of animals, and feeding daily, in addition to the whey, a certain proportion of shippings, or oil meal? In this way good calves can be raised, and at small expense. I have seen calves do quite as well upon whey, and a little oil meal or shippings, as in the usual way in which they are reared upon milk, and the cost comparatively was a mere trifle.

There is no time now to present a matured and well considered plan for erecting stalls and feeding-troughs, so as best to conduce to the health and thrift of the calves while at the factory; but the main suggestion is offered, with the confidence that among so many practical men it can be turned to good account.

That whey may be fed to calves in this way at more profit than when employed for swine there can scarcely be a doubt. Whey-fed calves the past fall have been sold in Herkimer county at twenty dollars apiece, and, at such prices, it is evident the whey could be turned to profitable account.

Dairymen:—I urge you, in good faith, to take action in this matter of raising stock; and I warn you that unless a general movement in this direction is taken the coming year, disastrous consequences will follow. You cannot go on as you have done, in a wholesale slaughter of calves, blindly exterminating a race of milkers, now nearly extinct, but which, had it been fostered and improved in years past, would have given you a reputation scarcely inferior to that which you have acquired in the manufacture of cheese. Had your best calves from deep milking stock been saved and improved upon, who can say but that to-day you would have had a type and race of milkers that would stand unchallenged for the dairy "the world over."

Now you scour the country, and throw away your money

upon scrubs and "stump-tail cattle," for the purpose of filling up the herds, realizing from them no profit, but wasting your substance and labor to no purpose. I tell you, my friends, the time has come when we must wake up from old notions and old systems, in order to meet the necessities of the age. We must have milkers that will turn out annually their 600 or 700 pounds of cheese per head. There is no difficulty in the matter, if we pay attention to the breeding and rearing of our own stock, and in securing the requisite food for their maintenance.

FOOD FOR THE PRODUCTION OF MILK.

I have but a word to say about food for the production of milk.

I know that there is difference of opinion in regard to which is most profitable, old or recently re-seeded pastures. But the fact is beyond dispute, that good old pastures will not only fatten cattle more rapidly, but produce a better quality of milk—that is, milk having a larger per centage of butter, than newly seeded grounds. Perhaps the quantity of milk from the same herd may not vary materially, but that from the old pastures has more butter in it, and is therefore more valuable. During the past two years I have traveled over a considerable portion of the New York dairy region, and made an examination of many farms, and when I have been able to get at statistics, I find it to be the general rule that the largest product of cheese on individual farms has been obtained where the cows fed upon old pastures.

CONCLUSION.

My friends: I have briefly alluded to some of the new features of the dairy, and what seems to be its present needs. None of us have, as yet, reached the end of improvement in dairy farming. Review, for a moment, the history of agriculture for the last twenty years. Mark the progressive improvements, which have become more numerous and more important every year, and you will not fail to be convinced that the tide of progress is rolling onward with an increasing power, and that our future advances will be even greater than the past.

You may rely upon it that dairy farming in all its features is destined, at no distant date, to become one of the most interesting branches of national industry, and in its prosecution the highest ability will be demanded. For this reason it becomes of the deepest interest that those engaged in its practice should be men of intelligence, having a clear knowledge of the processes of nature, with which they are so constantly brought in contact; for then they will be prepared to record their results with accuracy, and to deduce therefrom correct opinions, which will lead them forward to a perfect knowledge of the true principles upon which their practice is based.

"Contradiction *cannot* exist between the principles which science dictates, and the experience which is derived from practice. They are the same in their origin, as well as in their character. The laws of nature are fixed and definite, and a knowledge of these laws constitutes what we term science. But whilst the laws of nature are definite, it must be remembered that they modify each other; and the results consequently vary according to the several agencies which are called into operation. In proportion as we become more fully acquainted with the laws and operations of nature, so shall we be more competent to combine our opinions and form correct theories."

POULTRY: PROFITS AND MANAGEMENT.

[The demand for eggs and poultry in the markets of this country, to say nothing of their consumption in country families, is very great and is annually increasing. Still it is seldom that poultry is kept here in such a way that the owner can tell whether it is profitable or not. In Europe, especially in France and England, this business is often managed quite systematically. Near some of our large cities the keeping of poultry is lately engaging considerable attention. To make any business profitable, however, it must be understood. As serving to illustrate the principles involved in poultry-raising, the following extract from a lecture by Mr. J. A. Clarke, late of the English Royal Agricultural College, is transcribed:]

Fowls, like other living creatures, require a lodging. Royalty, nobility, and so on, may build palaces of stone-work, with verandahs, cupolas, fancy castings, ornamental wire-work, glass, &c., but birds, though beautiful themselves, are not gifted with æsthetic taste, and there is no need whatever for their home to be picturesque and genteel. Do not make an erection ugly, when the cost will be little more for a design that will be pleasant to the eye; but beware of building a sumptuous residence, that might easily swallow up in interest all the profit you can hope to make by its inmates. The shelter adapted for a farm-yard, and for a farmer who earns his living, need be only of a simple description. Arthur Young prescribes, in his "Farmer's Calendar," that, if a woman is kept purposely to attend to the fowls, she should have her cottage contiguous to the fowl-house, that the smoke of her chimney may play in the roosting and sitting rooms; poultry never thriving so well as in warmth and smoke—an observation as old as Columella, and strongly confirmed by the quantity bred in smoky cabins in Ireland. This is all very well, barring the smoke. What we should study is a warm situation and aspect, sheltered from and shut against north and north-east [and other cold] winds, with no sharp draught through the house, yet with a sufficient current from ventilation; and the higher the apartment the healthier for the birds. I think a plain structure of studs and weather-boarding quite as good as a brick building; the main defect with most farmeries being the small number of separate rooms and houses. It is not sufficient to have a sitting-house, roosting-house and laying-house for hens, a house for turkeys, another for ducks, and so on. Fowls require separation, according to sex and age, and you cannot have too many houses, boxes and pens about your premises, in order to accommodate them all. The roof should be perfectly weather-tight. The floor is not so well of brick or stone slabs as of earth, well rammed down, and covered with loose gravel. This is to avoid harboring the great pests of the hen-house, fleas. Dimensions will be very much matters of fancy; but shun overcrowding. Architects often plan roosting-houses with perches one higher than another, rising like a ladder from floor to ceiling, taking care that one is not placed directly over another, as in that case the droppings of the upper row would fall upon the birds below. But all lofty perches are objectionable; heavy fowls injure their feet in jumping down; for though they will fly up or walk up a ladder to bed, they will generally take the shortest cut down in the morning. The best plan is to have perches al on a level, two to two and a half feet from the ground; the best perch being a wooden bar of three or four inches in breadth; and, if supported by legs, like a stool, so as to be readily moved, so much the better. Clumsy birds, like Cochins, [Shanghais, &c.,] prefer to roost at even lower elevation, unless a very easy ascent is prepared for them. It is not necessary to have a separate house for laying, provided the nests be at the side, far enough from the perches. But a sitting-house should be prepared, in order that the sitting hens may not be disturbed by the other fowls. I need scarcely urge the importance of cleaning out the houses, say twice a week, and of once or twice in the summer cleaning and lime-washing the whole of the interior. Various notions are seen in the matter of nests. Some poultry-keepers have a number of wooden cells, like pigeon-holes on a large scale, with a hinged door, or a slide, in front, to fasten in unsteady sitters, and to keep out intruders. The nests in my own hen-house are simply rectangular cells, made of board, 20 inches high, and 18 to 20 inches long and broad, set upon the floor, and close to the wall—a bar running along the front edges of the boards, to keep the eggs from rolling out. But round shallow dishes of wicker are good; so also are shallow pans of earthenware, half filled with sand; and some managers prefer simple cells of loosely laid bricks. As to the proper fibrous or other material for bottoming the nest, avoid long straw, for this is liable to pull eggs out of the nest by getting entangled about the hen's legs. Hay, again, is safer, but harbors abundance of vermin. The best materials are cocoanut refuse or short straw, dusted with flowers of sulphur, to expel vermin, while a sod with rough grass on it makes a good and moist foundation for all. Where you have several sorts of fowls, of course you must have a number of distinct houses, each with its small enclosed "run," or yard. Wire netting, eight feet high, will keep most breeds, and you must have close boarding at the bottom, two feet in height, to prevent the cocks pecking at each other, and to keep birds of both sexes from spoiling their heads in the sharp meshes. But one of the greatest points in poultry management, even when you have only one sort, is to avoid congregating many birds in one building, or upon the same ground; neglect of this precaution often brings disease that depopulates whole yards. If only a single farm-yard is at your disposal, and your cottagers are afraid to take in young broods on account of their scratching propensities in gardens, you had better put up little houses, like enlarged dog-kennels, remote from each other, in all parts of your grounds as spaces about plantations, shrubberies duly fenced from the flower-garden, and so on. Here place little colonies of chicks, when their mothers forsake them, and you will be surprised to see how fast they will grow, with feeding added to the myriads of insects and seeds which they glean from their apportioned run. People have fancies about coops and rips. My hints are, have them large enough, cheaply constructed, able to keep out the rain without requiring pieces of sacking to be thrown over them, and closed at the ends, as well as at the back. You may add a wire front, to be shut at night against weasels and rats.

You can buy some of Mr. Baily's nobby poultry-fountains; but if you are not afraid of breakages, crockery ones will do. Or you may use a large flower-pot dish, with a flower-pot placed inside it to keep the chickens and ducks out leaving a ring of water for them to dip their bills in. Fowls also want a dust bath; that is to say, a box, or what is better, a glazed earthen-ware pan, of fine sand and wood ashes; in this the birds "rootle," dusting their plumage, and dislodging and destroying parasites. It is always well to have bricklayers' rubbish, slacked lime, burned oyster-shells, coal ashes, and gravel lying about a poultry-yard; besides being sweetening and sanitary, they afford the birds pieces of hard material, as fine stones and bits of mortar, so indispensable for the milling action of the gizzard.

I come now to the general management of fowls. When you keep hens for their eggs only, the proportion of hens to one cock is immaterial, infertile eggs being as good as others for the egg-cup and cookery. It is best, however, to let twenty or thirty hens follow a champion and protector, who takes care of them finds food for them, and often with true gentility, sees that all are supplied with pickings and scratchings before partaking of anything himself. For breeding strong, healthy chickens, give only six or eight hens to one cock, though a young bird may have ten. The old fashioned plan is to breed in-and-in, from the strongest "cockerels," (that is, cocks in their first breeding year; after arriving at the adult age of six months); rarely introducing a purchased bird for "change of blood." But prize-poultry men know very well that a dwindling progeny is a sure result of breeding from closely-related fowls, while there is no more common cause of disease. A cock will work well for a couple of years; if he be a favorite, you may keep him three years, if the young birds do not "whip" him and wear out his life. My pratice is to keep sixteen females in a farm-yard, with a second-season cock, (or "stag,") and a young cockerel for his first season; this difference of age insuring the mastery to one of the warriors, and so preventing repeated and desperate duels. It would be far better to place the two cocks, with eight hens each, in separate yards—so avoiding innumerable bad eggs. A pullet hatched early in spring begins to lay at the approach of winter, and pullets hatched late in summer begin to lay in the ensuing spring; and it is by saving a certain proportion of pullets from the early and late broods, that you make sure of winter eggs, a few very early hatched chickens for catching the highest markets, and a numerous flock of chicks the warm months, when rearing is least precarious.

The hen continues in her prime for two, and, at most, three years; therefore, save every year pullets equal to a third of your brood stock, selling off at a trifling price the same number of aged hens, or offering them up in a stewed dish or well-baked pie. However, I have no scruple about keeping a heavy, symmetrically-made, splendidly-feathered "partlet" for four years, for the sake of her stock. Many farmers grumble about their poultry, from not paying attention to such a simple matter as their not looking over their brood stock once a year, drafting all the old dames, known by the developed scales on their legs, and reserving from the market-basket the most promising young pullets raised during the season.

In a general way, it is not worth a farmer's while to try for very early chickens. For midsummer show purposes, and in the neighborhood of large cities, where 10s. or 12s. or more per couple can be obtained for extremely forward birds, it may pay well, but the labor and trouble demand great perseverance. A pullet saved from an early "clutch," will lay in December, and hatch in January or early in February; but she must sit on only seven to nine eggs, and if she hatches half a dozen chicks, you may consider it very good luck for that cold season. The clutch must be shut in a warm room, with dry earth, gravel, or ashes, to run on, as a stone or brick floor will cramp the chickens' legs almost as surely as wet earth or grass. The nights are so long that the time between one daylight feed and the next, would be starvation to the little creatures; so that you have to feed by candle-light, (without ever omitting,) late at night and early in the morning, laying the food upon a black-painted board, and shining the light upon it while the chicks are picking. March, April and May, hatching is a much easier matter, and the second brood, (for a good sitting breed hatches twice, and sometimes thrice, during the year,) will come in July, August and September. Late hatches should be avoided.

As laying time comes on with the opening year, when the combs of the pullets begin to redden and their bodies enlarge, be diligent and liberal with your feeding; more particularly because frost and snow often deprive the birds of their "shack," and insects, worms, &c., being scarce, animal diet should be provided in their place. Of course, grain is the staple food—as whole corn, with tail wheat, that usually has much "split" among it, and a proportion of bruised oats. Mashed potatoes, "creed" rice, soaked bread, garden vegetables, make good changes in the diet; and paste or barley-meal, or oat-meal, &c., is advisable for getting up and preserving "condition." To promote laying, give the hens the bones and scraps of meat and fat from the dinner-table; indeed, waste nothing eatable out of the kitchen and pantry, and do not scruple to rob the pig-wash tub in favor of your fowls. A capital addition is a quarter of a pound of horse beef among half a dozen hens, given three times a week. And bullock's liver, and again sheep's entrails, boiled, chopped and peppered, are supplied with excellent effect. Keep to regular feeding hours, twice a day being sufficient, but three times all the better, (I am speaking now of adult fowls,) and scatter no more food than the birds will eagerly and quickly devour. Extravagance leaves half the provender to be gleaned up by flocks of sparrows, and makes poultry-keeping expensive.

Look up eggs daily, or oftener if you please, for fear of thieves, or of frost in its season, of course leaving the necessary nest-egg. And you may use pieces of chalk, porcelain eggs, or eggs turned in wood and painted white, to entice the hen to her nest. One of the annoyances of fowl-keeping is being deceived by your eggs, having to throw them away rotten from under the patiently-sitting hen. Perhaps you cannot always guard against this evil. For the sitting-house may be warm enough, the nest not too dry, the eggs well preserved, and not too old, and yet failure ensue. In fact, cold weather will sometimes conspire against your management, and eggs will be infertile in spite of your proper mating of the sexes, your careful treatment of the eggs, and your good feeding the sitting hen to keep up the warmth of her body. But at any rate adopt every known precaution. Avoid shaking the eggs when selecting them, place them in boxes in preference to drawers, which shake all your eggs every time they are opened or shut. The slightest touch of frost is fatal; so place the eggs in bran or chaff, laying them on their side, and turning them over every day; because the hen almost always brings off a full clutch when she has "stolen" her nest in some secret retirement, and her eggs are laid on their side, and turned about by her getting on and off her nest. A good plan is to pencil-mark the day of the month on the side of each egg when you put it by; then you turn the marks down one day and up the next; and you can see the age of every egg you select for sitting. The fresher the egg the better; still you must always have a sufficient number in reserve, lest several hens should want to sit at one and the same time. Eggs for consumption may be packed in bran, or in salt, or kept in lime-water, for almost any length of time, placed with the small end downwards. Of course the parentage of an egg is the main point in determining the probable character and quality of the bird; but the size and shape are of some importance. Small, rounded eggs, laid by pullets, may bring fine birds; but their earliest eggs are not worth hatching. Choose an egg of medium size, (an extremely large one may contain two yolks, and prove an abortion,) well formed, without any rib or flaw, and with the air-vessel distinctly marked at the top of the egg when this is held end upwards between the air and a candle. Some persons pretend that the air-vessel when in the centre foretells a cock, while towards the side it betokens a pullet.

When a hen is "broody," or inclined to sit, she clucks, as if calling chickens—which perhaps she sees in imagination; and a young pullet had better be proved with an egg or two, whether she is a steady sitter, lest a seat of valuable eggs should be spoiled by her forsaking them; though eggs are not always ruined by getting cold, after a few days' sitting. Cruel means are sometimes resorted to for making a hen sit when she is not disposed, and still more unfeeling practices are adopted to prevent a hen sitting when she is wanted only for egg-laying. But I strongly condemn all attempts at confining a poor bird, and making a mother of her against her will; while the prevention of sitting is easily accomplished, (in case a seat of eggs turns out rotten, and the hen persists in her expectation of chicks,) by continually disturbing the hen, shutting her up where she can find no eggs, and by cooling her incubation fever with a cold-water bath. To make a hen sit in the place you choose, you have only to take her from her stolen nest at night, and cover her over for a time. Re-line a nest before sittting a hen, sprinkling a little sulphur to banish fleas as much as possible; and it is well to barricade her at first against being disturbed by other birds. The proper number of eggs in spring and summer will depend upon their size, and upon the size of the hen, ranging from eleven to sixteen, or even more. The hen will commonly leave her nest every day for food and water; but if you have boxed her in, you must take her off once a day, and bear in mind that as she has now no exercise to aid digestion, the food should consist of a little hard, but principally of soft substance, as oat-meal, or barley-meal paste, chopped cabbage, lettuce, and so on. If you find later eggs in the nest, remove these unmarked eggs, seeing that they would not hatch simultaneously with the others; this point, however, requiring most attention when you have crossed-bred hens among others of some valuable breed. Book the date of each sitting, and on the ninth or tenth day examine the eggs, (in Lincolnshire we call it "shiring,") by holding them between your eye and a beam of light—as a candle in a darkened room. If an egg is right it will appear quite dark, except a small clear disc at the top; if the egg appear semi-transparent throughout, it should be taken away, as it is infertile, would probably become rotten, and yet, at this stage of the proceedings, makes a good dinner, boiled hard and chopped up, for a brood of chickens. The hen sits twenty-one days, generally sitting very closely during the last week; but if through any accident the eggs are left to get cold (in that week) the birds may sometimes be hatched by another hen, or by artificial warmth. To avoid the common disappointment of chicks dead in the shell, damp the eggs daily during the last week, either dipping eggs in lukewarm water or sprinkling a little cold water on the eggs from a brush. Moistening the poros shells prevents the lining membrane from becoming so hard and dry that the poor little chicks cannot break through it; and you need not be afraid of the operation, as a hen generally damps her eggs in a stolen nest from getting her feathers trailed in wet or dewy grass and herbage. Look frequently at a hen as her term draws to an end—taking away any rotten eggs, which might explode and kill a half-hatched chicken; and remove the earliest chickens, to prevent the mother running off with them, and leaving the rest to die in the shells. Young managers are wont to feed their new-born treasures too soon, as if fancying that the little prisoners must be hungry because they had nothing to eat all the time they lay doubled up in their shell. But the rule is, no food of any kind for twelve hours; all they want is heat. Beware here of old wives' nostrums. If a baby is born it must at once learn that it has entered into the world of drugs, by swallowing a dose of castor-oil, just "to clear its little stomach." If a cow calves she cannot prosper until she has eaten the placenta; and a chicken must not only have the nib taken off its beak, and the beak dipped in water, (which is all right enough,) but must have a nasty, hard, black pepper-corn forced down its throat—I suppose to be conducive to its misery and destruction by at once irritating and weakening the digestive organs. Give the chicks plenty of bread soaked in milk, a few bread crumbs, and roughly ground wheat-meal, wetted with lukewarm milk (skim-milk will do,) of such a consistence that when a little ball or pellet of it is thrown upon the ground it will break and scatter about in particles. After a few days vary the diet with cheap chicken-rice, creed soft, and a scanty allowance of whole grain, which should be fine, small screenings of wheat. Vegetables—as cabbage and onion tops, chopped fine—make a nice mixture with other food (potato, however, is too scouring); and every other day you may give each clutch a hard-boiled egg or a little mutton suet, chopped fine. In fact, study frequent changes of diet. For the first fortnight chickens need almost hourly feeding. If they have a good "run" among grass and shrubs, in warm dry weather, thus picking up abundance of insects, they will want proportionately less food; but never offer them more than they eagerly run after. Both hen and chickens must have clean, often-renewed water within reach, arranged so that the chickens cannot get their legs in, and so the hen cannot upset it. Let the coop be daily moved to a fresh patch of ground. In warm weather the hen, after the first week, may be let out during the day, provided she be a good mother; for some wild and tiresome hens will trail their little ones to death, over-walking the poor little things, and at least hindering their growth. In cold or wet weather coop close, and place the clutch in a house at night. The length of time for cooping (say two or four weeks) depends upon the weather, the vigor of the chickens, and the quiet or straying habits of the mother

—some hens being awkward in a coop, trampling very young chicks to death, and so requiring plenty of room or earlier liberty. When two hens come off at the same time, let one take both broods, if in summer, that the other may lay again the sooner; but in cold weather one small clutch is plenty for one mother to cover and find food for.

A common error is to coop successive broods in the same small enclosure, probably because this is near to the kitchen-door, and convenient for the constant attention which is required. But separation is a main point in rearing healthy birds. Distribute your coops about your yards, of course choosing safe and sunny places; and if your early broods occupy a space before your house, you may put the later broods on a plot behind, and so on, always allowing a considerable interval to elapse before following upon the same ground, to avoid getting the walk "tainted," as it is termed, with liability to disease.

It is a modern practice to separate the sexes at two months old, or earlier, sending the cockerels to a yard by themselves, as they are found to thrive better, and live together without quarreling. And here comes in the advantage of having several yards at considerable distances apart; in fact, separate poultry establishments upon the same farm, which may often be contrived in connection with bailiffs' or laborers' cottages.

A well-fed fowl taken from the straw yard is very nice eating; but beyond this, you may have a very heavy and thoroughly fat as well as delicately-flavored fowl. This is when they have been "put up" to feed. At three or four months old—younger in summer and older in winter—shut the fowls in a confined space, as in a coop or hutch, giving the birds room to sit or stand, but to turn around and move about only with difficulty, the bottom being made of longitudinal round bars, on which the fowls perch, and between which their droopings fall. This coop must be under cover, and in a warm and rather dark place. A V-shaped trough of wood, or better of earthen-ware or glass, is placed along the front of the coop, receiving three times a day as much food as the birds will eat at once, and being immediately after cleared out.

Mr. Bailey prescribes oat-meal and milk, mixed slack, but not quite liquid, the consistence being such that if some of it is placed on a board it will slightly spread. Fresh water should be accessible in pans, and a little gravel given occasionally. It is indispensable to feed at sunrise, the birds making no progress if suffered to get hungry. Their term of confinement should be a fortnight, or rather less, if they were in good condition when put up, and if they have been kept quiet, without any introduction of a strange or quarrelsome companion. It is not often that birds will preserve their health for three weeks of such treatment.

Cramming is not a refined practice, but as money is made by it, and the punishment to the fowl is not worthy of mention in comparison with the horrors of caponizing, I must describe it. The oat-meal is mixed considerably stiffer than as last mentioned, and the milk of which it is made may have a little mutton suet boiled in it. The paste is formed into "crams," rolled up dry, each as thick as a little finger, and nearly a couple of inches long. Six or eight of these elongated boluses are administered morning and evening, being dipped in milk or pot liquor, to make them go down "slick" and easy.

Mr. Bailey's description of cramming is as follows: "The fowl is placed in the lap, the head is held up, and the beak being held open with the thumb and finger, a cram is introduced into the gullet; the beak is then closed, and the cram is gently assisted down, till it reaches the crop. Care must be taken not to pinch the throat, as ulceration would follow, and the fowl would be spoiled." Water and gravel should be provided, for the birds to help themselves; and if they seem to require it a little food may be placed before them at mid-day. "Before the second feed is given, the crop should be lightly felt, to ascertain if it is empty. If not, the morning meal has not been digested. The fowl must be taken out immediately, and the beak being held open, as if for cramming, some warm water or gruel shoud be poured down the throat, and the beak closed. This will soften the food; but if more food were forced into the crop, on that already hardening there, the bird would become crop-bound—*i. e.*, the food would become solid and indigestible, and the fowl would be totally spoiled for the table, if it did not die." A machine on the principle of a force-pump has been employed, by which one person can cram a dozen birds in seven or eight minutes.

You judge the fatness of a fowl by feeling if the breast is plump. The skin under the body should also be thick and fat, and fat may also be felt under the wings. Cadgers in the poultry markets are accustomed to nip the rump laterally with the finger and thumb: it should be thick, fat and firm.

When you have successfully bred, reared and fattened a prime young fowl, that is to be a delicate dish on your table, it is very disappointing to have all your pains nullified by the indiscretion of a cook. Tenderness is a quality that can be secured by keeping the bird long enough between the slaughtering and the spit; and to make it keep well for a couple of days in summer, or much longer in cool weather, fast the fowl twelve hours before bringing it to the knife.

DISEASES.—On the subject of diseases I shall add little. Poultry books are generally half-full of diagnosis and remedies; but in few farm-yards is a troublesome manipulation of cocks and hens, or an elaborate preparation of pills and drinks, likely to be followed up. A great deal of quackery, as well as a great deal of learning, has been printed on this subject. You can consult some of the valuable hand-books which great authors have published; and all I can do in this brief lecture is to point out a few of the commonest ailments, with the most effectual modes of treatment. For diarrhœa, mix cayenne pepper and chalk in gruel, or with meal. If a purgative is required, give a teaspoonful of castor oil, or a little jalop made into a pill with butter. For indigestion, when a chicken is suddenly taken with a convulsive fit, the legs straightening out, and the crop hard, pour warm water down the throat, and next day feed on soft food.

For mange or loss of feathers, scarring of the comb, etc., give small quantities of sulphur and nitre, mixed with butter. When birds suffer too much, and are long "on the moult," try a little extra stimulating diet, as hemp-seed, buckwheat, animal food, and that great restorative, bread soaked in ale. When chickens get the pip, gaping, with a horny excrescence on the tongue, tear off the hard substance with your thumb-nail, administer pills of rue and bread, or made of scraped horse-radish and garlic, with a grain of Cayenne pepper, and supply plenty of clean water. Roup is a very dangerous and infectious malady—a very plague among fowls. The premonitory symptom is, that the skin hanging from the lower beak and to which the wattle is attached, is inflated and emptied at every breath —the same hoarseness and difficulty of breathing as if from a cold. Give a table-spoonful of castor-oil, and a few hours after, give one of Baily's valuable "roup and condition pills." If there be rattling in the throat, with a fœtid discharge from the eyes and nostrils, wash the eyes, nostrils and inside of the mouth with vinegar. Mr. Ferguson Blair gives this prescription: "Take of dried sulphate of iron, in powder, half a drachm; capsicum, in powder, one drachm; extract of liquorice, a sufficient quantity to make a mess, which is to be divided into thirty pills; one to be given three times a day, continued to the end of the third day, and then followed by a second prescription. This is: Half-an-ounce of sulphate of iron and one ounce of Cayenne pepper, in fine powder. Mix carefully a teaspoonfull of these powders with butter, and divide into equal parts, one to be given twice a day."

Gapes is another common disease, arising from small white worms in the trachea. Grain, wetted with spirits of turpentine, is one medicine; camphor in the drinking water is another; but a complete means of cure is of a surgical kind. Take a hen's tail-feather, stripped all but an inch at the end; put it down the hen's windpipe (not the gullet), twist it once or twice round, and withdraw it, with the worms adhering to it. This is an operation, however, "more easily said than done."

A descriptive and historic account of the various popular breeds, with the special purpose for which each may be valuable, does not come within the present lecture;* and I now proceed to offer a few hints about other poultry besides fowls.

Ducks, clever as they are at taking care of themselves, are somewhat difficult to manage, as far as "good luck" with sittings is concerned. The wild duck being monogamous, shows that only a few ducks should be allotted to one drake—say five or at most six; four would be all the better. As the treading generally takes place upon water, the duck diving at the time, the birds must always have free access to their favorite element, not necessarily in a pond, for a tub a foot and a half deep will suffice. And as they are of very early habits, you must either provide a tub of water in their house, or else let them out very early in the morning. Certainly there are few districts where it is safe to have ducks out in a yard or wandering "worming" about the pastures all night. *Apropos* of the tub, bear in mind that a duck *can* be drowned as readily as any other animal; for, if too long in the water with the feathers saturated, the poor bird will sink; therefore, form your tub so that your ducks can easily get out. Ducks are wonderfully fastidious about their nests. In frosty weather you must take away the eggs; and as the ducks will lay thirty or forty eggs, you can hatch them under hens, which, indeed make by far the better nurses. March is early—April is a better month for ducklings to come off, as they like warmth no less than water. The duck must be closely cooped for the first week, or she will tire out, and so kill her young; she must be apart from any other duck, to prevent the little ones from going to the wrong coop, and being seized by the wrong mother's sharp bill; and she must be away from pond or stream, lest the ducklings should get their legs cramped with the cold. Let the duck have a saucer or dish to drink from, and let the ducklings paddle in a shallow tray

* The lecture was one of a series.

placed a yard or two from the coop, to prevent accidental slopping and soaking of the tender little birds. In very dry warm weather this discipline need not last more than a few days; then move the duck and coop to the margin of a pond (still apart from other ducks as they and drakes too, are very vicious, and apt to bill off a whole brood in a few minutes); and when the ducklings are a fortnight old they may be separated from their mother, driven to the water in the morning and shut up in a house at night. Beware of having deep pans or buckets of water where ducklings and chickens can have access to them keep none but very shallow drinking vessels for your poultry; empty your stable-buckets when not in use, and float pieces of board in your horse and cattle watering places. The first food for ducklings is bread soaked in milk, or paste made of barley-meal and new milk; malt flour is also used, as more fattening. You may give also boiled rice and potatoes, and small wheat soaked, with frequent treats in the way of flesh. But with muddy ponds to luxuriate in, they need little else than an opportunity of filling their crops with meal paste.

Turkeys require very great care and attention; yet, where the hen-wife makes them her pets, and studies their welfare in every way, she at any rate (whatever the farmer himself may say,) may find them profitable. The turkey-hen lays one egg every thirty hours, and should be put upon a dozen eggs, and fed with corn and water. She sits a month. When the chicks come off—taken one by one as they escape out of the shells, and wrapped in flannel—they are commonly made to swallow a pepper-corn each, as well as to drink a little water. They need no food for twenty-four hours, and will then pick what is placed before them. Their food should be hard-boiled eggs, chopped very fine, or curd with bread crumbs, and boiled nettles and green onions finely minced. Coop the hen for a fortnight, and then let her ramble with her young, being warmly housed at night; but beware of the least wetting by rain. A critical time with them, is at a little over two months old, when the male and female markings begin to appear, and the birds are called turkey "poults." Boiled vegetables, meal, grain, and various seeds are employed in feeding them. After harvest, they will range the stubbles, and many hen-wives " top-up " their favorites by cramming for Christmas markets.

I conclude this imperfect lecture, with two or three hints on the management of geese.

A gander should be mated with three geese—certainly not more than four,—and perhaps two would be a luckier number. In her first breeding season, the goose has few goslings; but after that, remains in her prime for years. She lays from twelve to twenty eggs, but with high feeding will sometimes lay thirty, or even forty. You should get two hatches in a year In the middle of February, the goose is commonly inclined to lay, and evinces her condition by running about with straws in her mouth, as if nesting. Watch her, and when she drops an egg, take the goose and the egg and fasten her for a while upon the place you have prepared for her laying and sitting. A few board boxes, with straw-thatched top, answer very well for geese, and are best placed beside a pond, and in a sheltered situation. She may sit upon from ten to fifteen eggs, according as she is a young or old bird. Her time of incubation, is one month; and a little aid in breaking the shell is sometimes necessary; but beware of making the partially hatched gosling bleed. If one goose comes off just about the time another is due, fasten the latter on her nest, to prevent her, perhaps, leaving her eggs to spoil, upon hearing the "croodling" cry of her neighbor's young ones. The goslings want no food for twelve hours; then give bread soaked, with boiled potatoes, &c., and provide a sod of grass for the little bills to pull at, with plenty of water for them to drink. Keep them out of the water for a few days, sunshine being their best food, and rain their fatal enemy. Shut them up for some days, and when they go out, watch them in windy weather, as a gosling blown upon its back cannot readily get on its legs again, and may die.

Grass and herbage are the main food of geese; but fatten them upon oats and meal. A goose put up to fatten, eats a pound of oats daily—for the first week—and three-quarters of a pound daily afterwards; a goose in good condition, off stubbles, being fattened on oats and water in three weeks.

When a goose's feathers are "ripe," they should be plucked off—an operation that gives but little pain to the bird if properly performed, and at the right time. The feathers under the wing are always left to hold up the wings, which would otherwise trail upon the ground. It is usual to pluck three times in the season, one goose yielding a pound of feathers in three pluckings.

In some well-watered districts, geese are profitable; and in a very growing season, they do little damage to the pastures. In dry summers, however, they are very injurious, pulling up much good herbage by the roots; and what is worse, in badly watered localities, fouling and spoiling the ponds for horses and cattle.

PUBLIC SHEEP-SHEARINGS:

ON WHAT PRINCIPLES SHOULD THEY BE CONDUCTED?

Although a chapter was given under this head in my report for 1865, the observations made during another year teach that more may be said on the subject before it is generally viewed in a proper light. A greater number of public shearings was, probably, held in the country in 1866, than in any former year, and the interest manifested in them does not appear to diminish.

The first question which presents itself in regard to these meetings is, What ends are sought to be accomplished by them? They are generally held under the supervision of agricultural societies, or wool-growers' associations, whose ostensible objects are the improvement of agriculture, or some branch of that interest. If it be asked, what constitutes improvement? it may be answered that in the case before us, it is the production of some marketable article at an increased profit. It may be an article of superior quality, for which an extra price is obtained, or the improvement may consist in producing an increased quantity of an article in proportion to the cost. In any view, it can have no reference to what is not intrinsically valuable.

Whether these principles have governed all persons who have been influential in getting up the so-called "sheep-shearing festivals," is a matter on which nothing need now be said; but it may be beneficial to the public to consider the management and results of these exhibitions. The leading idea in reference to them in the outset, seemed to be the display of fleeces of unusual weight as taken from the sheep in an unwashed condition. Little attention was paid to the quality of the wool, and less to the actual quantity (when separated from extraneous matter) which the fleece might contain. Some relation, however, between the weight of the body of the sheep and the weight of the fleece was early recognized, and premiums were offered for the heaviest fleeces, grown within a certain period, in proportion to weight of carcass. The effect of these premiums was of course to lead wool-growers to endeavor to obtain fleeces of the greatest weight, whether the weight consisted of wool or something else. It was soon found, however, that weight was more readily added by a substance which was not wool, and which did not increase the value of the fleece.

That the tendency of this course was to divert attention from the really valuable properties of sheep, and to establish in their place those of no value, except as a basis of mere speculation, was obvious to all persons capable of reflection. As a means of correcting the evil, it was proposed to offer premiums for scoured or cleansed fleeces of the greatest weight in proportion to the time of their growth and the live weight of sheep producing them. This was a step, and but a step, in the right direction. It would show how much real wool the fleeces contained; but it had no reference to the quality or value of the wool, or the cost of producing it. Like the premiums offered for the heaviest uncleansed fleeces in proportion to the live weight of the sheep, it only provided for taking the weight on the day of shearing, so that no light whatever was thrown on the average live weight of the sheep during the time the wool was growing—a fallacy which alone was sufficient to destroy the basis of comparison.

Previous to 1865, no attempts appear to have been made by any association to ascertain even the quantity of actual wool comprised in a fleece. That year a premium of fifty dollars was offered under the auspices of the New York State Wool Growers' Association, for the heaviest scoured fleece in proportion to weight of carcass, and considerable competition was brought out. The Jonesville Association in this State offered premiums for scoured fleeces the same year. The principal facts elicited in both these cases, were published in my report for 1865.

In 1866 the New York Association issued a programme for scoured fleeces on a more comprehensive scale, though still falling short of what is required to bring out all the important facts involved. The scale of prizes and the requisitions pertaining to them were substantially as follows:

1. Best Merino ram's fleece of about one year's growth, giving the greatest weight of scoured wool in proportion to the time of its growth and the live weight of the animal. 2. Best Merino ewe's fleece, under the same conditions as specified above for the ram's.

3. Best Merino ram's fleece of about one year's growth, giving the greatest weight and *value* of scoured wool in proportion to the time of its growth, without reference to the weight of the animal. 4. Best Merino ewe's fleece, under the same conditions as specified in the third case.

5. Best fleece of English long wool, of about one year's growth, giving the greatest weight and *value* of wool in proportion to the time of its growth, without reference to the weight of the animal.

6. Best fleece of English middle wool, with the same conditions as specified under the preceding head.

Prizes were awarded in these six classes, according to the prescribed rules. What can be learned from them, or what facts do they establish in regard to the comparative profits of the sheep to which the prizes were awarded? Take the prize under the first head. The "*best* Merino ram's fleece," might at first glance be thought to mean the fleece that is worth the most money "in proportion to the time of its growth, and the live weight of the animal;" but it must be observed that "the greatest *weight* of scoured wool in proportion to the time of its growth and the live weight of the animal," is the specification. It may be asked, what was the word "best," put in here for? If the premium was to be awarded to the fleece of the greatest *weight*, according to the time of growth and the weight of the animal, what has the word *best* to do with it? Why not simply say, for the heaviest fleece, &c.? If, however, it was intended to take quality into consideration, why not say the premium would be given for the fleece of the greatest *value*, &c.? In calculating the value, weight would, of course, incidentally come in. But the premium was undoubtedly intended to be awarded, and was awarded, without other reference to the value of the fleece than would be indicated by its weight. The public is, therefore, without any special information as to the value of the fleece, either considered by itself or as compared with any other in competition with it. As the prize awarded under the second head was based on the same principles as that under the first, nothing more in regard to it need be said.

The requisitions in the third and fourth classes are, that the fleeces shall give the greatest weight and *value* of scoured wool in proportion to the time of their growth, without reference to the weight of the animal. What idea can be obtained from this in regard to the profit of the fleeces to which premiums are awarded? No element of cost is considered except time. Again, why is it said "greatest *weight* and value of wool," if the premium was intended to be awarded, as seems probable, for the greatest aggregate value of fleece? If the object really was to ascertain which was the most valuable fleece, why couple with value the greatest weight? The fleece produced within the stated time that is *worth most* should have the premium, if that is the point aimed at, no matter whether it is the *heaviest* fleece or not. The *value* is the overruling principle, the weight merely incidental. But the committee probably ignored the ambiguity of the terms in which the premium was offered, for they seem to have been governed only by the value of the fleece, and that to which they awarded the premium was not the heaviest according to the time of growth. They gave the premium to a ram whose carcass after being shorn weighed 124.75 pounds; whose fleece, 338 days old, weighed, unwashed, 16.24 pounds; scoured, 5.12 pounds, valued at $1 per pound, making the value of the fleece for the year $5.52. A competitor which stood third in valuation, weighed 152 pounds; fleece, 364 days old, weighed, unwashed, 22.57 pounds; scoured, 6.635 pounds, valued at 80 cents per pound, making the value of the fleece for the year $5.32—twenty cents less than the value of the premium fleece, although the weight of scoured wool for a year's growth was more than a pound more. The premium was, therefore, awarded to the most valuable fleece grown within the specified time, though the fleece did *not*, in the language of the requisition, "give the greatest *weight* and value of wool in proportion to the time of growth."

Thus far, comprising the first four classes, the competition was restricted to Merinos. The fifth class included only English Long-wools. No distinction of age or sex was made, and the same ambiguous terms were employed as in classes three and four. The sixth class refers to English Middle-wools, though the only competitor presented—and no doubt seems to have been expressed as to his eligibility, for he took the premium,—was a South Down, the *shortest* wooled of all the English breeds.

The tables given in the report of the committee not being suited to our page, a table which presents the main facts in a more condensed form, is copied from the *Country Gentleman:*

1. *Merino Ram Fleeces in Proportion to Live Weight of Sheep.*

Animals in Order of Merit.	Weight of Carcass.	We't of Fleece Unwashed.	We't of Fleece Scoured.	Age of Fleece in days.	Quant'y grown in one year.	PRIZE COLUMN. Quantity produced by 1 lb. of animal in 1 year.	
1, ...	73.25	14.515	5 03	364	5.04	.08424	
2, ...	92.25	12.06	4.03	366	4.00	.04315	
3, ...	88.50	13.93	3.93	380	3.79	.04292	
2. Merino Ewe Fleeces in Proportion to Live Weight.							
1, ...	57.75	10.295	4.545	364	4.63	.08030	
2, ...	51.25	9.50	3.87	360	3.909	.07628	
3.	46.25	11.50	3.325	345	3.515	.07592	
4, ...	44.75	9.385	3.28	377	3.168	.07081	
5, ...	50.50	9.93	3.34	360	3.373	.06679	
9, ...	62.50	11.605	4.00	364	4.007	.06387	
7, ...	60.25	12.885	4.65	485	3.452	.05730	
7, ...	50.50	7.795	2.945	404	2.617	.05183	
3. Merino Ram Fleeces in Proportion to Value.							
						Per lb.	Total.
1, ...	124.75	16.34	5.12	338	5.5261	$1 00	$5 52
2, ...	123.50	17.96	5.28	355	5.4275	1 00	5 42
3, ...	152.00	22.57	6.635	364	6.6539	80	5 32
4, ...	110.00	16.695	5.21	344	5.5261	96	4 94
5, ...	116.25	12.87	5.03	345	5.2158	1 00	5 21
6, ...	93.00	12.765	5.635	405	5.0771	98	4 97
7, ...	127.00	19.71	5.265	360	5.1538	96	4 94
8, ...	115.00	15.37	5.105	394	4.7267	96	4 53
9, ...	105.75	17.21	5.03	407	4.4201	1 00	4 42
10.	87.50	13.135	4.84	410	4.2194	96	3 98
11, ...	115.25	15.00	3.65	345	3.8580	98	3 78
4. Merino Ewe Fleeces in Proportion to Value.							
1, ...	77.00	14.06	5.295	364	5.3071	98	5 20
2, ...	65.75	17.43	5.885	403	5.2633	96	5 05
3, ...	103.50	16.635	4.695	375	4.5698	1 00	4 56
5. Long Wool Ram Fleeces in Proportion to Value.							
1, ...	100.25	10.795	9.03	355	9.2819	77½	7 39
2, ...	209.00	13.575	8.135	335	8.8612	80	7 08
3, ...	125.00	11.65	8.03	355	8.2563	75	6 19
6. Middle Wool Ram Fleece.							
1, ...	161.75	8.105	4.75	340	5.9845	70	3 49

The animal which took the premium in class one, was owned by Theron Steele. In regard to him, the committee remark that he "was entered for the scoured-wool prize in 1865, but owing to the competition of ewes in the same class, was as low as No. 11 in the order of merit, though a comparison will show that he did better then than now."

The ewe which took the premium in the second class, was owned by A. H. Clapp. It is the same ewe which took the

"Moore prize" of $50,—the only prize offered by the Association—in 1865. Her weight after being shorn, was 57.75 pounds, being a gain of 8¾ pounds since she was shorn in 1865, at two years old. She gave that year, 9.6 per cent. of scoured wool in proportion to live weight. This year she gives 7.88 per cent. The committee remark that she came to the show a few days after having dropped her lamb. They also say that five different ewes which competed in this class, would have beaten the best ram, had they competed in the same class, as they did last year.

The owner of the ram which took the premium in the third class, was Wm. H. Pugsley, and the owner of the ewe which took the premium in the fourth class, was Wm. R. Pitts. It is proper to notice the course taken by the committee in making their decisions in these classes. They say that in determining the value of the wool, they placed the cleansed fleeces side by side on a table, "so that the comparison by eye and touch was easy and satisfactory. The relative value was the point aimed at, and the committee took one dollar per pound as the standard for the best fleeces, and rated the others accordingly, not intending to say what the wool would sell for." The committee state that of three ewes which competed in the fourth class, the one which took the premium, competed in 1865, then standing No. 4 in the order of merit. "It will be seen by comparing the tables that she has now produced more wool per day than in 1865." She is three years old; but it is not stated whether she has had a lamb. The ewe which is reported third in the order of merit, in this class, is stated to have been nine years old, "her age placing her at a decided disadvantage in the contest."

Two Cotswold rams and one Leicester were the only competitors for the prize in the fifth class, and it was taken by a yearling Cotswold, owned by E. Gazley. He weighed 100.25 pounds, after being shorn, in a condition called "fat;" fleece, 355 days old, weighed, unwashed, 10.795 pounds, scoured, 9.03 pounds, giving for a year's growth, 9.2819 pounds of scoured wool, valued at 77½ cts. per pound—$7.39. The fleece of the

32

other Cotswold ram in this class was valued at 75 cts. per pound, and that of the Leicester at 80 cts. The reasons for this difference are not obvious, especially why the Leicester wool was worth more than the Cotswold.

There was only one claimant for the prize in the sixth class —a South Down ram, age not mentioned, owned by J. Lynch. The requisitions in this class were the same as in classes three and four. The shrinkage of the fleece in scouring was very large for South Downs, being nearly fifty per cent.; yet it will be seen that the quantity of scoured wool produced in a year was greater than that of any Merino, except one. In valuation, however, it stands lowest of all to which that test was applied. The committee say: "Comparing the South Down with the Cotswold prize ram, we have sixty per cent. more of animal, and forty-seven per cent. less in value of wool."

The committee call particular attention to the weights of the sheep as compared with the weights of the cleansed fleeces; "because," they say, "they are important as indicating the cost of supporting the animal." But it must be borne in mind that these weights were only taken once during the year, and that at the time of shearing; which is far from affording satisfactory evidence of the average weight for the whole time the wool was growing.

The committee call attention to the fact, that in the Merino classes in which value of the scoured fleece is made the basis of the prize, there were eight fleeces of five pounds and less than six pounds each, with only sixty-three hundredths variation, while these same fleeces, uncleansed, varied *six pounds*. "This shows," continue the committee, "how valueless are the published weights of uncleansed fleeces, that abound in the newspapers. The business of the wool-grower is to raise wool, and he may well inquire whether the cost to him of these excessively heavy uncleansed fleeces, is not more than a prudent manufacturer can afford to pay."

The gentlemen composing this committee, were George Geddes, Chas. Tallman, Jas. M. Ellis, Wm. A. Duncan and H. D. L.

Sweet. It has been thought proper to thus notice the results brought out by the New York Wool-growers' Association, because the plan on which they were based approximates more nearly to what is wanted than any other as yet proposed, though still falling much short of perfection.*

It does not appear that any effort was made to institute a fair comparison of the aggregate profits of sheep—either those of different breeds or those of the same breed. The rules, in fact, do not comprise all the points necessary to show the relative profits of sheep in regard to their *wool*, while nothing is attempted in reference to the value of their carcasses for mutton. The great point in which the public is interested, is the aggregate profits of sheep, or the returns they give in mutton and wool, in proportion to the cost of keeping. It is desirable, of course, to know what profit they give in wool though this is but a part of the knowledge wanted.

Conceding the correctness of the basis assumed in the New York trials, some interesting comparisons may be instituted. For instance, on the supposition that all sheep consume food in proportion to their weight, and that the weight taken at the time of shearing is a fair criterion in reference to the average for the time the wool is growing, we may take the money value of the fleece in proportion to the weight of carcass, as the standard of profit in reference to wool. Comparing thus the Merino prize ram in class three with the Cotswold prize ram, we find that 100 pounds of the Merino gave $4.45 worth of wool, and that 100 pounds of the Cotswold gave $7.37. If we compare all the sheep whose fleeces were subjected to valuation, viz., fourteen Merinos, three Long-wools and one South Down, it will be seen that the per centage of value is in favor of the Long-wools; the Merinos standing next and the South Down considerably lowest. The great shrinkage in scouring of some of the heaviest Merino fleeces has already been noticed in extracts from the report of the committee. It was not, how-

*It is true that the prizes alluded to were offered by individuals, under the auspices of the New York Association; but this does not affect the principles involved.

ever, greater than in some other cases. In the report of a committee of the Illinois Wool-growers' Association, for 1866, it is stated that the fleece of a Merino ram shrunk in scouring 78½ per cent.

A large number of reports of sheep-shearings, or, "sheep-shearing festivals," so-called, held in this and other States in 1866, have been collected. Only one of those received from this State makes any reference to scoured fleeces; that one being the report of C. M. Fellows, Secretary of the Southern Washtenaw Wool-growers' Association, whose meeting was held at Manchester, on the 4th of May. Premiums were offered on scoured fleeces, both for Merinos and Long-wools. The wool was not subjected to valuation; rams and ewes competed together. In Merinos, the first premium was awarded to W. B. Dean, for a two-year old ram, whose weight after being shorn was 86 pounds, fleece (time of growth not stated) unwashed, 13 pounds 9 ounces; scoured, 6 pounds 9 ounces. The second premium was awarded to J. S. Wood, for a yearling ewe, weighing 60 pounds; fleece, unwashed, 10 pounds 4 ounces; scoured, 4 pounds 8 ounces.

In Leicesters, the first premium was awarded to C. M. Fellows, for a yearling ewe weighing 69 pounds; fleece, unwashed, 8 pounds, scoured, 5 pounds. The second to E. Wallington, for a yearling ewe weighing 90½ pounds; fleece, unwashed, 9 pounds 6½ ounces, scoured 5 pounds 14 ounces.

At the same exhibition a two-year-old Cotswold ram, owned by E. Wallington, weighed, after being shorn, 267 pounds, his fleece, unwashed, 17 pounds 8 ounces. A yearling Leicester ram, owned by C. M. Fellows, weighed 125 pounds; fleece, unwashed, 12 pounds. The fleeces of these animals were not scoured.

There were 141 sheep on exhibition, mostly Merinos. Only 41 were shorn to compete for the premiums, the weather being so cold that it was deemed unsafe to divest the sheep of the protection afforded by their fleeces. The premiums, except those above noticed, were awarded to the sheep giving the greatest weight of fleece, unwashed, in proportion to the weight of carcass. It does not appear, from the report, that any specifications were made in regard to the time of growth of the fleece, though that may have been considered by the committees.

For reasons which must be obvious from the foregoing remarks, it is not thought necessary to notice particularly awards made on this basis. They present nothing tangible in reference to the actual quantity of wool, its value, or the profit afforded by the sheep. As the writer was, however, present at this exhibition, he deems it proper to state that he has seldom seen at a similar gathering, so many sheep of equal merit, as were here collected. It is to be regretted that the rules of the Association were not such as to demonstrate to the public the superiority of those to which premiums were awarded.

It should be stated that the Michigan Central Agricultural Society held a sheep-shearing exhibition at the State Agricultural College, Lansing, in May last, at which there were many entries for premiums offered on scoured fleeces. But the destruction by fire of the factory at which the fleeces were to have been cleansed, defeated this object.

Can any better system than those hitherto noticed, be devised in reference to the offering of premiums at these public sheep-shearings? In considering this question, let it be decided in the first place, what facts it is desired the premiums shall bring out. If the subject is examined in a true light, it will be seen that the only proper basis for the premiums is the relative profits of the sheep in the production of either wool or mutton, or both combined. Keeping this constantly in view, it will not be difficult to arrange a programme. Several classes of premiums will be required, and it will be advisable to arrange the classes in reference to the purposes for which the different kinds of wool are adapted; as,

1. Felting wools adapted to the manufacture of fine broadcloths, of which the Silesian and Saxon may be taken as the type.

2. Felting wools adapted to the manufacture of goods of less fineness, but consumed largely for the manufacture of cassimeres, doeskins, &c., and represented by what is known in the market as full-blood Spanish Merino.

3. Wools adapted to the manufacture of delaine goods.

4. Long or combing wool, adapted to the manufacture of worsted goods, imitation alpacas, &c.

It may not in every case be expedient that premiums should be offered for all these classes; each association must decide for itself what kinds of sheep it will encourage the improvement of. It will be essential to ascertain the relative profits of the sheep for the production of wool, whether attention is given to the aggregate profits of wool and mutton or not. Premiums should be provided for the exclusive competition of sheep producing the same kind of wool. This should show which are most meritorious in reference to this object.

Having gone through with these classes, another should be established comprising *all kinds or varieties of sheep included in the general list*, premiums to be based on the *profits of wool and mutton.* A proper arrangement of the results will show the relative standing of the different competitors as to quantity and value of wool, quantity and value of mutton, and the aggregate value of these products. This, which may be called a *sweepstakes* class, will be the most important of all; because, if proper regulations are made and observed, it will show what sheep afford the greatest profit under the specified conditions.

The requisitions to be observed by competitors may be next considered. It has heretofore been assumed, in fixing the rules to be followed in the award of premiums at sheep-shearings in this country, that sheep consume food in proportion to their live weight. The principle is probably fallacious when applied to sheep of all breeds collectively, but may be generally correct in its application to those only of the same breed. Conceding its correctness in such cases, it affords a convenient basis for comparing the cost of sheep. If the object is to ascertain the quantity of wool produced in a given time, in proportion to the live weight of the sheep, it is not enough to weigh the sheep once only, and that at the time of shearing; they should be weighed at the commencement of the time specified, and with such frequency during the period of trial,—at least once a month,—as will furnish data for ascertaining the *average* live weight while the wool is growing. Animals of the same age should compete together, to make fair comparisons. It would afford a better idea of the positive merits of animals, if the amount or value of the product for which the premium is offered could be known for a longer time than one year; hence, besides offering premiums where only one fleece is produced by each competiter, it would be well to have a class embracing the product of the same animals for two or three years. This would be a pretty good test of the comparative value of the animals for the object in view.

The Committee of the New York Wool-growers' Association in their reports, notice the fact indicated by the trials under their supervision, that "for the mere production of wool, very large sheep are not desirable." This seems to be the case; but at the same time it may not be advisable to encourage for propagation, sheep of so small a size as may sometimes produce the greatest quantity of wool in proportion to live weight. To obviate this it may be well to fix on some weight which the competing sheep shall reach to entitle them to a premium. The standard may vary with different breeds—less weight being expected for a Merino than for the English breeds. Perhaps 50 pounds, without the fleece, for yearling Merinos, 60 pounds for South Downs, and 70 for Long Wools, with a corresponding weight for older animals, would be low enough.

The sweepstakes class would require most attention, and be necessarily attended with most expense. For this reason it will hardly be expedient for every association to attempt such an experiment as would be required. But the advantage of a fair comparison of breeds under similar conditions,—although it would not show positively their relative profits under all other conditions,—would be so important that associations having sufficient means at command, might accomplish much good by instituting and carefully carrying out such experiments.

The object should be to ascertain what breed or variety of sheep will return most money, in proportion to the expense of keeping, within a given time. In reference to this the fairest way would be to commence with the animals as near as practicable to the time of their birth, and turn them to the butcher at a given age—say two years old. It may be objected that this is rather an early age, but it should be remembered that quick returns are important in reference to profits, and it should be a prominent point in the experiment.

The sheep entered for competition should be placed in the hands of a person selected to conduct the experiment, under full and minute directions as to feeding and management. A given number—not less than three of each breed—should constitute a lot. The exact age should be known, and the different lots should be as near the same age as practicable. Lambs, taken at weaning-time—say four months old—would perhaps be the best subjects that could be had for a fair comparison. Let them be put on good grass, where all can have as much as they will eat, and if anything besides grass is allowed them—and it may be advisable to give something—let all have the same kind and quantity. It would, of course be most satisfactory to know just what each lot consumes; but while they are at pasture this is hardly practicable. In winter or house-feeding, however, this can be more readily ascertained; and it may be reasonably assumed that the proportion eaten by each lot during this season, might be taken as a fair basis of comparison for the time they are grazing.

When it is time to commence winter feeding, let the different lots or breeds be divided; all fed on the same kind of food, and an exact account kept of the quantity and cost of that eaten by each lot. All should have as much good hay as they will eat, with specific quantities of roots or grain. On a given day, as near to the time when the sheep are a year old as the season or weather will admit of, they should be sheared, the fleeces weighed in the dirt, and laid by until the second year's fleeces are ready.

All the sheep should have plenty of grass the second season, and during the second winter should be fed with a view to fattening them—all being allowed as much nutritious food as they will eat with a good appetite. A strict account of the food consumed by each lot should be kept, as during the first winter.

As near as practicable to the time when the second fleece has attained a year's growth, let the sheep be sheared again, and the fleeces weighed as before. Then let the fleeces produced in the two years be scoured, the quantity of cleansed wool in each fleece be ascertained, and the wool sold, or appraised by competent persons. Let all the sheep be slaughtered as soon as practicable after their second fleeces are taken off, and the carcasses sold to the best advantage.

The final account should show the live weight of the different lots of sheep at the commencement of the experiment; the cost of all the food they have eaten, except grass, the weight of wool in the dirt, and the weight and value of scoured wool produced by each sheep in the two years; the live weight on the day they were killed, and the dressed weight and value. The premium is to be awarded to the lot which shows the greatest profit.

It is not supposed that a single experiment of this kind would settle all the points involved; but if the experiment is fairly conducted, and several times repeated, various important facts would undoubtedly be established.

IMPROVED AGRICULTURAL IMPLEMENTS AND MACHINERY.

Perhaps no one thing has had a greater influence on the general welfare of the country, than the substitution of machinery for manual labor in agricultural operations, in connection with the various improvements of agricultural implements.

It can scarcely be realized by the younger portion of the agricultural community, that within the memory of persons still living, all the implements of the farm were of the most rude and clumsy description. The shovel was either of wood, or wood with a strip of iron doubled over the edge and riveted. In using it, the earth had to be loosened with a pick, and in some cases hauled on the shovel with a hoe. With no better tools than these did the soldiers of our Revolution dig their intrenchments. But they had the satisfaction of knowing that their enemies worked with no better tools, though they might have been better supplied as to numbers.

The first step towards a better kind of shovel, was the making of one of rolled iron, with an eye, into which was driven a straight stick for a handle. Even this was regarded as an important improvement. It was sometime afterwards before a shovel was made that could be forced into solid ground, or used to much extent except as preceded by the pick or iron bar. To Yankee ingenuity are we chiefly indebted for the modern shovel; and the name of Ames, which within the last sixty years has been stamped on millions that have been sent to every quarter of the world, is justly regarded as that of a public benefactor.

In priority of improvement, however, that important implement, the axe, may be said to have somewhat taken the lead.

In the demolition of the immense forests which lay before the American settler, the improvement alluded to seems to have followed on the principle that "Necessity is the mother of invention." The poet well describes the result:

> "With the pioneer axe what a conquest is made,
> What an empire of wealth has been won!
> What regions redeemed from the wilderness shade,
> Now rejoice in the beams of the sun!"

The vast work required to be done by this simple implement, rendered its utmost effectiveness a matter of great importance. Its principles were studied, and the ill-shaped English and Dutch axes were displaced by those whose form and weight comprised the proper points. Such was the contrast, that the American axe has acquired a name and fame unequalled by any similar implement.

Our mechanics also took the lead in the improvement of hay and manure forks, rendering them lighter, and of such shape that much more work could be done with them, with the same expenditure of strength, than with the old kind.

Improvements in ploughs within the present century, and chiefly within fifty years, have been of immense importance. The saving effected in both manual and team labor, is great. The old-fashioned wooden plough, whose mould-board was either left bare, or covered on the furrow-side with old hoes and other bits of iron, required double the force to drag it through the soil, that is required by our best iron and steel ploughs; and this extra team frequently made it necessary to add another driver. If the ground was much stony, a hand was required to follow the plough to bear on the beam in the worst places; and if it was sod ground, a man went along with a strong hoe, to aid the ploughman in turning the furrow-slices. With all this force, the work was not as well done as it is now.

Something has also been gained in the adaptation of ploughs to special purposes. Light soils require to be ploughed in a different manner from those which are too heavy, and ploughs of different construction are required for the respective objects. Quite different ploughs are also required for rough and uneven lands, and those which are smooth and level. Ploughs are now made with reference to the particular kind of work they are to do.

Great saving in manual labor has also been effected in the improved construction of horse-hoes, grubbers, cultivators, seed-drills, &c., resulting at the same time in better cultivation and an increased yield of crops.

But the most striking innovations on the old routine, have been those connected with the harvesting of crops—more particularly hay and the smaller grains. If the use of the mowing and reaping machine should be at once discontinued, it would produce a shock that would be felt over the civilized world. And yet the introduction of the machines in which such vast interests are involved, is quite recent. Without intending to raise the question of the date of invention, as between this and other countries, it may be safely assumed that in practical applications, the palm must be awarded to American mechanics; and scarcely twenty years have elapsed since the economical use of reaping and mowing machines in this country could be said to be an established fact. Ketchum's machine as a mower, and Hussey's as a reaper, may be considered the pioneers. The latter it is true was early used as a mower; but its work in grass was far from satisfactory.

At the show of the New York State Agricultural Society, at Buffalo, in 1848, Ketchum's machine was tried in second-crop clover. Farmers who witnessed the trial were hardly prepared to admit that the work was on the whole good enough to be tolerated as a substitute for the scythe. Some who had previously used it, stated that it would do very good work in straight, coarse grass, like timothy, but in fine, thick grass, was liable to clog. But the machine was soon improved in reference to its capacity of cutting lodged and fine grass.

In 1852, the New York State Agricultural Society instituted a trial of reaping and mowing machines, in connection with other farm machinery, at Geneva, in that State. Unrestricted competition was allowed. Seven machines were tried as mowers, and nine as reapers—three reaping machines which were entered for the trial not arriving on the ground till after the adjournment of the judges. Very few—not more than two or three—of the mowers were capable of equalling the scythe in quality of work; and even these, when brought to a stand, could not be started without backing and getting up speed. All the machines had an objectionable side-draft, and in some it was so great as to render their use very difficult, as well as severe to teams. There was difficulty in turning, and most of them were very liable to tear up the sward in the operation, notwithstanding that they required much room. To Manny's combined reaper and mower was awarded the first premium as a mower and the second as a reaper. Ketchum's machine took the second premium on mowers, and received nearly one-half the votes of the judges for the first premium. These were the only machines which as mowers showed themselves capable of cutting grass in a manner that would induce a good farmer to allow them to enter his fields.

Of the nine reapers tried, those of Burrall, Manny and Seymour & Morgan were given the preference by the judges, in the order here named. The work performed by them was quite satisfactory. The report of the judges states that a fair comparison of the work of the best machines with manual labor in the use of the cradle, shows a saving of 88¾ cents per acre in favor of the former.

But most of the reaping machines were very defective in regard to the execution of their work; the draft was very heavy, and the side-draft of some which in other respects were considered about the best, was "killing" on the horses. The only attempt at self-raking was made by Atkins's Automaton Reaper, which here made its first public exhibition. It left the grain in a tolerable condition for binding. Its complication and liability to derangement, were, however, apparent.

The results of this trial clearly indicated that the cutting of grass and grain by machinery was "manifest destiny." Many of the most inventive minds, and those of the most thorough mechanics, in all parts of the country were turned to this subject. Machines rapidly multiplied, and as they were brought before the public they were closely scrutinized, and the peculiar features of each taken due note of. Competition was a great stimulus to improvement, and the numerous machines, each possessing some novelty, aided to show the combinations necessary to a perfect model.

After the lapse of only five years from the Geneva trial, a general interest was manifested in regard to having one on a scale or plan that would bring together all the mowing and reaping machines in the country. A "national" trial was therefore held at Syracuse, N. Y., under the direction of the United States Agricultural Society, in 1857. Upwards of forty entries of mowing and reaping machines were made. When they were brought to the test, it was easy to see that great improvements had been made since the Geneva trial. Both the direct and side-draft were materially lessened, though the latter was still, in some machines, quite large. The ability of mowers to cut fine, thick grass was another point of improvement. Even the two which were so far ahead of the rest at the Geneva trial had gained something in this respect; while others had made a great advance. Still of the nineteen which were tried as mowers, only three could start from a stand in thick, fine grass without backing, or leaving grass imperfectly cut. The Buckeye mower, now and for several years past so widely known, competed in this trial, and received the first premium.

Perhaps the general improvement manifested in reapers was less striking than that in mowers. The most prominent point was self-raking. Besides the Atkins machine, several other self-rakers entered the trial, among which was that of Seymour & Morgan, of Rockport, N. Y., which even then gave hopeful indications of the success which it has since attained.

It is proper to say that during the five years that elapsed between the Geneva trial and that at Syracuse, various trials were held in different parts of the country, nearly every year;

but there was no trial which elicited competition from all sections. The same may be said in regard to several years subsequent to the Syracuse trial. But when nine years had passed, it was thought by many leading agriculturists that sufficient advance had been made to justify the bringing together the leading machines of the country.

The New York State Agricultural Society, through whose influence so much had already been done in originating and disseminating improvements in agricultural implements and machinery, resolved on holding a trial at Auburn, in that State, in the summer of 1866. The New York Legislature, appreciating the importance of the object, made an appropriation of $6,000 for defraying the expenses of the trial. It was commenced on the 10th of July. The number of entries for mowers, single and combined, was 44; for reapers, 30—making a total of 74. Nearly all these were tested. Comparing the machines with those in the Syracuse trial of 1857, it may be said that a general improvement was presented in finish and workmanship. The mowing machines in particular, were more compact; more simple in their construction, with fewer parts; generally lighter, though not less strong; running generally with less friction, and less draft, and, except in a few cases, with much less noise. The best machines at the Syracuse trial had, however, been improved but little—the difference being chiefly in the superior style of workmanship of the new ones. But the points of superiority possessed by a few machines at the Syracuse trial have been to a great extent adopted by others. This is the case in reference to their ability to cut tough grass, whether thick or thin, or tall or short, and to a considerable degree in cutting on uneven surfaces. Besides being tested in clover, in which upwards of forty machines were engaged, twenty were tried in a meadow where the surface of the ground and the character of the grass were such as to make a severe test of the cutting powers of the machines. The following extract from the Report of the judges will give some idea of the manner in which the machines acquitted themselves:

"Those who had been present at former trials, were astonished at the general perfection which had been attained by the manufacturers of mowing machines. Every machine, with two exceptions, did good work, which would be acceptable to any farmer; and the appearance of the whole meadow, after it had been raked over, was vastly better than the average mowing of the best farmers in the State, notwithstanding the great difficulties that had to be encountered. At previous trials, very few machines could stop in the grass and start without backing for a fresh start. At the present trial, every machine stopped in the grass and started again without backing, without any difficulty, and without leaving any perceptible ridge to mark the place where it occurred."

The Buckeye mowing machine, manufactured by Adriance, Platt & Co., of Poughkeepsie, N. Y., received the gold medal as the best mower. When it is considered that the Buckeye stood first at the Syracuse trial, and that after nine years of progress it still maintains its position, the genius and skill of its inventor must be admitted. It should be observed, however, that many more of its competitors in the late trial approximated to the position of *rivals*, than in the trial of 1857.

In reaping machines, the most prominent advance has been in making them *self-rakers*. Eight entries were made in this class, and seven machines were tried. It is doing no injustice to say that some of the self-rakers performed better in the various circumstances in which they were tried, than any of the hand-rakers. In the scale adopted for quality of work, the mark of 40 denoted perfection. The work of Seymour, Morgan & Allen's self-raker, called the "New Yorker," was marked, in standing wheat, 39; in lodged wheat, 38; in rye, 40; in barley, 40. The work of C. C. Bradley & Son's Syracuse self-raker, was marked as high in standing wheat, only one figure lower in lodged wheat and barley, and three lower in rye. No other reapers showed so good a record in quality of work—taking all their work.

On the whole, it seems to have been demonstrated that for the future it is inexpedient to offer premiums for hand-raking reapers, as self-rakers are capable of entirely superseding the employment of manual labor in this case. It may be well to say that the first premium for self-raking reapers at the Auburn trial, was awarded to Seymour, Morgan & Allen, of Brockport, N. Y. This is another instance of a machine that stood first of its kind in 1857, occupying not merely the same position in 1866, but having advanced to one of still greater importance. The second premium for self-raking reapers was awarded to C· C. Bradley & Son, of Syracuse, N. Y.

But though the most striking improvements in reaping machines, as shown by the Auburn trial, were those already alluded to, others of no trifling importance were obvious. Many of the machines, including several of the self-rakers, were able to cut lodged and tangled grain to much better advantage than any could nine years before. This was a point particularly noticeable. A leading New York farmer, witnessing the operation of some of the reapers in heavy wheat, that was apparently *twisted* down by a whirlwind, observed that he was then seeing what he had previously never expected to see—self-raking machines cutting clean grain, in such condition, and leaving it in a fair state for binding.

Another point, applicable alike to reapers and mowers, was doing away with the side-draft, which was formerly so serious an objection. Of sixty machines tested for side-draft, at Auburn, one was found to show 11 lbs., which was the highest; one showed 10 lbs., one 8¼ lbs., two 7½ lbs., while seventeen showed 5 lbs., or less—many standing as low as two to two-and-a-half pounds, and several showing none at all.

Before dismissing the subject of reaping machines, it should be mentioned that a machine was exhibited—though no provision was made for it on the programme—which was calculated to have men ride on it and bind the grain as fast as cut. It was from Illinois, and was called the Marsh Harvester. It did not work satisfactorily, the grain, perhaps, being too heavy and too much lodged down. It seemed to embody a good principle, and if more perfectly built might answer the purpose. In fact, it is stated that much grain has already been secured with it in Illinois. It is not, perhaps, improbable that this machine and some of the self-binders will be made useful.

Other implements and machines were brought out at this trial which deserve notice. The clover and grass having been cut by machines, whatever stirring it was thought necessary to give the hay before it was put in cocks, was done with tedders, of which two kinds were entered. Bullard's, which was the best, is spoken of in the report of the judges, as having been "thoroughly tested in clover, in timothy and in fine grass—in windrows as well as in swath. It received the unanimous approval of the judges, and we believe of all farmers who saw it in action. We think the introduction of this machine will be of the greatest importance to hay-makers. * * * * Every kind of hay, when worked over by the tedder, was cured with much less exposure to the sun than would otherwise have been possible. * * * * The machine tedded an acre of heavy clover easily in 15 minutes, while the horses were walking at a natural gait (for the driver was not aware that we were taking his time), and four acres an hour was the average time of all the trials which we made with it."

The hay having been cured and ready to be put in the barn, a trial of *machines for loading* was made. Two such were presented—one by Niles & Gillette, of Little York, Cortland county, N. Y., the other by Foust & Stratton, Evansburgh, Crawford county, Pa. A description of the machines will not be attempted here, as persons interested can apply to the patentees or venders for descriptive circulars. With the aid of the first mentioned machine, the report says: "Three men put a load of hay on a wagon in twenty-two minutes." With the other machine, "three men put a load of hay on the wagon in nine minutes. Two of these men were employed in spreading the hay upon the load, and one drove the wagon." The cost of loading hay by hand is computed at twenty cents a load, and the cost of loading with this machine at seven and a half cents a load. But the interest on the first cost of the machine and the repairs annually required are to be taken into account. In conclusion the report says: "We are of opinion that both of these machines show a gratifying progress in the right direction, but that they are not sufficiently mature, either in contrivance or in mechanical execution to warrant the award of the Gold Medal of the Society."

Proceeding in the usual order, the next thing to be done was to unload the hay, and this brought to the test *forks worked by horse-power.* Thus the grass was cut by horse-power, the hay tedded or stirred by horse-power, raked by horse-power, loaded by horse-power and unloaded by horse-power. In some instances, after all this has been done, the hay has been finally trodden in the mow by horses.

Five different forks were presented, which were classified by the judges as follows: The short-handled fork, of which Palmer's is the type; the long-handled, represented by Gladding's; the double fork, like the Raymond; the mixed kind, in which the central tine only is duplicated, like the Little Giant, which was entered for exhibition only and not for competition; and the harpoon fork, like that of Walker. The fork of A. B. Sprout, of Muncy, Pa., differed, however, from either of the others, it being a *hay-knife and fork* combined.

For working in hay only, some of the harpoon forks, including Sprout's, showed more rapid execution than any others. The latter, at the first test, pitched 1,810 pounds of hay over the beam at five pitches, in 2 minutes 30 seconds; in the second test, it pitched 2,360 pounds into the mow (not over the beam), at six pitches, in 2 minutes—one horse only being used.

Walker's improved horse-fork, exhibited by Wheeler, Melick & Co., Albany, N. Y., pitched 2,735 pounds of hay, over the beam, at 15 pitches, in 12 minutes 50 seconds; and 2,115 pounds, under the beam, at 7 pitches, in 2 minutes.

Some of the other forks were deemed better adapted to general purposes, especially to handling grain in the straw, than the harpoons. Gladding's, exhibited by J. L. Mansfield & Co., of Clockville, N. Y., to which was awarded the first premium, pitched, at the first test, at thirteen pitches, 2,120 pounds of hay, in 3 minutes 10 seconds; at the second test, 1,985 pounds, at ten pitches, in 2 minutes 10 seconds; at the third test, pitched over the beam, 1,500 pounds, at eleven pitches, in 3 minutes 20 seconds; and at the fourth test, pitched over a beam 22 feet 5 inches above the floor, and 5 feet 8 inches below the rafter, 1,990 pounds, in 8 minutes 50 seconds.

The judges awarded the first premium to the Gladding fork, because they considered it the "best for general purposes. It is light, cheap, durable, and rapidly and conveniently operated; it is adapted to various situations; can be used in narrower places than any other, and distributes the hay in the mow better."

The second premium was awarded to the Raymond fork, a description of which is given on a preceding page of this report.

A special premium was awarded for Sprout's combined knife and fork. The report says: "We give the second premium to the Raymond fork because it is applicable to barley and oats, as well as to hay, which has not been proved with respect to Sprout's fork. But we are much impressed with the value of this combination of the hay-knife and fork. For farmers who have nothing but hay to pitch, who have plenty of horse-power, and sufficient of room to swing in, we think there is no instrument in use better adapted for their purposes; while its excellence as a hay-knife is unsurpassed, and as a whole will prove a valuable instrument for any farmer. * * It enters the hay with ease and is tipped with celerity and certainty. It gathers a single pound of hay from the barn-floor as easily as an ordinary hand-fork, and holds it more securely. It is one of the best hay-knives we have ever seen. As a knife it will rapidly cut hay in the mow into blocks, and as a fork remove it to any place that may be desired. It is apparently indestructible, and will last a lifetime." It weighs 11 lbs. Price for fork alone, $9; for fork and 3 pulleys, $11; for fork, 3 pulleys and 80 feet of rope, $15.

Other machines were exhibited at Auburn,—as threshing machines, fanning-mills, straw-cutters, &c.,—presenting more or less improvement, though characterized by no special novelty.

The Prairie States have presented the widest field for the use of agricultural machinery, and well has it been improved. By the various planters, drills and broadcast sowers, Indian corn and the smaller grains have been deposited in the ground with no more hand-labor than is required to guide the team and manage the implement; and the hands thus employed, ride over the fields comparatively at their ease, the work being done well and with great dispatch. For crops which, like Indian corn, require cultivation while growing, "sulky" cultivators are provided, on which men ride and guide horses to do the work.

Taking a comprehensive view of the saving of labor in agriculture by the use of machinery and improved implements, there cannot be a doubt that it has had a most important bearing on our national interests, inasmuch as it has unquestionably aided, in a very essential degree, in carrying the Government through the great struggle in which it has lately been involved. By the use of this labor-saving apparatus, we have been enabled to send thousands of men to the field of battle, who would otherwise have been required on the fields of agriculture; while abundant subsistence has been furnished for our home population and our vast armies; thus enabling us to prosecute the war till all our domestic enemies were subdued, and foreign ones awed into respect.

In conclusion, we may glance at the influence which has been exerted through some of our inventions on the agriculture of other nations.

At the first International Exhibition at London, in 1851, McCormick's reaping machine made a very successful performance. The result was that an arrangement was made with an English company for the manufacture of the machines in that country. They were somewhat modified in construction, and some improvements were added to adapt them to the special wants of the English farmer. Great numbers of them have been introduced, and they have given great satisfaction.

A few years subsequently to this, Walter A. Wood & Co., of Hoosick Falls, N. Y., introduced into England, Wood's improved Manny machine—a combined mower and reaper. This, too, generally performed satisfactorily as a reaper, and was well received. But the success of this and all other machines then known in Britain, was not so flattering for cutting grass. The fine, thick short grass of the old meadows in that country, required a machine that could cut very close to the ground in order to save the whole crop. Certainty of execution, also, without the liability of clogging, or leaving the grass jagged and unsightly, was no less insisted on, while the draft was wanted to be brought fairly within the power of a pair of good horses.

W. A. Wood & Co. were the first to meet this want successfully, which they did with Wood's mower, in 1859. The result was a great sale for these machines throughout Great Britain and Ireland, which has continued to the present time.

Messrs. Wood & Co., as well as McCormick and other American manufacturers of reapers and mowers, have likewise introduced their machines into France, Russia and other countries of Continental Europe, where, at the present time, great numbers of them are in use. Thus has the ingenuity of our mechanics, and the enterprise of our manufacturers, aided in making our youthful nation known and respected among the older powers of the world.

RETURNS FROM AGRICULTURAL SOCIETIES.

Although no returns have been received from the Michigan State Society, the report of a committee of that Society appointed to award premiums for the best cultivated farms, is deemed of so much importance that it is herewith presented:

PREMIUM FARMS.

The committee appointed by the Execucutive Committee of the Michigan State Agricultural Society, to award the premiums offered for the best farms in the State, entered for competition previous to July 15, 1866, respectfully report as follows:

There were six farms entered, of which five were farms of 160 acres or over, and one was less than 160 acres, viz:

1. Farm of C. W. Greene, of Farmington, Oakland county, 160 acres.
2. Farm of Ezra D. Barnes, of Burns, Shiawassee county, 220 acres.
3. H. D. Benedict, of Essex, Clinton county, 280 acres.
4. H. B. Chapman, of Reading, Hillsdale county, 220 acres.
5. J. D. Adams, of Climax, Kalamazoo county, 360 acres.
6. B. Hathaway, Little Prairie Ronde, Cass county, 110 acres.

The farms were visited by the committee in the order they are enumerated above, the first being that of C. W. Greene, of Farmington. Each was inspected with the design of following out the instructions of the Society, as laid down in the conditions attached to the offer of the premiums, and statements of the owner were taken with the design of eliciting all the information necessary to explain the system followed by the farmer, and its results.

OAKLAND COUNTY.

The farm of Mr. Greene is situated about a mile and a half from the Grand River turnpike road, and is distant from Detroit 22 miles, that city being its market. It contains 160 acres of land, of which 130 are improved and under cultivation, the remaining 30 being a wood lot, containing fine fencing and building timber. The farm is divided into 14 lots. The house, barns and yards occupy the center of the north end, along which runs the road, east and west. A lane four rods in width extends from the barn-yard and in the rear of the house to the wood lot, which is at the extreme south end. Each of the fields on this farm communicates with the lane by gates well hung and painted, on which were marked the number of the field and the quantity of land it contained. On either side of the lane the proprietor had set out shade trees, and he had also set out forest trees of the hardiest and best varieties along the fences on the division lines and along the road. There were altogether upon this farm fully 1,500 rods of fence, 800 of which were nine rails high. The balance which comprised the dividing fences between the several fields were eight rails in height; not staked. These fences were remarkable for their workmanlike neatness, and a substantial, firm and solid appearance, and were well adapted to the wants of a farm on which all kinds of domestic animals were bred and kept. A large portion of the tract of land comprising the farm had been of a wet nature, abounding in springs, which had no outlet for the water, and which consequently overflowed and rendered the most valuable sections of little productive value. So full of these springs had been this farm that many of them were found bursting out on the upland, and forming small quagmires, or shaking bogs. Draining was an imperative necessity, and after much consideration, Mr. Greene entered upon a course of improvement which tile draining formed the basis. There has been laid down on this farm fully 2,000 rods of tile drains, one-fourth of which is five-inch sole tile, and the balance comprising the branch drains, is laid with three-inch sole tile. The general depth of each drain is not less than three feet below the surface at any point. The estimated average cost of these drains was 62½ cents per rod, which includes cost of tile and hauling them a distance of six miles from the kiln, which is situated at Northville. An examination of the drains showed that they were silently, but surely and steadily performing their work, and the luxuriant condition of the crops of corn, potatoes and oats, growing where but a few years ago there was little else but sedgegrass, flags and rushes, exhibited what energy and judgment could perform when applied to the amelioration of the soil.

The farm house was a handsome structure, well located in connection with the farm, the out-buildings and the yard. The grounds around it are well laid out, and with a liberal discretion, but are not yet complete. The yards and buildings and sheds were not perfect, but are being remodeled, and, in our opinion, are not yet calculated to accommodate fully the stock and crops. The orchard comprises five acres, mostly of old trees, in a healthy condition, and designed only to furnish fruit for the family.

The farm was fully stocked to its utmost capacity, there being kept the following:

Nine horses, including one working team, one pair of brood mares, five young colts of various ages, all with a large share of thorough-bred blood in them, Mr. Greene preferring the large, active thorough-bred for all purposes, and especially on account of his distance from market.

Of cattle there were nine head, comprising one yoke of working oxen, six milch cows and one bull, the cows being shorthorn, with a cross from the Devon, and selected for their milking qualities. Mr. Greene's rule is to keep one cow for every two persons in the family.

Of sheep there were 130 head, or one for every acre of improved land, of improved Merino fine-wool stock.

Of swine, 10 head, of a cross of a Suffolk boar on the Chester-white.

The system pursued by Mr. Greene is that which is called mixed farming, and he confines his attention to rendering every acre of his land productive, and making it pay its due proportion of income. The crops of the previous year consisted of ten acres of wheat, 15 acres of corn, 30 acres of hay, 10 of potatoes, 5 acres of oats, and 5 acres in pasture. This year there are 16 acres in wheat, 20 acres in corn, 15 acres in potatoes, 20 acres in hay, and 50 acres in pasture. The wheat and potatoes are the only crops sold; all the other crops are fed out on the farm, and are sold in the shape of wool, mutton, beef, horses and pork. The potato crop on this farm is an important one, the market being Detroit, to which it is hauled by teams over the excellent graveled Grand River turnpike. To keep the farm in the highest productive state, the utmost attention is paid to the increase of the manure pile and its application to the land; hence no feeding crop is sold. The amount of labor paid for, including repairs and tools, was only $260. The average family supported was ten persons, while by an examination of the returns given to the committee as the money sales of the farm, we find that each improved acre brought in a return of $22.59½. A most remarkable result, and one which the committee take great pleasure in recommending to the attention of the farmers of the State, and especially as in this case, the whole was the produce of legitimate farming business, not mixed in any way with nursery business, or the buying and selling of stock, or trading of any kind whatever.

SHIAWASSEE COUNTY.

The farm of Ezra D. Barnes is situated in the town of Burns, Shiawassee county, 10 miles south and west of Gaines Station, on the Detroit and Milwaukee railroad, and 18 miles from Corunna and Owosso, which are its principal markets.

This farm consists of a tract of land ot 220 acres, almost in the form of a square. The soil is a rich, strong loam, intermixed with gravel and stone, and its location is very choice, being on the southern slope of a ridge that extends with a gentle slope to a rich swale that lies across its lower section, while on the south-west corner it is bordered by a small lake. The public road runs through the farm east and west, and the fields mostly open into it. For richness of soil and beauty of location, this farm is unsurpassable, and it gives a very favorable impression of the land in the southeren portion of Shiawassee. It is divided in fields ranging from eight to 20 acres in size, the whole of which are neatly f nced in with substantial eight-rail fences, in good order, and with painted gates hung on heavy solid posts and well fastened. The whole number of acres under cultivation is 150, the remaining 70 being in wood. About 50 rods of stone under-drains have been laid to take the water out of some low places, but no other drainage was needed. The house was a handsome two-story frame building, surrounded with fruit and forest trees, and inside well planned and convenient. Attached to one wing was a neat workshop in the most perfect order. The barn was 50 by 36 feet, well designed for the use of the farm, and around it were the several yards for the accomodation of the large flocks of sheep kept on this place. The grounds around the house were ample, and numbers of evergreens and other trees had been set out at an early day by the present proprietor, who was the original settler. The vegetable garden is located at some distance from the house, and it is not disturbed by the poultry. It was neatly kept and in good order. The orchard contained about six acres, and was set out by Mr. Barnes when he first settled on the farm. He has thus one of the oldest and finest in the country. He keeps it up to a good standard by grafting in the new varieties from time to time. He also grows the plum, the peach and the pear successfully, and has even tried the apricot, but the frosts have not permitted the latter to do well.

The live stock on the farm consists of one pair of horses, six milch cows, three yearlings and one calf, bred from a cross of Devon and Durham stock; 300 sheep, of which 90 are breeding ewes, the bucks being obtained from Vermont, and 10 head of swine.

Mr. Barnes makes his sheep the principal basis of his system. The strong soil makes his pastures heavy and rich, and the grass on all the fields was thick and luxuriant, and in the opinion of the committee capable of sustaining a much larger amount of stock per acre than was placed upon it. He does not grow wheat to any extent, as the insect has rendered the crop uncertain in the neighborhood. The crops last year consisted of ten acres of wheat, eight acres of oats, five acres of corn, 80 acres of hay, leaving about 90 in pasture. The crops of the present year are wheat, 40 acres; corn, seven acres; peas, eight acres; oats, six acres; hay, 40 acres, and pasture 80 acres. He also has pasturage for 150 sheep during the season. The farm supports an average family throughout the year of 13 persons, and pays out for labor $190. The average amount received last year from each acre of improved land was $12 33.

CLINTON COUNTY.

The farm of Hiram Benedict is situated in the township of Essex, in Clinton county, about 15 miles northwest of St. Johns, which is on the Detroit and Milwaukee railroad, and is the principal market, and about a mile and a half east of Maple Rapids. This farm consists of a tract of land of 280 acres in extent, and of which 220 are under cultivation. The soil is the rich gravelly red loam, peculiar to opening land, and which makes the finest ot wheat growing lands. The farm is a plain, and in its quality for cultivation is almost perfect. The whole tract has not half an acre of waste land on it. The country around is equally rich and fertile, and must become one of the finest agricultural sections in the State. The farm is cut in two by the east and west public road, and the fields lying back of it are reached by lanes that extend north and south. The fences are mostly in good condition. There was only one piece of drain on this farm to get rid of the water in a low place, as the soil drained itself. The farm is divided into six 10 acre lots, and seven of 25 acres each. The house was an elegant two-story mansion, designed to overlook the whole plain on which the farm was located; as yet unfinished, convenient in its arrangement and accommodations. The barns, sheds and yards were ample and well adapted to the system of cultivation pursued, and admirably fitted by their arrangement for the keeping of either cattle or sheep. The grounds and yards connected with the house are as yet incomplete. The orchard is irregular and contains many large and old trees, but is not designed to furnish fruit for market. As an evidence of the mild nature of the climate, we noticed that the peach trees and plum trees in grounds around the house were bearing quite fair crops of fruit.

The live stock on this farm consists of 11 head of horses, six of which are kept for the work on the farm; the other five are young stock; six milch cows, one yoke of working oxen, six head of two year olds and four yearlings, and six head of swine. Mr. Benedict makes wheat the basis of his system, using plaster and clover. Two years in clover, followed by wheat seeded, is the rotation, and his general crop of wheat occupies about 50 acres. Oats are only treated as a catch-crop, hay being the next crop. The crop of the previous year had been largely winter-killed, so that the returns did not give a full average of the income. The crops of last year and this year exhibited the following as the productive capacity of the soil: 50 acres ofwheat, average production 20 bushels per acre; 18 acres of corn, 10 acres of oats, 40 acres in hay, 70 acres in pasture, and 10 acres in clover-seed. The farm supports a family of six persons as an average the year round, and there is paid out for labor about $450. The average income from the farm per improved acre gives $9 50.

HILLSDALE COUNTY.

The farm of H. B. Chapman is situated in the town of Reading, nine miles south of Hillsdale, on the Southern Michigan railroad, and contains 220 acres, 40 of which are a wood lot of magnificent timber. The farm is divided into 16 fields, ranging in size from 8 to 20 acres. The public road is the northern boundary. Two lanes connect the fields with the barnyards, and permit any of them to be occupied by pasture lots, a brook that has been made to run along one side of one of the lanes, furnishing an unfailing supply of water. The fences were clean, and had been well taken care of, having been laid 18 years ago, with 11 feet rails, at an angle of 3½ feet. All the fields were supplied with gates. A large portion of this farm had originally been very wet, the water lying upon the surface, and held there until it was evaporated by the heat of summer. It had also been very stony. Mr. Chapman, with the energy for which he is remarkable, had readily seen that he must get rid of the stone and water if he was to make land productive, and he made the one help to get rid of the other. To get rid of the swales and marsh holes which covered the best part of his land, he has constructed 1,260 rods of under-drains, about two-thirds of which are filled with stone, and the other third being made of split timber. These drains are sunk fully 2½ feet, and cost when finished an average of 75 cents per rod for the stone drains, and 40 cents for the wooden drains. This ditching has made his fields level and dry. All of them we found very clean, with the corners of the fences as level and neat as any part of the farm.

There are two dwelling houses on this farm, each being well planned. The main dwelling is a handsome, convenient story and a half frame building, with a cellar basement on the best order and supplied with every convenience and comfort, and to lighten the household labor. The house is surrounded by neat, well-kept gardens and yards, producing ample supplies of the smaller fruits, as well as vegetables. The barns and yards, wells, cisterns and other arrangements, were contrived and planned so as to promote the greatest economy in labor and in time. There seemed to be a place for everything. The large barn near the house had a capacity for 100 tons of hay, and all were filled to their utmost limits. One of the barns recently built was almost worthy of being a model, so well adapted was it for the ease with which all the stock could be supplied and fed, without loss of time and without going out of doors.

There were two orchards on the farm, one near the house, of small size, in which were a large number of varieties of pears, cherries and other fruits. The other was the main apple orchard, five acres in extent, and comprising some choice varieties of fall and winter apples, the trees being thrifty and in good order.

The live stock consists of nine horses, of which five are kept for work; the rest are young stock; five milch cows, seven head of three-year-old steers, six yearlings and two year olds. The sheep on the farm comprise 190 ewes, 120 lambs, 60 wethers; and there were sold since shearing time 201 head. There are five sows and thirty pigs, as the stock of swine.

The basis of the system on this farm is the wool and the live stock, Mr. Chapman purchasing cattle to feed up his large fodder and heavy hay crops. The crops are as follows: 20 acres in wheat, 15 acres of oats, 25 acres of corn, 80 acres of hay, 30 acres of pasture. During the past season he clipped 2,050 pounds of wool, and sold from his stock 201 head of sheep. Last year his clip was only 1,600 pounds and 112 sheep sold. His crop of wheat also was unusually light. The farm sustains an average family of 11 persons, and the amount paid out for labor last year was $300. The average income per acre of improved land last year was at the rate of $16.50, as given by the returns furnished to the committee.

KALAMAZOO COUNTY.

The farm of Jervis D. Adams is in the town of Climax, seven miles south of Galesburg, Kalamazoo county, on the Michigan Central railroad. The farm contains 360 acres, of which 340 are improved and cultivated, and only 20 are in wood. The fields range in size from 11 to 45 acres. The division is not remarkable for its system, but the fields are conveniently reached, the public roads being on two sides, and a lane two rods in width extending from the barnyard through the centre of the farm to each field. The fences are mostly old, having been laid about 14 years, but in good order and clean.

The house is a neat and commodious one-story building, surrounded by gardens and orchards, that for neatness and finish are almost models. The front yard is devoted solely to ornament, and is partitioned off by hedges of cedar and arbor vitæ that have been trimmed and trained with the utmost taste and care. West of the house is a vegetable garden, surrounded and protected by a hedge that forms also a screen for the house from the west winds. The yards in the rear of the house have been laid down with grass, and rolled till they are smooth as a perfect lawn, and the roadways, gates and fences are in the neatest and most perfect order. Beside the gardens immediately attached to the house, there is an orchard of 700 trees, comprising 64 varieties of apples, the trees being in the most healthy state of growth; a peach orchard of 200 trees, containing 14 varieties; a separate garden for the half-hardy fruits, such as plums, grapes, raspberries, strawberries, the Lawton blackberry, surrounded by hedges and protected by buildings. Around the orchard is a treble hedge, composed of peach trees, the Osage orange, and rows of evergreen and deciduous trees, which have been set out for protection. There is also a nursery of 14 acres, containing young trees, cultivated for sale. Shade trees have been planted along the roads on the farm at equal distances. The farm buildings and yards are arranged on the most commodious plan for the accommodation of the stock and crops. In each of the stock yards were barracks with sliding roof, holding an average of 10 tons of hay, while the grain and hay that could not be put under cover, were in stacks, which were almost models in form. All the appurtenances for sheltering and feeding large flocks of sheep and herds of cattle during our long winters, were very perfect and complete, as well as substantial.

The soil of the farm was a rich, somewhat light loam, that needed no draining or ditching. Mr. Adams had opened some ditches for the purpose of lowering the water on certain marshes, but he had no under-drains. The surface was almost clear of stumps, he having pulled the last of them the present season with a Willis stump puller. The fields were clean and in good order, the fences being kept clear from weeds and foul stuff of all kinds.

The live stock kept on the farm comprised 15 horses, nine of which were used for work, and the other six were colts bred on the farm for sale. Nine milch cows, 11 head of young cattle and five calves, 375 head of sheep and 20 head of swine.

The system of cultivation on this farm takes as a basis, the production of wheat and wool as the principal money crops, and with them are combined the nursery, fruit growing, and also the raising of some cattle and horses; but the principal consumers of the fodder crops are the large flocks of sheep, the cattle and horses being used simply as aids, and yet forming an important part, for the sales of cattle and pork combined, from this farm last year, were larger in amount than all the wool sold the same year. The crops for the present season well exhibit something of the system, but it was difficult to arrange the results on the farm, as Mr. Adams, besides the home farm, works and uses two other farms adjoining, which belong to him, but are not included in the home farm, but which contribute a certain proportion of income. The crops of the present year are wheat, 87 acres, corn 312 acres, hay 60 acres, oats 10 acres, potatoes 12 acres, pasture 120 acres. The family sustained by the farm averages nine persons all the year round. The returns of income for the past year indicate an average for each improved acre of $14.30.

CASS COUNTY.

The committee reports that but one farm of a size less than 160 acres was entered. This farm was owned by B. Hathaway, Esq., of Little Prairie Ronde, in Cass county. The size of the farm is 110 acres, of which 30 acres are in woodland, the remaining 80 being under cultivation. Of this 10 acres are used as a nursery for fruit trees, and about 10 acres more are used for grounds, gardens, orchards and yards, leaving only 60 acres under cultivation for crops. The nursery business, and the growing of small and large fruit are extensively practiced by the owner. The fences were composed for a large part, especially around the orchards and along the roads, of the Virginia thorn (*Cratægus Virginiana*) and were the best specimens of thorn hedge we have seen in the State. He finds this thorn the best plant for hedges. He trains by plashing, and his hedges were high enough for a shelter, and at the same time stout and close enough for a complete fence which no animal could break through. On the farm nearly all the native thorns, as well as many of deciduous and evergreen trees, had been tried as hedges, but all had to yield for utility to the Virginia thorn.

The buildings on the farm were good, but like many other farmers, Mr. Hathaway was making additions and improvements. The house was a neat building, with very elegant grounds around it, neatly planted with evergreens, and the flower-gardens ornamenting its front, surrounded with hedges of cedar and arbor vitæ. Besides a large apple orchard, there was a pear orchard of some extent, containing 36 standard trees and 64 dwarfs, and which showed that the owner had given it much attention.

There had been no draining found necessary on the farm, and only the plot planted with pear trees had been under-drained.

The live stock on this farm consisted of three horses, one yoke of working oxen, four milch cows, four head of young cattle and three calves, 50 head of sheep, and 20 head of swine. During the past year the crops have been 12 acres of wheat, nine acres of corn, 17 acres of hay, 15 acres of pasture, and an acre and a half of potatoes. The returns of last year show an income equal to $29.60 per improved acre, but out of this should be taken about $7.58 per acre, for returns obtained from nursery and small fruit business, that belongs rather more directly to horticultural than agricultural industry; still, as it was a part of the produce of the farm, it could not be separated from the general result.

Your committee would direct attention to the plantations of trees which are found on Mr. Hathaway's farm, on a larger scale than is known elsewhere to us. On portions of his woodlands which had been cut off, he had set out in rows, like the trees in an orchard, 810 hard maples, 250 white and blue ash trees, 250 black walnut, 150 butternut, 180 soft maples, 180 white pines, 30 Austrian pines, and 90 Norway spruces, which, added to 170 hard maples and 80 white pines planted by the roadside, make a total of 2,190 trees, a portion of which show a vigorous growth and form an experience in tree planting of which we do not know any other example in the State. Mr. Hathaway had also under progress some very interesting experiments with seedling plants and new varieties of fruit, which are deserving attention, and which, when perfected, will unquestionably prove not only of great interest, but of great utility to horticulturists. The committee would be pleased to refer at more length to these efforts of Mr. Hathaway, but the limits of this report preclude such extended notice as would do them justice.

The Award of Premiums.—The committee having submitted their report on the condition of the farms entered for the premiums, as above, recommend the adoption of the following resolution by the Executive Committee:

Resolved, That the premium of $100, be and is hereby awarded to Jervis D. Adams, Esq., of Climax, Kalamazoo county.

Resolved, That the premium of $75 be awarded to B. Hathaway, Esq., of Little Prairie Ronde, Cass county.

M. DORRELL,
S. O. KNAPP,
Committee.

In a circular which was sent to all the Agricultural Societies in the State, information was requested in regard to the yield of crops for 1866. It will be seen that in several instances the request has been complied with. Returns have been obtained from several societies not previously heard from; but it is a matter of regret that several from which returns were received for 1865, have failed to make any report for 1866. It is to be hoped that all societies will in future report their annual proceedings to the Secretary of the State Board of Agriculture.

BARRY COUNTY.

The Secretary of the Barry County Agricultural Society reports a falling off in the average yield of the *wheat* crop for 1866, of from one-fourth to one-third, owing to the ravages of the Hessian fly and the severe winter. On sandy soils the fly damaged the crop materially, while on heavy soils it was somewhat winter-killed. *Indian corn* did not ripen well, owing to the cool, wet weather of August and September, and it was probably damaged fully one-third by frost. *Hay* and *potatoes* were about an average with previous years. The *oat* crop was very abundant, estimated at nearly double the usual yield. *Apples* were about half a crop, and *peaches* not over one-fourth.

The Agricultural Society of this county held its Fourteenth Annual Exhibition on the grounds of the Society, in Hastings, on the 9th, 10th and 11th of October, and was well attended. Foul weather of the 9th and the morning of the 10th, together with the bad condition of the roads, prevented a full exhibition. The stock on the ground showed improvement in the line of *blood*. In sheep the improvement was very marked. The number of members was 350, and the number of articles about 400. The premium list offered amounted to about $400, and the premiums awarded were $186. The following is the financial statement for the fiscal year ending Dec. 20th, 1866:

RECEIPTS.

1865.		
Dec. 20.	To amount cash on hand	$145 53
1866.		
Oct. 10, 11.	To Receipts for Membership	350 00
" "	" " gate fees and licenses	256 00
		$757 53

EXPENDITURES.

1865.			
Dec. 31.	By Paid Premiums to date		$ 9 85
1866.			
Jan. 2.	"	Taxes	6 38
June 5.	"	for clearing grounds	25 00
July 7.	"	express on State Reports	2 45
Aug. 9.	"	for pine lumber	30 00
Oct. 8.	"	" lumber and hauling same	8 55
"	"	" labor and team-work on grounds	108 50
" 10, 11.	"	" feed for stock	16 50
"	"	" printing	53 00
"	"	" expenses of speaker	20 00
Dec. 20.	"	" premiums to date	173 50
"	"	" taxes on grounds	6 60
"	"	" cash on hand	291 20
			$757 53

Officers for 1867.—J. C. Hanna, President; J. M. Nevins, Secretary; S. C. Prindle, Treasurer.

BERRIEN COUNTY.

The Secretary of the Berrien County Agricultural Society reports the yield of *wheat* in this county, for 1866, as fully up to the average of past years, and from personal observation, he thinks it was equal if not superior to that of any county in the State. *Indian corn* good, though that which was late suffered some from wet weather. The *hay* crop was good. *Oats* much better than usual. *Apples* an average yield. *Potatoes* good; some varieties, including the Shaker Russets and Neshannocks, suffered from the rot—worse in heavy soil than elsewhere.

Taking all crops, it is thought that Berrien county was highly favored in 1866.

The Society held its sixteenth Annual Exhibition on the grounds of the Society, in Niles, on the 9th, 10th and 11th of October. The weather was very unfavorable for the first and the forenoon of the second day, which materially interfered with the exhibition, and kept many people away who would otherwise have attended. The number of entries was 896, which, considering the unfavorable weather, was much larger than the officers expected. The attendance on the first day was meagre; but on the afternoon of the second and the whole of the third day, the crowd was great, and the receipts correspondingly large. The amount offered in premiums was $1,500, a considerable increase from the previous year, and had the weather been favorable the entries would have been proportionately increased. Even under the various disadvantages, a very marked improvement was apparent in some departments; especially in machinery and domestic manufactures, "the display of which," says the Secretary, "was superior to anything of the kind I ever saw at any county show in Michigan."

The Society has purchased 20 acres of ground directly east of the city, which, before the next exhibition, is to be fitted up in good style. The natural beauty of the ground is seldom excelled. A half-mile track is to be graded, buildings erected, and no expense spared to make it an honor to the county and an ornament to the city. The premium-list will be still further increased, new classes added, and it is hoped that the exhibition of 1867 will mark a new era in the agricultural exhibitions of Western Michigan.

Sheep and wool-growing in the county is yearly attracting greater attention, and a friendly rivalry is springing up among the farmers as to who shall possess the best sheep in the neighborhood. The introduction of sheep has been greater during the past year than for any five previous years.

Officers for 1867.—D. O. Woodruff, President; N. Fitch, Vice-President; R. W. Landon, Secretary; R. C. Paine Treasurer.

BRANCH COUNTY.

The Secretary of the Branch County Agricultural Society, reports the yield of *wheat* in that county as largely below the average, not affording enough for ordinary consumption and for seed, and not one-tenth of an average crop. *Indian corn* light; was injured by frosts. *Potatoes* in sandy soil good; not a large crop; "but a real blessing, for it is a help to the farmers in view of the short wheat crop." *Oats* above an average yield —the best crop raised in the county for three years last past. *Hay* a short crop. *Apples* a short crop. *Buckwheat* a fine crop —the largest ever produced in the county. The Secretary remarks:

"We are not prospering in our agricultural interests in Branch county. It is no fault of our farmers. The crops have all been put in properly; the wheat was winter-killed, and many pieces of corn were frost killed in the fall. Full crops of wheat have been put in this fall, and with the blessing of God we hope to see a more prosperous year in 1867."

The receipts from the Annual Exhibition were less than $1,000. The comparatively small amount is attributed to an almost continuous rain of three days and three nights next preceding the exhibition. The address was delivered by Hon. J. W. Lanier, and was pronounced eminently practical.

The Society has erected on its grounds a "Floral Hall," the central part being 60 feet octagon, with three wings, two of which are 60 by 28 feet, and the other 30 by 28.

Officers for 1867.—Cyrus G. Luce, President; J. H. Gray, Vice President; Albert Chandler, Secretary; Ives G. Miles, Treasurer, with an Executive Committee consisting of five members.

CASS COUNTY.

No returns have been received from the Cass County Agricultural Society, but an answer to the circular of the Secretary of the Board of Agriculture was returned by the Seretary of the

VOLINIA FARMERS' CLUB.

He reports the *wheat* crop of that section a little below the average, perhaps a fourth; but thinks its increased price will far more than bring it up to the standard in value. The quality could hardly be improved. *Indian corn* from a fourth to a third below the average, more from the long-continued wet, cool weather than from frosts. *Potatoes* are stated to have suffered severely from the rot, nearly one-half the crop having been lost from that cause. The Peach-blow variety was least affected. *Apples* not more than half a crop, but the quality good.

This Club appears to be a very useful association, and it would be well for the interests of agriculture in the State if its example was generally imitated. The Secretary of the Club writes:

"Although our association has been organized but little more than a year, it has been as successful as the most sanguine anticipated. The meetings are held on the first Saturday in each month, and during the fall and winter months, semi-monthly. Each meeting has its subject arranged by programme for the year, taking each farm product as near its season as practicable. The fall and winter meetings are devoted mainly to discussions, with exhibitions of specimens of such products pertaining to the subjects under discussion, as members may see fit to bring forward. We sometimes have a show that would not disgrace the tables of some of our county agricultural societies.

"Each discussion is opened by an essay or address from a member chosen at the previous meeting, and this is followed by remarks by all who feel disposed to speak on the subject. An abstract record of the remarks is kept by the Secretary; also, all statistics, &c.

"The meetings during the summer months are devoted chiefly to sheep-shearing, trials of implements and machines, exhibitions, &c. They have met with decided success."

A. S. Rogers, of Volinia, is the Secretary of the Club.

GENESEE COUNTY.

The enterprising Agricultural Society of this county appears to be steadily advancing. The report of the Secretary shows that the list of premiums offered for 1866 amounted to $1,077, an increase over the former year of $112. The grounds of the Society have been improved. A hall for the exhibition of vegetables, grain, &c., has been erected, and also a commodious speaker's stand. A good well has been provided, and general repairs made on sheds, fences, &c. The entire cost of these improvements was about $900.

The Seventeenth Annual Exhibition was held on the 26th, 27th and 28th of September. Several days immediately previous were very rainy, but the days of the exhibition were very fine; the exhibition is reported as having been very good, and the crowd of visitors beyond precedent. The receipts from all sources were $1,636 38, being $28 02 more than those of the favorable year of 1865. The address was delivered by Prof. M. Miles, of the State Agricultural College, and is pronounced a valuable practical discourse.

The Annual Report of the Executive Committee of this Society presents a valuable synopsis of the yield of crops and the general condition of the agriculture of the county for the year 1866. The substance of the Report is as follows:

It will be recollected that in our last Annual Report we had occasion to speak of the very favorable season of 1865, for all kinds of agricultural products, and its influence in maturing fine and abundant crops. The weather of 1866 offers a great contrast. The Spring was cold and dry up to the middle of May. From the beginning of June, a wet time set in, constant and increasing rains with but little intermission as the season advanced, followed by early nipping frosts. These causes greatly retarded labor on the farm, checked the early growth of crops, and rendered it difficult to secure the harvest in good order.

Winter Wheat was, perhaps, the best crop raised in 1866. The yield was about an average, and the quality very fine. Owing to the backwardness of the season in April, less Spring Wheat was put in than would otherwise have been sown. It was a fair produce.

Oats afforded an average yield, but the crop was damaged at least twenty-five per cent. by the wet.

The growth of *Corn* was affected first by the coldness of the Spring and early Summer, and afterwards by the heavy rains, especially upon the low wet lands; and just before its time for maturity, the frost cut it down, spoiling the stalks for fodder. From these causes combined, the crop was diminished about one-fourth from what it otherwise ought to have yielded.

In consequence of the ungenial weather in Spring, less breadth of land was sown to *Barley* than usual. The produce per acre was a full average and the quality good.

A large yield of *Hay* would have been saved but for the wetness of the season, which probably caused a loss of one-third of the promised crop. An average amount, perhaps, was harvested.

Potatoes suffered from the same cause to a still greater extent. A large proportion has been affected by the rot, in consequence of which we cannot estimate them at more than one-third of an average crop.

The culture of *Hops* is annually increasing in importance in this county, and has grown to be a valuable and profitable branch of farm business. It is estimated that about 200 bales of 200 lbs. each, were packed the past season—principally in the Townships of Burton and Grand Blanc, and some in Flint and Richfield. So far as we can learn, no investment of industry on the farm yields a better return than the Hop-yard, in proportion to the land it occupies and the labor it requires. As a result of this, we observe a large increase in the breadth of ground set out for the next year's crop.

Sorghum.—In the month of January, 1866, the Michigan State Cane Growers' Association held their Annual Meeting in the city of Flint, as an inducement to which this Society contributed $150 towards the premiums offered. The meeting was well attended by our farmers, and much valuable information gleaned from the discussions and addresses, as well as from the exhibition of machinery and productions. The result was that quite an impetus was given to the culture of Sorghum in this county, leading to the construction of at least eight mills for the manufacture of syrup, all of which, we believe, have been kept busy at work during the season. The fact has been demonstrated that a very good article of syrup can be made here; but both the yield and quality were affected by the unfavorable nature of the weather for the growth and maturity of the plant, as well as by the want of experience as to what kinds of seed are best suited to this climate. Making allowance for the drawbacks incident to the establishment of any new branch of business, there is every encouragement to persevere in the raising and manufacture of Sorghum as a crop that will ultimately yield a large return.

Fruit.—The yield of Apples has been comparatively small, perhaps not over half an average crop, though the quality was good. The deficiency has been ascribed partly to spring frosts, and in some measure to the over-bearing of the trees the previous year. Pear trees did not produce well. Grapes, Plums and Peaches bore a fair fruitage.

Cattle.—We are pleased to observe something of a return to the interest felt a few years ago in keeping up the improved stock of Cattle, which has languished for a year or two past. Notwithstanding the temptation to sell, afforded by high prices, farmers are retaining their young Cattle to a large extent, so that the scarcity which has lately prevailed will not be allowed to continue. While the Durham and Devon bloods still preserve their places in the esteem of stock raisers, other varieties are being introduced more freely than formerly. Ayrshires continue to attract attention; and a fine herd of Galloways has been introduced by Hon. E. H. Thomson from Canada, since we made our last report on this subject. The condition of the Cattle throughout the county is about the average.

Horses.—the increase in valuable Horses keeps pace with the general progress in agricultural pursuits. As we observed last year, large Horses continue to be more sought after for business purposes than formerly; good draft Horses being in more demand than light fancy teams, although there is no lack of taste for handsome and showy animals.

Sheep.—Notwithstanding the depression in the wool trade, there is no falling off observable in the interest taken for some time back in the improvement of Sheep. We doubt if any county in the State can show finer flocks, and for a still nearer approach to perfection in the best points of the finer wool-bearing varieties, occasional importations continue to be made from the purest bloods of New York and Vermont. The Sheep Breeders' and Wool Growers' Association of the county are doing a good work in promoting the interest felt in this department of stock husbandry.

We are again under obligations to Wm. A. Morrison, Esq., of the city of Flint, for the following statistics and remarks on the wool trade of the past year:

" The whole amount of Wool marketed at Flint, for 1866, is 370,000 lbs.; estimated amount sold at other points on the line of the Detroit & Milwaukee Railroad, in this county, and including Holly, 250,00 lbs.; amount unsold, 200,000 lbs., making a total of 820,000 lbs., [which is about 120,000 lbs. over the reported and estimated clip of 1865.] The condition of Wool was about as in former years, except an improvement in the use of a light twine, and not quite so much stuffing. There is still great room for improvement in thorough washing, and it is in this that our farmers are behind those of parts of Ohio, Pennsylvania and Virginia; and when the same thorough washing and care is exercised, and nothing is put up but clean Wool, our farmers will get relatively the same price as the farmers of those States do for their extra and double extra Wools. The average of most of the Wool sold this season has been about 50 cents, though it has ranged from 62½ to 45; being influenced to the higher range by the proposed tariff, and declining as much from excessive importations of woolen fabrics, as from any other cause."

Hogs.—The supply of Hogs has again become abundant, and fully equal to the demand, with a marked improvement in the breeds. The Swine that meet the most favor seem to be the cross of Suffolk and Byfield with the Chester Whites.

Manufactures.—The manufacturing interests of the County are extending rapidly in value and importance. In addition to the Farming Implements heretofore made, Messrs. Hakes, Kimball & Co., of the city of Flint, have entered extensively into the manufacture of a superior Mowing Machine—the "Eagle" patent of E. F. Herrington, of Valley Falls, N. Y.—with which they supply the entire State. The shipments of Lumber from this County have been immense. Two Wooden Factories, at Fenton and Atlas, are doing a large business and manufacturing most excellent goods.

Officers for 1867.—C. H. Rockwood, President; F. H. Rankin, Secretary; Harlow Whittlesey, Treasurer; J. L. Gage, Oren Stone, Auditors, with twenty-one Vice-Presidents, and an Executive Committee consisting of seven members.

SHEEP-BREEDERS' AND WOOL-GROWERS' ASSOCIATION.

An association under this name has been formed in this county, which held its first Annual Sheep-Shearing and Exhibition on the grounds of the Agricultural Society, at Flint, on the 9th and 10th of May last. The exhibition of sheep was confined to Merinos, the number of which was 107. Besides these, the report states that there were some beautiful sheep from abroad; the owners of which entered them without competition. It is said there was not an inferior sheep upon the grounds. The awarding committees reported that the competition was in many cases so close as to make their decisions very difficult.

The Secretary in his Report estimates the increase in the number of sheep in the county within the past year at ten per cent.; which is mainly owing to the natural increase, though there have been introduced some choice Merinos and Leicesters.

"At the usual wool season the market ruled dull, and has not rallied; and those farmers who parted with their clips had generally to accept lower rates than those which prevailed in 1865. Buyers also exercised more discrimination as to the condition of the fleeces, than was previously the custom. This is a feature which we would recommend every careful wool-grower unhesitatingly to encourage. When carried on with judgment, its effect will be to give to those who shall be circumspect as to the cleanliness and make-up of their fleeces, a due compensation for the extra trouble it may entail. It is the manifest interest of every Sheep-breeder and Wool-grower of this Association, to establish and maintain a good character among buyers for the quantity and condition of the wool-clip of Genesee County; and no pains should be spared to accomplish this. Its result will be enhanced money value, and increased competition to secure the wool; which will afford an ample return in dollars and cents, as well as in reputation. We therefore heartily commend to the approval of wool-growers the distinction thus made by the buyers between clean and unclean fleeces, when exercised judiciously and reasonably. In this connection, we would draw the attention of wool-raisers to the fact that much of the inferior condition of otherwise choice wool is occasioned by allowing the sheep to run too long after washing and before shearing.

"The present condition of the flocks in this County, is not so good as it has been at this season for several previous years. This is owing to the long-continued wet weather, and inferior feed of the past summer and autumn.

"The number of members enrolled for the year 1865, was sixty-one, each of whom was entitled to bring in his family.

In addition to these, the sale of admission tickets would indicate that about 250 visitors who were not members had been upon the grounds at the time of the Festival. This is a good showing for the inauguration of a new project, at an unusual season of the year, with the nature of which the people had not yet become acquainted, and devoid as the exhibition is of the more varied attractions of a County Fair. The receipts of the Society were sufficient to defray all its expenses, so that no indebtedness exists, which is an unusually favorable result for the first year of such associations."

Hon. F. H. Rankin, of Flint, is the Secretary of this association.

GRATIOT COUNTY.

An Agricultural Society has lately been organized in this county, the Secretary of which reports that the *wheat* crop of the county gave an average yield this year. *Oats* good, but damaged materially by wet weather. *Indian corn* promised to be extraordinary, but the cold rains in August and September prevented its ripening, and the frost found it unprepared. *Potatoes* very good. *Hay* good. *Buckwheat* materially injured by the rains. *Apples, peaches* and *grapes* as good as could be expected considering the short time since the trees and vines were set out.

"It is eleven years this fall since the first tree was cut to give room for what is now our young but thriving village, Ithaca, which is the county seat; and four years of that time a good proportion of our able-bodied men were in the army. Our population has doubled during the past two years, and the cry is still they come."

The Agricultural Society was organized in June, 1866, and the First Annual Exhibition was held at Ithaca on the 4th and 5th of October. Good weather prevailed, and the number of entries was about 300. The various departments were well filled—the display of fruit being large and good. A hall 200 feet long by 20 wide was filled with vegetables, fruits and articles, tastefully arranged.

RECEIPTS.

From sale of tickets		$225 60
From Board of Supervisors		50 00
		$275 60

EXPENDITURES.

Paid in Premiums	$120 50	
" preparing Grounds	48 50	
		168 90
On hand		$106 70

Officers for 1867.—Frs. Nelson, President; W. E. Winton, Secretary; Emery Crosby, Treasurer, with fifteeen Vice Presidents, and an Executive Committee consisting of five members, who, with the President and Secretary, constitute a Board of Directors.

HILLSDALE COUNTY.

A paper has been received from the President and Secretary of the Hillsdale county Agricultural Society, which comprises a brief history of the agriculture of the county from its first settlement, together with an account of the organization and general course of the Society, and giving many facts of interest and value, which are well worthy of preservation. The main portion of the document is herewith presented:

There is probably no county in the State more highly favored in the oiginal distribution of timber and water, or one possessing a greater variety of soil than Hillsdale. Without the uniformity of soil which characterizes the Prairie States, we have, perhaps, all its depth and richness in some of the soils of our originally heavy timbered lands, with the opposite extreme in those which resemble the warm, quick soils of Long Island and New Jersey, as well as all the intermediate and intermixed varieties. The character of our farming was hence predetermined by the nature and variety of our soil. This, our people, being for the most part "original Yankees," were not slow to perceive—or that it was the course of wisdom and interest alike to develop and turn to its greatest account, the position which they found themselves to occupy. Hence the labor of our farms is not the routine work of the Prairie; but is of that character denominated *mixed farming*, giving variety to the farmer's labor, calling into exercise all the faculties of the mind, and developing all its perceptions, which under other circumstances might not be expected.

Hillsdale county contains within its limits the highest elevations of land, in the Lower Peninsula. Among these elevations are the sources of five of its principal rivers. As its name imports, its surface is sufficiently undulating to give these incipient streams a rapid motion. While, therefore, there is little land that is not supplied with water, in desirable quantities, there is little comparatively that is covered with water, little that is marshy and unfit for cultivation.

After heavy rains we can sooner take in hand the plow and cultivator, and we find that our elevated position often exempts us from the early frosts of lower lands. These facts which intuition might seem to point out, observation and experience have demonstrated. From all of which considerations we infer the capacity of this part of the State, when properly developed, to sustain a dense population.

From the year 1830, when the first settlement was made, until 1850, very little except wheat, corn and pork was produced or attempted. With that year it may be said a new era dawned upon us; for although the railroad had been opened to Hillsdale in 1843, it was only in such a way as to suggest the *nature* of a railroad without giving us the reality.

The practice during these previous years of constant and excessive cropping of our lighter soils, which had been selected and settled by the pioneer, because the easiest divested of the growing timber, began to demonstrate its ruinous tendency, and at once give direction to our incoming population towards the heavier timber lands, which were eagerly seized and speedily improved; while the earlier settlers, perceiving the mistakes of former years, began to supply the proper remedy, which with completed railroad facilities, giving a ready market and a supply of plaster, which before was unattainable, they were enabled now to do. As a result, it may be stated that our lighter soils, which in 1850, under the old system or *want* of system, showed sad deterioration, are to-day in all respects, equal in productiveness, and give equal if not greater net returns to the judicious farmer, than the best of our originally timbered lands under equally judicious management.

The year 1850 is memorable, too, for the introduction of improved stock into the county. The Devons, being the pioneers were introduced by Judge Miller, of Moscow, from Seneca county, N. Y. These were soon followed by the Durhams, Geo. C. Munro, Esq., of Jonesville, being the first to invest in a Kentucky-bred bull. About this time the Holderness, of Ohio, probably a cross of the genuine Holderness and native, were introduced in the town of Reading, making a decided improvement on the Michigan natives, giving us at our first Annual Fair, held in 1851, a very good representation of two distinct families and of one mixed family. The splendid herds of William Curtis & Sons, of Wheatland, which bore off the palm of superiority over all competitors at our late State Fair, and of Col. Fowler, of Reading, Whitebeck, of Pittsford, and Payne, of Somerset, not to mention others of less extent and notoriety in the different towns in the county, may be cited as the index of our present position in the department of cattle.

Our first exhibition was held on the public square in Hillsdale, and was free to all. The premiums offered were paid from a subscription raised for that purpose. Since then the Society has held its exhibitions annually, extending its influence and benefits quietly, but surely, numbering 125 life members and about 800 annual members.

It has been the aim of the Society to foster every interest and improvement, whether in breeding, in the drainage or tilling of the soil, in the construction of farm-buildings and farm-improvements, or in the mechanic arts. We think the results of the last two years demonstrate the fact that our Society is a success. Agricultural Societies become a success when they enlist the energies of the entire people in their behalf. This interest we think we have in a good measure secured; as will be evident from the fact that at our late Fair there were more than 1,000 entries made, on which 450 premiums were awarded, amounting to about $800. Our minor premiums are necessarily small in amount, and for the present must remain so; the growing interests of the Society requiring grounds and improvements centrally located, costing large sums of money. These it has been our object to complete and pay for, so far as possible, as we go.

In pursuance of this object, we have raised and expended on our grounds and buildings, within the last two years, nearly or quite $6,000. Our Fair grounds are situated within the corporate limits of the village of Hillsdale, and embrace 25 acres, at a cost of $3,500. On these grounds we have erected the past season "Floral Hall," at an expense of $3,500 more. The property of the Society has at the present time a cost value of not less than $12,000. Our indebtedness amounts to $2,500.

On the 15th of May last, the Society held a Sheep-shearing Festival, on which occasion there was a fine, active competition. The number of entries was 48; the heaviest fleece shorn, weighed 22 14-16 lbs. We deem this a success.

Our crops the past season have suffered materially. *Wheat* was badly winter-killed, giving us an average yield of not more than six bushels to the acre. The *Hay* crop was also light, owing to the clover being winter-killed. *Oats* were a good crop, and were well secured. *Potatoes*, in yield were good, but in some parts of the county they commenced rotting before digging. *Corn*, early in the season gave promise of an abundant crop; but the cold, wet weather of August arrested its growth to such an extent that the small amount of warm weather in September failed to to bring it forward, as a whole, to maturity. The result is much imperfect, unsound grain; about two-thirds of a crop. The *Apple* crop was very good, one dealer alone having shipped 5,000 barrels from here.

Our large interest, however, lies in our flocks, which we have reason to believe will compare favorably with those of any county in the State. This interest has for many years past been of far greater value to us than our wheat crop.

We cannot give you a better idea of the general interest taken in our Society, than by a brief statement of the entries and receipts of our late fair. Of cattle, there were 90 entries; of horses, 245; of sheep, 97 pens; of swine, 23 pens; of poultry, 28 coops; of teams for plowing, 4; of trotting teams, 16; of carriages, horses and farm implements, 90; of dairy products, 25; of fruit, 80; of garden products, 48; of domestic manufactures, "wool and cotton," and linen, 102; of needle-work and embroidery, 140; of paintings and musical instruments, 31. Total, 1,019 entries. The gross receipts of the Fair were $3,275.

We also add, as an item worthy, perhaps, of record, that a member of our Society, the past season, is said to have done the fastest and best mowing with a machine, that has hitherto been done in the United States, and for which he has received the premium. The machine was the Champion Mower, of Springfield, Ohio, manufacture, said to be an improvement on the Buck Eye. The amount of grain mowed, and time, were as follows: Eleven and 91-100 acres of heavy grass were mowed in 5 hours and 41 minues, or an average of an acre of ground to about every 28 minutes of time. If any other county in the State can beat this, we shall be glad to hear of it. If not, Hillsdale is ahead.

GEO. W. UNDERWOOD, *President.*

F. M. Holloway, *Secretary.*

Dec. 5th, 1866.

Farmers', Mechanics' and Stock-Breeders' Association of Jonesville.—The only public exhibition of this Association during the year, was one of horses, held on the 27th and 28th days of June, at which the receipts were $255 10 only, the weather being very unfavorable. Premiums were offered and paid to the amount of $400. The reason why no full exhibition was held, was the long-continued wet weather. Improvements have been made on the grounds of the Association during the year to the amount of between $200 and $300. It is contemplated to put up permanent buildings during the ensuing year to the value of $1,200 to $1,500. If this is done the money will be raised by assessments on the stockholders.

The yield of crops is given as follows: *Wheat*, through the county, not over one-third an average crop. Many fields were entirely cut off, and very few yielded more than five to ten bushels per acre. *Clover* was almost an entire failure, most fields being winter-killed. Crops were not generally injured by wet weather, except *Hay*, which was hurt to some extent. *Oats* were never better. *Corn* very good, but some fields injured by early frosts, though not to a great extent. Corn-fodder somewhat injured by frost.

Officers for 1867.—Geo. C. Munro, President; Richard S. Varnum, Secretary; E. O. Grosvener, Treasurer, with a Board of twelve Directors.

IONIA COUNTY.

The Tenth Annual Exhibition of the Ionia County Agricultural Society was held on the grounds of the Society, near Ionia, on the 3d and 4th of October. An increased interest was shown, and an additional number of memberships sold, notwithstanding an adverse influence in the village in favor of the race-course and horse-show, and also by the formation of another agricultural society in the county, which held its exhition on the same day. The exhibition of implements was the best ever made in the county. There was also a spirited competition in fine-wooled sheep. Other departments were very deficient. On the whole, it is thought the Society is making progress in the right direction.

RECEIPTS.

Balance on hand from last year		$ 17 38
From rent of Grounds		35 00
Receipts from Exhibition		385 00
		$437 38

EXPENDITURES.

Premiums awarded	$209 25	
Expenses	172 40	
		381 65
Balance on hand		$55 73

The address, which was delivered by Prof. M. Miles, of the State Agricultural College, is spoken of as plain, practical and to the point.

Officers for 1867.—E. P. Kelsey, President; P. H. Taylor, Secretary; Fred. Hall, Treasurer; with a board of five Directors.

E. H. Bliven, of Ionia, reports in regard to the crops of the county, that *wheat* was a very small crop. Ten bushels per acre is the estimated average for the county. *Indian corn* good, though some late-planted badly injured by frost. *Hay* crop excellent. *Oats* good. *Potatoes* not an average, *Apples* not a full crop.

Produce sold in Ionia at the following prices: Wheat, $2.25 to $3 per bus.; corn, 50 cts. to $1; apples, 75 cts. to $1; potatoes, 40 cts.; butter, 35 cts. per pound; hay, $12 per ton.

The chief products are wheat and wool. Some hops were planted this season; but from some unknown cause about one-third of the sets failed to grow. Hops will be more largely cultivated in the county, if present prices for the article continue. Broom-corn, sorghum, and peppermint are cultivated to some extent.

JACKON COUNTY.

The Secretary of the Jackson County Agricultural Society reports the yield of crops as follows: *Wheat* one-fourth of an average crop; *Indian corn* three-fourths of an average; injured by frost to the amount of one-third. *Oats* over an average. *Potatoes* an average. *Apples* an average. *Hay* an average.

The receipts and expenditures of the Society for the year 1866, are as follows:

RECEIPTS.

Balance on hand at the beginning of the year		$ 763 67
Received from sale of tickets at Annual Show		1,486 27
" rent of buildings		140 75
" from the county of Jackson		151 00
		$2,541 69

EXPENDITURES.

Paid expense account	$582 31	
Improvements on real estate	414 00	
Premiums	634 15	
		1,630 47
Balance on hand		$911 22

A list of the officers for 1867 is not given. W. Budington, of Jackson, is the Secretary.

KALAMAZOO COUNTY.

The Secretary of the Kalamazoo County Agricultural Society reports that the yield of *wheat* in 1866, for this county, was not an average, though the crop in the northern part of the county is thought to have been a full average, it being in some instances very large. One farmer proposed to enter a field yielding fifty bushels to the acre, in competition for a premium. In the south half of the county, the yield was not more than half an average, although it turned out better than was anticipated in the early part of the season. Taking the whole county, three-fourths of an average yield is considered a fair estimate. *Oats, hay and potatoes* gave a full average yield. *Apples* about one-half an average. *Indian corn* was never more promising than previous to the unpropitious "corn weather" of early autumn. The crop was more than an average in quantity; but was much injured by frost. Of good, well-matured corn, one-half an average is all that can be claimed.

"On the whole," writes the Secretary, "the toil of the husbandman, in this county, has been remunerative. If the products are not excessive, the prices are large. Farmers who have drawn a load of wheat to this market and sold it for $24, and perhaps that in 'store-pay,' have this year brought loads of the same quantity, and taken home $120 for each load, with a lively competition among buyers to obtain it."

The Annual Exhibition of the Society was held at Kalamazoo on the 26th—28th of October. It was not, in a pecuniary view, a success, and is said to have been far from creditable to the county. One of the causes of this was the very wet weather at the usual time of sowing wheat, which made it necessary for farmers to improve the first favorable time thereafter. "But another and more potent cause," it is said, "is the existence of the 'National Horse Association.'" The interest manifested in the horse-shows, greatly detracts from the interest which should be taken in the agricultural exhibitions of the county.

Statement of receipts and disbursements for the year 1866:

RECEIPTS.

Balance in treasury at the beginning of the year	$175 23
Total receipts of the Exhibition	525 90
Deficit	133 87
	$835 00

EXPENDITURES.

Premiums paid	$530 00
Expenses	305 00
	$835 00

Officers for 1867.—Chas. E. Stuart, President; Jas. Black, Vice President; Frank Little, Secretary, with an Executive Committee consisting of five members.

KENT COUNTY.

The Secretary of the Kent County Agricultural Society reports that the crops there for 1866 were generally bountiful. *Wheat* an average crop in quantity, and much more than average in quality. *Indian corn* about an average in quantity, but not so in quality. It was not injured by frost, but did not ripen well on account of the wet and cloudy weather. *Oats, rye* and *buckwheat* about an average. *Potatoes* an average in quantity but below an average in quality. *Peaches* three-fourths of an average crop, and of poor quality, owing to wet and cloudy weather at the time of ripening.

The interest in the Society and its exhibitions is said to have run down during the war, and a debt of over $700 was contracted. The Executive Board determined to make a strong effort this year to put the affairs of the Society on a better footing, and succeeded in a good degree. The premiums were raised, especially on those objects which most needed improvement. A premium of $75 was offered for the best bull; and the premiums on hogs and sheep were made three or four times what they had heretofore been; and for the encouragement of dairymen, a premium of $30 was offered on butter.

The result was, that when the exhibition took place, although from the lateness of seeding many farmers were kept away, the attendance was greater than ever before, and the Society was left with means to pay all premiums and expenditures and also to pay all indebtedness. The Society has now splendid grounds, with considerable improvements, all paid for. The croakers have "dried up," and a new interest has been awakened in the Society and the improvement of agriculture, from which even greater success is looked for in the future.

Considerable interest is said to be felt in reference to a thorough geological survey of the State, and the wish is expressed that the Legislature may take the steps required to accomplish this object.

A list of the officers of the Society is not given. The Secretary is L. S. Scranton, of Grand Rapids.

LAPEER COUNTY.

The Secretary of the Lapeer County Agricultural Society reports the yield of *wheat* for 1866 as about two-thirds of an average crop. *Potatoes* not over half an average. *Oats* very heavy. *Apples* not as plenty as in 1865. *Indian corn* considerably injured by frost; there was a large growth of stalks, but much soft corn. *Hay* was abundant; that which was cut early was well secured; but little was saved from flats and bottom lands, on account of the continuous rains and high water.

The Ninth Annual Exhibition of the Society was held at Lapeer on the 10th–12th of October. The show of cattle and sheep was large. The weather was unfavorable. The Society has been erecting a large Floral Hall, and also some horse-sheds, the past season, and is in debt about $300. The citizens of the counties of Oakland and Macomb are allowed to compete at the shows of this Society, and the citizens of Lapeer county have the same privilege at the shows of the Societies of Oakland and Macomb counties.

Officers for 1867.—John B. Wilson, President; R. G. Hart, Secretary; M. B. Smith, Treasurer, with a Board of seventeen Directors.

LIVINGSTON COUNTY.

The Secretary of the Livingston County Agricultural Society reports the yield of *wheat* in that county in 1866 at two-thirds of an average crop, but of superior quality. *Hay* a full average, and of good quality. *Potatoes* not an average, an eighth less, and somewhat injured by rot. *Apples* about half an average crop; quality very good. *Indian corn* injured to the amount of one-fourth its value by frost; though the number of bushels raised is greater than that of several previous years. The wet weather is said to have injured an immense amount of corn—thousands of bushels, husked, lying on the ground when heavy rain-storms came, and lay in that state for weeks, some of it rotting. *Oats* considered to have been the heaviest produced in the county for the last twenty years.

It is not stated when the Society held its last exhibition; but it is said to have been a "complete success." The grounds of the Society at Howell have been much enlarged an improved, and visitors and exhibitors find there many more conveniences than formerly. At the last exhibition, cattle, sheep and swine are said to have been exhibited in large numbers, while the other departments made a fine showing. The whole number of entries was 458, and the total amount of receipts was $922 70.

No list of officers for 1867 is given. The Secretary is Albert Tooley, of Genoa.

MACOMB COUNTY.

The Secretary of the Macomb County Agricultural Society reports the yield of *wheat* in that county in 1866, as about two-thirds of an average crop; the quality better than for some years previously. *Indian corn* was much injured by the wet, cold weather of the summer, and in some places badly injured by frost in the fall. *Buckwheat* was hurt from the same cause. *Barley* and *rye* an average crop. *Hay* an average, and of good quality. *Apples* not as large a crop as in 1865, but the quality much better, they being much less affected with worms than formerly. Orchards are being much increased in the county. *Potatoes* made a small crop, of poor quality, owing to the extremely wet weather and early fall frosts. On the timbered lands the crop rotted very badly. The Secretary was informed by several members of the Society, that they would have to buy all the potatoes they should use, their own crops being wholly lost. Of *turnips*, the Swedish or ruta-baga is most grown in the county; but the yield is not as large as usual, nor of as good a quality, owing to the cold, wet weather. Of *clover seed* there was but a small number of bushels raised in the county. Owing to the wet weather, it did not fill well.

The seventeenth Annual Exhibition of the Society was held at Romeo, October 3—5th. It was not as successful as some former exhibitions, though very respectable. The number of cattle exhibited was less than in some former years, but the quality was superior. Short-horns were well represented, the largest exhibitor being Geo. W. Phillips, of Armada. Devons were not numerous, but very good, and there was a small herd of Ayrshires, said to be good, owned by Mr. Patton, of Armada. Horses of the different classes were good, except roadsters, in which class the deficiency is said to have been owing to the premiums not being large enough to make it an object for the owners of the best horses to bring them out. The show of sheep was as good as any ever made by the Society, and in Long-wools and South Downs the best—specimens being probably as good as could be found in the State. Swine and poultry were good. There was a good show of vegetables, fruit and flowers, including a fine display of house-plants. In these articles the exhibition was better than any previous one. There was a large display of farm implements. The address was delivered by Rev. R. G. Beard, of Armada, and was listened to with great satisfaction by a large audience.

The number of entries was nearly 700. The receipts fell short some $300 of the amount received in 1865, which was due to many farmers being kept at home to sow their wheat, which they had been prevented from doing at the usual time, by constant and heavy rains.

RECEIPTS.

From the County—40th of a mill tax	$128 59
Receipts of the Exhibition	918 32
Balance on hand at last settlement with treasurer	458 22
	$1,505 13

EXPENDITURES.

Paid premiums and expenses	1,038 70
Balance on hand	$466 43

Officers for 1867.—Chas. Andrus, President; D. W. Briggs, Vice President; C. W. Whitney, Secretary; A. W. Sterling, Treasurer, with a board of four Directors.

MICHIGAN CENTRAL AGRICULTURAL SOCIETY.

This Society was organized in November, 1865. The First Annual Meeting was held January 31, 1866, at which Wm. A. Dryer was chosen President; L. B. Potter, Secretary; E. H. Whitney, Treasurer, with one Vice President and two members of the Executive Committee from each of the following counties: Ingham, Eaton, Clinton, Shiawassee and Livingston.

The Society has purchased a very fine tract of land of about 40 acres, lying on Grand River, 165 rods from the centre of the city of Lansing, and it has been enclosed with a good board fence, eight feet high, except on the river bank. Some temporary buildings have been erected, a half-mile track made and put in good condition, and other improvements commenced.

The Society held a very successful sheep-shearing on the grounds of the State Agricultural College, on the 23d and 24th of May. The only drawback to this, the first show of the Society, was the burning of Messrs. Parmelee & Co's woolen mill, where some forty fleeces of wool entered for a premium had been left for the purpose of being scoured.

On the 12—14th of September, the Society held its first Annual Exhibition, on the grounds before mentioned. The weather was rainy for some time preceding and on the day of opening of the exhibition, but was fair during the second and most of the third days. Considering the unfavorable weather, the newness of the grounds, and other disadvantages, the exhibition was highly creditable, and very encouraging in reference to the future. The receipts were about $1,300. An exhibition of horses was to have been held in October; but it was postponed on account of the continued wet weather.

The officers of the Society have labored under great embarrassments from want of necessary funds to carry on the Society through the first year. Another inconvenience is the fact of there being no law in the State authorizing the chartering of an agricultural society embracing several counties, as this does. With the requisite legal provision, and with funds to pay for the land, the ultimate success of the Society can hardly be doubted. The Society originated in no spirit of rivalry with any other society; its movers believed that there was here a field for improvement, which this association might occupy to the great benefit of the community. A year's experience fully justifies this belief; and the supporters of the Michigan Central Agricultural Society will continue to labor for its prosperity as a means of promoting the public good.

Officers for 1867.—I. H. Bartholomew, President; L. B. Potter, Secretary; E. H. Whitney, Treasurer.

OAKLAND COUNTY.

No regular returns have been received from the Oakland County Agricultural Society. The Secretary of the State Board of Agriculture had the pleasure of attending the last exhibition of this Society at Pontiac, and was much gratified with many things there brought to his notice. The show of Short-horn cattle was highly creditable, both as to the number and quality of the animals. That of Devons was good, and comprised some very fine specimens. Horses were numerous, and the classes for the carriage and farm, were unusually good for a county exhibition. There was also a very large and interesting show of implements.

The following valuable papers from C. W. Greene, of Farmington, a leading farmer of Oakland county, are understood to have been laid before the Society, the matters to which they relate receiving premiums:

DRAINAGE.

In all business transactions, where capital and labor may be judiciously concentrated at a given point, by the formation of stock companies, or by well organized associations, such as usually direct the business of manufacturing, trade and commerce, where every movement radiates from one centre, and where every interest is harmoniously united, it is not difficult to calculate or determine results, nor is the goal of success seen far in the distance.

But unfortunately the agricultural interest of this country, as yet, is in possession of no such advantages. Agriculturists have long since felt the force of concentrated capital and unity of action combined, but have not been able to wield that power in their own behalf, nor to protect themselves against its crushing influences. The acres we till are counted by millions, covering or extending over a vast area of territory, divided by mountain ranges, stretching through a diversity of climate, limited only by seas and deserts, dependent on uncertain markets at different points, not unfrequently at inconvenient distances. We vie with each other in the production of material wealth, and then without concert of action, forced into competition with each other upon the market, we too frequently perform the role of underbidders at the sale, thereby causing and witnessing our financial destruction.

These are some of the evils to which we are subjected; wrongs which press with ponderous weight upon us, but how, or when, these difficulties under which we now labor are to be removed or overcome, I leave for the wisdom of others or the future to determine. If we are to continue our individual efforts single-handed, unaided by combined skill and concentrated capital, against those organized monopolies which are attached to other branches of trade and industry, we shall need to base and conduct our diversified and fragmentary operations upon principles of sound policy, with an eye single to practical results.

In agricultural pursuits, there are at least three primary considerations, applicable to all cases in connection with successful cultivation, viz., draining, manuring and tillage. It is the object of this report more particularly to call attention to the first, referring briefly to some experiments, observations and final results. This subject is not introduced for its novelty; it is not new in theory, yet I apprehend its beneficial results are not appreciated in this country.

Argument, or extended remarks, upon the value of drainage, in this connection, are uncalled for; it being a question without a negative, its feasibility and importance having long since been established upon scientific principles, and reduced to successful practice by the leading agriculturists of all Europe.

In this country, we hear some inquiry and much talk, about reclaiming waste places, redeeming adhesive or clayey soils, and renovating worn lands by stocking down or taking up with certain prescriptions thrown in, such as lime, plaster, salt, alkalies and other mixtures; all well enough in their place if properly applied to soils prepared to receive them, while drainage, the first and primary consideration, the basis upon which all future successful operations must depend, is ignored, or treated with blind indifference and neglect.

But the question is often asked by the uninitiated, is all this expense and precision necessary, and will it pay? I apprehend that where there is a superabundance of surface-water flowing in from above, or springs breaking out from beneath, that no healthy vegetation can exist, and that draining is the only remedy.

That in adhesive or clayey soils, it is the only process of thorough amelioration, rendering the soil friable, and in proper condition.

That in worn or reduced lands, where the vegetable mould has been exhausted, it becomes necessary, preparatory to deeper tillage, more surface-soil being required while it is being restored to its original fertility; in short, all the benefit derived from a thorough system of drainage in other countries, is applicable to this, with some additional advantages—the growing season with us being short, by this process we may practically gain from two to three weeks, in bringing forward and ripening our produce, which in the aggregate would adds thousands, perhaps millions of dollars to the wealth of the State.

The question may be asked, do all our lands require such preparation? Perhaps not; but I imagine the quantity of land that would not be improved by such a system of manipulation, is much smaller than is generally supposed.

It is my conviction that one-half of the improved land, comprising at least five counties on the eastern border of this State, will not pay four per cent. net on the capital invested, until thus treated; and that every acre in said counties would be improved by the process, in the aggregate, over and above all expenses, within the space of five years.

In answering the question, "Will it pay?" and in complying with the rules of your Society concerning reports of this kind, it is obligatory that a minute, detailed, account be given of the field, or parcel of land entered in competition for your Society's premium, both as to location and condition previous to draining, the manner of doing this work, and the final result, which is as follows:

The tract or parcel of land is situated on the east side of what is known as the gravel-ridge. It is comparatively level, with slight inclination to the southeast. Soil very diversified; sand, gravel, loam and vegetable mould prevailing; all resting on clay subsoil, but varying from one to ten feet in depth.

Mound or bog springs of the most troublesome character frequently appear, from one to five feet above the surface level. Three separate water courses break out from the ridge above, and spread out into swales or basins, varying from ten to twenty rods in width. These swales were formerly productive of the coarsest vegetation, viz: bog-grass, flags, rushes, and other worthless rubbish. My method of reclaiming this field, and all other lands like conditioned, is by under-draining with sole tile.

The following statement represents the plan and mode of operations:

The field or parcel of land referred to was first surveyed and stakes set, noting the distance from point to point; the relative condition of the surface as to elevation or depression was then ascertained by the use of the level. Other things being equal, the lowest depressions which would admit of the largest cuts were selected for the principal or main drains, running parallel to each other, ranging from thirty-three to sixty-six feet apart, according to the condition of the land or the amount of water to be supplied by side cuts or collateral drains.

The side cuts, or feeders, are placed at such distance apart as the condition of the land and the necessity of the case would indicate, connecting with the main drains at any angle less than a right angle, according to circumstances. The trenches were cut about fifteen inches wide at the top, and from three to five inches at the bottom, according to the size of the tile used, and not less than three feet in depth. Five-inch tile were used for the main drains, and three-inch for the collaterals.

The bottom of the ditch was made even, the inclination corresponding to the fall or descent required. The tile were then evenly laid upon the bottom of the ditch, and the joints having been well pressed together, a light covering of straw was thrown in upon the tile to prevent the sand from washing into the joints of the tile, previous to the earth being firmly settled around them. The ditches were filled by the use of the plow and scraper, where the earth was sufficiently firm to permit the team to stand, and the shovel in all other cases.

This field contains seventy-five acres of land, and eight hundred rods of sole tile have been laid down in the manner above described, at an expense of about sixty cents per rod, or four hundred and eighty dollars in the aggregate.

The following figures represent the results for the years 1865 and 1866, respectively, including the expense of seed, cultivation, harvesting, and interest on land valued at seventy-five dollars per acre, and I submit the same respectfully in answer to the query "Will it pay?" For the year 1865, the field was divided into three parcels, and planted as follows: two acres in wheat, nine acres in potatoes and fourteen in corn:

Dr.

To two acres of wheat	$ 40 00
" nine acres of potatoes	190 00
" fourteen acres corn	180 00
" interest on same in the aggregate	131 25
Total	$541 05

Cr.

By two acres wheat, 85 bushels, at $2 per bus	170 00
" straw, three tons	10 00
" fourteen acres corn, 800 bushels, 50c per bus	400 00
" corn fodder, 20 tons, at $5 per ton	100 00
" nine acres potatoes, 1,800 bus., at 50c per bus.	900 00
Amount	$1,580 00
All expenses subtracted as above	541 05
Cr. balance	$1,038 95
The cost of draining deducted	480 00
Leaves a balance in favor of draining, of	$558 95

for the year 1865.

For the year 1866:

Cr.

By ten acres potatoes, 1,800 bus., 50c per bus.,	900 00
" ten acres corn, 400 bus., 75c per bus	300 00
" corn fodder, 15 tons, at $5 per ton	75 00
" four acres sown corn for fodder, ten tons, at $10 per ton	100 00
" one acre sorghum	50 00
Amount	$1,425 00
Dr. aggregate expenses, including interest on land.	550 00
Giving a balance in favor of draining of	$975 00

for the year 1866.

It will be observed that there is a little falling off in the yield per acre, from '65 to '66. This was caused by the ravages of worms and insects, more particularly the wire-worm, which is usually very destructive the second year after draining and breaking up sward-lands, as they are forced to the surface for subsistence.

It is worthy of note that the early frosts of the past season, which proved so destructive generally, did not materially affect vegetation on my drained lands, while it was most destructive on other lands adjacent. This fact alone would seem to be sufficient to arrest the attention of farmers, and offers additional inducements to further investigation upon this subject.

The above suggestions are respectfully submitted to those who are interested, hoping that none will hastily leave rich lands, good timber, pure springs, and flowing streams, until an effort is made commensurate with the privileges which surround them, and the undeveloped resources of material wealth which exist in their county at home.

C. W. GREENE.

POTATOES.

In compliance with the rules of your Society, I respectfully submit the following report pertaining to a parcel of land containing five acres, planted to potatoes during the past season:

The soil is composed of sand, gravel and loam, intermixed in various proportions, resting upon clay subsoil. It was underdrained by tiling in the Spring of '64, and planted to corn. In the Spring of '65, it received at the rate of eight cords or sixteen loads of barn-yard manure per acre, plowed under eight inches deep, and planted to corn and potatoes.

Last Spring, '66, it was plowed ten inches deep by ten in width, and again planted to potatoes in the manner hereinafter described. They were selected from the Peach-blow variety, of medium size, cut into from two to three pieces each. The dropping proceeded with the plowing, one piece for a hill on the side of the furrow-slice, about four inches below the surface and twenty-four inches apart in the drill row, every fourth furrow being used for the drill, making the position of each hill twenty-four by forty inches apart. This mode of planting required at the rate of ten bushels per acre.

The plowing and dropping process being through, the field-roller was used in order to pack the surface more firmly upon the tubers. As the sprouts began to make their appearance, the surface was thoroughly harrowed, in order to check the weeds until the vines should get the start, or of sufficient substance for the cultivator.

The after tillage was by the use of harrow and cultivator, the operation being performed at intervals as the case might require, until the vines had completely covered the ground, preventing the use of any implement altogether. The few remaining weeds that appeared late in the season, were pulled by hand.

For the want of a machine, which I could not obtain, to which I could attach horse-power, I was obliged to dig the crop with the potato-fork, which I secured in good condition the last of October.

The following represents the final results in detail:

Dr.

To seed, ten bus. per acre, 50 bus.	$25 00
" plowing five days, $2 50 per day	12 50
" dropping two days, $1 25 per day	2 50
" cultivating and rolling five days, $2 00 per day	10 00
" pulling weeds by hand five days, $1 25 per day	6 25
" digging thirty-three days, $1 25 per day	41 25
" interest on land at $75 00 per acre	26 25
	$123 75

Cr.

By 1,125 bus. potatoes, at 50 cts per bus.............	562 60
Subtract..................................	123 75
Balance..................................	$438 75

C. W. GREENE.

SHIAWASSEE COUNTY.

The Secretary of the Shiawassee County Agricultural Society reports that the *wheat* crop of the county was an average yield, and of superior quality. *Oats* very heavy. *Indian corn* was an average yield, but there was considerable soft corn, on account of the early frost. The *potato* crop was small, and of an inferior quality, with some rot on heavy land. The crop of *hay* was good. The extent of land seeded to winter wheat in 1866, was not more than two-thirds as much as usual.

The Society has enlarged its show-grounds at Owosso, to nearly double their former extent. They comprise a half-mile track. A new office, committee-room, &c., have been built. The entire expense of the improvements was about $800. The Annual Exhibition, held October 23—25th, was not as good as was expected, on account of the unfavorable weather. The receipts were $850. The address was delivered by Sanford Howard, Secretary of the State Board of Agriculture.

Officers for 1867.—Geo. W. Slocum, President; G. R. Lyon, Secretary; A. B. Chipman, Treasurer; with an Executive Committee of five members.

VAN BUREN COUNTY.

The Van Buren County Agricultural Society held its Sixteenth Annual Exhibition at Paw Paw, October 10th–12th, 1866. The printed list of premiums awarded indicates that there was a good competition. The Society was organized in 1851. The number of members for 1866 was 300. The financial affairs are stated as follows:

RECEIPTS.

Cash in treasury previous to Exhibition	$325 35
Received on county order	78 28
Receipts at last Exhibition	623 00
	$1,026 63

EXNENDITURES.

Paid orders	$536 21
Incidentals	2 60
Cash on hand	487 82
	$1,026 63

Officers for 1867.—F. M. Manning, President; J. J. Woodman, Vice President; O. H. P. Sheldon, Secretary; E. G. Butler, Treasurer, with an Executive Committee consisting of six members.

There is another society in this county, under the name of the

LAWRENCE TOWN AGRICULTURAL SOCIETY.

It was organized in 1862, and has at present 76 members. It has held four Annual Exhibitions; is in a prosperous condition; has good show grounds, and is free from debt.

Officers for 1867.—E. E Chadwick, President; H. A. Pond, Secretary; John H. White, Treasurer; with a Board of seven Directors.

WASHTENAW COUNTY.

The President of the Washtenaw County Agricultural Society, H. Arnold, of Ann Arbor, reports the yield of crops in that county, for 1866, as follows; *Wheat* about two-thirds of an average yield. *Oats* and *barley* very abundant, the former injured to some extent by rain. *Potatoes* about two-thirds of an average. *Apples* one-half an average. *Hay* quite an average. *Indian corn* not a full crop, and not more than two-thirds of it sound. *Buckwheat*, not a large breadth sown, but the yield moderate.

The Society held its Annual Exhibition at Ann Arbor, October 9—11th. Its success was quite flattering, the receipts amounting to about $1,800. The Society is free from debt, with a surplus on hand of about $600.

REGISTER OF
METEOROLOGICAL OBSERVATIONS,
FOR THE YEAR 1866,
TAKEN AT THE
State Agricultural College of Michigan,
BY R. C. KEDZIE,
Professor of Chemistry.

LATITUDE, 42° 42′ 24″; LONGITUDE, 7° 33′ 19″ WEST OF WASHINGTON.

Height above the Sea, 895 Feet.

METEOROLOGICAL OBSERVATIONS FOR THE MONTH OF JANUARY, 1866.

Day of Month.	Thermometer in the open air. 7 A. M.	2 P. M.	9 P. M.	Mean.	Rain and Snow. Time of beginning of rain or snow.	Time of ending of rain or snow.	Amount of rain or melted snow in gauge in inches.	Depth of snow, in inches.	Clouds. 7 A. M. Percentage of cloudiness.	Kind of clouds.	2 P. M. Percentage of cloudiness.	Kind of clouds.	9 P. M. Percentage of cloudiness.	Kind of clouds.	Winds. 7 A. M. Direction.	Force.	2 P. M. Direction.	Force.	9 P. M. Direction.	Force.	Max. Thermometer.	Min. Thermometer.	Barometer Height Reduced to Freezing Point. 7 A. M.	2 P. M.	9 P. M.	Mean.	Force or Pressure of Vapor, in Inches. 7 A. M.	2 P. M.	9 P. M.	Relative Humidity, or Percentage of Saturation. 7 A. M.	2 P. M.	9 P. M.
1	26	23	15	21⅓	......	......	......	......	50	Cir.St.	50	Cu.St.	90	Cu.St	S W	4	W	2	W	1	26	6	28.982	29.121	29.148	29.083	.105	.089	.040	75	72	46
2	13	24	25	20⅔	......	......	......	......	90	Cu.St.	10	St.	90	Cu.St.	S W	1	W	1	S W	2	25	6	29.104	29.035	28.943	29.027	.062	.061	.066	81	47	49
3	24	31	22	25⅔	......	......	......	......	100	Cu.St.	80	Cu.St.	100	Cu.St	S W	1	W	2	S W	3	31	8	28.859	28.855	28.923	28.879	.094	.118	.101	73	68	66
4	14	13	5	10⅔	......	......	......	......	100	Cu.St.	80	Cu.St.	10	St.	N W	3	N W	3	W	1	14	−3	29.005	29.891	29.183	29.092	.051	.048	.027	63	62	49
5	11	15	13	13	......	......	......	......	100	Cu.St.	60	Cir.Cu	100	Cu.St	N W	3	S W	3	S W	2	14	6	29.151	29.152	29.210	29.171	.042	.055	.063	59	64	61
6	14	29	13	18⅔	......	......	......	......	100	Cu.St.	90	Cir.St.	80	St.	S E	1	E	1	N E	2	29	0	29.171	29.183	29.271	29.191	.067	.105	.63	81	66	81
7	6	12	7	8⅓	......	......	......	......	100	Cu.St.	30	Cu.	100	Cu.St.	N E	2	N E	2	N E	2	12	−11	29.601	29.745	29.933	29.759	.043	.045	.045	75	60	76
8	−6	9	−3	0	......	......	......	......	00	......	0	......	0	......	E	1	E	2	S W	1	9	−13	30.079	30.084	29.958	30.037	.033	.036	.038	100	56	100
9	−7	23	20	12	......	......	......	......	40	St.	90	Cir.St.	30	Cir.St.	S E	1	S W	2	S W	2	23	−12	29.820	29.690	29.619	29.708	.032	.073	.075	100	59	70
10	24	30	28	27⅓	In night	11 A. M.	.40	4	100	Nim.	100	Cu.St.	100	Cu.St.	S W	4	S W	3	S W	1	30	20	29.265	29.069	29.015	28.119	.129	.148	.135	100	89	88
11	31	39	34	34⅔	3 P. M.	......	......	......	100	Nim.	100	Nim.	100	Nim.	S E	1	S E	1	S E	3	39	28	29.032	28.953	28.881	28.988	.174	.216	.196	100	91	100
12	35	39	39	37⅔	......	11 P. M.	.06	......	100	Nim.	100	Nim.	100	Nim.	S E	3	S E	1	S W	4	39	29	28.618	28.478	28.530	28.544	.204	.238	.238	100	100	100
13	32	31	19	27⅓	......	......	......	......	100	Cu.St.	100	Cu.St.	100	Cu.St.	S W	3	S W	3	S W	2	32	−3	28.611	28.738	28.945	28.764	.162	.155	.103	89	89	100
14	3	11	10	8	......	......	......	......	80	Cu.St.	40	Cu.	30	Cir.	N E	3	N E	2	N E	2	11	−3	29.251	29.328	29.280	29.286	.050	.038	.054	100	49	78
15	13	19	26	19⅓	12 M.	......	.40	......	100	Cu.St.	100	Nim.	100	Nim.	E	3	E	4	S E	4	28	8	29.091	28.716	28.810	28.702	.048	.087	.141	62	84	100
16	20	23	23	22	......	12 M.	.05	......	100	Nim	100	Cu.St.	100	Cu.St.	S W	5	S W	4	W	3	23	12	28.524	28.761	28.862	28.715	.108	.106	.106	100	86	86
17	17	32	26	24⅔	......	......	......	......	80	Cir.St.	100	Cu.St.	100	Cu.St.	S W	2	W	4	W	2	32	13	28.816	28.534	28.677	28.675	.094	.143	.185	100	79	100
18	19	30	22	23⅔	......	......	......	......	100	Cu.St.	100	Cu.St.	30	Cu.St.	W	1	S W	2	....	0	30	11	28.691	28.688	28.691	28.690	.103	.130	.118	100	78	100
19	52	39	47	39⅓	11 P. M.	......	......	......	100	Cu.St	100	Cu.St.	70	Cu.St.	S E	1	S W	2	S W	2	50	3	28.596	28.627	28.485	28.569	.181	.216	.323	100	91	100
20	9	10	1	6⅔	......	1 A. M.	.42	......	100	Cu.St.	90	Cu.St.	30	St.	S W	6	S W	6	S W	5	10	−6	28.815	29.079	29.171	29.021	.051	.054	.032	77	78	70
21	5	15	8	9⅓	......	......	......	......	70	Cu.St.	100	Cu.St.	80	Cu.	S W	4	S W	4	S W	3	15	−3	29.138	29.136	29.048	29.124	.027	.063	.062	49	81	100
22	10	19	15	14⅔	......	......	......	......	40	Cu.	30	Cir.	40	Cir.St.	W	2	W	2	S W	1	19	4	29.045	29.134	29.133	29.105	.054	.071	.070	78	69	52
23	17	24	15	18⅔	......	......	......	......	100	Cu.St.	100	Cir.St.	80	Cir.St.	S E	1	S E	1	N E	1	25	5	29.141	29.114	29.1[illegible]4	29.139	.078	.129	.066	83	100	100
24	12	27	25	21⅓	In night	......	.10	1	90	Cu.St.	70	Cu.St.	100	Cu.St.	N E	1	E	3	E	3	27	8	29.142	29.017	29.008	29.055	.075	.063	.117	100	63	87
25	22	28	26	25⅓	......	......	......	......	100	Cu.St.	50	Cu.St.	100	Cu.St.	N E	1	E	1	W	1	28	10	28.798	28.824	28.863	28.830	.118	.117	.141	100	76	100
26	23	30	16	24	......	......	......	......	90	Cu.St.	10	St.	00	......	N E	1	N	2	N	1	30	4	28.890	28.929	28.939	28.919	.123	.130	.070	87	78	83
27	8	29	17	18	......	......	......	......	10	St.	90	Cu.St.	0	......	....	0	....	0	....	0	29	3	28.996	29.032	29.201	29.166	.062	.142	.078	100	88	83
28	22	29	26	25⅔	12 M.	7 P. M.	.15	1½	100	Cu.St.	100	Nim.	30	Cir.St.	W	3	S W	2	....	0	30	18	28.842	28.763	28.781	28.795	.118	.160	.141	100	100	100
29	30	38	34	34	......	......	......	......	100	Cu.St.	100	Cu.St.	100	Cu.St.	S W	1	S W	2	S W	2	38	27	28.848	28.861	28.745	28.818	.167	.208	.175	100	91	89
30	33	37	29	33	......	......	......	......	100	Nim.	70	Cu.	0	......	W	2	W	4	W	3	37	22	28.639	28.748	28.800	28.775	.168	.116	.160	89	58	100
31	25	35	31	30⅓	......	......	......	......	10	St.	80	Cu.St.	40	Cir.St.	S W	2	S W	3	W	4	35	20	28.796	28.679	28.569	28.681	.100	.127	.118	74	62	63
Sums	...	...	...	......	......	......	2.03	6½	......	......	......	......	......	......	....	..	....	..	....	..	......	......	......	......	......	......	......	......	......	......	......	......
Means	...	...	...	21.16	......	......	......	......	82	......	73	......	69	......	....	..	....	..	....	..	20°.2	7°.75	......	......	......	29.013	.094	.113	.107	86	75	85
Average,									74																		104			82		

METEOROLOGICAL OBSERVATIONS FOR THE MONTH OF FEBRUARY, 1866.

Day of the Month	Thermometer in the open air: 7 A. M.	2 P. M.	9 P. M.	Mean.	Rain and Snow: Time of beginning of rain or snow	Time of ending of rain or snow.	Amount of rain or melted snow in gauge in inches.	Depth of snow, in inches.
1	24	25	20	23	......	......	......	......
2	21	22	12	13⅓	Snow	squalls.	.10	1
3	14	12	12	12⅔	......	......	......	......
4	4	14	8	8⅔	......	......	......	......
5	5	12	12	9⅔	......	......	......	......
6	14	23	17	18	......	......	......	......
7	21	35	31	29	......	......	......	......
8	25	23	23	23⅔	7 A. M.	3 P. M.	.10	1
9	23	31	35	29⅔	......	......	......	......
10	24	39	33	31⅓	3 P. M.	......	......	......
11	21	25	12	19⅓	......	8 A. M.	.40	4
12	18	25	19	20⅔	......	......	......	......
13	20	32	25	25⅔	9 P. M.	......	.30	3
14	26	31	5	20⅔	......	5 P. M.	.20	2
15	–4	8	–3	0⅓	......	......	......	......
16	–15	13	1	–1⅔	......	......	......	......
17	17	31	25	24⅓	......	......	......	......
18	25	31	20	25⅓	7 A. M.	3 P. M.	.11	2½
19	29	35	23	29	......	......	......	......
20	21	27	18	22	......	......	......	......
21	21	39	42	34	......	......	......	......
22	43	54	42	46⅓	3 P. M.	......	.40	......
23	32	36	40	36	......	9 P. M.	.02	......
24	25	32	31	29	[illegible]	......	.06	½
25	7	13	8	9⅓	......	......	......	......
26	6	25	23	18⅔	......	......	......	......
27	14	37	32	27⅔	......	......	......	......
28	32	47	48	42	......	......	......	......
29	...	...	...	......	......	......	......	......
30	...	...	...	......	......	......	......	......
31	...	...	...	......	......	......	......	......
Sums.	...	...	...	......	......	......	2.33	14
Means	...	...	...	22°.71	......	......	......	......
Average,					......			

Day of the Month	Clouds 7 A. M.: Percentage of cloudiness.	Kind of clouds.	2 P. M.: Percentage of cloudiness.	Kind of clouds.	9 P. M.: Percentage of cloudiness.	Kind of clouds.	Winds 7 A. M.: Direction.	Force.	2 P. M.: Direction.	Force.	9 P. M.: Direction.	Force.
1	100	Cu.St.	20	Cu.	0	......	W	3	W	4	S W	2
2	100	Cu.St.	80	Cu.St.	50	Cu.St.	S W	3	S W	5	N W	3
3	100	Cu.St.	80	Cu.St.	50	Cu.St.	W	5	W	5	S W	4
4	30	Cu.St.	80	Cu.	100	Cu.St.	W	2	N W	3	S W	2
5	100	Cu.St.	100	Cu.St.	100	Cu.St.	S W	2	S W	4	S W	4
6	100	Cu.St.	40	Cir.St.	30	Cu.St.	N W	1	S W	1	S E	2
7	90	Cu.St.	100	Cu.St.	100	Cu.St.	S W	2	S W	3	S W	1
8	100	Nim.	100	Nim.	100	Cu.St.	N E	2	N E	3	....	0
9	100	Cu.St.	100	Cu.St.	100	Cu.St.	S E	2	S E	3	S W	2
10	90	Cu.St.	100	Cu.St.	100	Nim.	S E	1	N E	1	N E	1
11	100	Nim.	80	Cu.	0	......	N E	2	N E	1	....	0
12	100	Cu.St.	20	Cu.St.	40	Cu.St.	N E	3	N	1	....	0
13	100	Fog.	100	Cu.St.	100	Nim.	S W	1	S E	1	E	1
14	100	Nim.	100	Nim.	50	Cu.St.	S W	1	S W	2	S W	6
15	60	Cu.St.	100	Nim.	30	Cu.St.	S W	2	S W	4	S W	3
16	80	St.	80	Cu.St.	10	Cu.St.	S W	3	S W	5	S W	5
17	30	St.	40	Cir.St.	0	......	S W	4	S W	4	S W	4
18	100	Nim.	100	Nim.	30	Cu.St.	S W	3	S W	1	S W	1
19	100	Cu.St.	100	Cu.St.	0	......	S W	2	S W	3	S W	3
20	40	Cu.	40	Cu.	30	Cu.St.	S W	3	S W	5	S W	2
21	100	Cu.St.	70	Cir.St.	0	......	S E	2	S W	3	S W	5
22	70	Cu.St.	60	Cu.St.	100	Nim.	S W	3	S W	4	S E	1
23	100	Nim.	100	Nim.	100	Nim.	E	2	E	2	S W	3
24	100	Cu.St.	70	Cu.	80	Cu.	W	3	W	4	W	3
25	80	Cu.St.	30	Cu.	80	Cu.	W	4	S W	4	W	3
26	70	Cir.St.	90	Cu.S.	80	Cir.Cu.	S W	1	S W	3	S W	2
27	70	Cir.St.	10	St.	0	......	....	0	....	0	....	0
28	100	Cu.St.	100	Cu.St.	100	Cu.S.	S	2	S E	1	S W	1
29	......	......	......	......	......	......	....	..	....	..	....	..
30	......	......	......	......	......	......	....	..	....	..	....	..
31	......	......	......	......	......	......	....	..	....	..	....	..
Sums.	......	......	......	......	......	......	....	..	....	..	....	..
Means	83	......	75	......	57	......	....	..	....	..	....	.
Average,	71						......					

Day of the Month	Max. Thermometer.	Min. Thermometer.	Barometer Height Reduced to Freezing Point: 7 A. M.	2 P. M.	9 P. M.	Mean.	Force or Pressure of Vapor, in Inches: 7 A. M.	2 P. M.	9 P. M.	Relative Humidity, or Percentage of Saturation: 7 A. M.	2 P. M.	9 P. M.
1	25	15	28.631	28.659	28.693	28.661	.094	.092	.091	73	64	85
2	23	4	28.700	28.633	28.759	28.697	.086	.101	.075	85	86	100
3	14	0	28.832	28.774	28.869	28.826	.051	.075	.075	63	100	100
4	14	–2	28.903	29.039	29.264	29.068	.038	.051	.034	73	63	54
5	13	0	29.358	29.257	29.346	29.320	.041	.045	.045	74	60	60
6	29	10	29.413	29.386	29.315	29.371	.051	.106	.078	61	86	83
7	35	21	29.156	29.085	29.057	29.082	.096	.142	.136	85	70	78
8	25	17	29.016	28.959	28.955	28.943	.135	.118	.112	100	100	88
9	35	17	28.802	28.615	28.555	28.677	.036	.155	.142	22	89	70
10	40	17	28.663	28.664	28.750	28.695	.036	.173	.175	22	73	94
11	25	8	28.856	29.038	29.077	28.990	.095	.117	.060	85	87	80
12	26	13	29.103	29.077	29.015	29.067	.058	.117	.163	100	87	100
13	33	17	29.032	28.997	28.875	28.968	.108	.181	.135	100	100	100
14	31	–3	28.538	28.631	28.703	28.666	.141	.155	.041	100	89	74
15	10	–14	28.971	28.083	29.277	29.068	.026	.033	.025	100	100	66
16	8	–22	29.283	29.217	29.143	29.214	.033	.036	.031	100	72	52
17	31	12	29.114	29.032	29.036	29.063	.047	.155	.141	50	89	100
18	34	19	29.032	28.799	28.631	28.824	.089	.156	.147	72	79	84
19	37	17	28.546	28.560	28.657	28.587	.142	.142	.069	88	70	72
20	27	5	28.743	28.957	29.063	28.921	.080	.093	.098	71	63	100
21	48	18	29.093	29.040	28.996	29.043	.066	.131	.222	85	55	82
22	54	30	28.956	28.964	29.013	28.981	.278	.206	.207	100	49	100
23	40	31	28.019	28.697	28.567	28.427	.181	.222	.246	100	100	88
24	33	3	28.701	28.771	28.872	28.781	.117	.143	.094	87	79	73
25	13	6	29.290	29.319	29.401	29.339	.060	.063	.048	100	81	77
26	25	1	29.479	29.403	29.224	29.363	.063	.109	.113	100	74	88
27	41	11	29.193	29.253	29.222	29.215	.072	.115	.143	91	58	70
28	49	31	29.090	29.019	28.959	29.016	.181	.219	.249	100	77	77
29	......	......	......	......	......	......	......	......	......	......	......	......
30	......	......	......	......	......	......	......	......	......	......	......	......
31	......	......	......	......	......	......	......	......	......	......	......	......
Sums.	......	......	......	......	......	......	......	......	......	......	......	......
Means	31°.1	9°	......	......	......	28.970	.095	.124	.118	81	73	84
Average,	......		......				.112			81		

METEOROLOGICAL OBSERVATIONS FOR THE MONTH OF MARCH, 1866.

Day of the Month.	Thermometer in the open air. 7 A. M.	2 P. M.	9 P. M.	Mean.	Rain and snow. Time of beginning of rain or snow.	Time of ending of rain or snow.	Amount of rain or melted snow in gauge in inches.	Depth of snow, in inches.	Clouds. 7 A. M. Percentage of cloudiness.	Kind of clouds.	2 P. M. Percentage of cloudiness.	Kind of clouds.	9 P. M. Percentage of cloudiness.	Kind of clouds.	Winds. 7 A. M. Direction.	Force.	2 P. M. Direction.	Force.	9 P. M. Direction.	Force.	Max. Thermometer.	Min. Thermometer.	Barometer height reduced to freezing point. 7 A. M.	2 P. M.	9 P. M.	Mean.	Force or pressure of vapor, in inches. 7 A. M.	2 P. M.	9 P. M.	Relative humidity, or percentage of saturation. 7 A. M.	2 P. M.	9 P. M.
1	45	56	49	50	In night.		.20		90	Cu. St.	100	Nim.	80	Cu.	S W	1	S W	3	0	..	57	43	28.931	28.949	28.943	28.941	.204	.282	.298	68	63	92
2	46	53	51	50	4½ P. M.	10 P. M.	.11		70	Cu. St.	100	Cu. St.	100	Nim.	S W	1	S W	2	S W	2	54	28	28.905	28.910	28.913	28.909	.311	.321	.374	100	80	100
3	30	36	28	31⅓					20	St.	10	Cir. Cu	0		S W	3	S W	4	S W	5	36	14	29.000	28.064	29.041	29.035	.167	.129	.099	100	61	64
4	19	25	20	21⅓					100	Cu. St.	90	Cu.	20	Cu. St.	W	4	N W	5	N W	4	27	13	29.094	29.131	29.220	29.145	.087	.100	.075	84	74	70
5	15	31	23	23					0		10	Cu.	0		S W	1	S W	4	W	2	31	11	29.246	29.251	29.254	29.250	.070	.100	.084	82	57	71
6	14	37	31	27⅓					20	St.	100	Cu. St.	100	Cu. St.	S W	1	S W	2	W	3	38	17	29.275	29.232	29.175	29.227	.082	.157	.174	100	71	100
7	21	28	10	23					10	Cu. St	70	Cu.	0		N W	3	N W	4	N W	5	28	11	29.134	29.153	29.236	29.175	.064	.117	.09	56	76	85
8	16	33	27	25⅓					40	St.	50	Cir. St.	0		W	1	W	2	W	1	33	13	29.286	29.286	29.270	29.280	.058	.113	.147	65	60	100
9	24	27	17	22⅔	7 A. M.	12 M.	.05		100	Nim.	90	Cu. St.	0		S W	1	N E	3	N	1	30	2	29.028	29.033	29.274	29.111	.129	.093	.078	100	63	83
10	8	32	32	24	9 P. M				0		40	Cir. St.	100	Nim.	S W	1	S W	3	S E	3	32	5	29.276	29.210	28.790	29.092	.048	.143	.143	77	79	79
11	30	41	37	39		3 P. M.	.31		100	Nim.	100	Nim.	100	Cu. St	S W	4	S W	3	0	..	42	26	28.536	28.717	28.746	28.666	.223	.241	.199	95	95	90
12	31	33	34	33⅔	In night.		.12	⅓	100	Cu. St.	100	Cu. S.	100	Cu. St.	N E	1	W	3	N E	1	39	29	28.908	28.903	29.067	28.959	.155	.149	.155	89	71	79
13	30	35	32	32⅓	7 P. M.				100	Cu. St.	100	Cu. St.	10	Nim.	N E	1	N E	2	N E	3	37	27	29.028	29.195	29.150	29.091	.167	.142	.181	100	70	100
14	33	33	33	32⅔		8 P. M.	.02		100	Nim.	100	Nim.	100	Cu. St.	N E	1	....	0	....	0	33	28	28.991	29.019	29.067	29.025	.181	.168	.168	100	89	89
15	33	35	32	33⅓	3 P. M.	6 P. M.	.03		100	Cu. St.	100	Cu. St.	100	Cu. St.	N E	1	E	1	S W	[illegible]	35	23	29.013	28.884	28.841	28.912	.175	.183	.181	94	90	100
16	27	29	19	25	Snow	squalls.	.05	½	100	Cu. St.	100	Cu. St.	70	Cu.	S W	3	S W	4	S W	5	29	4	28.737	28.664	28.745	28.715	.111	.142	.087	75	88	84
17	9	13	9	10⅓					40	Cu. St	60	Cu.	0		W	3	W	5	W	2	13	2	28.927	29.058	29.059	29.014	.051	.048	.065	77	62	100
18	16	30	26	24	6 A. M.	10 A. M.	.02	¼	100	Nim.	80	Cu.	100	Cu. St.	S W	3	S W	4	W	1	30	12	28.836	28.773	28.826	28.818	.074	.130	.105	83	78	75
19	12	27	26	25					100	Cu. St.	80	Cu. St.	100	Cu. St.	N E	1	N E	1	E	2	27	15	28.893	28.95[illegible]	28.820	28.888	.084	.129	.105	71	88	75
20	20	[illegible]	31	[illegible]	5 P. M.	11 P. M.	1.10		100	Nim.	100	Cu. St.	100	Nim.	E	3	E	2	E	3	31	15	28.828	28.068	28.931	28.809	.091	.135	.174	85	88	100
21	20	29	23	24					100	Cu. St.	80	Cu.	0		N W	2	W	3	W	4	30	15	28.641	28.878	28.417	28.645	.108	.147	.106	100	91	86
22	16	35	33	32	In night.		.13		80	Cu. St	100	Cu. St.	90	Cu. St.	S W	1	S	1	E	3	35	22	29.096	29.074	29.054	29.075	.135	.162	.150	100	80	80
23	37	33	29	33					100	Nim.	100	Cu. St.	100	Cu. St	W	2	W	3	N W	3	37	20	28.681	28.779	28.812	28.757	.221	.168	.142	100	80	83
24	25	32	21	26	11 A. M.	5 P. M.	.08		80	Cu. St.	100	Nim.	40	Cu.	S W	1	S W	2	W	4	33	7	28.888	28.735	28.[illegible]59	28.800	.135	.181	.080	100	100	71
25	11	19	12	14	3 A. M.	8 A. M.	.07	1	100	Nim.	40	Cu.	0		N W	2	N W	5	N W	2	19	5	28.901	28.995	28.821	28.905	.062	.0807	.060	89	84	80
26	13	28	24	21⅔					0		20	Cu.	0		W	1	N W	2	W	1	29	13	29.204	29.251	28.945	29.100	.063	.099	.100	81	69	57
27	22	34	31	28⅔					40	Cir St.	60	Cu. St.	100	Nim.	E	1	E	2	E	1	33	20	29.283	29.262	29.196	29.247	.118	.196	.123	100	100	77
28	27	33	28	29⅓	3 A. M.	11 P. M.	.42	4	100	Nim.	100	Nim.	100	Nim.	E	2	E	1	W	1	35	27	28.991	29.177	29.200	29.089	.120	.188	.135	88	100	88
29	5	34	27	28⅔					90	Cu. St.	60	Cu. St	0		W	2	W	1	W	1	35	25	28.556	28.953	28.188	28.4[illegible]9	.117	.12[illegible]	.111	82	61	75
30	27	37	31	31⅔	4 A. M.	8 P. M.	.03		20	St.	100	Nim.	100	Nim.	S W	1	S W	[illegible]	S E	1	40	27	28.941	28.796	28.985	28.907	.129	.084	.155	83	38	89
31	33	46	39	41					90	Cu. S	90	Cu. St.	100	Cu. St.	S E	2	S W	2	S W	2	47	29	28.31[illegible]	28.488	28.655	28.486	.180	.262	.233	81	84	100
Sums.							3.39	6.25																								
Means				29.°6					71		81		63								34°.1	17°.6				28.979	.126	.152	.144	90	77	88
Average,									71																		.140			83		

METEOROLOGICAL OBSERVATIONS FOR THE MONTH OF APRIL, 1866.

Day of Month.	Thermometer in the open air. 7 A. M.	2 P. M.	9 P. M.	Mean.	Rain and Snow. Time of beginning of rain or snow.	Time of ending of rain or snow.	Amount of rain or melted snow in gauge in inches.	Depth of snow, in inches.	Clouds. 7 A. M. Percentage of cloudiness.	Kind of clouds.	2 P. M. Percentage of cloudiness.	Kind of clouds.	9 P. M. Percentage of cloudiness.	Kind of clouds.
1	25	43	37	38⅓	7 P. M	......	......	......	40	Cu.	20	Cir.St.	100	Nim.
2	34	41	37	37⅓	......	10 A. M.	1.00	......	100	Nim.	90	Cu. St.	100	Cu. St.
3	33	64	63	53⅓	......	......	......	......	80	Cu.	10	St.	100	Cu. St.
4	43	74	65	62½	......	......	......	......	30	Cir.Cu	100	Cir.Cu	20	Cu. St.
5	48	44	35	42⅓	......	......	......	......	100	Cir.Cu	100	Cu.	100	Cu.
6	31	36	30	32⅓	......	......	......	......	100	Cu. St.	90	Cu.	100	Cu.
7	29	37	35	33⅔	......	......	......	......	100	Cir.Cu	100	Cu.	100	Cu.
8	32	40	31	34⅓	......	......	......	......	0	......	50	Cu.	0	......
9	30	47	39	35⅓	......	......	......	......	10	St.	0	......	10	St.
10	35	55	30	40	......	......	......	......	100	Cu. St.	100	Cir.Cu	100	Cu.
11	31	64	56	50⅓	......	......	......	......	50	Cu.	70	Cir.Cu	0	......
12	53	63	45	53⅔	2 P. M.	5 P. M.	.145	......	100	Cu. St.	100	Cu.	0	......
13	33	52	45	45	......	......	......	......	80	Cir.St.	10	Cu.	20	St.
14	44	58	41	47⅔	......	......	......	......	100	Cir.Cu	100	Cir.Cu	0	......
15	36	55	44	45	......	......	......	......	80	Cir.St.	100	Cir.St.	10	St.
16	37	66	54	52½	......	......	......	......	40	Cir.St.	10	Cir.	0	......
17	52	74	64	63⅓	......	......	......	......	100	Cir.St.	90	Cu. St.	30	Cu. St.
18	58	78	6[illegible]	66⅓	7 P. M.	8½ P. M.	.220	......	90	Cir	100	Cu.	100	Nim.
19	60	69	66	65	9 A. M	5 P. M.	.042	......	90	Cir Cu	100	Cu.	100	Cu.
20	64	67	61	64	......	......	......	......	100	Nim.	100	Cir Cu	0	......
21	56	65	53	57⅓	......	......	......	......	10	Cu.	100	Cir.St.	10	St.
22	46	61	54	63⅔	......	......	......	......	20	St.	80	Cir.	80	Cir.St.
23	41	50	47	46	......	......	......	......	100	Cu.	100	Cir.St	80	Cir.St
24	39	51	45	41⅔	......	......	......	......	10	Cu.	10	Cu.	100	Cir.Cu
25	37	51	43	43⅔	......	......	......	......	10	Cu.	0	......	0	......
26	36	56	42	45⅓	......	......	......	......	0	......	10	Cir.St	0	......
27	41	63	63	60	......	......	......	......	70	Cir.Cu	70	Cir.	20	Cu. St.
28	67	65	40	57⅓	......	......	......	......	70	Cir.St.	70	Cir.Cu	0	......
29	44	62	50	52	......	......	......	......	10	St.	10	Cu.	10	Cir.Cu
30	42	56	50	49⅓	......	......	......	......	10	Cir.St.	70	Cir.Cu	100	Cir.Cu
31	..	..	..	......	......	......	......	......	......	......	......	......	......	......
Sums	..	..	..	......	......	......	1.407	......	......	......	......	......	......	......
Means	..	..	..	48° 94	......	......	......	......	60	......	65	......	46	......
Average,									57					

Day of Month.	Winds. 7 A. M. Direction.	Force.	2 P. M. Direction.	Force.	9 P. M. Direction.	Force.	Max. Thermometer.	Min. Thermometer.	Barometer Height Reduced to Freezing Point. 7 A. M.	2 P. M.	9 P. M.	Mean.	Force or Pressure of Vapor, in Inches. 7 A. M.	2 P. M.	9 P. M.	Relative Humidity, or Percentage of Saturation. 7 A. M.	2 P. M.	9 P. M.
1	....	0	E	1	E	3	43	32	29.9 1	29.037	28.990	28.992	.204	.164	.221	100	50	100
2	E	3	E	4	E	3	41	30	28.952	28.932	29.050	28.944	.196	.225	.199	100	91	90
3	S E	2	S	3	S	2	64	35	28.945	28.862	28.810	28.875	.208	.4[illegible]3	.365	91	73	76
4	S W	1	S	2	S	2	75	44	28.801	28.769	28.713	28.767	.310	.497	.259	92	59	58
5	S W	2	S W	3	S W	4	48	26	28.721	28.949	29.063	28.904	.310	.218	.127	92	76	63
6	S W	3	N W	3	N W	2	35	18	29.085	29.103	29.172	29.120	.174	.212	.167	100	100	100
7	W	1	W	2	....	0	37	20	29.165	29.132	29.085	29.127	.160	.178	.127	100	81	62
8	N E	1	N E	2	....	0	40	18	29.099	29.091	29.091	29.093	.162	.097	.137	69	89	78
9	....	0	W	2	N W	1	48	28	29.198	29.077	29.077	29.117	.111	.112	.110	67	34	46
10	S	1	S W	2	....	0	55	26	28.961	28.785	28.807	28.851	.142	.193	.167	70	44	100
11	...	0	S W	2	S	2	31	64	28.872	28.815	28.796	28.827	.155	.208	.255	89	34	97
12	S	3	S W	4	S W	1	66	32	28.712	28.574	28.733	28.673	.244	.416	.251	60	72	84
13	....	0	S E	2	S	2	56	36	29.098	29.090	29.066	29.068	.186	.183	.204	81	47	68
14	S	2	S W	4	....	0	59	32	28.795	28.754	28.916	28.821	.218	.229	.212	76	47	82
15	N E	2	E	2	E	1	56	30	29.030	29.017	29.002	29.013	.129	.155	.196	61	34	63
16	N E	1	E	2	E	1	66	35	29.002	28.977	28.945	28.974	.178	.203	.206	81	32	49
17	S E	2	S E	2	S	2	74	50	28.969	28.956	28.954	28.959	.334	.163	.433	86	66	73
18	S	2	S	3	...	0	78	54	28.978	28.951	28.961	28.963	.403	.550	.676	67	58	100
19	....	0	N E	1	N	3	73	57	28.967	28.904	28.906	28.925	.518	.564	.536	100	79	84
20	S W	3	S W	3	S W	2	72	54	28.706	28.673	28.613	28.664	.520	.489	.35[illegible]	89	75	66
21	W	4	W	4	W	1	62	40	28.539	28.537	28.521	28.532	.282	.216	.244	63	37	60
22	W	1	W	3	....	0	63	37	28.597	28.584	28.590	28.590	.215	.216	.231	69	40	55
23	N E	3	N W	4	N W	3	50	32	28.479	28.460	28.509	28.482	.135	.117	.133	91	32	41
24	W	3	S W	3	W	2	52	30	28.548	28.509	28.503	28.520	.090	.087	.138	38	22	46
25	N W	2	N W	3	N W	2	57	27	28.513	28.599	28.718	28.610	.084	.047	.058	38	12	21
26	....	0	N W	2	....	0	68	28	28.866	28.843	28.817	28.842	.0[illegible]9	.083	.155	28	19	38
27	S W	3	S	3	S	2	67	42	28.843	28.734	28.619	28.732	.236	.261	.349	70	38	51
28	S W	1	S W	4	....	0	62	28	28.554	28.701	28.925	28.726	.425	.330	.203	64	53	82
29	E	1	W	2	E	1	58	28	28.998	28.947	28.952	28.965	.241	.101	.117	84	18	32
30	E	1	W	3	E	1	58	33	28.957	28.826	28.767	28.850	.155	.179	.139	58	40	39
31	....	..	....	..	....	..	......	......	......	......	......	......	......	......	......	......	......	......
Sums	....	..	....	..	....	..	......	......	......	......	......	......	......	......	......	......	......	......
Means	....	..	....	..	....	..	53°.8	34°.8	......	......	......	28.848	.219	.247	.232	76	53	63
Average,													236			64		

METEOROLOGICAL OBSERVATIONS FOR THE MONTH OF MAY, 1866.

Day of the Month.	Thermometer in the open air. 7 A. M.	2 P. M.	9 P. M.	Mean.	Rain and Snow. Time of beginning of rain or snow.	Time of ending of rain or snow.	Amount of rain or melted snow in gauge in inches.	Depth of snow, in inches.	Clouds. 7 A. M. Percentage of cloudiness.	Kind of clouds.	2 P. M. Percentage of cloudiness.	Kind of clouds.	9 P. M. Percentage of cloudiness.	Kind of clouds.
1	38	35	35	36	2 A. M.	5 P. M.	1.182	4	100	Nim.	100	Nim.	100	Nim.
2	35	48	41	41⅓	....	....	....	....	0	......	60	Cu.	0	......
3	40	53	48	47	....	....	....	....	70	Cu. St.	90	Cu.	0	......
4	46	59	45	50	....	....	....	....	10	St.	100	Cu.	0	......
5	43	63	50	51⅓	10½ P. M.	....	....	....	100	Cu.	20	Cu.	70	Cu.
6	44	60	43	51⅔	....	3 A. M.	.010	....	0	......	30	Cu.	0	......
7	50	68	55	57⅔	....	....	....	....	10	St.	90	Cu.	10	Cu. St.
8	53	50	58	53⅓	9 A. M.	7 P. M.	.320	....	100	Cir. St.	100	Nim.	100	Nim.
9	49	63	54	67	....	....	....	....	100	Cu.	30	Cu.	0	......
10	52	69	53	58	....	....	....	....	100	Cu.	100	Cu.	0	......
11	57	73	56	62	....	....	....	....	0	......	70	Cu.	0	......
12	66	64	63	64⅓	2 P. M.	9½ P. M.	.126	....	70	Cir. Cu	100	Nim.	100	Nim.
13	50	56	43	51⅓	....	....	....	....	100	Cir. St.	10	Cu.	0	......
14	41	56	47	48	....	....	....	....	0	......	10	Cu.	0	......
15	54	79	53	60⅔	4½ P. M.	....	....	....	90	Cir. Cu	90	Cu.	100	Cu.
16	41	50	43	44⅔	....	3½ A. M.	.390	....	100	Cu.	70	Cir. Cu	0	......
17	44	63	50	52⅓	....	....	....	....	0	......	90	Cir. St.	100	Cu.
18	63	73	63	68	....	....	....	....	50	Cir. Cu	50	Cir. Cu	0	......
19	56	80	73	69⅔	....	....	....	....	70	Cir. St.	0	......	0	......
20	73	70	61	68	....	....	....	....	70	Cir. St.	10	Cu.	0	......
21	52	56	46	51⅓	....	....	....	....	0	......	50	Cu.	0	......
22	41	59	48	49⅓	....	....	....	....	0	......	10	Cu.	0	......
23	49	61	47	52⅓	....	....	....	....	0	......	20	Cu.	0	......
24	59	69	55	58	....	....	....	....	0	......	10	Cu.	0	......
25	63	76	55	65	....	....	....	....	0	......	100	Cu.	80	Cir. Cu
26	51	72	61	61⅓	11 P. M.	....	....	....	100	Cu.	60	Cir. St.	100	Cu. St.
27	43	43	46	47⅓	....	4 P. M.	.980	....	100	Nim.	100	Nim.	100	Nim.
28	52	61	48	53⅔	7 P. M.	....	....	....	10	Cir. Cu	90	Cu.	100	Nim.
29	45	56	49	50	....	4 A. M.	.460	....	100	Cu.	90	Cu.	40	Cir. Cu
30	57	71	58	62	....	....	....	....	90	Cir. St.	70	Cir. Cu	100	Cu.
31	45	67	48	53⅓	....	....	....	....	10	St.	50	Cir. Cu	50	Cir. St.
Sums.	..	..	..	....	....	....	3.478	4	......	......	......	......	......	......
Means	..	..	..	55.°04	....	....	....	....	50	......	60.6	......	37	......
Average, ...									49.2					

Day of the Month.	Winds. 7 A. M. Direction.	Force.	2 P. M. Direction.	Force.	9 P. M. Direction.	Force.	Max. Thermometer.	Min. Thermometer.	Barometer Height Reduced to Freezing Point. 7 A. M.	2 P. M.	9 P. M.	Mean.	Force or Pressure of Vapor, in Inches. 7 A. M.	2 P. M.	9 P. M.	Relative Humidity, or Percentage of Saturation. 7 A. M.	2 P. M.	9 P. M.
1	N E	3	N E	2	N	1	38	27	28.471	28.436	28.678	28.528	.208	.183	.183	91	90	90
2	N W	2	W	3	N E	1	49	24	98.838	28.847	28.866	28.851	.142	.143	.126	70	43	49
3	....	0	N W	3	....	0	54	34	28.925	28.874	28.853	28.884	.175	.100	.120	69	25	36
4	W	2	W	3	....	0	59	31	28.841	28.799	28.763	28.801	.169	.190	.204	54	38	68
5	....	0	W	3	N W	1	59	31	28.816	28.832	28.807	28.819	.186	.203	.210	67	43	63
6	N E	1	E	2	....	0	61	30	29.019	29.013	29.019	29.017	.218	.177	.136	76	34	70
7	....	0	S W	2	S W	1	63	44	29.099	29.028	28.971	29.032	.158	.260	.269	71	42	62
8	S W	1	N E	1	....	0	60	42	28.888	28.749	28.643	28.761	.244	.323	.310	60	65	92
9	S W	1	S W	2	....	0	67	44	28.756	28.711	28.724	28.727	.297	.290	.282	85	42	67
10	S E	1	....	0	...	0	71	38	28.882	28.773	28.757	28.787	.282	.336	.3[illegible]1	73	47	80
11	....	0	S	1	....	0	75	44	28.743	28.751	28.721	28.73[illegible]	.378	.376	.363	81	47	81
12	S W	2	S W	3	S W	2	73	45	28.736	28.731	28.732	28.749	.407	.464	.478	63	77	63
13	N	3	N W	3	N W	2	57	23	28.797	28.842	28.953	28.864	.139	.131	.143	39	29	43
14	N W	2	N	2	N	2	63	39	29.030	28.973	28.894	28.967	.147	.179	.202	57	40	62
15	S	3	S W	3	S W	2	71	37	28.766	28.566	28.556	28.62	.206	.293	.423	49	40	88
16	N E	2	N E	2	N	2	50	27	28.707	28.843	28.870	28.808	.212	.186	.121	82	51	43
17	N	1	S	1	S	1	63	42	28.878	28.789	28.660	28.775	.196	.270	.282	68	47	63
18	S W	2	S W	3	....	0	77	40	28.632	28.625	28.658	28.638	.416	.375	.386	72	39	67
19	S	1	S	2	S W	1	85	56	28.754	28.735	28.6[illegible]4	28.704	.336	.561	.681	75	55	72
20	W	3	S W	4	S W	3	73	40	28.603	28.645	28.795	28.684	.545	.263	.242	67	36	45
21	N	2	N W	4	....	0	55	30	28.836	28.881	28.940	28.852	.282	.155	.139	60	34	54
22	N W	1	N	2	....	0	59	27	29.048	28.902	28.964	28.971	.169	.140	.143	65	28	43
23	S W	1	N W	2	....	0	63	26	29.033	28.972	28.98[illegible]	28.962	.247	.164	.179	71	30	55
24	S W	2	W	3	S W	1	69	45	29.034	28.886	28.850	28.923	.234	.163	.243	65	23	56
25	S W	2	W	4	....	0	76	44	28.744	28.652	28.628	28.674	.270	.273	.3[illegible]1	47	30	71
26	S	1	N E	3	N E	3	72	43	28.604	28.481	28.393	28.49[illegible]	.293	.358	.297	79	46	55
27	N [illegible]	3	N E	4	N E	3	52	42	28.1[illegible]1	28.184	28.390	28.231	.335	.325	.286	100	100	92
28	N W	1	W	3	N W	1	64	40	28.601	28.579	28.585	28.588	.308	.242	.285	79	45	85
29	W	2	S	2	W	1	60	39	28.644	28.764	28.690	28.699	.251	.336	.272	84	75	78
30	W	2	S W	3	N	3	72	32	28.677	28.590	28.708	28.658	.3[illegible]2	.371	.309	69	49	64
31	N	2	N W	2	E	1	69	43	28.942	28.958	28.937	28.945	.182	.274	.137	61	71	40
Sums.	....	..	....	..	....	..	......	......	......	......	......	......	......	......	......	......	......	......
Means	....	..	....	..	....	..	64°.09	37°.45	......	......	......	28.823	.266	.262	.256	69	47	61
Average, ...													.261			59		

METEOROLOGICAL OBSERVATIONS FOR THE MONTH OF JUNE, 1866.

Day of Month.	Thermometer in the open air. 7 A. M.	2 P. M.	9 P. M.	Mean.	Rain and Snow. Time of beginning of rain or snow.	Time of ending of rain or snow.	Amount of rain or melted snow in gauge in inches.	Depth of snow, in inches.	Clouds. 7 A. M. Percentage of cloudiness.	Kind of clouds.	2 P. M. Percentage of cloudiness.	Kind of clouds.	9 P. M. Percentage of cloudiness.	Kind of clouds.	Winds. 7 A. M. Direction.	Force.	2 P. M. Direction.	Force.	9 P. M. Direction.	Force.	Max. Thermometer.	Min. Thermometer.	Barometer Height Reduced to Freezing Point. 7 A. M.	2 P. M.	9 P. M.	Mean.	Force or Pressure of Vapor, in Inches. 7 A. M.	2 P. M.	9 P. M.	Relative Humidity, or Percentage of Saturation. 7 A. M.	2 P. M.	9 P. M.
1	56	75	53	63	...	...	...	...	90	Cir.Cu	30	Cu.	10	Cu.	S E	2	S E	2	S	1	76	45	28.965	28.891	28.858	28.904	.336	.484	.452	75	66	94
2	60	76	54	62	...	...	...	...	80	Cir.St.	80	Cir.Cu	70	Cir.St.	S E	1	S E	3	...	0	77	51	28.881	28.695	28.698	28.758	.453	.436	.362	88	49	87
3	66	71	61	66	7½ P.M.	...	...	...	100	Cir.Cu	90	Cir Cu	100	Cu.	E	1	E	3	E	2	74	56	28.623	28.550	28.543	28.571	.438	.331	.505	88	39	94
4	80	63	64	64	...	8 A. M.	.026	...	100	Nim.	100	Cu.	100	Cu.	S E	1	N E	2	E	1	71	58	28.516	28.525	28.560	28.539	.518	.543	.529	100	79	89
5	64	76	67	69	5 P. M.	7½ P.M.	.422	...	100	Cu.	90	Cu.	100	Cu.	S E	1	S W	3	S W	2	77	52	28.551	28.530	28.466	28.515	.569	.614	.333	97	68	50
6	58	59	59	58⅔	5 A. M.	10 A. M.	.318	...	100	Cu.	100	Nim.	100	Nim.	S W	3	S W	3	S W	3	61	55	28.452	28.449	28.585	28.495	.423	.439	.469	88	88	94
7	6[illegible]	71	59	63⅓	...	...	...	...	100	Cu.	100	Cu.	80	Cu.	S W	1	W	3	...	0	72	54	28.766	28.790	28.755	28.770	.462	.537	.420	91	71	68
8	70	86	76	77⅓	10 P. M.	...	...	...	70	Cu.	70	Cir.Cu	10	Cu.	S W	2	S	2	S W	1	88	62	27.761	28.678	29.634	28.69[illegible]	.523	.605	.772	72	65	66
9	66	73	66	68⅓	...	6 A. M.	.320	...	100	Nim.	100	Cir	10	Cu.	W	2	W	2	...	0	76	43	28.760	28.855	28.912	28.842	.639	.449	.301	100	56	49
10	57	78	65	66⅔	...	...	...	...	50	Cir.	50	Cir.	10	Cu. St.	N	2	N W	2	N	2	83	45	29.062	29.068	29.068	29.066	.433	.369	.551	73	41	75
11	64	76	65	63⅓	3 P. M.	4 P. M.	.220	...	10	Cir.St.	50	Cir.	10	Cu. St.	E	2	S	2	S E	3	78	55	29.110	28.953	28.938	29.003	.295	.514	.389	63	54	83
12	71	86	75	77⅓	...	...	...	...	90	Cu.	10	Cir.	10	Cu.	S	2	S W	3	W	3	83	65	28.978	28.856	28.837	28.887	.280	.805	.732	37	65	90
13	75	79	73	75⅔	12½ A.M	3 A. M.	.466	...	70	Cu.	0	...	20	Cu.	S W	3	S W	3	S W	2	80	57	28.647	28.704	28.634	28.662	.745	.612	.595	86	62	76
14	67	72	62	67	...	...	...	...	100	Cir.Cu	100	Cu.	20	Cu.	S W	3	S W	4	S W	2	73	48	28.688	28.720	28.683	28.698	.425	.595	.396	64	76	76
15	60	70	60	63⅓	...	...	...	...	10	Cu.	100	Cu.	10	Cu.	S W	3	S W	3	S W	1	71	50	28.738	28.690	28.700	28.790	.426	.385	.370	82	53	66
16	59	65	52	58⅓	11¼ A.M	12 M.	.183	...	100	Cu.	100	Cu.	10	Cu. St.	S W	2	S W	3	...	0	65	42	28.704	28.716	28.682	28.634	.410	.289	.335	82	73	80
17	53	60	54	55⅔	...	...	...	...	100	Cu.	100	Nim.	100	Cu.	N	1	N E	2	N E	3	62	42	28.722	28.717	28.692	28.719	.348	.310	.308	86	60	74
18	46	54	54	51⅓	2 A. M.	2½ P.M.	1.080	...	100	Nim.	0	...	100	Cu.	N W	3	N W	3	...	0	56	41	28.465	28.455	28.604	28.508	.311	.355	.256	100	84	61
19	53	70	54	59	...	...	...	...	100	Cu. St.	0	...	0	...	W	2	N W	2	...	0	73	42	28.745	28.837	28.894	28.825	.295	.353	.216	73	48	85
20	[illegible]5	73	65	69⅓	...	...	...	...	20	Cir.	20	Cu.	10	Cu.	S W	2	S W	3	...	0	81	62	28.982	28.868	28.866	28.912	.420	.514	.536	68	54	84
21	[illegible]3	74½	76	71	2 P. M.	3 P. M.	.155	...	40	Cir.	100	Nim.	100	Cu.	S W	1	S W	4	S W	3	82	59	28.793	28.712	28.742	28.749	.617	.712	.543	77	83	79
22	65	79	64	69⅓	...	...	...	...	0	...	10	Cu.	0	...	S W	1	S W	1	...	0	81	55	28.858	28.834	28.856	28.848	.583	.537	.489	94	54	75
23	70	74	67	70⅓	9 A. M.	2 P. M.	1.650	...	100	Cu.	100	Cu.	0	...	S	1	S W	2	...	0	78	63	28.880	28.773	28.788	28.813	.658	.771	.501	90	95	51
24	76	86	79	80⅓	...	...	...	...	50	Cu.	10	Cir.	0	...	S W	2	S W	3	S W	1	87	68	28.832	28.847	28.879	28.852	.812	.719	.785	91	58	100
25	8[illegible]	79	72	77	10½ A.M	11½ A.M	.210	...	50	Cir.	100	Cir.Cu	0	...	S W	3	S W	1	...	0	87	64	28.885	28.934	28.954	28.924	.800	.813	.717	78	82	77
26	76	83	77	78⅔	9¼ P.M.	10 P. M.	.050	...	100	Cir.Cu	90	Cir.Cu	100	Cu.	S W	2	S W	2	S W	3	84	59	28.847	28.798	28.811	28.218	.652	.637	.666	73	56	77
27	64	70	55	63	...	...	...	...	0	...	60	Cu.	100	Cu.	S W	3	W	3	W	2	70	38	28.745	28.788	28.891	28.808	.464	.616	.348	77	70	86
28	49	60	53	54	...	...	...	...	0	...	100	Cu.	100	Cu.	S W	2	N W	2	...	0	65	47	28.908	29.066	29.017	28.990	.229	.255	.354	67	49	50
29	58	61	60	59⅔	2 P. M.	5½ P.M.	.240	...	100	Cu.	100	Nim.	100	Cu.	S W	2	S W	2	S W	2	75	46	29.020	28.948	28.959	28.975	.372	.537	.396	78	100	76
30	60	74	67	67	...	...	...	...	100	Cu.	70	Cu.	50	Cu.	W	2	S W	3	...	0	77	48	29.000	29.000	29.032	29.010	.479	.463	.303	84	56	46
31	...	...	...	...	...	...	...	...	...	...	...	...	...	...	...	...	...	...	...	...	...	...	...	...	...	...	...	...	...	...	...	...
Sums	...	...	...	...	...	...	5.366	...	...	...	...	...	...	...	...	...	...	...	...	...	...	...	...	...	...	...	...	...	...	...	...	...
Means	...	...	...	66°.6	...	...	...	...	70	...	77	...	47	...	...	...	...	...	...	...	74°.9	53°.1	...	...	...	28.783	.480	.399	.466	80	65	77
Average,	...				...				64						...						...		...				.483			74		

METEOROLOGICAL OBSERVATIONS FOR THE MONTH OF JULY, 1866.

Day of the Month.	Thermometer in the open air. 7 A. M.	2 P. M.	9 P. M.	Mean.	Rain and Snow. Time of beginning of rain or snow.	Time of ending of rain or snow.	Amount of rain or melted snow in gauge in inches.	Depth of snow, in inches.	Clouds. 7 A. M. Percentage of cloudiness.	Kind of clouds.	2 P. M. Percentage of cloudiness.	Kind of clouds.	9 P. M. Percentage of cloudiness.	Kind of clouds.
1	68	72	63	67⅔	....	......	....	....	100	Cu.	100	Cu.	100	Cu.
2	65	77	69	70⅓	....	....	....	....	100	Cu.	40	Cu.	50	Cu.
3	66	74	62	67⅓	2½ P.M.	....	....	....	100	Cir. Cu	50	Cu.	50	Cu.
4	65	78	69	70⅔	....	2 A. M.	.140	....	100	Cu	90	Cu.	10	Cu.
5	75	85	76	78⅔	....	....	....	....	10	Cir. Cu	10	Cir. Cu	10	St.
6	78	88	75	80⅓	....	....	....	....	10	Cu.	50	Cu.	10	St.
7	78½	89	74	77⅙	2½ P.M.	....	....	....	80	Cir.	90	Cir. Cu	100	Cu.
8	71	75	65	70⅓	....	2 A. M.	2.610	....	100	Cu.	90	Cu.	10	St.
9	62	72	60	64⅔	....	....	....	....	90	Cir. Cu	50	Cir. Cu	0	......
10	62	75	60	65⅔	....	....	....	....	10	St.	10	Cu	0	......
11	63	82	69	71⅓	....	....	....	....	10	Cu.	0	......	0	......
12	70	84	70	74⅔	....	....	....	....	0	....	10	Cu.	0	......
13	77	89	73	80⅓	....	....	....	....	0	......	50	Cir.	10	St.
14	77	90	75	80⅔	....	....	....	....	90	Cir.	20	Cir.	0	......
15	83	90	79	84	....	....	....	....	0	......	30	Cu.	0	......
16	80	90	81	83⅔	3¼ P.M.	4 P. M.	.224	....	40	Cir. St.	60	Cu.	10	Cu. St.
17	79	86	75	80	....	....	....	......	10	St.	90	Cu.	100	Cu.
18	72	66	79	72⅓	1 A. M.	3 P. M.	.530	....	100	Nim.	100	Nim.	0	......
19	62	72	61	65	....	....	....	....	70	Cir. Cu	100	Cu.	70	Cir. St.
20	62	76	67	68⅓	During	night.	.042	....	80	Cir. Cu	90	Cu.	100	Cu.
21	66	74	72	70⅔	4 P. M.	5 P. M.	.160	....	100	Cu.	100	Cu.	100	Cu.
22	70	81	71	74	....	....	....	....	Foggy	......	30	Cu.	20	Cu. St.
23	66	78	71	71⅔	....	....	....	....	100	Cu.	90	Cu.	10	Cir. St.
24	71	83	74	76	7½ P.M.	8½ P.M.	.050	....	90	Cu.	90	Cir. Cu	60	Cu.
25	73	82	71	75⅓	....	....	....	....	30	Cir. St.	80	Cir. Cu	50	Cir. Cu
26	69	84	72	75	....	....	....	....	90	Cir. St.	50	Cu.	100	Cu. St
27	75	81	71	75⅔	....	....	....	....	100	Cir. Cu	100	Cir. Cu	70	Cir. Cu
28	73	80	70	74⅓	12½ P.M	2 P. M	.280	......	10	Cu.	20	Cu.	100	Cu.
29	69	82	68	73	6½ P.M.	7 P. M.	.158	....	80	Cir. Cu	20	Cu.	10	Cir. Cu
30	66	77	68	70⅓	....	....	....	.... ..	70	Cir. Cu	50	Cu.	10	St.
31	64	79	75	72⅔	....	....	....	....	30	Cir. Cu	100	Cu.	100	Cu.
Sums.	....	..	..	....	....	....	4.194	....	......	......	......	......	......	......
Means	....	..	..	71.°72	....	....	....	....	58	......	63	......	37	......
Average,				....	....	....	....	....	52					

Day of the Month.	Winds. 7 A. M. Direction.	Force.	2 P. M. Direction.	Force.	9 P. M. Direction.	Force.	Max. Thermometer.	Min. Thermometer.	Barometer Height Reduced to Freezing Point. 7 A. M.	2 P. M.	9 P. M.	Mean.	Force or Pressure of Vapor, in Inches. 7 A. M.	2 P. M.	9 P. M.	Relative Humidity, or Percentage of Saturation. 7 A. M.	2 P. M.	9 P. M.
1	S W	2	S W	2	S E	3	75	60	29.084	29.079	29.005	29.054	.476	.489	.446	69	62	77
2	S W	2	S W	3	S W	2	82	62	28.932	28.918	28.906	28.918	.516	.601	.529	84	65	75
3	S W	2	S W	3	S W	2	75	60	28.813	28.722	28.658	28.731	.570	.568	.491	89	67	88
4	S W	2	S W	3	S W	2	79	60	28.593	28.635	28.673	28.633	.583	.514	.564	94	54	79
5	S W	2	S W	3	S	2	86	70	28.758	28.792	28.793	28.787	.785	.691	.731	90	57	81
6	S W	2	S W	3	S	2	88	68	28.877	28.842	28.750	28.823	.626	.692	.628	65	52	73
7	S W	3	S W	3	S W	1	84	66	28.834	28.863	28.774	28.823	.834	.677	.758	88	66	90
8	S W	1	E	2	N W	2	78	53	28.845	28.977	28.957	28.926	.720	.577	.389	95	64	63
9	N E	2	N E	2	....	0	74	49	29.068	29.086	29.091	29.088	.491	.322	.456	88	29	88
10	....	0	W	2	E	1	82	49	29.166	29.103	29.069	29.112	.491	.415	.487	88	48	94
11	W	1	W	2	....	0	86	56	29.073	29.064	29.050	29.062	.416	.691	.635	72	63	90
12	S W	2	S W	3	...	0	86	63	29.076	29.038	28.976	29.030	.658	.623	.685	90	53	100
13	S W	2	W	2	....	0	90	66	28.990	28.940	28.916	28.948	.717	.809	.626	77	59	65
14	S W	2	S W	3	...	0	92	65	28.937	28.914	18.918	28.923	.758	.751	.785	82	53	90
15	S W	2	S W	4	....	0	90	69	28.954	28.936	28.950	28.946	.802	.707	.813	72	51	82
16	S W	2	N W	3	S W	1	91	68	28.984	29.003	28.983	28.990	.758	.707	.745	74	51	70
17	S W	2	N W	2	....	0	87	68	28.991	28.947	28.893	28.943	.818	.762	.745	82	62	86
18	S W	2	N E	2	....	0	73	49	28.840	28.835	28.901	28.858	.785	.570	.500	100	89	100
19	N E	2	N E	2	....	0	74	52	29.006	28.998	28.971	28.992	.556	.559	.537	100	72	100
20	N E	2	E	2	E	1	76	60	29.000	28.933	27 878	28.940	.523	.614	.566	94	68	84
21	S W	1	S	2	E	1	78	60	28.855	28.802	28.769	28.808	.659	.641	.745	100	77	95
22	....	0	S W	3	S W	2	81	61	28.783	28.754	28.768	28.768	.695	.624	.608	95	59	80
23	N E	1	E	2	....	0	81	57	28.818	28.842	28 845	28.835	.570	.626	.603	89	65	80
24	S	2	S E	1	....	0	85	60	28.918	28.904	28.882	28.901	.644	.717	.751	86	64	88
25	....	0	N E	2	....	0	84	59	28.961	28.964	28.970	28.965	.617	.497	.720	77	45	95
26	E	1	W	1	....	0	83	56	29.001	28.975	28 942	28.972	.599	.584	.706	85	50	90
27	S E	2	S E	2	S E	1	83	53	28.950	28.934	28 875	28.918	.666	.664	.682	77	62	90
28	...	0	S W	1	S	1	84	58	28.867	28 809	28.824	28.833	.732	.758	.695	90	74	95
29	....	0	N W	2	....	0	84	57	28.830	28.726	28.779	28.778	.671	.572	.612	95	52	90
30	N E	2	N E	2	....	0	78	53	28.867	28.945	28.880	28 897	.604	.457	.577	94	49	85
31	S	1	S W	2	S	2	81	53	28.914	28.811	28.717	28.814	.464	.574	.554	77	58	64
Sums.	....	..	....	..	....	..	......	......	......	......	......	......	......	......	......	......	......	......
Means	....	..	....	..	....	..	82°.2	60°.9	......	......	......	28.905	.637	.626	.624	85	55	84
Average,	....						......		....				.629			74		

METEOROLOGICAL OBSERVATIONS FOR THE MONTH OF AUGUST, 1866.

Day of Month.	Thermometer in the open air. 7 A. M.	2 P. M.	9 P. M.	Mean.	Rain and Snow. Time of beginning of rain or snow.	Time of ending of rain or snow.	Amount of rain or melted snow in gauge in inches.	Depth of snow, in inches.	Clouds. 7 A. M. Percentage of cloudiness.	Kind of clouds.	2 P. M. Percentage of cloudiness.	Kind of clouds.	9 P. M. Percentage of cloudiness.	Kind of clouds.	Winds. 7 A. M. Direction.	Force.	2 P. M. Direction.	Force.	9 P. M. Direction.	Force.	Max. Thermometer.	Min. Thermometer.	Barometer Height Reduced to Freezing Point. 7 A. M.	2 P. M.	9 P. M.	Mean.	Force or Pressure of Vapor, in Inches. 7 A. M.	2 P. M.	9 P. M.	Relative Humidity, or Percentage of Saturation. 7 A. M.	2 P. M.	9 P. M.
1	71	78	64	71	1 A. M.	6 A. M.	.040		100	Cu.	10	Cu.	10	Cu.	S W	3	S W	4	....	0	77	54	28.650	28.671	28.788	28.703	.682	.443	.464	90	46	77
2	60	73	58	63⅔					90	Cu.	50	Cu.	50	Cu.	W	3	N W	3	....	0	74	48	28.771	28.868	28.938	28.859	.426	.376	.452	82	47	94
3	65	72	62	66⅔	9½ P.M.				100	Cu.	100	Cu.	100	Cu.	S W	2	W	2	N E	2	76	53	28.954	28.921	28.743	28.872	.483	.524	.523	78	66	94
4	59	69	58	62		4 A. M.	.772		100	Cu.	50	Cu.	50	Cu.	N W	2	N E	3	....	0	71	44	28.917	28.991	29.036	28.981	.439	.398	.394	88	56	82
5	60	72	63	65					20	Cir.St.	50	Cu.	50	Cu.	N W	2	W	3	W	2	73	42	29.078	29.041	29.036	29.051	.396	.358	.386	76	46	67
6	58	72	66	65⅓					50	Cir.	90	Cir.St	90	Cir.St.	W	1	W	2	W	1	73	42	29.080	29.051	29.014	29.048	.394	.422	.438	82	54	68
7	63	70	62	65					100	Cu.	100	Cu.	100	Cu.	W	1	W	2	....	0	71	57	29.014	29.001	29.947	28.987	.570	.482	.523	88	66	94
8	63	65	62	63⅓	9 A. M.	10 P. M.	.764		100	Cu.	10	Nim.	100	Nim.	E	2	E	2	N W	3	77	54	28.846	28.616	28.598	28.686	.543	.618	.576	94	100	100
9	59	70	64	64⅓					100	Cu.	50	Cu.	50	Cu.	W	1	W	3	W	2	72	48	28.849	28.878	28.876	28.867	.439	.482	.497	88	66	83
10	57	75	65	65⅔					100	Cu.	80	Cir Cu	80	Cir.Cu	....	0	E	1	W	1	75	56	28.955	28.946	28.948	28.949	.466	.554	.549	100	64	89
11	66	75	65	68⅔	3 P. M.				100	Cu.	100	Cu.	100	Cu.	S W	1	S	1	S	3	75	50	29.989	29.033	23.971	28.989	.604	.666	.604	94	77	94
12	66	77	70	71		6 A. M.	.350		100	Nim.	100	Cu.	100	Cu.	S W	2	S W	3	....	0	77	64	28.881	28.785	28.746	28.803	.639	.758	.733	100	82	100
13	69	76	66	70⅓	2 A. M.	3½ A.M.	.588		100	Cu.	100	Cu.	100	Cu.	W	2	N W	3	...	0	75	59	28.765	28.754	28.763	28.760	.671	.652	.604	95	73	94
14	62	79	67	69⅓					100	Cu.	40	Cu.	40	Cu.	W	1	W	2	N W	2	80	55	28.843	28.829	28.893	28.855	.556	.691	.457	100	69	69
15	61	64	52	55⅔					100	Cu.	50	Cu.	50	Cu.	N E	2	E	3	....	0	65	36	29.059	29.123	29.165	29.115	.505	.403	.334	94	67	86
16	49	67	52	56					0		0		0		N E	1	E	2	....	0	69	39	29.209	29.154	29.137	29.166	.322	.362	.361	92	55	93
17	55	73	61	63					0		20	Cir.Cu	20	Cir.Cu	S W	2	S W	2	....	0	75	44	29.128	29.036	29.019	28.061	.405	.510	.505	94	63	94
18	57	71	64	64	6 P. M.	12 P. M.	.222		90	Cir.Cu	100	Cu.	100	Cu.	....	0	N W	2	W	1	73	55	28.975	28.876	28.851	28.900	.466	.503	.596	100	66	100
19	60	67	55	60⅔					Foggy		50	Cu.	50	Cu.	N	2	N	2	....	0	67	42	28.824	28.821	28.836	28.827	.487	.393	.405	94	59	94
20	51	58	55	54⅔	1 P. M.	8 P. M.	.258		90	Cir.St.	100	Nim.	100	Nim.	S W	1	W	3	....	0	68	42	28.877	28.818	28.804	28.867	.374	.452	.433	100	92	100
21	54	66	57	59					10	Cu.	60	Cu.	60	Cu.	W	2	N W	3	S W	1	67	43	28.817	28.773	28.749	28.779	.390	.407	.407	93	63	87
22	49	61	48	52⅔					100	Cu.	100	Cu.	100	Cu.	N	2	N W	2	....	0	61	36	28.830	28.838	28.819	28.829	.272	.297	.335	73	55	100
23	48	58	48	51⅓					100	Cu.	50	Cu.	50	Cu.	N	2	W	2	S W	1	59	44	28.828	28.827	28.845	28.833	.285	.329	.335	85	41	100
24	59	61	50	53⅔					100	Cu.	100	Cn.	100	Cu.	W	2	S W	3	....	0	60	34	28.878	28.875	28.904	28.885	.309	.150	.309	85	22	85
25	48	62	47	52⅓					100	Cu. St.	50	Cir.Cu	50	Cir.Cu	S W	1	S W	2	....	0	64	41	28.951	28.912	28.919	28.927	.310	.166	.298	92	20	92
26	58	63	59	61⅔					90	Cu.	100	Cu.	100	Cu.	S W	2	S W	3	S W	2	68	53	28.841	28.812	28.787	28.813	.452	.305	.469	94	34	94
27	61	73	57	63⅔					10	Cu. St.	100	Cu.	100	Cu.	S W	1	S W	2	S W	1	75	46	28.795	28.778	28.786	28.786	.442	.552	.543	83	75	94
28	57	76	61	64⅔	3½ P.M.	4 P. M.	020		10	Cu. St.	30	Cu.	100	Cu.	....	0	N E	1	N E	2	75	51	28.797	28.775	28.828	28.800	.466	.577	.505	100	64	94
29	55	70	62	62⅓					Foggy		30	Cu.	50	Cu	....	0	S W	2	....	0	72	53	28.897	28.706	28.846	28.846	.433	.549	.491	100	61	88
30	60	68	64	64	5 A. M.	4 P. M.	.438		100	Nim.	100	Nim.	100	Cu.	S W	1	S E	1	....	0	72	56	28.834	28.785	28.843	28.820	.578	.612	.596	100	90	100
31	64	77	70	70⅓					100	Cu.	90	Cu.	100	Cu.	S E	1	S E	2	S E	3	78	61	28.766	28.725	28.698	28.729	.597	.678	.658	100	73	90
Sums.							3.442																									
Means				62°.6					75		69		56								71°.4	48°.2				28.884	.448	.466	.480	91	62	90
Average,									66																		464			81		

METEOROLOGICAL OBSERVATIONS FOR THE MONTH OF SEPTEMBER, 1866.

Day of the Month.	Thermometer in the open air. 7 A. M.	2 P. M.	9 P. M.	Mean.	Rain and Snow. Time of beginning of rain or snow.	Time of ending of rain or snow.	Amount of rain or melted snow in gauge in inches.	Depth of snow, in inches.	Clouds. 7 A. M. Percentage of cloudiness.	Kind of clouds.	2 P. M. Percentage of cloudiness.	Kind of clouds.	9 P. M. Percentage of cloudiness.	Kind of clouds.	Winds. 7 A. M. Direction.	Force.	2 P. M. Direction.	Force.	9 P. M. Direction.	Force.	Max. Thermometer.	Min. Thermometer.	Barometer Height Reduced to Freezing Point. 7 A. M.	2 P. M.	9 P. M.	Mean.	Force or Pressure of Vapor, in Inches. 7 A. M.	2 P. M.	9 P. M.	Relative Humidity, or Percentage of Saturation. 7 A. M.	2 P. M.	9 P. M.
1	70	73	68	70⅓	2¼ A. M.	4 P. M.	1.180	......	20	Cu.	100	Nim.	20	Cu.	S	2	S W	3	S	2	80	65	28.655	28.760	28.628	28.647	.733	.771	.648	100	95	95
2	70	73	63	68⅔	10 P. M.	11 P. M.	.020	......	70	Cir.Cu	10	Cu.	100	Cu.	S W	2	W	3	W	1	73	56	28.773	28.785	28.865	28.807	.621	.409	.510	85	50	88
3	62	73	56	65	......	......	......	......	100	Cu St.	20	Cu.	10	St.	....	0	S W	2	....	0	74	41	28.912	28.906	28.912	28.910	.556	.510	.449	100	63	100
4	61	67	67	69	9 A. M.	12 M.	.614	......	100	Cu. St.	100	Cu.	100	Cu.	S E	1	S W	1	....	0	71	53	28.863	28.720	28.723	28.772	.505	.626	.626	94	95	95
5	57	67	53	63	......	......	......	......	90	Cir.St.	80	Cir.Cu	0	......	W	2	W	3	....	0	70	42	28.977	28.891	28.922	28.930	.466	.425	.375	100	64	93
6	51	74	61	62⅔	10½ P.M	......	......	......	60	Cir.Cu	90	Cir.Cu	100	Cu.	....	0	E	1	....	0	74	51	28.960	28.941	28.944	28.948	.390	.463	.505	93	56	94
7	57	64	67	57	......	11 P. M.	.432	......	100	Nim.	100	Cu.	100	Nim.	E	1	N E	2	....	0	67	49	28.872	28.783	28.774	28.809	.466	.464	.662	100	77	100
8	53	65	52	56	......	......	......	......	50	Cu.	70	Cu.	0	......	W	2	S W	3	S	1	67	43	28.877	28.943	29.028	28.949	.403	.376	.361	100	59	93
9	51	65	52	61⅔	......	......	......	......	60	Cir.Cu	100	Cir.St.	90	Cu.	....	0	N E	2	....	0	65	54	29.134	29.130	29.095	29.119	.374	.470	.388	100	63	100
10	56	69	60	65	3½ P.M.	......	......	......	100	Cu.	100	Cu.	100	Nim.	S W	1	N E	1	S E	2	70	57	29.046	28.944	28.804	28.931	.449	.529	.518	100	75	100
11	62	72	61	63⅔	......	......	......	......	100	Nim.	100	Cu.	60	Cu.	S E	1	S W	2	S W	3	73	43	28.567	28.506	28.511	28.514	.556	.706	.537	100	90	100
12	62	66	63	54	......	3 A. M.	.826	......	100	Cu.	100	Cu.	20	Cu.	W	3	S W	4	S W	2	67	43	28.519	28.558	28.677	28.586	.523	.316	.510	94	49	88
13	50	64	50	51⅔	......	......	......	......	20	Cu. St.	20	Cu.	10	Cu. St.	S W	2	S W	3	....	0	64	45	28.837	28.871	28.837	28.848	.361	.403	.361	100	67	100
14	50	60	45	45⅓	......	......	......	......	80	Cu. St.	100	Cu.	0	......	S W	2	S W	4	....	0	60	28	28.805	28.920	29.003	28.909	.361	.283	.251	100	54	84
15	37	53	46	56⅓	6 P. M.	......	......	......	10	St.	30	Cu.	100	Nim.	....	0	S	2	S	2	56	36	29.179	29.134	29.104	29.139	.199	.244	.311	90	60	100
16	52	57	61	50⅔	......	10 P. M.	1.426	......	100	Nim.	100	Cu.	100	Nim.	S	3	S W	2	S W	2	61	44	28.949	28.864	28.778	28.863	.388	.466	.537	100	100	100
17	48	54	50	48⅔	6 P. M.	......	......	......	100	Cir.St.	100	Nim.	100	Nim.	N E	2	N	1	....	0	56	44	28.980	28.950	28.919	28.949	.260	.282	.335	78	67	93
18	48	50	48	51	......	6 P. M.	.202	......	100	Nim.	100	Cu.	100	Cu.	N	1	E	2	N E	1	50	44	28.865	28.820	28.819	28.834	.335	.335	.310	100	93	92
19	48	55	50	45⅔	......	......	......	......	100	Cu.	100	Cu.	100	Cu.	N E	2	N E	2	....	0	55	39	28.886	28.914	28.976	28.925	.310	.295	.283	92	63	75
20	45	47	45	44	1 A. M.	11 P. M.	.464	......	100	Nim.	100	Nim.	100	Nim.	N E	2	N E	2	N W	2	46	36	28.889	28.882	28.872	28.881	.275	.323	.300	92	100	100
21	41	53	38	45	......	......	......	......	100	Cu.	100	Cu.	0	......	N W	2	N W	2	....	0	56	27	28.934	28.966	39.017	28.972	.235	.219	.208	91	54	91
22	36	55	44	52⅓	......	......	......	......	0	......	50	Cu.	100	Cir.Cu	S W	1	E	2	....	0	61	32	29.076	29.038	29.021	29.045	.170	.295	.196	80	58	68
23	45	61	51	55⅓	......	......	......	......	100	Cu.	50	Cu.	0	......	E	2	S	2	S W	2	66	41	29.000	28.953	28.934	28.962	.275	.325	.343	92	61	93
24	58	66	52	55⅓	8 A. M.	8¾ A.M.	.100	......	100	Cu. St.	100	Cu.	100	Cir.St.	S E	3	S W	3	S	1	53	48	28.801	28.919	28.836	28.852	.423	.570	.382	88	89	96
25	52	47	46	48⅓	6 A. M.	6½ P.M.	.542	......	100	Cu. St.	100	Nim.	100	Cu.	E	2	N W	2	....	0	60	32	28.965	28.958	29.016	28.979	.338	.298	.311	100	92	100
26	36	60	45	47	......	......	......	......	0	......	0	......	10	St.	....	0	S W	2	....	0	60	36	29.164	29.056	29.048	29.089	.170	.283	.204	80	54	68
27	47	70	53	56⅔	......	......	......	......	0	......	10	Cu.	0	......	....	0	S W	2	....	0	70	39	29.103	29.091	29.087	29.093	.298	.335	.375	92	53	93
28	44	70	52	54⅔	......	......	......	......	0	......	0	......	0	......	....	0	S W	2	....	0	69	38	29.145	29.091	29.097	29.111	.289	.449	.388	100	61	100
29	43	63	52	54⅓	......	......	......	......	10	St.	0	......	10	St.	....	0	S W	2	....	0	69	38	29.119	29.090	29.090	29.100	.254	.380	.388	92	56	100
30	50	65	52	55⅔	......	......	......	......	10	St.	20	Cir.St.	10	St.	....	0	N E	1	....	0	67	38	29.101	29.083	29.093	29.089	.374	.451	.361	100	73	93
31	..	..	..	......	......	......	......	......	......	......	......	......	......	......	....	..	....	..	....	..	......	......	......	......	......	......	......	......	......	......	......	......
Sums.	..	..	..	......	......	......	5.866	......	......	......	......	......	......	......	....	..	....	..	....	..	......	......	......	......	......	......	......	......	......	......	......	......
Means	..	..	..	55.°8	......	......	......	......	66	......	63	......	58	......	....	..	....	..	....	..	64°.3	42°.7	......	......	......	28.956	.381	.443	.497	94	70	93
Average,				......	......	......	......	......	64						......						......	......	......				.407			85		

METEOROLOGICAL OBSERVATIONS FOR THE MONTH OF OCTOBER, 1866.

Day of Month.	Thermometer in the open air. 7 A. M.	2 P. M.	9 P. M.	Mean.	Rain and Snow. Time of beginning of rain or snow.	Time of ending of rain or snow.	Amount of rain or melted snow in gauge in inches.	Depth of snow, in inches.	Clouds. 7 A. M. Percentage of cloudiness.	Kind of clouds.	2 P. M. Percentage of cloudiness.	Kind of clouds.	9 P. M. Percentage of cloudiness.	Kind of clouds.	Winds. 7 A. M. Direction.	Force.	2 P. M. Direction.	Force.	9 P. M. Direction.	Force.	Max. Thermometer.	Min. Thermometer.	Barometer Height Reduced to Freezing Point. 7 A. M.	2 P. M.	9 P. M.	Mean.	Force or Pressure of Vapor, in Inches. 7 A. M.	2 P. M.	9 P. M.	Relative Humidity, or Percentage of Saturation. 7 A. M.	2 P. M.	9 P. M.
1	43	69	51	54⅓	......	......	......	......	0	......	0	......	0	......	....	0	S W	1	....	0	69	41	29.087	29.009	28.965	29.030	.278	.462	.343	100	65	93
2	54	73	51	59⅓	......	......	......	......	0	......	100	Cu.	100	Cu. St.	....	0	S W	3	N E	3	73	33	28.885	28.821	28.883	28.863	.418	.510	.245	100	63	65
3	37	56	47	46⅔	......	......	......	......	10	St.	0	......	100	Cu.	....	0	E	2	....	0	57	35	29.077	28.967	28.980	29.008	.214	.282	.273	95	63	85
4	45	59	43	49	......	......	......	......	100	Cu. St.	100	Cu.	90	Cu.	N E	2	E	3	E	1	59	26	29.147	29.158	29.217	29.171	.228	.190	.209	76	38	75
5	32	55	40	42⅔	......	......	......	......	20	Cir. St.	20	Cir. St.	0	......	S W	1	S	2	....	0	55	29	29.359	29.318	29.281	29.319	.143	.269	.203	79	62	82
6	54	65	50	49⅔	......	......	......	......	0	......	0	......	0	......	E	1	S W	2	....	0	65	32	29.263	29.149	29.152	29.188	.196	.403	.335	100	67	93
7	59	72	54	61⅔	......	......	......	......	70	Cir. Cu	80	Cu.	0	......	S W	2	S W	3	S W	1	72	47	29.151	29.088	29.055	29.098	.500	.559	.418	100	72	100
8	53	72	61	62	6½ P. M.	......	......	......	10	Cu. St.	100	Cu.	100	Nim.	....	0	S W	3	S W	2	72	51	29.006	28.894	28.864	28.921	.403	.516	.537	100	70	100
9	55	61	53	56⅓	......	......	......	......	100	Cu.	100	Cu.	100	Cu.	...	0	S W	2	....	0	64	49	28.855	28.827	28.767	28.816	.405	.473	.375	94	88	93
10	55	65	56	58⅔	......	......	1.112	......	100	Nim.	100	Cu.	100	Nim.	N E	2	E	3	N E	2	65	52	28.780	28.848	28.922	28.850	.433	.483	.449	100	78	100
11	55	58	55	56	......	8 A. M.	.092	......	100	Nim.	100	Cu.	100	Cu.	N E	2	E	3	N E	1	58	51	28.969	28.959	28.948	28.958	.433	.452	.433	100	94	100
12	55	58	54	55⅔	......	......	......	......	100	Nim.	100	Cu.	100	Cu.	E	2	N W	2	N E	2	59	50	28.960	28.945	28.935	28.946	.433	.423	.390	100	88	93
13	54	60	47	53⅔	......	......	......	......	100	Cu.	100	Cu.	0	......	N E	1	E	2	....	0	60	33	29.040	29.040	29.086	29.055	.390	.367	.298	93	71	92
14	39	60	48	49	......	......	......	......	10	St.	0	......	0	......	....	0	N E	2	....	0	61	34	29.197	29.204	29.272	29.224	.238	.263	.310	100	54	92
15	42	65	46	51	......	......	......	......	Foggy	......	0	......	0	......	E	1	N W	2	....	0	65	33	29.387	29.354	29.378	29.373	.267	.272	.286	100	44	92
16	37	70	45	50⅔	......	......	......	......	0	......	0	......	0	......	....	0	S W	1	....	0	70	31	29.436	29.313	29.208	29.319	.221	.323	.300	100	44	100
17	36	68	40	48	......	......	......	......	10	St.	0	......	0	......	....	0	S	3	....	0	68	32	29.147	29.027	29.010	29.061	.212	.290	.248	100	42	100
18	37	73	65	58⅓	......	......	......	......	10	Cu. St.	20	Cir. St.	100	Cir. Cu	....	0	S W	2	S	3	73	36	29.576	28.891	28.854	29.103	.221	.313	.323	100	39	65
19	59	60	54	57⅔	9 A. M.	......	......	......	100	Cu. St.	100	Nim.	90	Nim.	S W	2	S W	2	....	0	62	48	28.872	28.939	28.955	28.922	.323	.487	.390	65	94	93
20	58	69	61	62⅔	......	8 P. M.	.662	......	50	Cir. Cu	80	Cu.	100	Cu.	....	0	S	4	S	1	70	50	28.958	28.941	28.881	28.926	.483	.496	.537	100	70	100
21	63	66	61	63⅓	10 A. M.	8 P. M.	.166	......	100	Cu.	100	Cu.	100	Cu.	S	3	S W	4	S	4	66	45	28.698	28.704	28.459	28.620	.446	.502	.442	77	78	83
22	49	54	46	49⅔	......	......	......	......	100	Cu.	60	Cu.	30	Cu.	S W	4	S W	3	S W	3	54	36	28.561	28.782	28.701	28.634	.272	.157	.19[illegible]	78	38	62
23	39	37	34	36⅔	......	......	......	......	100	Cu.	100	Nim.	100	Cu. St.	S W	3	N W	2	S W	2	45	29	28.680	28.746	28.860	28.762	.216	.199	.175	91	90	89
24	33	40	36	36⅓	......	......	......	......	100	Cu.	100	Cu.	100	Cu.	W	2	S W	2	....	0	40	29	28.946	28.995	29.022	28.987	.168	.118	.149	89	48	71
25	34	42	36	37⅓	2 P. M.	......	......	......	100	Cu. St.	100	Cu.	100	Nim.	S E	1	S W	3	....	0	44	31	29.041	28.990	28.916	28.983	.175	.199	.191	89	74	90
26	37	43	37	39	......	8 P. M.	.620	......	100	Nim.	100	Cu.	100	Cu.	S W	2	S W	3	S W	2	43	32	28.776	28.786	28.922	28.828	.221	.231	.208	100	83	91
27	37	45	37	39⅔	4½ P. M.	10 P. M.	.470	......	100	Cu. St.	100	Cu.	100	Nim.	S W	1	S W	2	S	2	46	33	29.041	29.060	29.056	29.051	.199	.204	.221	90	68	100
28	45	49	51	48⅓	7½ A. M.	8 P. M.	.444	......	100	Cu. St.	100	Nim.	100	Nim.	S	3	S W	3	S	3	49	38	28.848	28.753	28.719	28.773	.228	.319	.374	76	96	100
29	41	43	40	41⅓	......	......	......	......	100	Cu. St.	100	Cu.	100	Cu.	S W	2	S W	2	S W	3	48	35	29.756	28.777	28.774	28.769	.212	.254	.263	82	92	82
30	43	42	35	38⅓	......	......	......	......	100	Cu.	50	Cu.	100	Cu.	S W	2	W	3	N W	3	43	26	28.712	28.726	28.885	28.774	.208	.199	.162	91	74	80
31	32	39	36	35⅔	......	......	......	......	100	Cu.	60	Cu.	100	Cu.	S W	2	S W	3	S W	2	48	28	29.021	29.045	29.017	29.027	.143	.110	.129	79	46	61
Sums	..	..	..	......	......	......	3.566	......	......	......	......	......	......	......	....	..	....	..	....	..	......	......	......	......	......	......	......	......	......	......	......	......
Means	..	..	..	49°.5	......	......	......	......	64	......	66	......	68	......	....	..	....	..	....	..	60	37°.5	......	......	......	28.979	.288	.334	.301	91	67	88
Average, ...					......				66						......						......		......				.307			82		

METEOROLOGICAL OBSERVATIONS FOR THE MONTH OF NOVEMBER, 1866.

Day of the Month.	Thermometer in the open air. 7 A. M.	2 P. M.	9 P. M.	Mean.	Rain and Snow. Time of beginning of rain or snow.	Time of ending of rain or snow.	Amount of rain or melted snow in gauge in inches.	Depth of snow, in inches.	Clouds. 7 A. M. Percentage of cloudiness.	Kind of clouds.	2 P. M. Percentage of cloudiness.	Kind of clouds.	9 P. M. Percentage of cloudiness.	Kind of clouds.	Winds. 7 A. M. Direction.	Force.	2 P. M. Direction.	Force.	9 P. M. Direction.	Force.	Max. Thermometer.	Min. Thermometer.	Barometer Height Reduced to Freezing Point. 7 A. M.	2 P. M.	9 P. M.	Mean.	Force or Pressure of Vapor, in Inches. 7 A. M.	2 P. M.	9 P. M.	Relative Humidity, or Percentage of Saturation. 7 A. M.	2 P. M.	9 P. M.
1	38	54	57	47⅔					100	Cu.	60	Cir.St.	60	Cu.	S W	2	S	3	S W	2	55	32	28.673	28.619	28.674	28.722	.144	.206	.270	63	49	72
2	38	45	33	38⅔					100	Cu.	100	Cu.	10	St.	S W	1	W	3	S W	1	46	22	28.982	29.065	29.067	29.038	.123	.138	.181	54	46	100
3	29	42	38	36⅓					100	Cir.St.	90	Cu.	60	Cu.	....	0	N E	2	N E	1	42	27	29.206	29.236	29.278	29.240	.142	.134	.144	88	50	63
4	35	40	36	37					100	Cu. St.	100	Cu. St.	100	Cir.	N E	1	N E	2	N E	3	40	22	29.342	29.351	29.346	29.343	.162	.160	.149	80	64	71
5	26	42	28	32					10	St.	00	......	00	......	...	0	E	2	....	0	42	16	29.558	29.549	29.527	29.545	.123	.155	.135	87	58	88
6	21	46	32	33					[illegible]0	....	20	Cir.Cu	20	St.	....	0	S E	2	...	0	46	24	29.462	29.349	29.285	29.365	.096	.125	.143	85	40	79
7	26	56	40	40⅔					[illegible]0	......	10	Cir.St.	00	......	....	0	S W	2	....	0	56	26	29.201	29.067	29.020	29.076	.070	.336	.203	39	75	82
8	45	53	48	48⅔					100	Cu. St.	100	Cu.	100	Cu.	S W	2	S W	2	S W	2	53	38	28.956	28.969	28.944	28.956	.132	.321	.335	61	80	100
9	42	57	44	46⅓					100	Cu.	00	......	00	......	S W	2	S W	3	S W	1	55	23	29.029	29.003	29.024	29.018	.267	.216	.203	100	46	82
10	23	48	41	39	3 P. M.				00	......	100	Cu.	100	Nim.	....	0	S E	1	N E	3	48	25	29.015	28.940	28.640	28.886	.153	.212	.257	100	63	100
11	40	44	39	41		4 P. M	.54		100	Cu.	100	Cu.	100	Cu.	S W	3	S W	3	S W	3	44	33	28.588	28.710	28.888	28.728	.225	.241	.216	91	84	95
12	39	45	31	38⅓					100	Cu.	10	Cu. St.	00	......	W	2	S W	2	....	0	45	23	29.043	29.105	29.146	29.098	.195	.182	.155	82	61	89
13	30	42	40	37⅓					80	Cir.St.	100	Cu. St.	10	St.	S E	1	S E	3	S E	3	45	28	29.150	29.060	28.953	29.054	.167	.222	.203	100	83	82
14	43	51	38	44					100	Nim.	100	Cu.	100	Cu.	S W	3	S W	3	....	0	51	34	28.823	28.812	28.747	28.998	.254	.296	.165	92	79	72
15	37	39	39	38⅓	1 P. M.	8 P. M.	.24		100	Cu.	100	Nim.	100	Cu. St.	....	0	W	1	W	1	41	30	28.708	28.525	28.438	28.557	.199	.225	.216	90	91	91
16	36	41	39	38⅔					100	Cu. St.	100	Cu. St.	100	Cu. St.	S W	2	W	3	W	2	41	30	28.357	28.403	28.584	28.448	.191	.190	.195	90	74	82
17	38	45	36	39⅔					100	Cu. St.	70	Cu.	20	St.	S W	1	S W	3	S W	1	46	31	28.710	28.730	28.722	28.720	.165	.204	.170	72	68	80
18	37	48	45	43⅓					80	Cir.St.	30	Cir.Cu	60	Cir.Cu	....	0	S W	2	E	1	48	33	28.748	28.736	28.715	28.733	.199	.236	.228	90	70	76
19	42	43	42	42⅓	3 A. M.	7 P. M.	.86		100	Nim.	100	Nim.	100	Cu. St.	N E	1	N	1	N	2	43	35	28.672	28.477	28.527	28.558	.267	.254	.267	100	92	100
20	39	48	38	41⅔					100	Cu. St.	70	Cu.	70	Cu.	N W	1	N W	2	N W	1	48	30	28.548	28.660	28.719	28.642	.216	.212	.229	91	63	100
21	25	42	32	33	4⅓ P.M.				50	Cu.	50	Cu.	100	Nim.	N W	1	S W	1	S E	1	42	25	28.885	28.781	28.664	28.776	.135	.177	.181	100	66	100
22	32	35	30	32⅓		5 P. M.	.60	7	100	Nim.	100	Nim.	50	Cu	N E	1	N	1	N	1	35	9	28.503	28.646	28.834	28.661	.143	.142	.148	79	70	89
23	22	35	31	29⅔					100	Cu. St.	100	Cu. St.	100	Cu. St.	....	0	N	1	....	0	35	10	28.904	28.925	28.989	28.952	.118	.142	.118	100	70	68
24	20	34	30	28					90	Cir St.	100	Cu. St.	100	Cu. St.	S E	1	S W	1	S W	2	34	13	29.022	28.983	29.017	29.007	.108	.175	.111	100	89	67
25	18	36	29	27⅔					20	Cu. St.	10	St.	10	St.	S E	1	S W	1	S W	1	30	20	29.092	29.013	28.930	29.012	.098	.129	.123	100	61	77
26	30	37	38	35					80	Cir.St.	100	Cu. St.	100	Nim.	S E	1	....	0	....	0	38	24	28.878	28.923	28.913	28.906	.130	.199	.208	78	90	91
27	38	44	49	43⅔	10 A. M.		.28		50	Cu. St.	100	Mim.	100	Nim.	N E	1	N E	1	N E	1	49	38	28.879	28.783	28.715	28.792	.208	.289	.322	91	100	92
28	52	41	34	42⅓		12 M.	.08		100	Nim.	90	Cu.	100	Nim.	N E	1	W	1	W	1	62	28	28.629	28.594	28.616	28.613	.388	.235	.196	100	91	100
29	32	35	30	32⅓					100	Cu. St.	100	Cu. St.	100	Cu. St	S W	1	S W	1	W	2	35	22	28.659	28.655	28.614	28.642	.162	.183	.148	89	90	89
30	27	24	31	30⅔					100	Cu. St	100	Cu. St.	60	Cu.	S W	1	S W	2	W	1	34	22	28.698	28.794	28.994	28.828	.129	.155	.155	88	79	89
31																																
Sums.							2.60	7																								
Means				37.°94					78		73		64								44°.	26°.1				28.946	.172	.203	.192	86	71	86
Average,									71																		.189			81		

METEOROLOGICAL OBSERVATIONS FOR THE MONTH OF DECEMBER, 1866.

Day of Month.	Thermometer in the open air. 7 A. M.	2 P. M.	9 P. M.	Mean.	Rain and snow. Time of beginning of rain or snow.	Time of ending of rain or snow.	Amount of rain or melted snow in gauge in inches.	Depth of snow, in inches.	Clouds. 7 A. M. Percentage of cloudiness.	Kind of clouds.	2 P. M. Percentage of cloudiness.	Kind of clouds.	9 P. M. Percentage of cloudiness.	Kind of clouds.	Winds. 7 A. M. Direction.	Force.	2 P. M. Direction.	Force.	9 P. M. Direction.	Force.	Max. Thermometer.	Min. Thermometer.	Barometer height reduced to freezing point. 7 A. M.	2 P. M.	9 P. M.	Mean.	Force or pressure of vapor, in inches. 7 A. M.	2 P. M.	9 P. M.	Relative humidity, or percentage of saturation. 7 A. M.	2 P. M.	9 P. M.
1	29	34	28	30⅓	....	....	....	....	100	Cu. St.	100	Cu. St.	00	......	....	0	S W	1	....	0	36	22	29.110	29.081	29.074	29.088	.142	.155	.153	88	79	100
2	25	43	38	35⅓	....	....	....	....	10	St.	20	Cir.St.	00	......	S W	1	N E	2	S	2	43	22	29.003	28.932	28.914	28.949	.117	.142	.229	87	51	100
3	42	43	42	42⅓	....	....	....	....	70	Cu. St.	100	Nim.	100	Nim.	S	2	S	1	S E	2	43	36	28.779	28.623	28.585	28.662	.155	.254	.244	58	92	91
4	41	43	29	37⅔	....	....	....	....	100	Cu. St.	70	Cu. St.	00	......	S E	2	S W	1	....	0	43	20	28.548	28.634	28.824	28.668	.212	.254	.142	82	92	88
5	26	44	39	36⅓	....	....	....	....	80	Cir.St.	30	Cir.Cu	80	Cir.St.	....	0	E	1	....	0	44	22	29.013	29.075	29.141	29.076	.141	.241	.216	100	84	91
6	39	47	44	43⅓	....	....	....	....	100	Cu. St.	100	Cu.St.	100	Cu.St	E	1	S E	1	....	0	47	34	29.051	28.932	28.946	28.986	.216	.273	.289	91	85	100
7	40	43	41	41⅓	1 A. M.	....	.68	....	90	Cu.	100	Nim.	50	Cu. St.	S E	1	S	1	S E	1	50	34	28.977	28.908	28.666	28.850	.203	.231	.235	82	83	91
8	52	39	28	39⅓	....	10 P. M.	.17	1½	90	Cu.	100	Nim.	100	Nim.	S	2	S	3	W	4	52	16	28.229	28.229	28.561	28.339	.388	.195	.153	100	82	100
9	24	25	12	20⅓	....	....	....	....	100	Cu.St.	90	Cu.	00	......	S W	3	S W	4	W	3	25	2	28.651	28.652	28.704	28.669	.100	.117	.045	79	87	60
10	10	16	15	13⅔	....	....	....	....	30	Cu.St.	90	Cu.	100	Cu. St.	S W	2	S W	3	S W	2	16	3	28.738	28.801	28.840	28.793	.057	.059	.025	79	65	29
11	14	16	14	14⅔	....	....	....	....	100	Cu. St.	100	Cu. St	100	Cu.St.	S	2	S W	3	S W	2	18	6	28.843	28.831	28.927	28.867	.051	.074	.063	63	83	81
12	13	17	16	15⅓	....	....	....	....	100	Cu. St.	70	Cu.	50	Cu.	W	2	S	1	S	1	17	7	28.975	29.011	29.100	29.028	.063	.078	.059	81	83	65
13	14	22	9	15	10 A. M.	5 P. M.	.10	1	30	Cu. St.	100	Nim.	30	St.	....	0	....	0	N W	1	22	-3	29.136	29.039	29.089	29.088	.057	.118	.048	72	100	77
14	6	22	13	13⅔	....	....	....	....	10	Cu. St.	40	Cu.St.	00	......	....	0	S E	1	S E	1	21	-5	29.265	29.367	29.387	29.319	.041	.036	.048	74	31	62
15	17	20	19	18⅔	10 P. M.	....	....	....	100	Nim.	100	Nim.	90	Cu. St.	S E	1	N W	1	S E	2	20	10	29.328	29.167	29.031	29.175	.068	.091	.071	75	85	69
16	23	28	26	25⅔	....	5 P. M.	.50	5	100	Nim.	100	Nim.	100	Cu. St.	W	1	N E	2	S E	1	28	11	28.644	28.530	28.538	28.570	.106	.135	.105	86	88	75
17	17	30	29	25⅔	....	....	....	....	10	Cu. St.	50	Cu.	100	Cu. St.	N W	1	N W	1	S W	1	30	10	28.786	28.902	29.006	28.898	.063	.130	.123	67	78	77
18	21	25	27	24⅓	....	....	....	....	80	Cu. St.	90	Cu St.	20	Cu.	S	1	S E	2	S W	2	29	13	29.081	29.009	28.958	29.016	.096	.135	.111	85	100	75
19	32	34	21	29	3 A. M.	3 P. M.	.10	1	100	Nim.	100	Nim.	100	Cu. St.	E	1	N W	1	....	0	34	4	29.084	29.008	29.163	29.052	.181	.155	.096	100	79	85
20	10	16	7	11	....	....	....	....	90	Cu.	10	St.	30	St.	E	1	E	1	E	1	16	-1	29.366	29.414	29.346	29.385	.068	.074	.043	100	83	76
21	14	24	23	20⅓	....	....	....	....	90	Cu. St.	100	Cu. St.	100	Cu. St.	E	2	E	1	....	0	32	8	29.244	29.158	28.985	29.129	.057	.111	.089	63	86	72
22	34	38	36	36	7 A. M.	....	.20	....	100	Nim.	100	Nim.	100	Nim.	E	2	S E	1	S E	1	38	30	28.802	28.621	28.520	28.647	.155	.208	.191	79	91	90
23	40	39	36	38⅓	....	....	.15	....	100	Nim.	100	Nim.	100	Nim.	....	0	N W	1	N W	1	40	25	28.350	28.228	28.323	28.300	.248	.238	.191	100	100	90
24	31	30	24	28⅓	....	Slight	Snow.	....	100	Nim.	100	Cu. St.	100	Cu. St.	N W	2	N W	2	N W	1	31	13	28.429	28.452	28.562	28.481	.136	.167	.129	78	100	100
25	30	24	16	23⅓	....	Slight	Snow.	....	100	Nim.	70	Nim.	00	......	W	1	N W	1	....	0	30	4	28.703	28.757	28.837	28.765	.148	.111	.059	89	86	65
26	24	28	18	23⅓	....	Slight	Snow.	....	100	Cu. St.	100	Cu. St.	30	Cu.	S E	1	N W	1	N W	2	28	6	28.736	28.660	28.678	28.691	.111	.135	.082	86	88	84
27	13	19	14	15⅓	....	....	....	....	40	Cu. St.	90	Cu. St.	10	......	N W	1	N W	2	N W	2	19	3	28.812	28.909	28.946	28.889	.048	.087	.051	62	84	63
28	10	19	13	14	....	....	....	....	10	Cu. St.	100	Nim.	00	......	N W	1	N W	3	W	1	19	3	29.018	29.050	29.073	29.050	.039	.087	.063	57	84	81
29	14	18	14	15⅓	....	....	....	....	90	Cu. St.	100	Nim.	100	Cu. St.	N W	2	N W	2	N W	2	25	7	29.140	29.028	29.064	29.073	.051	.082	.051	63	84	33
30	13	16	15	14⅔	....	....	....	....	100	Cu. St.	50	Cu. St.	90	Cu. St.	S W	1	E	1	....	0	16	7	29.114	29.073	29.004	29.063	.048	.090	.055	62	100	64
31	15	23	21	19⅔	....	....	....	....	100	Cu. St.	100	Cu. St.	100	Cu. St.	S E	1	S W	1	W	2	23	0	29.076	28.973	29.017	29.022	.055	.106	.096	64	86	85
Sums.	..	..	..	....	....	....	1.90	....	......	......	......	......	......	......	....	..	....	..	....	..	......	......	......	......	......	......	......	......	......	......	......	......
Means	..	..	..	25°.53	....	....	....	8.5	82	......	86	......	62	......	....	..	....	..	....	..	30°.2	11°.9	......	......	......	28.893	.116	.140	.114	79	83	75
Average, ...					....				76						....						....		....				123			79		

WINDS.

This is for the record of the direction *from* which the wind is blowing as indicated by a vane, and its force by estimation. The direction is entered in eight points of compass: N., N. E., E., S. E., S., S. W., W., N. W. The force is to be estimated and registered by the following table, in figures from 1 to 10:

1. Very light breeze,	2	miles	per hour.
2. Gentle breeze,	4	"	"
3. Fresh breeze,	12	"	"
4. Strong wind,	25	"	"
5. High wind,	35	"	"
6. Gale,	45	"	"
7. Strong gale,	60	"	"
8. Violent gale,	75	"	"
9. Hurricane,	90	"	"
10. Most violent hurricane,	100	"	"

ABSTRACT OF METEOROLOGICAL OBSERVATIONS FOR 1866.

Mean Height of Barometer (at 32°) inches,	28.913
Mean temperature,	45°.61
Mean maxium. temperature,	50°.77
Mean min. temperature,	32°.25
Per centage of cloudiness,	.65
Total rain and melted snow, inches,	39.51

APPENDIX.

APPENDIX.

At a special meeting of the Michigan State Board of Agriculture, held at the office of the Board, in Lansing, January 8th, 1867, the following resolution was unanimously passed:

Resolved, That T. T. Lyon and the Secretary of this Board, prepare a memorial to the Legislature on the subject of the injurious destruction of Forest Trees in this State, the importance of checking this evil, and the expediency of encouraging the planting of trees as a means of shelter and protection to crops, fruit trees, &c.

In pursuance of this resolution, the following Memorial was presented to the House of Representatives, by whom it was referred to a Special Committee, which made thereon the report herewith appended:

To the Honorable, the Legislature of the State of Michigan:

Your memorialists would respectfully represent, that, owing to the original abundance of the timber growth of our State, and the obstacle it consequently presented to the occupation of the soil for agricultural and other purposes, together with a very general failure to appreciate its modifying influence upon our climate, a most reckless, improvident, and as your memorialists believe, injurious warfare, has, from the earliest settlement of our State, been waged against our forests, opening to the free sweep of winds, in many cases, extensive stretches of country, and thereby injuriously affecting still broader regions, by subjecting them, from such course, to more sudden and extreme changes of temperature, and at the same time increasing the liability to frost and drought, by not only diminishing the amount of rainfall, but also by accelerating evaporation from the surface, accompanied as it must ever be, by a corresponding rapid diminution of temperature.

The momentous importance of this subject may be appreciated

if we consider that within the last five years, the damage to the wheat crop of our State alone, from lack of shelter, can hardly be less than many millions of dollars; while the loss of fruit trees and their products, within that period, from the same cause must at least be an equal sum.

Believing, as your memorialists do, that this process is still going on, and that its continuance must involve still more extensive and injurious effects upon the climatology of our State, we may be allowed to invoke your careful consideration of the subject, for the purpose of devising if possible, a remedy. And, as a means of securing so desirable a result, we may be allowed to suggest the importance of a general diffusion of information on the subject, the encouragement by legislation for the preservation of spare timber in belts along the exposed sides of our farms, and the planting of trees as windbreaks where lands have been already opened; and to facilitate this last process, the modification of our highway laws, the better to facilitate the shutting up of stock from the highways, and the planting and preservation of roadside trees, whenever the people of a town so desire—and, in any and every feasible manner, the encouragement of the planting of trees as windbreaks, about buildings, yards, orchards, fields, farms and highways, till this country shall become checkered over with windbreaks, either natural or artificial, breaking up and diminishing the force of our prevailing winds, attracting and retaining the tribute of passing clouds, and still further improving the equability of the temperature, by checking the two free radiation of heat from the soil.

With this state of affairs in process of realization, we shall no longer be subject to the imputation that we are, by the recklessness of our people in this respect, entailing upon ourselves and our descendants, the severities of the prairie winters, while the inhabitants of the prairies, having the subject brought feelingly to their consideration, are, through a prudent foresight in this respect, already beginning to reap the benefits of the opposite course.

Your memorialists would request that in consideration of the peculiar nature of the subject, and the object to be secured, it be referred to such committee of your body, as from previous acquaintance with the matter in its various bearings, shall be best qualified to give it due consideration.

T. T. LYON,
SANFORD HOWARD,
Sec. Mich. State Board of Agriculture.

REPORT OF THE COMMITTEE.

Your committee, deeply impressed with the importance of this subject, have sought to give it the thoughtful and conscientious investigation which is due to a subject which deeply affects the agricultural productions and the general welfare of a great commonwealth. The interests to be subserved, and the evils to be avoided by our action on this subject have reference not alone to this year or the next score of years, but generations yet unborn, will bless or curse our memory according as we preserve for them what the munificent past has so richly bestowed upon us, or as we lend our influence to continue and accelerate the wasteful destruction everywhere at work in our beautiful State.

With an abundance of valuable forest trees, such as has blessed no other State east of the Rocky Mountains, our people have been disposed to regard this legacy of the slow-paced centuries, not as a blessing to be prized and cherished, but an enemy to be destroyed. Before this blind impulse of destruction, nothing is regarded as worthy of protection. The trees which should adorn the farmer's lawn, shade his home, border his lanes and roads, and afford a grateful shade in his pastures, are all made to pass under the axe. Even trees which would soon bring him wealth as lumber are often sacrificed to that insatiate monster "improvement." Thus the black walnut and cherry in many parts of the State, have been split into rails or burned in log-heaps. Pines are cut down for a few bolts of shingles or a single saw-log, and the balance left to rot; oaks fit for the ribs of mighty navies, are burned up to rid the ground of an encumbrance, and to-day the exquisitely beautiful "bird's-eye maple," fit to adorn the palaces of kings, is burned as fire-wood, or thrown into the log-heap, an unconscious burnt-offering to the god of Folly. Instead of preserving in any proper measure these blessings of God's own planting, man seems to take delight in wasting his fair heritage, and as tree after tree falls beneath his blows, he exclaims, "one enemy less in the land." Thus fields and homes, highways and bye-ways, are smitten with one common treeless doom, and the dreary monotony of the desert threatens a land that was once like the Eden of old, where "God made to grow every tree that is pleasant to the sight and good for food." We have forgotten that the bountiful Father has declared that "the *tree of the field is man's life.*"

It is not claimed that it is wrong to sacrifice some portion of forests to form arable field and meadow. The forest, as such, yields no food for man, or nothing adequate to sustain a dense population; but to cut down the forest just as we would attack any nuisance, merely to destroy it,—to lay it waste to form new fields while the old fields are only partially and inefficiently cultivated from lack of labor, means, or energy—this is mere vandalism—the destruction of treasures which, the destroyer knows not how to prize.

The wealth of the United States in forest growths, is a matter of just pride to those who have compared our forest growths with those of other countries. Thus, according to Clave, the forest trees of France comprise only about twenty species, and according to Rossmäsler, there are only about fifty-seven species in Germany, but of these, many are mere shrubs, or fruit trees, so that it is safe to say that the forest trees of Europe, of economical value, do not exceed forty or fifty species; while, according to Dr. Cooper, the species in the United States exceed two hundred and thirty; and in the North American Sylva, by Michaux, with supplement by Nuttall, there are described as natives of the United States, one hundred and ninety-four species, of which the trees average a height over thirty feet, and eighty-six species with average height over fifty feet. Of the trees in the United States which would be classed as first and second class forest trees, there are twenty-two species of oaks, eleven of walnuts, ten of maples, eleven of birches, and forty-seven of evergreens, as pines, &c.; or the evergreens alone, of the United States, which are classed as first and second class forest trees, equal the species of all Europe combined. But not only is the United States, as a whole, thus rich in its arboreal growth, but there is no State east of the Rocky Mountains so rich in its forest wealth as Michigan. Indeed, too many have regarded this wealth as so abundant as to amount to the actual poverty of its possessor, to be got rid of at any sacrifice. With all such, the statement of Hon. Geo. P. Marsh, in his very valuable work "Man and Nature," (p. 301,) should have great influence: "I greatly doubt whether any one of the American States, except, perhaps, Oregon, has at this moment more woodland than it ought permanently to preserve, though no doubt a different distribution of the forests in all of them might be highly advantageous."

But rich as we are in this treasure, when we see how rapidly we are parting with it—when we learn how vast is our market —that the government buildings at Nashville, Chattanooga, and Nashville were built with pine lumber taken from Saginaw,— when we see that Chicago has become the first lumber market in the world, and all her treasures drawn from our State, that every river and stream on our western border is made to pour this forest wealth into the Chicago market, to supply the comparatively treeless region which stretches to the foot of the Rocky Mountains—when we see these "portable steam saw-mills," like "flying artillery," sweeping over our State, at every cross-roads, opening their guns upon the trees still left in the settled portions of the State—your committee think our people should ponder, and ask themselves whether they are not "killing the goose that lays the golden egg." While the people of this State feel a great pride in their mineral resources—in their copper, which stands confessedly at the head of all produced in the world for its purity, so that when European Physicists, when requiring copper of absolute purity, say that "Lake Superior copper must be used for this instrument,"—its iron which acknowledges no superior, and must search far and wide, for an equal—its salt, plaster, and marble, which will soon take the rank "first among equals"—yet, in the estimation of your committee, Michigan is richer in her forests than in all her mineral resources combined—and it is eminently proper that attention should be called to the fearful waste which is squandering this priceless treasure.

But however important this subject, and worthy of the attention of the land-owners of this State, it is the duty of your committee to call the especial attention of the farmers and fruit-growers, to the effect of the destruction of these forests on the climate of our State.

Forests act as a balance-wheel of the land climate, contributing powerfully to an equability in the three most important elements of climate, viz: heat, moisture, and wind.

Your committee will consider these subjects in the order indicated.

TEMPERATURE.

The tendency of climate in this latitude, far removed from the controlling influence of the oceanic bodies of water, is to tropical heat in summer, and arctic cold in winter, and hence the necessity of some agent which will control the power of the one, and moderate the rigor of the other.

The question is often asked whether our climate has changed since this State was first settled? and your committee regret that they have no meteorological observations reaching back far enough to settle this important question, but there are some facts which seem to indicate that our winters have greatly increased in severity within the last forty years, and this increased severity seems to move along even-paced with the destruction of our forests. Your committee will make a short extract bearing on this point, from the report of 1865, of the Secretary of the Board of Agriculture, p. 244:

"Thirty years ago the peach was one of the most abundant fruits in this State : easy to cultivate, and the tree bearing early, it was planted everywhere, and everywhere yielded its luscious harvest. This was emphatically true of the South-Eastern part of the State. At that time a frost injurious to corn at any time from May to October was a thing unknown. Thirty years ago I plucked in abundance spring flowers in the open fields in Lenawee County in January. Now, the peach in all that region is a most uncertain crop. The contingency of frost enters into the farmer's calculations concerning the corn-crop, and curious boys do not hunt the fields for flowers in January. Fourteen years ago I settled in Eaton County, and there again found the peach in all its pride of honey and gold, but there too it is fast passing away, till a good crop of peaches comes 'like angels visits.' A similar change is observed in almost all of the older-settled parts of the State, till the peach seems destined to take up its final abode in a narrow strip skirting the eastern shore of Lake Michigan."

The destruction of the wheat as well as the corn crop, is becoming a matter of great anxiety to our farmers in many sections, and the winter-killing of the clover in the eastern part of the State last winter, not by "heaving," but apparently frozen dead in the ground, and appearing black and rotten in the Spring, may be another proof of climatic changes of grave significance to the farmers and dairymen.

While there is this strongly marked tendency to increased severity in our winter cold, there seems an equally strongly marked tendency to excessive summer heat. The heat of the sun is moderated chiefly by three causes: radiation, evaporation, and ærial currents or winds. The heat of the sun, if not mitigated by radiation or evaporation, would render a large part of our globe uninhabitable. Thus Herschel at the Cape of Good Hope, in mid-winter, cooked eggs by the heat of the sun alone—not by concentrating it, but simply by confining it, and preventing its radiation. Radiation takes place only from the surface of bodies, and the more extended the surface, the greater the capacity for radiation.

The trunk, branches, and leaves of a tree, present a larger surface than the ground they cover. Dr. Gray tells us, "the Washington Elm, at Cambridge—a tree of no extraordinary size—was some years ago estimated to produce a crop of seven million leaves, exposing a surface of two hundred thousand square feet, or about five acres of foliage." With such a vast increase of radiating surface, no one will wonder at the refreshing coolness of the forest shade, and no one will doubt but that a country abounding in forest trees must enjoy comparative exemption from excessive summer heat; but where this is wanting, as in some of the sandy deserts, where the summer glare is unbroken by a shadow, and only the sandy surface radiates the intolerable heat, travelers tell us that "the soil is fire and the wind is flame." We have here, indeed, a concurrence of circumstances tending to produce a high temperature—the absence of moisture in the soil, and consequently no evaporation, the absence of clouds to intercept the sun's rays, and the small surface of the sandy plains. The reverse of all these conditions we find in forests; and with the destruction of its forests, every country is liable to deterioration from excess of summer heat.

Excess of radiating surface would tend to increase the severity of our winters, but with the approach of winter this enormous increase of surface vanishes with the fall of the leaves, and the leaves themselves become an admirable covering for the cold and freezing earth. Thus the forest leaves shed their cool and dewy blessings upon the earth in summer heat, and cover it up tenderly and warmly from the winter cold. Even when the leaves by process of decay have passed into the condition of vegetable mold, their protecting influence does not cease, for this substance is an excellent non-conductor of heat. Even in the compact form of swamp muck the non-conducting property is strongly marked. Thus in the winter of 1865, in making excavations for laying pipes to convey water to the Reform School in this city, the ground was found frozen in some places to the depth of four feet, yet on the muck bed at the Agricultural College, in a position equally exposed, the frost extended to a depth of less than eight inches. While our open fields, which by process of cultivation have been deprived of their covering of leaf mold, become frozen to a great depth in our protracted winters, the forest grounds retaining this covering of leaves and mold, are often protected from frost altogether, or frozen only superficially.

Forests exert, indirectly, a controlling influence over the temperature of a country through their relations to evaporation and precipitation of moisture, and this subject will be again alluded to, when discussing the relations of forests to evaporation and precipitation.

It is believed by many that there is an intimate relation between the ratio of evaporation to precipitation, and the fertility of any region. Exceptions to this are found when natural or artificial irrigation remedies the absence of rain. But in general terms where evaporation is so greatly in excess of precipitation, that all precipitation is removed by evaporation, and none is drained off by rivers, barrenness is the general rule. Whenever, therefore, the amount of rainfall is deficient, or tends to deficiency, anything which tends to increase evaporation, will tend to the agricultural impoverishment of that region. The usual annual fall of rain in the central part of our State, is about 29 inches. In the year 1866 there was a large excess over this amount, being 39½ inches; but this is 10 inches in excess of the average. We are beyond the latitude of the excessive precipitation of the returning trade-wind. This S. W. wind, although our most prevailing wind, over-balancing in frequency all the other winds which blow in the central part of the State, reaches us as a comparatively dry wind. Thus it appears from the observations taken at the Agricultural College for nearly four years, that the rainy winds are easterly winds.

If you call the winds from the SW. W. and N. W. the westerly winds, and those from NE. E. and S. E. the easterly winds, from observations taken three times a day, viz: at 7 A. M., 2. P. M., and 9 P. M., we find that in 1863 every 11.2 easterly winds gave one inch rain; and every 70.1 westerly winds gave one inch rain; in 1864, every 12 easterly and 66½ westerly winds gave one inch rain.

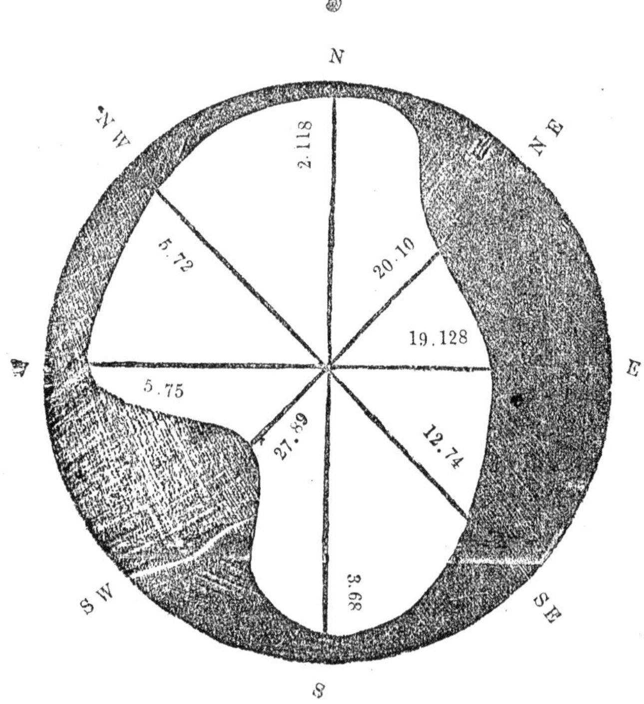

RAIN ROSETTE FOR 1863–1866.

In 1865—every 14½ easterly, and every 60½ westerly winds gave 1 inch rain.

In 1866—every 12 easterly, and every 32 westerly winds gave 1 inch rain.

Or, on the average, ever 12.4 observations of winds from the east, give 1 inch rain, and every 57.3 observations of westerly winds give 1 inch rain. The observations are taken thrice daily.

Investigations designed to determine the relation of evaporation to precipitation in this latitude, have developed some startling facts. Observations for this purpose were made at the Agricultural College, for the years 1865, and 1866, from March to November, of each year. The observations were made by exposing a vessel with vertical sides, so as to expose the same surface to evaporation and precipitation. This vessel was exposed to the action of the sun and wind, being placed on the surface of the open ground, away from buildings and trees. In this vessel was placed water to the depth of one inch, and whenever it approached dryness, an inch additional of water was placed in the vessel, or if it was like to overflow, an inch in depth was removed. As rain would fall into this dish, as well as water evaporate out of it, the difference between the water added and that taken out would give the difference between evaporation and precipitation. In the year 1865, during the eight months, from March 15th to Nov. 14th, the evaporation exceeded the rain-fall by 6½ inches, or the rain-fall for 8 months was 25.35 inches, while evaporation was 30.85 inches.

In 1866 the rainfall for the corresponding 8 months was 29.78 inches, while the evaporation for the same time exceeded this by 2¼ inches or a total evaporation of 32.03 inches. It will be understood that in these observations the evaporations took place from a *saturated surface*, and consequently greatly exceeded the evaporation which takes place from the surface of the ground which is seldom saturated with water during the growing months.

Since the above was written one member of your committee received from I. A. Lapham, LL. D., of Milwaukee, an account of similar investigations made at Milwaukee, and extending through five years. Dr. Lapham made his investigations by exposing a basin of water in the open air, and measuring the amount of evaporation by means of a micrometer screw turned down every morning until the point of the screw touched the surface of the water. His observations are given for the year by months, but as the observations at the Agricultural College were taken only from March 15 to Nov. 14 for each year, one-half of Dr. Lapham's observations for March and November, both of the evaporation and rainfall will be taken, which will give an approximation of the true result. We find that the average rain for this period for five years at Milwaukee is 23.61 inches, while the average evaporation for the same period is 32.58 inches, or the evaporation exceeds the precipitation by 8.97 inches, while at the Agricultural College the average excess of evaporation is only 4.37 inches. In other words the excess of evaporation over precipitation for 8 months at Milwaukee surpasses that at Lansing by 4.60 inches.

Undoubtedly the relations of evaporation to precipitation will be found to vary in different parts of our State. The noble inland seas which clasp our borders must have a large control over the meteorology of their shores. Notwithstanding this control, the tendency to excess of evaporation over precipitation in this latitude shows that any process which will increase this tendency should be viewed with alarm. Even with the present large extent of the surface of our State covered with forest, the evaporation is found to be in excess of precipitation. Will not the further destruction of our forests tend to increase still more this disparity? May not the excess of evaporation over precipitation in Wisconsin be accounted for by her limited forests and extended prairie surface?

Forest growths are regarded by many of our ablest physicists as exerting a marked influence over the amount of rainfall in such a region. The fact that all countries abundantly clothed with forests are also well supplied with rain, and the rain is equally distributed through the season of vegetable growth, would naturally lead to the conclusion that forest growths have some agency in determining this rainfall. Others have claimed that the equable rainfall was the effect of other causes, and that the abundant forest growth was the *effect* of the abundance and distribution of the rain, and not the *determining cause* of the rain. But whichever we may place as antecedent, or consequent, we find that abundant and well distributed rain is associated with large forest growths, and if these forest growths are extensively removed, the rains diminish, or become capricious, droughts and floods alternating, while in regions destitute of all vegetable growth, rain is unknown, as in the strong lines of the poet, quoted by Marsh:

> "Afric's barren sand,
> Where naught can grow because it raineth not,
> And where no rain can fall to bless the land,
> Because, naught grows there."

Humboldt, while speaking of the effect of removing forests, says: "In felling the trees which covered the crowns and slopes of the mountains, men in all climates seem to be bringing upon future generations, two calamities at once—a want of fuel and a scarcity of water."

Herschel enumerates among the influences unfavorable to rain, "absence of vegetation in warm climates, and especially of trees. This is no doubt one of the reasons of the extreme aridity of Spain." What the real condition of Spain is, may be seen by the following extract quoted by the Detroit Daily *Post*: "Aridity and barrenness, indeed, is the general characteristic of the whole country. The insane folly which has caused the people to denude the country of trees, has modified no doubt unfavorably, a climate already too dry, which strikes with astonishment and horror one new from the delicious freshness and verdure of England. The Spaniard, and above all, the Castilian, has an innate hatred of a tree; if he does not cut it down for firewood, he cuts it down because it harbors birds that eat his grain. Forests and brushwood alike disappear before the inevitable axe, until, as often occurs in Castile, the traveler may look for leagues over the country, without seeing a tree or brush to break its uniformity. This foolish extinction of the forests has been the source of innumerable evils to the country—evils which are continually acting upon and augmenting each other. Unrestrained by any vegetation, the rain water rushes down the steep sides of the hills and over the plains, wearing them into deep gullies, and carrying off the finer and most valuable parts of the soil. The rivers, terrible and dangerous torrents in times of rain, shrink and dry up almost immediately after this is passed over; the water, for which the country is gaping, hurried off to the sea, becomes lost for all useful purposes; an extreme aridity of the atmosphere is the consequence, a continually diminishing rainfall, and a continually impoverished country, which nothing can now remedy but a strong energetic action on the part of the people to replant and irrigate it."

Asbjörnsen, quoted by Marsh, says: "Numerous examples show that woods exert an influence in producing rain, and that rain fails where they are wanting; for many countries have, by the destruction of their forests, been deprived of rain, moisture, springs, and water courses, which are necessary for vegetable growth. In Palestine, and many other parts of Asia, and Northern Africa, which in ancient times were the granaries of Europe, fertile and populous, similar consequences have been experienced. These lands are now deserts, and it is the destruction of the forests alone, which has produced this desolation.

"On the other hand, examples of the beneficial influence of planting and restoring the woods are not wanting. In Lower Egypt, both at Cairo and near Alexandria, rain rarely fell in considerable quantity—for example, during the French occupation of Egypt, it did not rain for sixteen months—but since Mehemet Ali and Ibrahim Pacha executed their vast plantations, (the former alone having planted more than twenty millions of olive and fig trees, cottonwoods, oranges, &c.,) there now falls a good deal of rain, especially along the coast, in the months of November, December and January; and even at Cairo it rains both oftener and more abundantly, so that real showers are no rarity."

Boussingault, a most careful observer and guarded writer, says: "In my judgment, it is settled that very large clearings must diminish the annual fall of rain in a country."

SPRINGS AND STREAMS.

It is a matter of common observation that springs are frequently dried up by clearing the ground above and adjacent to them. A great many instances might be adduced in proof, but only two will be mentioned here. Marschand, quoted by Marsh, says: "The Wolf Spring, in the commune of Soubey, furnishes a remarkable example of the influences of the woods upon fountains. A few years ago this spring did not exist. At the place where it now rises, a small thread of water was observed after very long rains, but the stream disappeared with the rain. The spot is in the middle of a very steep pasture, inclining to the South. Eighty years ago, the owner of the land perceiving that young firs were springing up in the upper part of it, determined to let them grow, and they soon formed a flourishing grove. As soon as they were well grown, a fine spring appeared in the place of the occasional rill, and furnished abundant water in the longest droughts. For forty or fifty years this spring was considered the best in the Clos du Doubs. A few years since the grove was felled and the ground turned into a pasture. The spring disappeared with the wood, and it is now as dry as it was ninety years ago."

Dr. Piper, in his "Trees of America," says: "Within half a mile of my residence there is a pond, upon which mills have been standing for a long time, dating back, I believe, to the first settlement of the town. These have been kept in constant operation until within some twenty or thirty years, when the supply of water began to fail. The pond owes its existence to a stream which has its source in the hills which stretch some miles to the south. Within the time mentioned, these hills which were clothed with a dense forest, have been almost entirely stripped of trees; and to the wonder and loss of the mill-owners, the water in the pond has failed, except in the season of freshets; and what was never heard of before, the stream itself has been entirely dry. Within the last ten years a new growth of wood has sprung up on most of the lands formerly occupied by the old forests, and now the water runs through the year, notwithstanding the great droughts of the last few years."

The influence of the forest in promoting springs and small streams is not difficult to understand. In the first place evaporation is checked both by excluding winds and by shading the ground from the direct rays of the sun, so that but little evaporation takes place except what is transpired or evaporated from the leaves. In the second place the fallen leaves and the leaf mold readily absorb, and tenaciously retain the rains which fall upon them, so that the rain water flows from such grounds but very slowly, the great mass being absorbed by the soil and reappearing at places more or less distant as springs and rivulets.

INUNDATIONS.

A rain may fall on a hay-stack or thatched roof for hours before any will be seen to trickle down its sides; but if it fall upon a clean shingle roof, the eaves begin to drip at once. So the slowness with which rain-water, falling on forests, finds its way into water-courses, as compared with the impetuosity with which it rushes from the open fields, shows clearly that forests have a restraining influence upon the inundations which naturally follow any unusual rain-fall. The danger in such inundations arises not so much from the quantity of the rain-fall, as the rapidity with which it finds its way into the water courses. If the period of egress of such waters can be extended, the danger is proportionately diminished, or disappears altogether. On the other hand, any system of husbandry which accelerates this efflux of a rainfall, whether it be by destroying the natural absorbent surface of the soil, and substituting therefor the comparatively non-retentive surface of pastures and meadows, or by ditches or other means affording a more rapid escape for such rainfall, increases by so much the danger from inundations.

Were not the remarkable inundations which occurred in the State of Ohio during last year, with their attendant destruction of property, the natural result of opening up the avenues of escape into the water courses, so that the rainfall which in a wooded country, would be many days in escaping, might now flow off in a few hours? If the farmers of Ohio had cherished their Sylvan friends and protectors, would they not have secured immunity from so great a calamity?

But the most usual season of danger from these freshets is when the snow, which has accumulated through the winter, is carried off by a rain and warm wind. In such cases the beneficial influence of the forest is very great, for there is not only the absorbing and retaining influence of the forest soil with its natural covering, but the rapidity with which the snow melts in the woods is much less than in the open grounds where the warm winds have full sweep. Mr. Marsh quotes an instance from Dr. Piper which clearly confirms this view: "A body of snow one foot in depth, and sixteen feet square, was protected from the wind by a tight board fence about five feet high, while another body of snow, much more sheltered from the sun than the first, six feet in depth, and about sixteen feet square, was fully exposed to the wind. When the thaw came on, which lasted about a fortnight, the large body of snow was entirely dissolved in less than a week, while the smaller body was not wholly gone at the end of the second week." In this case the snow fully exposed to the wind melted more than twelve times faster than that sheltered from the wind. If the melting of our snow in the spring, instead of being completed in a few hours, could be extended through a period twelve times as long, the violence of our spring freshets would disappear under all ordinary circumstances, and be greatly mitigated under all extraordinary circumstances. The most feasible means for securing this result, is by availing ourselves of the protecting influence of forest growths, and thereby controlling the sweep of the wind.

Allusion has been made to the incidental control of temperature exercised by forests. This arises from the relations of watery vapor to radiant heat, and in consequence of the greater dampness of the forest climate. Tyndall, in his beautiful researches on heat, has shown that water-vapor has a most remarkable power of restraining the radiation of heat, and by a series of experiments, perfectly convincing, has demonstrated that an atmosphere saturated with watery vapor, acts as a screen, to cut off almost entirely the escape of heat by radiation. There are well known facts which confirm the deductions from the philosophical researches of Tyndall and Count Rumford. Thus travelers assure us that in the rainless deserts, such as Gobi and Sahara, while the sands by day reach a temperature almost unendurably hot, yet the nights are almost as unendurably cold, for the atmosphere over these parched wastes is so destitute of moisture that radiation is almost entirely unchecked, and the temperature which by day often reaches 130°, at night often falls below the freezing point. This connection of drought and frost was noticed centuries ago: thus Jacob in his spirited reply to Laban, in summing up the hardships of his shepherd life said, "in the *day the drought consumed* me, and the *frost by night*, and my sleep departed from my eyes."

In our own State, autumnal droughts are almost always soon followed by frosts. Thus the frosts which cut the corn in September, 1863, was preceded by a drouth, there being less than nine-tenths of an inch of rain in that month. So important is atmospheric humidity in checking radiation of heat, and thus preventing frost, that Tyndall makes the following statement: "The withdrawal of the sun from any region over which the atmosphere is dry, must be followed by speedy refrigeration. The winters of Thibet are almost unendurable from the same cause. Even the absence of the sun at night, causes powerful refrigeration when the air is dry. The removal, for a single summer's night, of the aqueous vapor from the atmosphere which covers England, would be attended by the destruction of every plant which a freezing temperature could kill. In short, it may be safely predicted, that whenever the air is *dry*, the daily thermometric range will be great."—*Tyndall on Heat, p.* 405.

The gardener who wishes to preserve his tree from spring frost, places a tub of water under it, and the watery vapor rising from this in a still night envelopes the tree in an invisible blanket to cover it from frost. The autumnal frosts which have injured our crops in years past, have inflicted no injury in the vicinity of rivers and lakes where the exhalations arising from these bodies of water have spread their protecting mantle over the adjacent lands. The great specific heat of water has undoubtedly much to do with this protecting influence, but more still is done to this peculiar influence of the watery vapor. As the atmosphere becomes dryer by clearing away the forest, frosts during the growing season, become more frequent and more destructive. This has been the general experience in clearing up a new country, and is an urgent plea for the preservation of a portion, at least, of our forests.

WINDS.

One of the most important offices of the forest is the control of winds. With the exception of mountain ranges, no terrestrial object has such marked control over the violence of winds as forest trees; and there are numerous instances to show that the destruction of the forest has opened the country to the disastrous influence of the pitiless wind. Thus Dussard, as quoted by Marsh, maintains that the *mistral*, the dreaded N. W. wind of France, whose chilling blasts are so fatal to tender vegetation in spring, "is the child of man, the result of his devastations. Under the reign of Augustus, the forests which protected the Cevennes, were felled or destroyed by fire in mass. A vast country, before covered with impenetrable woods —powerful obstacles to the movement and even the formation of hurricanes—was suddenly denuded, swept bare, stripped, and soon after, a scourge hitherto unknown struck terror over the land from Avignon to the Buches du Rhone, and thence to Marseilles, and along the whole maritime frontier. The people thought this wind a curse sent of God. They raised altars to it, and offered sacrifices to appease its rage."

Prof. Rosa, in the Polytechnic Journal for Dec., 1861, gives the following: "To supply the extraordinary demand for Italian iron occasioned by the exclusion of English iron in the time of Napoleon I. the furnaces of the valleys of Bergamo were stimulated to great activity. The ordinary production of charcoal not sufficing to feed the furnaces and the forges, the woods were felled, the copses cut before their time, and the whole economy of the forest was deranged. At Piazzatore there was such a devastation of the woods, and consequently such an increased severity of the climate, that maize no longer ripened. An association formed for the purpose effected the restoration of the forest, and maize flourishes again in the fields of Piazzatore."

Similar ameliorations have been produced by plantations in Belgium. Thus Bande in the *Reveu des Deux Mondes*, makes this statement: "A spectator placed on the famous bell tower of the cathedral at Antwerp, saw not long since, on the opposite side of the Schelde, only a vast desert plain; now he sees a forest, the limits of which are confounded with the horizon. Let him enter within its shade. The supposed forest is but a system of regular rows of trees, the oldest of which is not forty years of age. These plantations have ameliorated the climate which had doomed to sterility the soil where they are planted. While the tempest is violently agitating their tops, the air a little below is still, and sands far more barren than the plateau of La Hague, have been transformed, under their protection, into fertile fields."—(Man and Nature, p. 152.)

But we need not go beyond the limits of our own State for proof of the ameliorating influences on climates, of the destruction of forests. Attention has already been called to this by the failure of the peach crop all over our State, save a narrow strip under the lee of Lake Michigan, and by the partial destruction of our clover crop last winter. But a still more serious loss is the great damage to our wheat crop, especially in our old and well improved counties. The following extract from a valuable lecture delivered at Jackson, before a meeting of the agriculturists of Michigan, in 1864, by that veteran in the pomology of our State, T. T. Lyon, Esq., and quoted in the report of the Secretary of the State Board of Agriculture, for 1865, p. 251, places this subject in a clear light. "The natural result of this wholesale destruction, is manifesting itself in the higher winds, the more sudden changes, and the more extreme cold of our winters. Although in consequence of this state of affairs the peach, once almost as sure throughout our State as the apple, is now, in effect, driven under the lee of Lake Michigan; and although even our staple grain crop, wheat, was but two years since almost a total failure from want of shelter and protection, and though we have reason to fear that we have not yet seen the worst, the process of destruction yet goes on unchecked, and with a strange fatuity. Although the subject is one that deeply concerns us all, no measures are being taken or even seriously contemplated, to stay the growing calamity.

"Two years since, at a similar meeting, I availed myself of the opportunity to urge upon the Agriculturists of the State the importance of action in this matter. During the next winter the wheat crop of the entire State, from the want of the usual covering of snow, and the general lack of shelter from wind and sun, was diminished in amount more than one-half,—a loss to the State in a single year of more than five millions of bushels. The present winter threatens a repetition of the same calamity; and with the great breadth of wheat sown, we shall be fortunate if the amount of loss be not essentially greater than before."

Last year the loss on all that part of the State lying south of the Michigan Central railroad,—a region deprived of the ameliorating influence of Lake Michigan on the south-west wind,—and comprising the richest agricultural portion of the State, was estimated at no less than three-fourths of the entire wheat crop! From what inquiries your committee have been able to make, the loss on the wheat crop alone, of this State, for the last four years, is not less than $20,000,000.

Your committee would be most happy to believe that this enormous loss springs from causes evanescent in their nature, and destined speedily to pass away, to return nevermore. But your committee are fearful that these vast losses "are but the beginning of sorrow," and that the improvidence which laid open our fields to that scourge of God, the S. W. wind, by the wholesale destruction of our forests, is now only beginning to reap the fruit of that want of forethought, and that these losses can be avoided only by restoring, in part at least, the natural barriers against the wind.

If it is conceded that protection from the wind is desirable. the practical question arises from which wind should the farmer especially seek to guard himself? This question may require different answers in different parts of the State, but for the central part of the State, the meterological observations taken at the State Agricultural College, enable your committee to answer this important question. From these observations it appears that for the winter months, for four years, the wind from W. was 169 times, N. W. 96, N. 24, N. E. 52, E. 60, S. E. 132, S. 30, and S. W. 369. A diagram is presented, in which the darkly shaded portion will present to the eye at a glance the comparative frequency of the wind from the different points of the compass. These observations of the winds it will be understood, were made three times a day.

WIND ROSETTE FOR MONTHS OF DECEMBER, JANUARY AND FEBRUARY, FOR THE YEARS 1864, 1865, 1866, AND JANUARY, 1867.

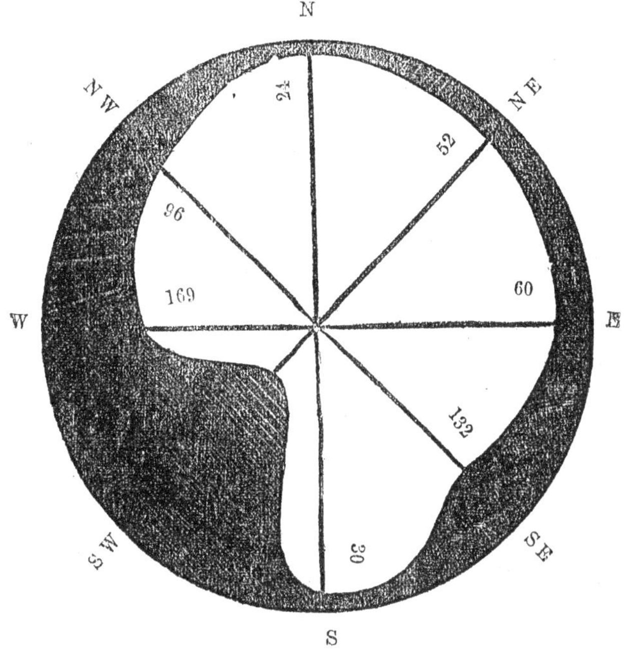

COLD WINDS.

But not only is our S. W. wind the most prevalent wind in the central part of our State, but, also, it is during our cold season our coldest wind. Thus, for the four years past, the Register Thermometer at the Agricultural College has indicacated a temperature at or below zero 54 times, the observations being made once a day. Of these 54 observations, the air was still or variable, 9 times. Wind from W. 3 times; from N. W. 5 times; from N. once; from N. E. twice; from E. twice; from S. E. 4 times; from S. none; from S. W. 28 times. The diagram marked Winter Rosette, presents a comparative view of the frequency of winds in any point of the campass, with the thermometer at or below zero of Farenheit's Thermometer.

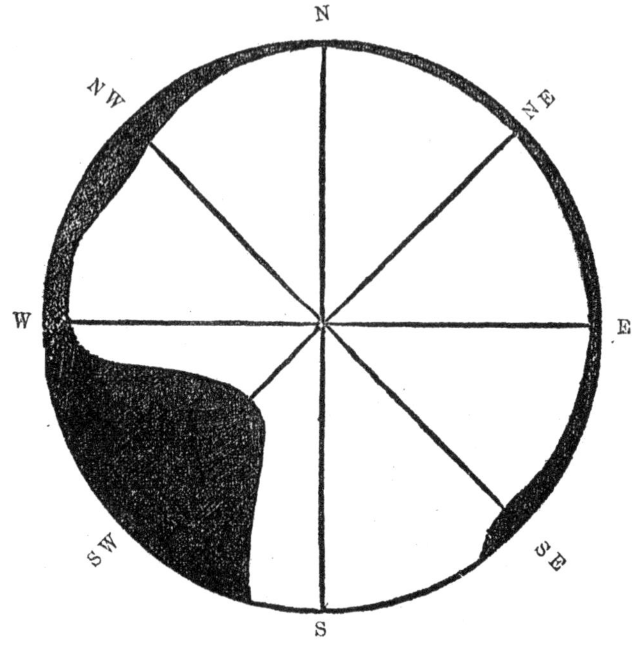

WINTER ROSETTE.

1 N., average -11°.
2 N. E., average -7°.
2 E., average -7°.
4 S. E., average -3°.
28 S. W., average -8°
3 W., average -3⅓°.
5 N. W., average -5° 4′.
9 No wind, or variable, average -5° 8′.

54 times in all the thermometer below zero

Both of these diagrams show how fearful a scourge is this S. W. wind, in the central part of our State, and answer with remarkable distinctness the question, from what wind should the farmer especially seek to guard himself?

That it is shelter from this wind that is needed to protect the farmer and fruit-grower, is shown by several facts. It is matter of frequent observation in this vicinity that the peach tree growing in a situation protected from the S. W. wind frequently produces fruit, while trees not thus protected are usually unfruitful. Some remarkable instances have been noticed in this city. A peach tree in Kalamazoo city was in large part exposed to the action of this wind, and produced no fruit, but one branch which lay upon the roof of an out-house and was covered with snow during a few very cold nights produced an abundant crop of fruit.

Even very slight barriers exert a surprising influence in guarding from the effect of wind. Thus Becquerel states, "In the valley of the Rhone, a simple hedge, two metres in height, is a sufficient protection for a distance of twenty-two metres," or a wind-break will protect a width of space eleven times its height. This is strikingly shown in the case of the wheat crop in this State. Mr. Lyon states in Report of the Secretary of the State Board of Agriculture for 1865, page 252: "I is presumed that during the season alluded to, few of us failed to observe that even the protection of a ridge or dead-furrow, running north and south through a field of wheat, was sufficient to preserve a streak of green, where all else was brown and bare; and that the shelter of a fence was the means of preserving a still greater breadth; while the interposition of a hedge of oak grubs or a body of timber invariably secured the preservation of a fair crop over a still greater breadth of ground, often amounting to an entire field."

In many parts of this State, it is found that if farmers harrow in their wheat, and then roll the ground smooth, the crop is usually an entire failure; if harrowed and not rolled, a partial crop is secured, but if plowed in with gang plows, the furrows running north and south, a good crop is almost certain. The reason why a good crop is secured when protected from the wind, is not hard to find. In the first place, it is shielded from the bitter biting S. W. wind; and in the second place, it is protected by a mantle of snow which lodges in the furrows or behind the fence and timber belts, and thus covers up the wheat from the destroying cold, for God has made no warmer winter covering for the cold and freezing earth than the snow. Whenever the ground is covered with this mantle, dropped from Heaven, the vegetation is safe from the deadly cold. But we are not sure of the presence of this covering, nor of its equal distribution over the surface of the ground so long as land is laid open to the sweep of the fierce S. W. wind, or even if it falls, it may rapidly disappear before the wind, either being swept off bodily, or evaporated in the rapidly changed and dry air of the winter winds.

DEPREDATIONS OF INSECTS.

Many countries are fearfully wasted by the depredations of insects. Thus the locust and grasshopper have, for time immemorial, devoured the vegetation of some countries at the east. In certain portions of our own country the grasshopper threatens to be as great a scourge, as in Asia. The chinch-bug of the prairies, if not as widely known, is equally dreaded. Other forms of insect life will probably appear to scourge the land, from which is driven out the forest, and the forest-loving birds. The following extract from Marsh, indicates an additional control of insect life connected with the forest: "The insects most injurious to rural industry do not multiply in or near the woods. The locust which ravages the east with its voracious armies, is bred in vast open plains, which admit the whole heat of the sun to hasten the hatching of the eggs, gather no moisture to destroy them, and harbor no bird to feed upon the larvæ. It is only since the felling of the forests of Asia Minor and Cyrene, that the locust has become so fearfully destructive in those countries; and the grasshopper which now threatens to become almost as great a pest to the agriculture of some North American soils, breeds in seriously injurious numbers only when a wide extent of surface is bare of woods."—Man and Nature, p. 291.

Your committee have thus called the attention of this honorable body to some of the results of this reckless and violent disturbance of the forest economy of our State. Your committee are painfully conscious that they have only very imperfectly and inadequately presented a most important subject, but they hope public attention will be aroused on a subject so intimately connected with the future welfare of our State, and that our intelligent farmers and land owners, may devise some means to stay a great and growing evil. It is time that unthinking destruction should stay its ruthless hand, and preserve for future generations a portion of the blessings we so richly enjoy. Cicero describes his ideal old man as busy in planting trees, who, when asked why he planted trees whose fruit he would never taste, replied "Others planted, and I have eaten the fruit: why should not I plant for the generations to come?" The forests of our noble State were planted by our father, God, and why should we not preserve a portion at least for the generations coming after us, or when our wasteful improvidence has stripped the earth of this inestimable blessing, why should we not restore in part, that other generations may receive a portion of that which was too bountifully bestowed upon us?

The necessity for the landowners of this State to adopt some efficient means for the preservation of our forests, becomes evident from another consideration. Among other nations, large tracts of land are kept in forest, either as parks and game preserves, or as government reserves for timber. These are the property of the State, and are carefully preserved from destruction, or re-planted as fast as the timber is removed. The nobility also take a just pride in their parks and forests. In these ways large portions of many countries are preserved in forest. But there are no such conservative influences at work in our State. The Government has no permanent timber reserves, parks or game forests. The care and preservation of the forests are entirely in the hands of individuals, and hence the greater responsibility resting upon them. The only *landed nobility* in America is the *farmer*, and he must preserve his parks and forests, or else forfeit his title of *a noble-man!*

REMEDIAL MEASURES.

The task of remedying these evils, by legislation, is a subject beset with many difficulties. The title of the great body of the land resting with individuals *in fee simple*, government can exercise over it no direct control whatever, and the ends to be sought by legislation on this subject must be secured by indirect methods. The Legislature have no constitutional power to forbid the destruction of forests on lands whose absolute ownership is vested in individuals, and this inability to control the individual in the management of his private affairs, is inherent in our American idea of the liberty of the citizen. In countries under despotic sway, direct legislation and control over the cutting of forests are matters of frequent occurrence, and it is acknowledged that such interference has been a good inFrance. Let it be f or Americans to show that liberty and intelligence can accomplish all the good that despotism can hope to secure, and without its ponderous machinery.

Among the methods suggested for preserving a portion of our forest, and especially for controlling the action of the wind, it has been proposed to exempt timber belts of moderate width, running north and south, from all taxation while left in forest. This, if generally adopted by our farmers, would unquestionably be productive of much good, but it is open to objection.

A more feasible method is legislation which will remove the necessity for such large use of timber in fences. Probably three-fourths of all the fences in this State are wasted in the effort to *fence out stock*, for one-fourth of our present fences would better accomplish all the good sought, if used to *fence in the stock.*

In a newly settled country the advantages of free pasturage in the woods, and the small extent of arable ground, with the abundance of rail timber, have led the inhabitants to let their stock run at large and to fence in their fields. But in a thickly settled region, the disparity between the forest lands and arable grounds and meadows is constantly increasing until the only grounds which lie in commons are the highways and the pasturage of this scanty surface is only secured by keeping up a vast amount of fence, and thus the farmers are heavily taxed to *fence in their farms in order to fence out their roads.* If the farmers, on the other hand, would fence in the comparatively small amount of land used for pasture, and leave all the rest of their farm unenclosed, the larger part of the timber now used in fencing would be saved; one heavy drain upon our forests would be stopped, and a heavy tax upon the farmer would be removed. This system would be practicable only in the older settled portions of our State. To compel the settler in the dense forests of our State to enclose pasture for his stock while thousands of acres of forest afford excellent grazing free of cost, would be manifestly oppression, and in such a community such a law if enacted would remain a dead letter.

But even in our older settled counties, where it might seem desirable that stock should be restrained from running at large, if one township should shut up its stock in pastures, and leave the other fields open, and an adjoining township should allow its stock to run at large, the stock of this second township might stray into the tempting fields of this first township, and much evil result.

Your committee propose therefore, that the question of what stock shall run at large in any county of this State for any ensuing year, shall be settled by a vote of the Board of Supervisors of that county, at their meeting in October, at which time the Board of Supervisors may decide whether horses, cattle, sheep and swine, shall be permitted to run at large the next year.

If no vote is taken at such meeting of the Board of Supervisors, or if any or all these classes of animals are not permitted to run at large for the ensuing year, then in that county, for such animals, for such year, the law of the State of New York on this subject, shall be in full force.

A uniformity on this subject will thus be secured in each county for any year, while the inhabitants of the different sections can restrain their stock or permit them to run at large, as they shall find conducive to their interests. The exclusion of cattle and swine from the highway will be a favor to those who wish to line the roadside with shade trees.

SHADE TREES BY THE ROADSIDE.

The section lines of this State are, usually, and the quarter section lines are frequently the lines of highways. This generally brings the lines of our highways within a mile of each other each way, and frequently within half that distance. In this way our State is checkered with roads. Over these lines of highways we can exercise direct legislation, and this is the only direct method by which we can reach this subject. If, throughout our State, these roads were lined on each side with shade trees, the winds would be greatly mitigated in their force, and a serious and constantly increasing evil would be abated in part. The roads themselves, in many instances, would be benefitted by such lines of shade trees; the comfort of travelers and teams secured, and the beauty of the country enhanced.

As our highways are sixty-six feet wide, if eight feet on each side were planted with forest trees, ample space for roadway would still be left. There would be but small inducement to plant shade trees in the highway, unless cattle were excluded therefrom, and the trees thereby preserved from destruction. Trees thus planted should be guarded by stringent legislation, from willful or malicious injury in any way, whether by cutting or girdling the same, or by hitching horses or cattle to them; and overseers of highways and all other persons should be forbidden to cut or remove any trees planted at a distance equal to, or exceeding twenty-five feet from the center of the highway.

To secure the planting of such shade trees it might be declared lawful for any person to plant trees along his own premises in the edge of the highway; or any person might be authorized to pay a certain per centage of his highway tax by planting trees in the border of the highway adjacent to his premises; or the overseer of the highway might cause a certain per centage of the highway tax to be so expended.

If by these or similar means, the highways of our State could be permanently flanked by compact lines of forest trees, an important and valuable restraint would be placed upon the sweep of our pitiless winds; and although the means may at first seem slight, and inadequate to produce any sensible result, yet their general adoption would unquestionably produce a marked effect in a few years.

Your committee have freely availed themselves of the valuable information contained in the work by Hon.Geo. P. Marsh, "Man and Nature." We wish this valuable book could be placed in the hands of every farmer and land owner in our State.

Your committee ask leave to introduce two bills, viz:

A bill to prevent animals from running at large in the public highways, except in certain cases;

Also,

A bill relating to the planting of trees in the highways, being a bill to amend section 1111, being section 2, of chapter XXV. of the compiled laws, and to add two new sections thereto;

And ask to be discharged from the further consideration of the subject.

R. C. KEDZIE,
J. J. WOODMAN,
O. H. FELLOWS.

LANSING, Feb. 12, 1867.

LAWS RELATING TO AGRICULTURE.

Passed by the Legislature of Michigan, 1867.

AN ACT to amend section ten, of act number one hundred and eighty-eight, of session laws of eighteen hundred and sixty-one, entitled "an act to re-organize the Agricultural College of the State of Michigan, and to establish a State Board of Agriculture.

SECTION 1. *The People of the State of Michigan enact,* That section ten, of act number one hundred and eighty-eight, of session laws of eighteen hundred and sixty-one, be so amended as to read as follows:

Sec. 10. The Secretary shall report to the Legislature, at every regular session thereof, and to the Governor on the first Wednesday in January in each year when the Legislature is not in session, which report shall embrace all such statements, accounts, statistics, prize essays, and other information relative to agriculture in general, proceedings of the State Board of Agriculture, of the State Agricultural College and farm, of the State Agricultural Society, and of the county and district agricultural societies, to be approved by the Board, and shall cause to be printed six thousand copies of said report for the year eighteen hundred and sixty-six, and the same number for each year thereafter. Two thousand copies of said report shall be placed in the hands of the Secretary of State, for disbursement through the Department of State, and four thousand copies shall be placed at the disposal of the State Board of Agriculture; one thousand copies of the same to be distributed by the Secretary of the said State Board of Agriculture, as the Board shall direct, and the remaining three thousand copies of the same shall be distributed by the first of June in each year, by the Secretary of the Board, to the secretaries of all the various county and district agricultural societies, as equally as may be according to the population of said counties, to be by said secretaries distributed among the various viewing committees of county and district fairs, giving one volume of such report to each of said committees who shall be present and discharge the duties of his office on the days of the county and district fairs. And if after distributing to the said committees there shall be any of said report left in the said secretaries hands, they shall distribute them as equally as may be among the farmers of their respective counties.

Sec. 2. This act shall take immediate effect.

Approved February 27, 1867.

AN ACT to prevent the adulteration of milk, and to prevent the traffic in impure and unwholesome milk.

SECTION 1. *The People of the State of Michigan enact,* That any person or persons who shall knowingly, with intent to cheat or defraud, sell, exchange or deliver, or offer for manufacture at any cheese factory, any impure, adulterated or unwholesome milk, shall be deemed guilty of a misdemeanor, and shall forfeit and pay, on the first conviction, twenty-five dollars and the costs of suit or prosecution, and shall be at once committed to the common jail of the county, until the same be paid. On the second conviction for the like offense, he shall forfeit and pay fifty dollars and the costs of suit or prosecution, and shall be committed as aforesaid until the same be paid. On the third and every subsequent conviction, he shall forfeit and pay one hundred dollars and costs of suit or prosecution, and shall be committed as aforesaid until the same be paid.

Sec. 2. Any person who shall adulterate milk with a view of offering the same for sale, exchange or manufacture, or shall keep cows for the production of milk for market, or for sale, exchange or manufacture, in an unhealthy condition, or feed the same on food that produces impure, diseased or unwholesome milk, shall be deemed guilty of a misdemeanor, and on conviction thereof shall be liable to the same penalties as provided for the violation of the preceding section of this act: *Provided,* That on the first conviction for the violation of either this or the preceding section of this act, such person shall not be held committed for more than ten days; for the second conviction not more than twenty-five days, and for the third and every subsequent conviction, not more than fifty days.

Sec. 3. Any person who shall sell or deliver at any cheese factory, or to any cheese manufacturer, to be made into cheese, any milk from which any cream has been taken, or any milk known as skimmed milk, or any milk from which that part thereof known among dairymen as strippings, has been withheld or kept back with intent to cheat or defraud such manufacturer, or with intent to cheat or defraud any other person or persons, contributing or delivering milk to such factory or cheese manufacturer, to be made into cheese, shall be deemed guilty of a misdemeanor, and shall be punished therefor as provided in section two of this act.

Sec. 4. The addition of water to milk, with intent to cheat or defraud, is hereby declared to be an adulteration.

Approved February 7, 1867.

AN ACT to authorize the formation of corporations for manufacturing cheese and other products from milk.

SECTION 1. *The People of the State of Michigan enact,* That corporations for the purpose of manufacturing cheese and other products from milk, with a capital stock of not less than one thousand dollars, may be formed under and in compliance with the provisions of an act entitled "an act to authorize the formation of corporations for mining, smelting or manufacturing iron, copper, mineral coal, silver or other ores or minerals, and for other manufacturing purposes," approved February fifth, eighteen hundred and fifty-three; and every such corporation and the officers, directors and stockholders thereof, shall hav and possess all the rights, and be subject to all the liabilitie conditions and obligations in and by said act, and the act amendatory thereof, provided and imposed upon corporatior formed thereunder, and upon the officers, directors and stocl holders, except as herein otherwise provided.

Sec. 2. Every corporation organized pursuant to the provisio and by authority of this act, shall, by its corporate name, ha power to acquire, own and hold all such real and personal esta as may be necessary or convenient for the purpose of carryi on the business of such corporation, and the same, or any p thereof, convey, lease or demise, mortgage, use and dispose at pleasure.

Sec. 3. Corporations formed under this act shall be subj to all general laws of this State relating to corporations t may be applicable thereto, and the Legislature may amend repeal this act at any time.

Sec. 4. This act shall take immediate effect.

Approved March 26, 1867.

AN ACT for the better promotion of the interests of agr ture, manufactures and the mechanic arts.

Section 1. *The People of the State of Michigan enact,* Th any county in this State where the inhabitants thereof organized and established more than one society for the couragement and advancement of agriculture, manufac and the mechanic arts, in accordance with the provisio section sixteen hundred and eighty-seven of the compiled the board of supervisors of said county may apportio amount raised by tax in said county, by the provisions o tions sixteen hundred and eighty-seven, sixteen hundre eighty-eight, and sixteen hundred and eighty-nine of the piled laws, among each of said societies, as they may equitable and just.

Sec. 2. When the inhabitants of parts of two or more counties lying adjacent to each other, have united in organizing and establishing a society for the encouragement and advancement of agriculture, manufactures and the mechanic arts, in accordance with the provisions of section sixteen hundred and eighty-seven of the compiled laws, the board of supervisors of each of the said counties may apportion to such society so much of the amount raised by tax in their respective counties, by the provisions of sections sixteen hundred and eight-seven, sixteen hundred and eighty-eight and sixteen hundred and eighty-nine of the compiled laws, as they may deem equitable and just.

Sec. 3. This act shall take immediate effect.

Approved February 7, 1867.

AN ACT to prevent the running at large of bulls, stallions, boars and rams.

Section 1. *The People of the State of Michigan enact,* That if the owner of any bull, stallion, boar or ram shall allow the same to go at large out of his enclosure, he shall forfeit the sum of five dollars for such offense, to be recovered on complaint before any justice of the peace of the county in which such owner may live, and twice that amount on any subsequent conviction: *Provided,* That such complaint shall be prosecuted within thirty days next after such animal shall be found at large as aforesaid.

Sec. 2. In addition to the penalty prescribed in the foregoing section, the owner of said bull, stallion, boar or ram thus found going at large, shall be liable to the owner of any cow, mare sheep or swine, for any and all damages arising from the going at large of such animals as aforesaid, to be recovered on any suit brought before any court of competent jurisdiction.

Approved March 20, 1867.

AN ACT to provide against nuisances.

Section 1. *The People of the State of Michigan enact*, That if any person or persons shall put any dead animal or part of the carcass of any dead animal, into any lake, river, creek, pond, road, street, alley, lane, lot, field, meadow or common, or in any place within one mile of the residence of any person or persons, except the same and every part thereof be buried at least two feet under ground, and if the owner or owners thereof shall knowingly permit the same to remain in any of the aforesaid places, to the injury of the health, or to the annoyance of the citizens of this State, or any of them, every person so offending, shall be deemed guilty of a misdemeanor, and upon conviction thereof, shall forfeit and pay a sum of not less than five dollars nor more than ten dollars, together with the costs of prosecution, and in default in the payment thereof, shall be imprisoned in the county jail of the county in which such conviction may be had, not exceeding ten days, to be imposed by any court of competent jurisdiction; and every twenty-four hours said owner may permit the same to remain after such conviction, shall be deemed an additional offense against the provisions of this act, and upon conviction thereof shall forfeit and pay a further sum of not less than ten dollars and not more than thirty dollars, together with the costs of prosecution, to be recovered as aforesaid, and in default in the payment thereof, be imprisoned as aforesaid not more than thirty days, or be punished by both such fine and imprisonment, in the discretion of the court.

Approved March 20, 1867.

AN ACT relating to the planting of trees or shrubs in the highway, being a bill to amend section (1111,) eleven hundred and eleven, being section two, of chapter twenty-five, of the compiled laws, and to add two new sections thereto.

Section 1. *The People of the State of Michigan enact*, That section two, of chapter twenty-five, of compiled laws, be amended so as to read as follows:

(1111.) Sec. 2. Any person or persons owning or occupying land adjoining any highway not less than three rods wide, may plant or set out trees or shrubs on each side of said highway contiguous to his land, which trees or shrubs shall be set in regular rows, at a distance of not less than six feet from each other, and within eight feet of the margin of the highway: *Provided*, That in incorporated villages or cities the common council of such cities or villages may fix and determine the distance that such trees shall be set from the margin of the highways therein; and any such person owning or occupying land contiguous to any highway, and who is assessed any highway or poll tax, may cause to be paid of such tax a sum not exceeding twenty-five per cent. for any year, by planting trees or shrubs in the margin of the highway, in a space not exceeding eight feet in width from the margin of the highway, which sum, when so paid, shall be credited upon his highway or poll tax for that year; and any overseer of the highway may cause a portion, not exeeeding ten per cent. of the highway tax in his road district, to be expended in setting out trees or shrubs in a space not exceeding eight feet in width from the margin of the highway.

Sec. 2. Any person who shall (except as hereinafter provided) willfully injure, deface, tear or destroy any tree or shrub thus planted along the margin of the highway, or purposely left thoro for shade or ornament, shall forfeit a sum not less than five nor more than one hundred dollars for each offense, which sum may be recovered in any court of competent jurisdiction: *Provided*, That whenever it shall appear to the board of commissioners for highways in any town in this State, that any shade or ornamental trees or shrubs are an obstruction or an injury to any highway, said trees or shrubs may be cut down or removed, by order of the aforesaid board of commissioners of highways.

Sec. 3. Any person who shall negligently or carelessly suffer any horse or other beast driven by or for him, or any beast belonging to him, and lawfully in the highway, to break down, destroy or injure any tree or shrub not his own, standing for use or ornament in any highway, or negligently or willfully, by any other means, shall break down, destroy or injure any such tree or shrub, shall be subject to an action for damages in a sum not less than one nor more than twenty-five dollars for each offense, to be recovered at the suit of the owner or tenant of the land in front of which such tree or shrub stands, or of the overseer of the highway in whose road district such tree or shrub may be situated.

Sec. 4. This act shall take immediate effect.

Approved March 27, 1867.

AN ACT to amend section one, of act number two hundred and sixteen, of the session laws of eighteen hundred and sixty-one, entitled an act to provide for the drainage of swamps, marshes and other low lands.

Section 1. *The People of the State of Michigan enact*, That section one, of act number two hundred and sixteen, of the session laws of eighteen hundred and sixty-one, entitled an act to provide for the drainage of swamps, marshes and other low lands, be amended so as to read as follows:

Section 1. *The People of the State of Michigan enact*, That the board of supervisors in any organized county in this State, shall at their annual meeting in the year eighteen hundred and sixty-seven, appoint three discreet freeholders, each of whom shall be an elector and an inhabitant of a different township from the others, to be known as drainage commissioners of such county; one for the term of one year, one for the term of two years, and one for the term of three years, each to hold his office until another shall be appointed in his place and duly qualified; and at their annual session in each year thereafter, the board of supervisors shall appoint one commissioner for three years and until his successor is chosen and qualified; such commissioners shall superintend the drainage of such swamps, marshes and other low lands in their respective counties, and also to clear out the streams when the current is obstructed by falling timbers, according to the provisions of this act as in their judgment affect injuriously the health of the inhabitants; and in case of the neglect or refusal of the board of supervisors of any such organized county, so to appoint such commissioners, it shall be obligatory upon them to make such appointment upon the presentation to them of a petition signed by fifty resident freeholders of the county, praying that such commissioners be appointed.

Approved March 27, 1867.

AN ACT to amend an act entitled "an act to provide for the draining of swamps, marshes and other low lands," approved March fifteenth, eighteen hundred and sixty-one, by adding thereto a new section.

SECTION 1. *The People of the State of Michigan enact*, That an act entitled "an act to provide for the drainage of swamps, marshes and other low lands," approved March fifteenth, eighteen hundred and sixty-one, be amended by adding thereto a new section, to stand as section twenty-eight, and read as follows:

Sec. 28. Whenever any drain shall be laid along or near the boundary line of any city or village, under the provisions of this act, and any lands within said city or village shall be benefited thereby, the said commissioners shall make an estimate of the sum that ought to be levied on each parcel of land so benefited, in the same manner, and the same proceedings shall be thereupon had as if said lands had been included within a township; and whenever said commissioners shall find it necessary, they may, with the consent of the common council or trustees, lay or construct any drain commenced in a township, through or into the limits of a city or village; and may in like manner estimate the sums that ought to be levied on any parcel of land within such city or village that shall be benefited by such drain, and the same proceedings shall be thereon had, and the sums collected in the same manner, as if said lands were situated in a township.

Sec. 2. This act shall take immediate effect.

Approved February 5, 1867.

AN ACT to repeal sections four and five, of act number two hundred and sixteen, of the session laws of 1861, entitled an act to provide for the draining of swamps, marshes and other low lands, approved March 15th, 1861, and to substitute two new sections therefor.

SECTION 1. *The People of the State of Michigan enact,* That sections four and five, of an act entitled an act to provide for the drainage of swamps, marshes and other low lands, approved March fifteenth, eighteen hundred and sixty-one, be and the same are hereby repealed, and two new sections substituted therefor, to stand as sections four and five, and which shall read as follows:

Sec. 4. Said commissioners shall appoint a time, at which they will meet at some convenient place or places, for the purpose of contracting for the performance of the construction and excavation of such ditch or drain, at which time, place or places, the owner, or his or her agent or attorney may appear, and make and execute a contract, with good and sufficient security, for the faithful performance of the construction and excavation of so much of said drain as shall run across his or her or their lands, or so much as the said drain commissioners shall adjuge or set off of said drain to such lands, if they, in their judgment, should judge that any subdivision of land should not excavate the amount of such ditch running across such subdivision of a section or part of section; and in case such owner or occupant, his, her or their agent or attorney, shall not appear and execute such contract, then it shall be lawful for such commissioners, and it shall be their duty, to let the same to the lowest responsible bidder, who shall file such a contract as aforesaid with said commissioners, and the expenses of such construction shall be levied upon such land, but such contracts shall be upon reasonable public notices, published in some newspaper published in the county; and also said drain commissionors shall post up three or more notices, either printed or written, and signed by them, along the line of such drain, or adjacent thereto, and such other places as they shall deem necessary.

Sec. 5. Said commissioners shall make an estimate of the sum necessary to be raised to pay the incidental expenses of making such ditch or drains, and also make an estimate of the sum that ought to be levied on each section, or part of section, or parcel of land on such marshes or low lands, in such proportion as they shall deem just, according to the benefit that will accrue to each, by making any such ditch or drain; and they shall cause maps of said lands to be made, designating thereon the length, depth, width, position and direction of every ditch or drain by them laid out and established by them; said map shall also contain a description of every section, or part of section or parcel upon which estimates have been made, with the amount of such estimates, also the aggregate amount to be collected in each township.

Sec. 6. This act shall take immediate effect.

Approved March 27, 1867.

AN ACT to prevent animals from running at large in the public highways.

Section 1. *The People of the State of Michigan enact*, That from and after the year one thousand eight hundred and sixty-seven, it shall not be lawful for any cattle, horses, sheep or swine to run at large in any public highway of this State: *Provided*, That this act shall be operative only in those counties or parts of counties in which it shall be so determined by resolution passed by the board of supervisors of such county.

Sec. 2. In case the board of supervisors in any county shall pass a resolution prohibiting any of the classes of animals named in section one of this bill to run at large in the public highway, then, in such county, after the year one thousand eight hundred and sixty-seven, the following sections of this act shall be in full force; but otherwise, they shall be null and void.

Sec. 3. It shall be lawful for any person to seize and take into his custody and possession any animal which may be in any public highway, and opposite the land owned or occupied by him, contrary to the provisions of the foregoing section. And it shall be lawful for any person to take into his custody and possession any animal which may be trespassing upon premises owned or occupied by him.

Sec. 4. Whenever any such person shall seize and take into his custody or possession any animal under the authority of the next preceding section, it shall be the duty of such person to give immediate notice thereof to a justice of the peace or a commissioner of highways of the town, city or village in which such seizure and possession shall have been taken, and such justice or commissioner shall thereupon give notice by affixing the same in six public and conspicuous places in said town, city or village, one of which shall be the district school-house nearest the residence of such justice or commissioner, that such animal or animals will be sold at public auction, at some convenient place in said town, city or village, not less than thirty nor more than sixty days from the time of the affixing of such notice, to be specified in such notice; the same justice or commissioner shall proceed to sell the said animals for cash, and out of the proceeds thereof shall, in the first place, retain the following fees and charges for his services in giving said notice and making said sale, viz: For every horse sold, one dollar; for every cow or calf, or other cattle, one-half dollar; and for every sheep or swine, twenty-five cents; and shall then pay to the person who shall have seized the said animal or animals, the sum following, that is to say: For every horse so seized or sold, one dollar; for every cow or calf, or other cattle, one-half dollar; and for every sheep, ten cents; for every swine, twenty-five cents; together with a reasonable compensation, to be estimated by such justice or commissioner, for the care and keeping of said animal or animals, from the time of the seizure thereof to the time of sale. If there shall be any surplus money arising from said sale, the said justice or commissioner shall retain the same in his hands, and pay the same to the owner or owners of said animals, after a reasonable demand therefor and satisfactory proof of such ownership: *Provided*, Such owner or owners shall appear and claim such surplus moneys within one year after sale. And if the owner or owners of such animal or animals shall not appear and demand such surplus moneys within one year after such sale has been made, he shall be forever precluded from recovering any part of such moneys, and the same shall be paid to the treasurer of the town for the use of the town, and his receipt therefor shall be a legal discharge to said justice or commissioner: *Provided*, That any animal sold in pursuance of this act may be redeemed any time within the year following such sale, by paying the expenses of such custody and sale, and a reasonable compensation for keeping the same.

Sec. 5. Any owner of any animal which shall have been seized under and pursuant to the foregoing provisions, may at any time before the sale thereof, demand and shall be entitled to the possession of such animal, upon the payment by him of the several sums hereinbefore required to be paid to the said justice or commissioner, and to the person by whom the seizure aforesaid shall have been made, together with a reasonable compensation to the person making such seizure for the care and keeping of such animal, to be estimated and fixed by such justice or commissioner, and upon making to such justice or commissioner satisfactory proof of ownership. And if such owner shall make such demand and proof at least three days before the time appointed for such sale, he shall be entitled to the custody and possession of such animal, upon paying one-half of the several sums above mentioned, together with the whole amount of compensation awarded by the said justice or commissioner.

Sec. 6. In case the animal so seized under the foregoing provisions of this act, shall have been so running at large or trespassing by the willful act of any other person than the owner, to effect that object, such owner shall be entitled to the possession of such animal by making the demand therefor, and the proof required in the next preceding section, and paying to the person making such a seizure the amount of compensation fixed by such justice or commissioner, for the care and keeping of such animal, and without paying any other charges; and the person committing such willful act shall be liable to a penalty of twenty dollars, to be recovered in an action at law at the suit of the owner of such animal, or the person making such seizure.

Sec. 7. All acts or parts of acts inconsistent herewith are hereby repealed.

Sec. 8. This act shall not apply to that portion of this State lying north of the tier of townships twelve north, unless so ordered by the board of supervisors of any county lying north of said tier of towns.

Approved March 27, 1867.

CONTENTS.

APPENDIX.

ERRATA.

On page 8, twenty-second line from the top, for "nineteenth century," read "sixteenth century."

On page 9, thirteenth line from top, for "less that a score of years," read "half a score," &c.

On page 73, in the note of Prof. Holmes, for "tar," read "tan."

On page 167, fifth line from the top, for "sulphate of soda," read "sulphite of soda."

www.ingramcontent.com/pod-product-compliance
Lightning Source LLC
LaVergne TN
LVHW020600110826
845149LV00002B/327

9781418188184